MASTERS OF MANAGEMENT

MASTERS OF MANAGEMENT

HOW THE BUSINESS GURUS AND THEIR IDEAS HAVE CHANGED THE WORLD—FOR BETTER AND FOR WORSE

ADRIAN WOOLDRIDGE

With a Foreword by John Micklethwait

HARPER
BUSINESS

An Imprint of HarperCollins*Publishers*
www.harpercollins.com

FIRST HARPERCOLLINS EDITION

A previous edition of this book was published by Crown Business in 1996 under the
title *The Witch Doctors*.

Designed by Renato Stanisic

Library of Congress Cataloging-in-Publication Data has been applied for.

ISBN: 978-0-06-177113-2

11 12 13 14 15   OV/RRD   10 9 8 7 6 5 4 3 2 1

Contents

PART IV: THE GREAT DEBATES

PART V: WORKERS OF THE WORLD

Acknowledgments

I am most grateful to Scott Moyers, formerly of the Wylie Agency, for suggesting that I should produce a new version of *The Witch Doctors*, which John Micklethwait and I published in 1996, and for gently persuading my publishers to put up with my slow progress; and to Andrew Wylie and the Wylie Agency in general for looking after my book-related life so wonderfully.

Writing this book has proved both more difficult than I had anticipated and more fulfilling. More difficult because I was guilty of underestimating the force of Heraclitus' observation that you cannot step into the same river twice, particularly in an age when the river has turned into a raging torrent. More fulfilling because the business landscape has been transformed dramatically over the past fifteen years, shaken by the Internet, the rise of emerging markets, and sundry smaller changes. Having spent the first decade of this century writing about American politics, I was happy to turn to a world where problems are routinely addressed, rather than just swept under the carpet, and where progress is a condition of staying in business.

It is a pleasure to be able to acknowledge my debt to the dozens of people whose brains I have picked during the writing of this book: Antoine van Agtmael, Sir Ronald Cohen, Ge Dingkun, Suren Dutia, Wim Elfrink, Juan Antonio Fernandez, Bill Fischer, V. G. Govindarajan, Lynda Gratton, Michael Hay, Daniel Isenberg, Joe Lassiter, Michael Jacobides, Rosabeth Moss Kanter, Tarun Khanna, Vinod Kumar, A. S. Lakshminarayanan, Robert Litan, Sandeep Maini, Arnoud De Meyer, George McKinnon, Nitin Nohria, Charles Ormiston, Jaideep Prabhu, C. K. Prahalad, Gideon Rachman, Navid Radjou, Sumanth Raman, V. Raja, Michael Roberts, Carl Schramm, Richard Straub, A. R. Srinath, Donald Sull, Ratan Tata, Jianmao Wang, and Dongsheng Zhou. They are not only masters of management but paragons of generosity, too.

At HarperCollins, I am most grateful to Hollis Heimbouch and her team. Hollis was everything an errant author could hope for: she identified gaps in my coverage, suggested innumerable improvements, and guided my re-editing, and all without raising her voice or ruffling any of my feathers.

I am grateful to numerous colleagues at *The Economist* who have had to put up with me at close quarters while I was distracted by this book, and who did me various kindnesses, large and small, in particular Joel Budd, Robert Guest, Daniel Franklin, Ludwig Siegele, Tom Standage, Rachel Horwood, and Sheila Allen. I am also grateful to *The Economist* for allowing me to reuse some passages that I originally wrote for its pages. *The Economist* continues to be what it has always been in the twenty-odd years that I have worked there, a perpetually engaging and endlessly stimulating seminar that somehow manages to produce a magazine every week, and, these days, a torrent of Internet commentary as well. John Micklethwait supported this book in much the same way that I support the Church of England: as a buttress from the outside.

The burden of book writing inevitably falls on those closest to you. I am eternally grateful to Amelia, who had to do more than her fair share of labor involved in moving continents and supervising building operations; and to Ella and Dora, who put up, not altogether uncomplainingly, with my book-writing duties. My dogs, Louis and Dolly, were constant sources of delight.

Foreword

What if the Female Manager of a High School Baseball Team Read Drucker's "Management" is hardly the catchiest title for a novel. But in 2010, What if . . . became one of the great success stories of the Japanese publishing industry, selling more than a million copies. The novel, by Natsumi Iwasaki, told the story of a teenage girl, Minami, who becomes a go-fer dogsbody for a baseball coach. Horrified by the team's lack of ambition, she sets about putting some steel into its collective spine, setting the team the goal of reaching the high school championships. But how can she turn second-rate rabble into a prize-winning team? As she searches for inspiration, she stumbles across Peter Drucker's 1973 masterpiece, Management: Tasks, Responsibilities, Practices. Minami quickly learns the importance of setting clear objectives. ("Objectives are not fate," Drucker wrote, "they are direction.") She then embraces Drucker's various principles as embodied in the titles of the book's chapters: "Minami addresses marketing," "Minami tries to harness people's strengths," "Minami takes on innovation," "Minami thinks about what integrity is."

Drucker has long been venerated in Japan, as a man who helped teach Japanese managers how to run businesses (and also explained Japan to the world). Minami's antics quickly produced a Drucker boom. *Management* sold some 300,000 copies in the first half of 2010, three times more than it had sold in the previous twenty-six years. Iwasaki donated some of her royalties to the Japan Drucker Workshop and the Peter Drucker and Mastoshi Ito Graduate School of Management. But the novel did more than this: it promoted a salutary debate about the business habits of a country that, thanks in part to Drucker, had shaken up the business world in the 1960s and 1970s with a succession of management innovations, such as "lean production" and "just-in-time delivery," but has been locked in a recession for two decades. Should Japanese companies set themselves clearer objectives rather than wallowing in consensus? And should they adopt clearer structures rather than sprawling into dozens of businesses? Five years after his death, Drucker still mattered.

In 1996, Adrian Wooldridge and I published a book on the management gurus called *The Witch Doctors*. It did not sell quite as many copies as *What if . . .* , but it did well. We were lucky in our timing. Over the previous decade the management theory industry had been rapidly expanding its empire. Reengineers were tearing apart companies—and sacking thousands of workers in the process—in the name of corporate efficiency. Tub-thumping gurus such as Tom Peters and Gary Hamel were wowing managers with lectures on how they ought to leap on the latest management theory bandwagon or face destruction. Business schools and management consultancies had their pick of the world's best and brightest.

But as we wrote *The Witch Doctors*, management theory's empire was afflicted by crises on almost every front. *Business Week* revealed that one of the leading reengineering firms was involved in a scheme to push one of their books up the best-seller list by buying thousands of copies and storing them in tractor-trailers. Companies were beginning to complain of "corporate anorexia" as they realized that the "fat" that the reengineers denounced was in fact essential to survival. At the same time, Japan, a country that had been counted as one of the great successes of management theory, was stuck in a recession (from which, sadly, it has not really emerged).

The Witch Doctors tried to do two things. One was to audit management theory: to work out which ideas, among the hundred being proffered, were useful—to find the jewels in the mud. And we did indeed argue that there were jewels—that the work of men like Drucker helped explain some of the great revolutions of the modern world. Many of the people who have since bought the book saw it as a useful filter: Adrian and I had read all this stuff, so they didn't need to do so. The other aim of the book was to describe the huge industry that had emerged to sell those ideas. We had spotted a phenomenon—and many reviewers were aghast at the size of it. Titles matter, and soon we became known as the people who had damned consultancies and gurus as "witch doctors." We were also quickly (and we can hardly claim unfairly) bracketed with other guru-questioning books such as *Fad Surfing in the Boardroom: Managing in the Age of Instant Answers*, by Eileen Shapiro, and *Dangerous Company: The Consulting Powerhouses and the Businesses They Save and Ruin*, by James O'Shea and Charles Madigan. Since then many more have followed, most notably Phil Rosenzweig's *The Halo Effect* in 2007, which justly upbraided *The Witch Doctors* for being too kind to Asea Brown Boveri and its former boss Percy Barnevik, and Matthew Stewart's *The Management Myth: Debunking Modern Business Philosophy*.

A couple of years ago, Adrian presented me with the idea of producing a new edition of *The Witch Doctors*. What had happened over the past fifteen years? Were the same gurus still laying down the law, or had new ones taken their place? Had management theory overcome its addiction to fads after the reengineering debacle, or had new ones been invented to take its place? And what about the rise of the Internet revolution and the rise of the emerging world? What were the gurus making of these momentous changes?

Listening to Adrian's pitch, I decided it had both an insight and a defect. The insight was that a follow-up to *The Witch Doctors* should focus more on the audit of management ideas than attacking the guru industry. There were many more ideas—including the Internet and emerging markets—to examine; by contrast, the idea that consultants could be greedy was now well understood. The hitch was that he thought this would be easy. Adrian suggested it would involve no more than a bit of clever tweaking and cunning substitution ("All we have to do is cross out the word 'Microsoft' and replace it with 'Google'" was one of his selling points). I realized, not for the first time, that he was talking nonsense—that the book would take far more work than he thought, given the pace of change in the business world, and that, given my day job at *The Economist*, I simply did not have time to do the work. So I gave him my blessing and suggested that he should do this particular book on his own.

Reading what he has done is a bit like revisiting a home that you lived in for several years of your life—but that has been not just renovated but rebuilt by a new owner. It has certainly not been a bit of modest updating. Many rooms have been massively expanded; others have shrunk; and some are gone completely. Staircases have appeared; doors have moved; windows have disappeared. Everything has been modernized. It has been a much more dramatic makeover than just changing a few names. Of course, I don't like everything—there is the editorial urge to put the sofa back where it belonged. But even from my egotistical perspective, it has clearly been improved. Adrian has made it relevant again, but he has kept most of the good bits of the original book and its spirit—of honest criticism.

So what has changed and what has stayed the same? To generalize wildly, the industry has stayed the same, but the ideas have changed.

The continuing influence of the gurus comes through. It is not just Peter Drucker's posthumous clout. Michael Porter is still king of the Harvard Business School. Tom Peters continues to give speeches on the importance of "letting go" and "delivering wow." More generally, management gurus remain what they were when we wrote about them in 1996—"the unacknowledged legislators of mankind." They still help to shape a huge range of institutions, from companies to charities to governments, and they still define the frequently hideous language of modern organizational life. Consultancies are even more active, and there are even more business schools than when we wrote about them. George W. Bush, America's first president to boast an MBA, appointed five businesspeople to his first cabinet, and he honored Peter Drucker with the Presidential Medal of Freedom on July 9, 2002.

This is all the more remarkable given what has happened. Since we wrote *The Witch Doctors*, the gurus have suffered two great embarrassments. One was Enron. The oil trading firm that collapsed in 2002 had been a darling of the management industry: staffed by MBAs from the world's leading business schools, starring in numerous case studies, and with close links to McKinsey (Jeff Skilling, Enron's CEO, originally came to the firm as a McKinsey consultant). The other was the 2008–09 financial crisis. Many of the financial techniques at the heart of the crisis were cooked up in business schools, and many of the toppled titans of finance, including Dick Fuld at Lehman and Andy Hornby at HBOS, held MBAs.

There has been soul searching because of this, and a desire to get rid of some of the oversell and hype. But management theory remains a hodgepodge. There are still gems, but there is also a lot of mud—most obviously the pseudoscientific gobbledygook, but also the faddism. Adrian has a merry time skewering the industry that has grown up to sell "corporate social responsibility" in the same way that we once looked at reengineering. Even the best gurus have a weakness for overselling themselves. The worst are often little better than hucksters. Management theory remains a porous industry in which serious thinkers rub shoulder to shoulder with products of the university of life.

Why has this continued? I still think the answer is the same one we put forward fifteen years ago. Business people are desperate for competitive insight (and so, increasingly, are bureaucrats). They need answers, help, anything. And they also know two things: that some of this stuff works, and that ignoring it completely can be fatal. Much as we might want to mock the fad for corporate social responsibility and recoil at a lot of the worthy tripe produced under that banner, companies that turned their back on issues like the environment and the employment habits of their suppliers have often been trounced by events. And even if business people have no need to apologize for what they are doing, they can still learn from what social entrepreneurs are up to.

So the basic market for management ideas has not changed. But what about the ideas themselves? Here I think there has been more of a shift. We remarked in *The Witch Doctors* on how the same ideas keep recurring—especially the debate between hard management techniques that usually aim to save money (and thus often involve sacking people) and soft ones that look to exploit talent and opportunities. That still exists. There are chapters here on strategy, organization, and globalization, but it is noticeable to me how much the pace has changed. For instance, taking advantage of a global market without being destroyed by it seems a much bigger challenge than it did in 1996, now that the entrepreneurial revolution has reached most corners of the world. The same goes for talent. The battle for brainpower has both intensified and universalized: across the emerging world, companies are locked in a brutal struggle for the best brains. The question of how you manage yourself has moved from the world of self-help into the halls of academia. In today's more flexible economy, where the average American worker has been with his or her current employer for only two years, employees have no choice but to take more responsibility for their own career development.

Two things account for many of the more startling changes between this book and *The Witch Doctors*. One is the rise of the Internet. In 1996, the Web was mostly used by academics and Google had not yet been invented. Today more than 80 percent of Americans have access to the Internet, and Google worries that it is suffering from a midlife crisis. The Internet—particularly the mobile Internet—has dramatically speeded up many of the changes we discussed in the book, from globalization to the unbundling of corporations. It has produced a new breed of cyber-gurus as well as its own cyber-fads, such as the current craze for "co-creation."

The other change is the rise of the emerging world—especially emerging Asia. Most of the Asian business thinkers we discussed in *The Witch Doctors* were Japanese. Some of the best bits of this book cover the new waves of innovation in China and India. What Adrian makes clear is that emerging Asia is not just copying; it is improving. The emerging world is rapidly becoming a center of innovation as well as a source of cheap hands and brains. The companies there—both local and Western—are rethinking everything, from talent management to core competencies. Adrian points to a radical new management idea—"frugal innovation"—which, he argues, will change the world in the same way that Japanese lean manufacturing once did. Frugal innovation radically redesigns products and services to make them much cheaper for the emerging middle class—and then re-exports them to the West. Examples include things as different as cars, telephone banking, and heart surgery.

This book has been substantially rewritten as a result of these developments. There are whole chapters on subjects that we did not mention in 1996 (corporate social responsibility; the war for talent; the spread of the entrepreneurial ideal; and the new models in the emerging world). The examples have also changed substantially. But at its heart, I would like to claim that the overall argument is based on the same three points.

First, management gurus are the powers behind the throne. Today's global elite are shaped by management theory in much the same way that the Victorian elite were shaped by classical culture. Second, management theory is an immature discipline, unusually open to charlatans, or semi-charlatans, and congenitally prone to fads. But, third, management theory also contains a great deal of good. The world is a much better place because of innovations such as management by objectives, lean manufacturing, and frugal innovation. And you need to know about them.

So the management gurus are like Caliban, a mixture of good and bad. In our last book, we chose a title that emphasized their dark side—the fact that far too much of the time gurus are witch doctors. Perhaps that was a little unfair. This time Adrian has decided to emphasize the more uplifting side: that the gurus are sometimes masters of management. You might argue that it is too generous. But if you don't like what is written here, complain to Adrian, not me. It is now his book. And I think it is a good one.

—*John Micklethwait*

Introduction: The Unacknowledged Legislators

On April 8, 2008, some three thousand masters of the universe descended on the Harvard Business School to celebrate their alma mater's hundredth birthday. They looked on admiringly as Jay Light, the school's ninth dean, served up a supersized portion of waffles and syrup. ("The need for leadership in the world today is at least as great as it has ever been. The need for what we do is at least as great as it has ever been.") They strolled around the school's forty impeccably maintained acres, reminiscing about old times and chatting with old mentors and new students. And—the highlight of the day for these congenital strivers and suck-ups—they crammed into the school's classrooms to discuss a specially prepared case study on "HBS at a hundred." What had the school done to earn its success in its first hundred years? And what did it need to do to stay on top over the next hundred?

Dean Light and Co. had plenty to be proud of. Over the past century HBS has transformed itself from a humble trade school—and a blot on the landscape, according to the old guard—into one of the most revered educational institutions in the world. HBS was not only considerably richer than any other business school in the world, with an endowment of $2.8 billion and annual revenues of $405 million. It was considerably more successful, too: as the school celebrated its centennial its alumni included the president of the United States and his next-door neighbor in Lafayette Square, the secretary of the Treasury; the president of the World Bank; the mayor of New York City; the bosses of General Electric, Goldman Sachs, and Procter & Gamble; 20 percent of the heads of Fortune 500 companies; and legions of hedge fund kings and private equity honchos. But even this list of alumni understates the institution's importance: HBS was responsible for developing the intellectual machinery of capitalism as well as training the people who operated that machinery.

Yet the timing of the birthday bash was less than perfect. Lehman Brothers was already looking shaky (the company lost 73 percent of its share-price in the first six months of 2008). And as the school continued to celebrate its birthday over the rest of the year, the capitalist system began to unravel. The collapse of Lehman Brothers almost took down the rest of the banking system, and the world was plunged into the most gut-wrenching depression since the 1930s.

The crisis brought down many of the school's most celebrated products, such as Stan O'Neal, the head of Merrill Lynch, and Andy Hornby, the head of HBOS (who, incidentally, had graduated top of his class). But it did more than this. Critics lambasted Harvard (and its fellow business schools) for inventing doomsday machines like collateralized debt obligations and for failing to give their charges any sense of risk and responsibility. The *Financial Times* headlined an article on the school's centenary "blame it on Harvard."[1] Philip Delves Broughton suggested that his fellow

Harvard MBAs should be known as "masters of the apocalypse" rather than masters of business administration. "If Robespierre were to ascend from hell and seek out today's guillotine fodder," he wrote, "he might start with a list of those with three incriminating initials beside their names: MBA."[2]

Unacknowledged Legislators

The story of Harvard Business School's hundredth birthday party is also a story of management theory in general: a story of extraordinary success compromised by equally extraordinary failure. Shelley once remarked that poets are "the unacknowledged legislators of mankind." These days that honor belongs to management theorists. Names such as Drucker and Hamel may not have the same noble ring as Wordsworth or Keats, yet wherever one looks, management theorists are laying down the law, reshaping institutions, refashioning the language, and above all, reorganizing people's lives. We have grown accustomed to finding people with MBA degrees clustered at the top of businesses and banks. But today you can find MBAs wielding power in charities, churches, and much of the public sector (the Harvard MBA who sat in the White House when Dean Light was making his speech claimed to practice "management by objectives" and packed his Cabinet with former chief executives).[3]

The rise of management theory is one of the most striking—and one of the least analyzed—developments of the past hundred years. The first recognizable management guru was Frederick Taylor, the father of stopwatch-based "scientific management." In the early 1900s, his books sold in the millions, and Taylor's consultancy fees were $35 a day—or $630 in today's money. Taylor's worker-as-machine theories always had their critics (Charlie Chaplin lampooned them memorably in *Modern Times*), but that did not stop them from being adopted by many leading American businessmen, including Henry Ford, or from spreading around the world. Lenin ordered his minions to adapt "the Taylor system" to socialist ends. The idea of "five-year plans" was dreamt up by one of Taylor's leading acolytes, Henry Gantt. A steady procession of management thinkers has followed in Taylor's path. After the Second World War, W. Edwards Deming, the pioneer of "total quality management," was dubbed the most revered American in Japan after General Douglas MacArthur.

Interest in management theory went into overdrive in the 1980s as the rich world in general, and America in particular, tried to come to terms with the rise of Japan, the spread of computers, and the invention of new financial techniques. For a new breed of increasingly evangelical management theorists, led by Tom Peters, the accompanying corporate self-analysis proved a bonanza. In the summer of 1982, Peters and another consultant from McKinsey & Company, Robert Waterman, published *In Search of Excellence*, which boldly (and correctly) told American businessmen that they were in better shape than they thought. The book sold more than five million copies, staying at the top of the *New York Times* best-seller list for more than two years and turning its authors into millionaires. What had traditionally been a business-to-business market, with consultants talking to other consultants, had been transformed into a business-to-consumer one.

Ever since *In Search of Excellence*, the guru industry has boomed. In America, the market for business books is worth some $750 million a year, and the market for online materials, DVDs, podcasts, and lecture courses is even bigger. In China, business books by the likes of Jack Welch and Tom Friedman take pride of place over the latest excrescences from Dan Brown and Co. In India, management gurus are treated with a reverence that once was reserved for spiritual gurus. Successful management gurus whizz around the world in first-class splendor, charging $60,000 a speech to tell middle managers in Barcelona or Bangalore where the world is heading and why.

The gurus themselves are only the most visible tip of a much larger management iceberg that incorporates business schools, management consultancies, and much of the business press. American universities award almost 150,000 graduate degrees in business every year, about one-quarter of all the graduate degrees they award, and people with MBAs can be sure of starting their new jobs with a significantly fatter pay packet than ordinary mortals. The cult of the MBA has spread from America to the rest of the world. Every year, a quarter of a million people the world over take the Graduate Management Admissions Test in the hope of gaining admission to an MBA program. Business schools are spreading rapidly across the emerging markets of Asia and Eastern Europe; they have even reached Oxford and Cambridge, though it took a nasty fight to put them there.

It is impossible to think of any other academic discipline that can match management theory's success in building an industry around itself. Guru breeding grounds, such as McKinsey and the Boston Consulting Group, have offices wherever firms lose money. Big-ego executives, who like to present themselves as masters of the universe, creep off in the afternoon to spend an hour with their "coaches." Even in cynical old Blighty, dozens of companies provide adventure-based management training, obliging fat merchant bankers and balding bond traders to swing across rivers and, later in the evening, around campfires, tell their colleagues what they really think about them.

More than any other branch of intellectual life, management theory has learned how to tap into two primal human instincts: fear and greed. It is usually one of these two emotions that persuades a middle manager at O'Hare Airport to pick up yet another book on leadership or tempts a chief executive in Ohio to blow yet another million dollars on consulting fees. However, it is also clear that management theory is bound up with three revolutions that directly or indirectly affect all of us: the reinvention of companies, the reinvention of careers, and the reinvention of the state.

Nowadays, companies everywhere are going through contortions that their predecessors could scarcely have imagined. The attrition rate of companies is spectacular—only about one-third of America's five hundred leading companies on a 1970 listing still exist today. So far the twenty-first century has proved to be terrifyingly turbulent. Three of America's five biggest investment banks have disappeared, and scores of other banks and mortgage companies have imploded. Two of America's "Big Three" carmakers have filed for bankruptcy, dragging dozens of suppliers with them, and America's manufacturing sector as a whole has shed almost a third of its jobs. Even the best companies, terrified that they will end up in this ever more crowded corporate graveyard, are reorganizing themselves. This applies not only to job-slashers such as General Motors but also to job-creators such as Google and Facebook.

Even when such contortions are not directly inspired by management theory, they tend to drive managers back into the gurus' arms. Management theory, after all, is the study of business. It explains not just what this or that firm is doing but what whole groups of firms are doing, and why. The old argument, that business people only need to know how to cultivate their own gardens, and that other people's gardens are none of their concern, no longer holds true. Industry borders are blurring everywhere: between publishers and Internet companies; between banks and mobile-phone companies; between broadcasters and cable companies. Even the most no-nonsense managers are having to come to grips with ideas like synergy and alliances—and the challenge of managing disparate, multicultural organizations. All these paths lead to management theory.

As companies change, so do careers. Jobs are being reinvented in much the same way that businesses are. Gone are the days when a man (and it usually was a man) could expect to spend his entire career working for the same company, starting as an apprentice, climbing up through the ranks, and retiring, after forty years of uninterrupted employment, to enjoy an index-linked pension, a corporate gold-watch, and a mention in the company history. In 2009, the average length of job tenure in the American retail sector, which now employs far more people than manufacturing, was a mere three years.[4] Members of the millennial generation expect to spend their lives hopping from boat to boat rather than finding a comfortable berth on a single ship. And the female half of that generation expect their careers to be more complicated still, with lots of off-ramping and on-ramping, plenty of flexitime and working at home.

What is more, the number of people who need to know something about management is growing relentlessly. The U.S. Bureau of Labor Statistics predicts that the number of Americans employed in "management" of one kind or another will increase by 11 percent by 2018, while the number of people employed in "production" will decline by 3 percent. In the long run, it seems, we will all end up not so much taking in each other's washing as collectively managing the "laundry in-taking process." Nor is it just white-collar workers who have to know their TQM (total-quality management) from their JIT (just in time): nowadays, even the lowliest factory worker in the Western world knows that his most valuable asset is his brain rather than his hands.

Just as companies have been forced by competitors and share-holders to question how they manage themselves, so have governments, prodded by growing budget deficits and angry taxpayers. This has led to a wave of privatization and contracting out. The U.S. government now employs far more contract workers than federal employees. It has also produced a wave of rationalization: countries around the world are trying to renegotiate public-sector contracts in order to improve working practices and lighten the burden of pensions. The men and women from McKinsey and Accenture have long ago extended their empires from the private sector to the public sector.

The Management Theory Paradox

Does the gurus' influence—their apparent status as the unacknowl-edged legislators of mankind—make sense? One obvious answer is that management theory matters because management matters. Put simply, it changes companies and the way that people work; and in a world where some companies are bigger than some countries and where most people spend more of their waking hours at work than at home, that changes lives—often dramatically. While most other academics—even scientists and economists—have to wait decades to see their work have any practical impact, the gurus' ideas are often tested immediately. There are few other academic disciplines that can claim to be so "alive."

Yet there is a catch. Management theory continues to be be-deviled by a paradox: a discipline that matters as much as any is very far from respectable. Many of the most thoughtful management theorists admit as much. The late Peter Drucker liked to quip that people use the word "guru" only because they cannot spell "charlatan." Henry Mintzberg used to have a motto pinned to his wall: "The higher a monkey climbs the more you see its ass." Management theory clearly has more than its fair share of tub-thumping charlatans ("Transform your company in three days for $10,000") who have jumped onto the management theory bandwagon because there is no longer any room left on the bandwagons peddling advice on sex or dieting.

But there is more to the management theory paradox than this. The management theory industry has a perfectly respectable wing: the journals published by the American Academy of Management are just as scholarly—or just as dull, if you prefer—as the journals published by other academic organizations. Many management scholars can vie with the best when it comes to the narrowness of their specialization and the laboriousness of their research methods.

The real problem with the management theory industry is that there are grave doubts about the serious canon of management theory. Too much of it seems to lack what Yorkshire folk like to refer to as "bottom." Generalizations are built on rickety foundations. Blueprints are applied without proper testing. And brilliant theories are suddenly unmasked as being little more than con tricks. Talk to academics who have not taken the industry's shilling and you are likely to hear all sorts of doubts about its intellectual credentials.[5] Watch ordinary business people attending seminars on TQM and the rest of it and you can see their eyes rolling. Sooner or later, in virtually every case, the word "bullshit" appears.

Witnesses for the Prosecution

The most uncompromising case against management theory is that its devotees are nothing more than economic vandals—and jargon-spewing ones at that. Look at the greatest economic disasters of the twenty-first century, from the implosion of Enron to the global credit crunch, and you will find products of the management theory industry not just at the scene of the crime but with their fingerprints all over the evidence.

At Enron Jeff Skilling, the company's CEO when it went up in flames, was a product of the two greatest engines of the management theory industry, Harvard Business School and McKinsey. Enron hired 250 MBAs from the world's greatest business schools and was a sucker for the latest management fads. McKinsey advised the company throughout its decade-long transformation from a humble natural gas pipeline company into a trading goliath with far-flung interests in everything from water to the Internet, and Skilling first caught Lay's eye when he was one of dozens of McKinseyites who were permanently camped in the company's Houston headquarters. Senior managers cited *In Search of Excellence* to justify the system of "loose-tight management" that gave callow young MBAs the freedom to try all sorts of "outside the box" ideas. They also used *The War for Talent*, by three McKinsey consultants, to justify the company's enthusiasm for "ranking and yanking" its employees—sacking the bottom tenth and giving huge rewards to the most successful, including personal invitations from Skilling to join him glacier hiking in Patagonia or off-road motorcycling in Mexico.

The management theory industry returned this admiration. A series of articles in the *McKinsey Quarterly* lauded Enron's "asset-lite strategy" and its "new breed of tightly focused and vertically specialized petropreneurs."[6] Harvard Business School published a dozen case studies praising the company to the rafters. In *Leading the Revolution*, Gary Hamel, of the London Business School, praised the company for pioneering a management revolution.[7] (Around the time of the collapse, Hamel was due to appear with Ken Lay at a high-profile guru fest called "the revolutionaries' ball.") *Fortune* magazine ranked Enron as the most innovative company in the United States for six consecutive years.

The 2008–09 economic crisis is usually blamed on overexuberant economic theories, not management ones. But many of the principal villains, including Dick Fuld at Lehman, John Thune at Merrill Lynch, and Andy Hornby at HBOS, were products of the world's best business schools. At the height of the boom more than 40 percent of the graduates of America's top business schools ended up on Wall Street. These young MBAs devoted themselves to applying the highly sophisticated financial techniques that they had learned from the world's smartest finance thinkers. They sliced mortgages into tiny slithers and then sold them to financial institutions all around the world; they pioneered new ways of massaging risk out of existence; and all the time they lost sight of the fact that they were building their financial castles on foundations of sand. Ray Soifer, boss of Soifer Consulting and himself a product of Harvard Business School, has even created an all-purpose indicator of financial disasters: if more than 30 percent of the products of HBS's graduating class end up in market-sensitive jobs, including investment banking, private equity, and hedge funds, it is a long-term signal to sell stocks.

All very embarrassing. But the problem with trying to indict management gurus on the basis of Enron or Lehman Brothers is that these examples look just as arbitrary as the successful companies that the gurus themselves are in the habit of citing. Most

MBAs had nothing to do with Potemkin companies such as Enron or Lehman. Financial booms and busts had been going on for centuries before the first MBA was awarded.

The appalling behavior of some high-profile MBAs also needs to be set against the good works of thousands of less-celebrated people. To put it simply: management theory can be useful. Two economists, Nick Bloom of Stanford and John Van Reneen of the London School of Economics, have conducted a thorough investigation of the impact of management ideas on productivity in a wide range of countries. They concluded that companies that use the most widely accepted management techniques, of the sort that are taught in business schools, outperform their peers in all the measures that matter, such as productivity, sales growth, and return on capital. But you can make the same point by looking at the circulation of management ideas. Japanese companies overran Western ones in the 1980s because they had better management systems, especially lean-production ideas. Western companies caught up with their Japanese rivals and boosted their productivity by copying these ideas.

Still, even if you reject the "apostles of the apocalypse" charge, there are plenty of lesser charges left in the docket. Four, in particular, stand out: that the discipline is constitutionally incapable of self-criticism; that it favors terminology that confuses rather than educates; that it rarely rises above the level of basic common sense; and that it is faddish, fickle, and bedeviled by contradictions that would not be allowed in more rigorous disciplines. The implication of all four charges is that, even if they are not jargon-spewing economic vandals, management gurus are con artists, the witch doctors of our age, playing on business people's anxieties in order to sell snake oil. Modern management theory is no more reliable than tribal medicine. Witch doctors, after all, sometimes got it right—by luck, by instinct, or by trial and error.

The first charge against management theory—that it is incapable of self-criticism—is half wrong and half right. Some of the best management gurus have subjected their discipline to fierce criticism. Henry Mintzberg, of McGill University, has enjoyed a successful career as one of the world's leading management gurus *and* one of the world's leading critics of management gurus. Phil Rosenzweig, a professor at IMD, the International Institute for Management Development in Lausanne, Switzerland, has suggested that management theory is often no better than a religious cult. Gurus spot a company that happens to be doing well for the moment—such as Asea Brown Boveri (ABB) or Enron—and make extravagant claims about the quality of their management systems and the brilliance of their CEOs. But a few years later the companies have collapsed and the gurus are applying "the halo effect" to a different set of companies.[8]

The criticism has been particularly fierce when it comes to management education. In 2005, in an article that was published just after his death, Sumantra Ghoshal, of the London Business School, penned an angry "*J'accuse*" against his fellow business academics, particularly those who were enthralled by free-market economics. "Business schools do not need to do a great deal more to help prevent future Enrons," he argued. "They need only to stop doing a lot of what they currently do. . . . Much of the worst excesses of recent management practices have their roots in a set of ideas that have emerged from business school academics over the last thirty years."[9] Jeffrey Pfeffer and Henry Mintzberg have been equally outspoken in the same cause. And Rakesh Khurana, of Harvard Business School, has launched an even more wide-ranging attack on business school education, lamenting its lack of rigorous professional standards and comparing it unfavorably with other professional educational programs, such as those in medicine and engineering.[10]

The economic crisis of 2007–08 has shaken the industry's confidence in itself still further—and persuaded many of its leading lights that they have no choice but to rethink management theory from the ground up. Harvard Business School has elected a new dean—Nitin Nohria—with a mandate to enact radical reforms. The management literature has been full of effusive mea culpas and elaborate plans for reform. In the aftermath of the financial crisis, MBA students across the country embraced the idea of taking "the MBA pledge," a voluntary oath to "serve the greater good" and otherwise act ethically.

The management theory industry is also surrounded by "frenemies" who simultaneously criticize the industry while feeding off its fat (I happily admit to being one of these creatures myself). Philip Delves Broughton and Matthew Stewart have made careers out of writing exposés about their experiences at Harvard Business School and an unnamed consultancy, respectively.[11] Lucy Kellaway uses the management pages of the *Financial Times* to lambast managers for producing so much "shameful, outrageous bilge."[12]

Yet so far none of this has cured the industry of its ailments: for every sinner who repents, there are thousands who sin more enthusiastically than ever. Management writers continue to fall victim to the "halo effect": books with titles like *What Would Google Do?* (by Jeff Jarvis) have replaced *ABB: The Dancing Giant* (by Kevin Barham and Claudia Heimer) on ambitious managers' shelves. Management professors continue to sell their pet theories to MBA students as if they were universal truths. Management fads continue to rise and fall. Management students continue to be the most money-obsessed people in universities (only about 20 percent of HBS students took the oath in 2009, when it was at the height of its fashion, and the proportion has been falling ever since).[13] And management prose continues to disfigure the language in ever more disgusting ways.

Which brings us to the second charge: that much management writing is incomprehensible gobbledygook. This is clearly a charge that nobody in his right mind could challenge—indeed one of the purposes of this book is to translate "managementese" into something approaching English. There seems to be something in the water in business schools or at management conferences that destroys people's capacity to speak plainly or write clearly. No metaphor goes unmixed. No jargon goes unused. No infinitive is left unsplit. This matters, because style can never be separated from substance. As George Orwell put it in 1946 in "Politics and the English Language," language "becomes ugly and inaccurate because our thoughts are foolish, but the slovenliness of our language makes it easier for us to have foolish thoughts."

What, then, of the third charge: that, underneath this convenient cloud of obfuscation, most of what the gurus are saying is blindingly obvious? Too often, to outside eyes, management gurus seem to be dealing in applied common sense ("the customer is king"); many of their catchphrases ("total-quality management") now seem trite. They often claim to be predicting the future when all they are doing is describing the present. Just as Lenin's *Imperialism, the Highest Stage of Capitalism* (1917) majestically predicted the outbreak of the First World War three years after it had actually happened, management gurus are forever prophesying a future that has already arrived. As Matthew Stewart, a disillusioned former management consultant, has put it, "aspiring gurus seem to understand that the road to riches is paved with garbled clichés and transparently unsubstantiated pseudotheories. No sentiment is too obvious or banal to count as management wisdom, provided it makes use of one or two bits of jargon and is followed by an exclamation point!"[14]

There is an element of truth in this, but less than critics allege. Some of the things that strike us nowadays as blindingly obvious were anything but obvious when farsighted management theorists began to talk about them. Peter Drucker, for example, was predicting the decline of the blue-collar worker and the rise of the "knowledge worker" back in the 1950s, when the trade unions were in their pomp and the Communist Internationale was still planning to create a worker's paradise. People have stopped preaching about total-quality management not because quality has gone out of fashion, but because everybody is striving for it. Besides, there is nothing inherently wrong with stating the obvious. One of the arguments for hiring management consultants is that they can see what is obvious to an outsider but incomprehensible to an insider. To quote Orwell again: "to see what is in front of one's nose needs a constant struggle."

However, the most common criticism of management theory focuses on the fourth charge: its faddishness. Management theorists have a passion for permanent revolution that would have made Leon Trotsky or Mao Zedong green with envy. Theorists are forever unveiling ideas, christened with some acronym, tarted up in scientific language, presented in jaunty, can-do, world-conquering terms that are supposed to "guarantee competitive success" (Lew Gloin has even invented a "systematic buzz word generator," based on a lexicon of thirty buzzy words, that allows you to launch your own management fad: anyone for total transitional flexibility? Or balanced logical capability?)[15] A few months later, with the ideas tried out and "competitive success" still as illusory as ever, the theorists unveil some new idea. The names speak for themselves: management by objectives, brainstorming, T groups, lean manufacturing, the balanced scorecard, reverse innovation, customer relationship management, corporate social responsibility, and so on.

The fashion in theories is mirrored by a fashion in companies. Gurus are forever discovering companies that seem to have stumbled on the secret of competitive success. A few years later, these miracle organizations are faltering, troubled, or even bankrupt (Rosenzweig rightly criticizes John Micklethwait and myself, in the first edition of this book, for buying into the hype about Asea Brown Boveri and Percy Barnevik).[16] Toyota and BP were once regarded as apogees of excellence. Now Toyota has faltered on the very thing that it was supposed to have mastered—total-quality management—and BP's claim to be "Beyond Petroleum" is the butt of jokes (Beyond Parody, etc.). The people who once boosted Toyota and BP have now moved on to the likes of Google and Best Buy. How long can it be before these modern miracles trip up and fall—and the gurus who were once praising them start writing books on where they went wrong and why?

Despite all this, these theories continue to command a large, if confused, audience among managers. In 2009 a survey by one of the leading management consultancies, Bain & Company, of what use managers made of twenty-five leading management techniques found that the average company used eleven techniques, with European companies even keener to use them than American ones. Management fashions seem to be growing ever more fickle, with new methods exploding onto the scene from nowhere. Tools such as customer relationship management (CRM), which involves compiling vast quantities of information about customers and then making business decisions on the basis of that information, can come from nowhere one year to reach top of the pops the next.[17]

Humble businessmen trying to keep up with the latest fashion often find that by the time they have implemented the new craze, it looks outdated. The only people who win out are the theorists, who just go on getting richer and richer. Indeed, it is not hard to construct a conspiracy theory to explain what is going on. Established gurus, with jet-set lifestyles to support, are always looking for ways to update their arguments; would-be gurus, be they overworked management consultants dreaming of spending some time with their families or underpaid business professors dreaming of first-class travel, are always trying to invent the revolutionary ideas that will establish their reputations; and everybody in the business is desperate to keep the wheel turning. Hence the paradox at the heart of the management theory industry: a surplus of overhyped new ideas and a dearth of level-headed criticism.

The Contradictory Corporation

Yet many of the complaints about faddism miss the point. There is nothing necessarily wrong about trying out new ideas. Rather like jogging or pumping iron, a new theory can force companies to exercise their corporate muscles. (Jack Welch of General Electric even dubbed one of his management systems "workout," implying that managerial change is good for corporate health.) The problem comes when these ideas contradict each other. The deeper objection to management theory is that it is pulling institutions and individuals in conflicting directions.

For every theory dragging companies one way, there are two other theories dragging it in another. One moment the gurus are preaching total-quality management, stressing the importance of checking quality and reducing defects; the next, they are insisting that what matters is speed (which means being a little less painstaking about checking quality) or innovation (which means having the courage to make mistakes). One moment they are saying that what gives a company its edge is its corporate culture, the more distinctive the better; the next, they are ordering companies to become more "multicultural" in order to be able to hold a mirror up to the rest of society. One moment companies are urged to agree on and then follow a single strong "vision"; the next, they are being warned that they live in an "age of uncertainty" where following any single vision can be suicidal. One moment companies are being urged to "reengineer themselves"—which is often a polite way of saying "sack the slackers"—and the next they are told about the importance of being socially responsible. Most management theorists have not worked out whether it is important to be global or local, to be big or small, to be run in the interests of shareholders or stakeholders. Usually, they end up telling managers to be all things to all people, covering up their intellectual confusion with bland phrases about "doing well by doing right." The surprise is not that great companies such as Toyota can falter in the face of all this contradictory advice but that they can operate at all.

The contradictions are particularly poisonous when they involve a company's relations with its staff. One of the more fashionable words in management theory is "trust"—it is this, the theory holds, that will keep "knowledge workers" loyal and inspire them to come up with ideas. Yet the gurus also preach the virtue of "flexibility," which is usually shorthand for firing people. Indeed, there is a growing contradiction between the interests of companies and those of their employees. What companies do to make themselves secure—laying off workers, putting them on short-term contracts, or introducing flexible work schedules—is precisely what makes those workers feel insecure. Meanwhile, the only person who could sort out these contradictions is the one who—thanks to all that de-layering—has the least time to do it: the boss.

These contradictions within firms reflect a deeper intellectual confusion at the heart of management theory: it has become not so much a coherent discipline as a battleground between two radically opposed philosophies. Management theorists usually belong to one of two rival schools, each of which is inspired by a different philosophy of human nature; and management practice has oscillated wildly between these two positions. Scientific management is based on the idea that the average worker is a lazy slob who is redeemed only by greed. The job of the manager is to break down jobs into their component parts so that even the stupidest persons can master them, and design incentive systems so that even the laziest will exert themselves. Humanistic management, on the other hand, is based on the idea that the average worker is a Promethean figure—intelligent, creative, and self-motivating. The job of the manager is to ensure that the work assigned is interesting enough to bring out the best in the firm's employees, by dint of devolving decisions to shop-floor workers, creating self-managing teams, and encouraging workers to make suggestions about how the company might be improved. This, in essence, is the debate between "hard" and "soft" management.

The first theory, in the guise of scientific management, held sway until the Second World War. The second theory gained ground in the 1950s and 1960s, under the banner of the "human-relations movement." The rival theorists have been advancing and retreating ever since. The humanists advanced in the 1980s with the fashion for Japanese management, but fell back in the 1990s as the fashion for reengineering gained ground. The humanists advanced again in the first decade of this century, as companies embraced empowerment and corporate social responsibility, but retreated once again as the global economy went into meltdown—and the hard-nosed job-slashers and restructurers moved back in.

The Contradictory Corporation has had two alarming effects. The first is the reinforcement of anxiety. The recession has made life difficult enough without gurus doing their bit. But management theorists are constantly cooking up new ways of dealing with our problems, from "nurturing talent" to sacking everybody and moving operations to Bangalore. *The Harvard Business Review* even sends a "management tip of the day" to anyone who subscribes to its email list—suck down as well as up! Build bridges to your enemies! Make sure you keep your nails clean!—though anybody who tried to follow all this advice would quickly be driven insane.

The second effect concerns language—and commitment. As contradictory theories zip past them, managers have learned how to pay lip service to theories without really understanding them, let alone bothering to implement them. Like the Soviet bureaucrats of old, and the North Korean bureaucrats of the present, many managers are living in a dual world: the real world and the world of officially sanctioned ideology. Thus, they talk about "empowerment" while habitually hoarding power or boast about "corporate social responsibility" while continuing to move jobs to the cheapest possible places.

This doublespeak matters, because management theory is the language of the international elite. An increasing number of people who rule companies and countries speak in its terms. For the young and ambitious, a business school education is looking more and more like a necessity, and a spell at a consulting firm more of a probability. Eavesdrop in the business-class lounge of any airport from Shanghai to San Francisco and you will hear a familiar vernacular. In politics, the old battles between left and right no longer seem to matter. In the last British election it was difficult to tell the difference between the policies of New Labor and New Toryism—let alone to understand where the Liberal Democrats fit into the equation. Instead, the battleground has become one of managerial efficiency: Who will "manage" the economy best? Who will "restructure" government most efficiently? Who has the necessary leadership skills to master the crisis? If this debate is carried out in terms that are contradictory or empty, then everyone suffers.

With a Scalpel, Not a Hatchet

Some would argue that all these contradictions indicate that management theory is itself a contradiction in terms. I prefer to see it as an immature discipline, prevented from growing up, partly, by its enormous financial success.

Management theory is in roughly the same state that economics was a century ago. Many of its fundamental tenets have yet to be established. The discipline still awaits its Joseph Schumpeter or John Maynard Keynes. It lacks rules of debate, so the discipline remains open to anybody with an axe to grind—much as economics was open to the likes of Karl Marx. However, just as anybody wanting to know about economics a hundred years ago could draw on writers such as Alfred Marshall, Adam Smith, and David Ricardo, management theory already has its founding fathers—among them, Alfred Sloan and Peter Drucker. Management theory has also generated debates on such momentous subjects as globalization, the nature of work, and the changing structure of companies. Despite its adolescent excesses, the discipline has generated ideas that work. Japanese manufacturers trounced American ones in the 1980s because they embraced quality. Indian companies have become outsourcing giants in part because they have learned how to apply techniques that were originally designed for the manufacturing sector to the service sector.

Dig into almost any area of management theory and you will find, eventually, a coherent position of sorts. The problem is that in order to extract that nugget, you have to dig through an enormous amount of waffle. This book is an attempt to extract those nuggets.

Needless to say, it would have been much easier (and often far more pleasurable) to have trashed the industry. There is a wealth of material for anybody hoping to produce a hatchet job. What is actually needed, however, is a "scalpel job," which is what I attempt to do in the following pages: I try to separate the good (or, at any rate, the influential) from the bad and the irrelevant—and to look at its effect on companies and society around the world. By definition, this has been an exclusive rather than an inclusive task. If ideas or thinkers fail the test completely, I have usually left them out, rather than wasting ink on people who have already spilt too much of it.

The first part of *Masters of Management* looks at how the industry works. Chapter one examines the life cycle and significance of one of the most influential management fads of the moment, corporate social responsibility (CSR), and compares it with another great fad from the 1990s, reengineering. Chapter two turns to the enormous industry that produces and sells management theory: the business schools, consultancies, publishing houses, and stand-alone gurus. The second part looks at some of the people who have defined modern management theory. Peter Drucker (chapter three) is the father of modern management and a natural introduction to most of the big debates of our time. Tom Peters (chapter four) has been the most influential guru of the past two decades, not just because of what he has said, interesting though that is, but also because of the way that he has said it. In recent years the subject has been redefined by a group of journalists (such as Tom Friedman and Malcolm Gladwell) and non–business school academics (such as Richard Florida and Robert Reich) who have jumped on the bandwagon. They are the subject of chapter five.

Part three examines the forces that are shaping the current management revolution. Chapter six looks at the way that traditional corporate structures, particularly top-down systems of command and control, have been reconfigured in the past three decades. Chapter seven traces the rise of a new kind of entrepreneurial capitalism, first in the United States and now in most of the rest of the world, that puts much more emphasis on startups, venture capital, and risk-taking than the old model of managed capitalism. Chapter eight examines the way that companies from emerging markets, most notably India and China but also Brazil and Mexico, are turning many of our long-established assumptions about business upside down. I have little doubt that we are at the beginning of a new management revolution that will shift the global balance of power just as powerfully as the rise of Japan did thirty years ago.

Part four takes a closer look at the great debates that this management revolution has unleashed. How do you combine knowledge, learning, and, perhaps the greatest management buzzword of the current era, innovation (chapter nine)? How do companies steer a straight course in an era when old-fashioned strategic planning has fallen out of favor and the gale of creative destruction is raging as never before (chapter ten)? What does globalization actually mean for today's hassled business people (chapter eleven)? Chapter twelve ponders what all this means for the boardroom. Are all these management ideas putting too much pressure on boards and making leadership impossible? And what exactly are companies for? Are they responsible to their shareholders alone or to a wider group of stakeholders? Chapter thirteen turns to management theory's colonization of the public sector, a colonization that is being speeded up by the sovereign debt crisis. Doctors now have to decide whether treating sick people is one of their "core competencies"; generals talk about war being "the ultimate benchmarking exercise"; governments call in McKinsey to redesign their state apparatus.

Part five looks at the subject from the other end of the telescope and asks what all these corporate gyrations mean for the workers of the world. How is the world of work changing? How are careers being reconfigured in a more uncertain era? Why do companies simultaneously preach de-layering while giving people ever grander titles, or spread anxiety while also urging their front-line workers to smile all the time (chapter fourteen)? Chapter fifteen looks at the growing "war for talent" and attempts to turn "talent management" into a science. Where can you get bright people? How can you make the best use of your "human resources"? And how is the war for talent changing the balance of power between individuals and organizations? Finally, chapter sixteen turns from the macro to the micro picture. How do we manage ourselves in a world where so many of the traditional landmarks are disappearing?

I have conducted my audit—or rather re-audit—with two groups of readers in mind. The first is the huge number of people who work in management or business but who find the world of the gurus faddish and off-putting. More and more people are assuming management responsibilities of one sort or another, and more and more are having their lives turned upside down by business practices that started far from home. I have consequently included as many case studies as possible from the emerging world as well as from the traditional heartland of management theory, the United States. The second group consists of "normal" readers who are vaguely aware of management theory but who blanch at picking up all those business books. This category encompasses an astonishing range of people—from entrepreneurs in Shanghai who are scanning the horizon for new opportunities, to political activists who want to know why everyone keeps telling them that the earth is flat, to spouses who want to understand why their husband or wife is being reengineered out of a job.

My aim has been to challenge the specialist readers without confusing the generalists. If any piece of jargon has somehow slipped through my net, I apologize. Time and again, confronted by a theory or a passage in a book, I have returned to three questions: Is it intelligible? Does it add up to more than mere common sense? Is it relevant? In short, I have tried to judge the gurus on the same terms that the foremost of them—such as Peter Drucker and C. K. Prahalad—have themselves insisted that they wish their theories to be judged: as a serious intellectual discipline.

PART I

HOW IT WORKS

1

The Fad in Progress: From Reengineering to CSR

Buying thousands of copies of your own book might sound like a particularly eccentric form of vanity. But what if the authors are backed by a deep-pocketed consultancy? What if getting onto the *New York Times* best-seller list can guarantee a lot of buzz? And what if that buzz can drive customers to the consultancy and speaking gigs at $30,000 a pop to the authors? Suddenly eccentric vanity looks like sound business.

This was the logic behind one of the most risible management scandals of the 1990s. In August 1995, *Business Week* revealed that CSC Index, an ambitious young management consultancy, and two would-be gurus with close ties to the consultancy, Michael Treacy and Fred Wiersema, had been employing methods that are more often associated with the grubbier parts of the record industry to turn *The Discipline of Market Leaders*, a slim and rather banal volume, into a best-seller.[1] They had brought so many copies of the book—always making sure to use small bookshops that were tracked by the *New York Times* in compiling its best-seller list—that thousands of copies had to be stored in tractor-trailers.

The *Business Week* exposé was one of the final chapters in the most remarkable management story of the 1990s, the story of the rise, triumph, and eventual fall of business-process reengineering, or reengineering for short. Reengineering was the most successful business fad of the Clinton era—a fad that persuaded companies around the world to break themselves up into their component parts and then put themselves back together from the ground up. It was also the most ambitious: Michael Hammer, the man who invented the idea along with James Champy, liked to give his job description as "reversing the industrial revolution."

The fad started off with an acute insight: that information technology (IT) had changed the business world so completely that companies needed to go back to the drawing board. Why break up a job into its component parts and disperse those parts around the organization, as companies had been doing since the industrial revolution, when a single computer-empowered worker could do it better and faster? It also generated a great deal of genuine excitement. Michael Hammer's "Reengineering Work: Don't Automate, Obliterate" was one of the most popular articles the *Harvard Business Review* ever published. *Reengineering the Corporation* (1993), which he wrote with Champy, sold more than two million books in seventeen languages.[2]

Reengineering was soon sweeping all before it. *Time* magazine argued that *Reengineering the Corporation* had "set in motion a revolution the likes of which hadn't been seen since Henry Ford introduced the assembly line." By 1994, 78 percent of Fortune 500 companies and 68 percent of FTSE 100 firms were engaged in some form of reengineering, according to PriceWaterhouseCoopers, a consultancy. William Bratton, the man who turned around the New York Police Department, was one of dozens of public-sector figures who championed the idea. Hammer proclaimed that he was doing if not God's work, then at least that of the angelic host: "I think this is the work of angels. In a world where so many people are so deprived it is a sin to be so inefficient."[3]

Reengineering undoubtedly did some good—streamlining cumbersome work processes, fine-tuning throaty organizations, and pruning unnecessary jobs. But even more than other business fads, it suffered from a combination of hubris and insensitivity. Reengineers failed to grasp that organizations are human rather than mechanical entities. Reengineered companies found that they were soon suffering from "corporate anorexia" as they lost some of their most vital people (including middle managers who, far from being surplus, embodied corporate lore and wisdom). They also experienced a catastrophic collapse in levels of trust as the workers who survived the pruning turned against their masters. For most people, reengineering was demonic rather than angelic.

Even more than other business fads, it was also corrupted by greed: as the movement's momentum began to wane, and the critics discovered more and more design faults, the reengineers resorted to ever more desperate methods to keep the hype going and the business rolling in—hence the fiasco with *The Discipline of Market Leaders*.

History Rhymes

The story of reengineering is of more than just antiquarian interest. It also throws light on the most influential business fad of the current decade: corporate social responsibility, or CSR. This claim might sound eccentric at first blush—it would be hard to come up with two more different management ideas than reengineering and CSR. Reengineering is the ultimate "hard" management tool; CSR is all soft and fluffy. Reengineering is all about making things more machine-like; CSR is about proving that there is a soul in the capitalist machine.

But in fact the two have a surprising amount in common. They are both classic business fads—ideas that contain a kernel of truth but which are oversold by ambitious gurus and greedy consultants and which eventually collapse under the weight of unrealistic hype and inflated expectations (though CSR's demise is hardly likely to be as dramatic as reengineering's). They both take a half-truth and treat it as a whole truth—reengineering by making a fetish of efficiency and CSR by exaggerating the importance of good works. And their fates are subtly intertwined: just as CSR's rise owed much to reengineering's excesses, so CSR's current woes will help to pave the way for another burst of reengineering. In the over-leveraged noughties, fair-trade coffee may have become a staple of most consumer lives and CSR a fixture in every boardroom. With the age of austerity upon us, consumers are watching their pennies and companies are scything back on the fluff.

Be Responsible, My Son

Corporate social responsibility has a short history but a long pre-history. Corporate philanthropists such as Cadbury and Rown-tree in Britain and Hershey and Kaiser in the United States built model communities to house their workers (at one point the U.S. had more than 2,500 company towns, housing 3 percent of the population).[4] In Germany and Japan, industrialists embraced a stakeholder model of capitalism in which workers were involved in decision-making. But by the 1970s company towns were withering across the Anglo-Saxon world, and share-holder capitalism had become bureaucratized. For many business people, corporate social responsibility meant nothing more than throwing some money at the local opera (and getting a few seats in return for the senior managers).

The pioneers of modern CSR—the idea that companies should embrace social responsibilities as a central part of their strategy rather than just a feel-good add-on—were an eccentric bunch: cranky business people such as Anita Roddick, the founder of Body Shop, and woolly intellectuals, such as the people associated with Business in the Community.[5] CSR types were much mocked by people from both sides of the political spectrum—by left-wingers for trying to provide capitalists with fig leaves of respectability and by right-wingers for thinking that capitalists needed fig leaves in the first place. Most business people followed the C. Montgomery Burns approach toward their trade: "I'll keep it short and sweet. Family. Religion. Friendship. These are the three demons you must slay if you wish to succeed in business."

Today the picture could not be more different. Most of the world's biggest companies trumpet their commitment to social responsibility. Some have even adopted a "triple bottom line" (people, planet, profits) to ensure that CSR is encoded in their DNA. And most of the world's great and good have signed up to the program. The United Nations Global Compact for corporate responsibility, launched at Davos in 1999, has more than three thousand corporate supporters. America has created a National Corporate Philanthropy Day (February 25), which even has its own colors, blue and green. Britain's 2006 Companies Act requires companies to report on social and environmental questions. China has created a Chinese Federation for Corporate Social Responsibility. As Clive Crook, a former colleague of mine at *The Economist*, has put it, "CSR is the tribute that capitalism everywhere pays to virtue."[6]

This tribute to virtue is paid in gold as well as hot air. No major consultancy is complete without a CSR practice. Some consultancies sell nothing but CSR: a group called the Ethical Corporation provides "business intelligence" on CSR to more than three thousand multinational companies, publishes a CSR-themed magazine and website, puts on a huge conference every year, and compiles an ever-expanding library of case studies on corporate irresponsibility, including studies of Exxon Valdez, Toyota, and McDonald's.[7] There are CSR performance indexes (such as the Dow Jones Sustainability Index); CSR professorships (more than half of U.S. MBA programs require their students to know something about the subject); CSR websites, newsletters, and professional organizations; and year in and year out, hundreds of CSR conferences, discussion groups, and other jamborees.

The CSR industry is by no means as corrupt as the reengineering industry became, but there are revolving doors and secret handshakes. Nongovernmental organization activists chastise multinationals for their failure to implement CSR and then take jobs with the same multinationals to advise them on how to implement it. Liberal professors write books chastising multinationals for their business practices and then create consultancies that advise the companies on how to escape future chastisement. Many journalists would have been keener on puncturing the movement's pretensions if they weren't invited to so many CSR conferences in exotic places.

What explains CSR's extraordinary success? Why has an idea that was once associated with a few eccentrics become mainstream? The simplest answer is reputation management. Joint-stock companies have always provoked profound suspicion, on the grounds that they have all the legal rights of individuals without any of the responsibilities. Sir Edward Coke complained in the seventeenth century that "they cannot commit treason, nor be outlawed or excommunicated, for they have no souls." A century later, another jurist, Edward Thurlow, worried that "corporations have neither bodies to be punished, nor souls to be condemned, they therefore do as they like."[8]

These suspicions have grown louder in recent years. Ordinary people expect ever-higher standards from their corporate masters. A survey by McKinsey in 2007 discovered that 95 percent of companies felt that "society" had higher expectations than it did five years ago.[9] Academics, whistle-blowers, journalists, NGOs, professional malcontents—all delight in exposing the malefactors of great wealth. Hollywood has produced a stream of corporate-bashing films: *The Constant Gardener* (pharmaceuticals), *Sicko* (healthcare), *Blood Diamond* (precious stones), *Supersize Me* (fast food), *Syriana* (big oil), *Michael Clayton* (corporate law), and *Capitalism, a Love Story* (business in general, courtesy of the man who made the best business-bashing film of all, *Roger and Me*, Michael Moore).

CSR is a way of fighting back, a way of managing your reputation in a reputation-shredding age. It is an ad campaign and an insurance policy rolled into one. It is no accident that some of the leading proponents of CSR are companies that have been embroiled in scandals or companies that operate in scandal-plagued industries such as oil and gas. CSR is both a ready-made advertising campaign and an insurance policy. Joseph Schumpeter once complained that "the public mind has by now so thoroughly grown out of humor with business, as to make condemnation of capitalism and all its works almost a requirement of the etiquette of the discussion."[10] CSR gives companies a seat at the table.

Globalization has given new urgency to the trend. Given that a company based in Boston can see its reputation shattered by heinous practice in Borneo, it is advisable to build ethical considerations into their supply chains (such as paying their subcontractors a living wage). So has environmentalism. Companies have taken to appointing chief sustainability officers, producing sustainability reports full of pictures of green fields and blooming flowers and generally revising their behavior to reduce their production of world-warming gases. In 2005, Walmart, the world's biggest retailer, committed itself to becoming a zero-waste business (it pledged to double the fuel efficiency of its vehicle fleet by 2015). In the same year, General Electric adopted an "Ecomagination Strategy" that involved slashing its output of greenhouse gases and investing heavily in "clean" technologies. Tesco and Sainsbury, two of Britain's biggest retailers, are locked in a fierce battle to prove who is greener. Even BSkyB, the British satellite outpost of the distinctly brown Murdoch empire, has declared itself "carbon-neutral."

Companies have been forming some surprising alliances in the name of CSR—and blurring the line between for-profit and nonprofit organizations in the process. Companies have taken to striking deals with governments to slay various monsters such as corruption (a particularly common practice in the mining industry) or blood diamonds (the Kimberley process). Limited Brands, a clothing company, has even lobbied the government of Alberta, Canada, over threatened caribou habitats. But the bread and butter in CSR deal-making is provided by NGOs. Coca-Cola has formed an alliance with the World Wild Life Fund to conserve freshwater river basins and with Greenpeace to eliminate carbon emissions from its coolers and vending machines.

The CSR boom is driven by a single obsessively repeated formula: that "being good is good business," as Anita Roddick of the Body Shop put it—that you can do well by doing right, as a thousand public relations professionals have put it since. CSR can improve the bottom line in four ways, at the very least, the argument goes: by attracting better workers and boosting overall morale; by appealing to socially conscious consumers, who are happy to pay a bit more for ethically sourced products; by identifying new business opportunities, particularly at the bottom of the pyramid; and by engaging socially responsible investors. CSR boosters have no shortage of examples to back up their arguments. One in nine American investment funds claims to have a "socially responsible element." There is evidence that people will buy a "fair and square" product over a plain vanilla one. In 2005, ABC Home Furnishings allowed two Harvard researchers to conduct an experiment on two sets of identical towels in one of its New York stores. One set of towels carried a "fair and square" logo and a message about how this towel was good for society. The researchers tried swapping the logo from one towel to the other. They discovered that not only did the sales of towels increase when they carried the label; they increased even more when the store raised the price of the towel.

Corporate Candy Floss

What should we make of all this? Is CSR an inspired formula for creating a better world, as its proponents claim? Or is it corporate candy floss, as its critics insist? Is it a conspiracy against shareholders (who end up footing the bill for all this CSR), as free-marketers argue? Or is it a gigantic con trick—an attempt to paint a human face on the snarling devil of corporate capitalism—as left-wingers suspect?

It is tempting to answer "all of the above." One of the many problems with CSR is that it is an inherently muddled philosophy—a feel-good mishmash rather than a coherent position—and one that is adopted by different people for different reasons. Some entrepreneurs are gripped by social problems; others see them as great advertising. Some companies are serious about CSR; others treat it as just another corporate ritual. This muddle is one reason for the movement's extraordinary popularity. But it also exposes it to a wide range of criticisms.

The least convincing arguments come from the left. Here the view is that CSR is nothing more than a con trick. Phrases such as "greenwashing" and "window dressing" abound. Companies devote only a miserable 2 percent of their income to philanthropy, almost exactly the same proportion that they devoted before the CSR boom. "Socially responsible" investment funds account for only 2 percent of investment funds in the United States and less than 1 percent of funds in Europe. The quintessential corporate villain, Enron, was one of the first big companies to adopt a "triple bottom line," and piled up environmental awards with the same panache that it piled up unfunded liabilities. Companies that are happy to embrace CSR when it coincides with their business ambitions suddenly lose interest when it comes into conflict with them.

The more subtle version of this argument is that CSR is nothing more than a polite mask that companies put on smart business decisions. Why does Whole Foods fill its shelves with organic food and "natural" washing powder? Not because it is more responsible than Giant, but because it has identified a lucrative market niche. Why does Starbucks offer health insurance to its baristas? Not because it is a good corporate citizen, but because it wants to reduce labor turn-over. Why have Mars and Cadbury become obsessed with "sustainable" sources of cocoa? Not because they have got religion, but because they are worried that supplies of cocoa may run out. In this view, what many corporate types regard as the strongest argument in favor of CSR—that it is just smart business—is in fact proof that it is just an optical illusion.

The problem with the left-wing assault on CSR is that it is based on the erroneous assumption that there is a fundamental conflict between the interests of companies and the interests of societies as a whole—and that companies are therefore engaged in a relentless game of greenwashing and window dressing. Of course, there are plenty of corrupt companies, some spectacularly so, such as Enron; and, of course, some companies make terrible mistakes, as BP did. But as a general rule, companies have done at least as much to advance human progress as any other social organization. The proliferation of companies from the midnineteenth century onward coincided with the most rapid economic progress in human history. The United States, with more than five million companies, has the world's highest standard of living; North Korea, with no companies worthy of the name, has the lowest.

Companies bring people together in a voluntary association in order to solve problems and create things that people want. Launching a new company is a leap in the dark and an act of faith. Investors risk their capital; managers and workers risk their time and effort. Failed companies are punished by bankruptcy. Successful ones produce new products and processes that raise productivity. Walmart's brutally efficient supply chain may have meant that it has pushed a lot of smaller retailers out of business, but American shoppers save at least $50 billion on food alone every year by shopping in its stores.

Companies produce direct benefit in terms of jobs. General Electric employs 320,000 workers with 700,000 dependents. But, as Ann Bernstein points out, that is only the tip of the iceberg. The company helps to support 600,000 company pensioners and five million shareholders, many of them retirees. More than 660 million people a year travel on aircraft that are powered by its engines, and 230 million have scans on its imaging machines. The company helps to generate more than one-third of the world's electricity and is constantly investing in innovative new products. GE also pays dividends that supplement the income of millions of people and provides financing for universities and other public-sector organizations.[11] The triple bottom line: we should start out by assuming that companies are good things rather than bad.

That argument sets up a much more powerful line of criticism—from the right. Here the accusation is also of a con trick—but a trick played not by companies on the public but by managers on their shareholders. Corporate executives do not own the companies that they run. They are employed by the firm's real owners—the shareholders—to maximize the long-term value of their assets. If managers want to be honored at charity dinners, they should reach into their own pockets, rather than those of their shareholders.

That argument has been at the heart of the conservative critique of corporate do-goodery ever since Milton Friedman first voiced it in 1970,[12] but over the years other conservatives have added new twists. One is that CSR is based on all sorts of questionable assumptions. To whom exactly are companies responsible—the places where they have their operations, or society at large? And if they are responsible to "society at large," what on earth does that mean? Does "society" really have a common collective interest, or is it an arena of competing individuals and interest groups? And if it is an arena of competition, who determines to which interests companies are responsible? People from different parts of the world have strikingly different ideas of what CSR means: in China, the hallmark of a "socially responsible company" is safe, high-quality products; in Germany it is secure employment; and in South Africa it is the company's contribution to healthcare and education.

Then there are those pesky NGOs. What right do these organizations have to speak for society as a whole? Nobody elects them. Nobody holds them to account. And nobody subjects them to the sort of hard-headed analysis that they apply to companies (they seem to have as much of a vested interest in producing outrage as Coca-Cola has in producing fizzy drinks). The entire world of NGOs has a Potemkin-like quality: slither-sized organizations are forever issuing reports and referring to other slither-sized organizations. When Ralph Nader decided to swap the Potemkin world of pressure groups for electoral politics in 2000, he won only 3 percent of the vote, enough to put George W. Bush in the White House but not enough to prove that he had any popular legitimacy.

And what about the claim that companies can do well by doing good? The trouble is that words are cheap: exhaustive studies have demonstrated that for all their claims to the contrary, shoppers and investors are not willing to put their money where their mouths are. Philip Morris is still one of the best-performing stocks in the world. A study by the Wharton Business School, at the University of Pennsylvania, found that "ethical" funds underperform the general market by 31 points a year. A study by the European Union showed that while 75 percent of consumers said they were willing to adjust their shopping habits in the light of ethical and environmental considerations, only 3 percent had actually done so. "If there was a dolphin-safe can of tuna next to a regular can," J. W. Connolly, a former boss of Heinz, has noted, "people chose the regular product. Even if the difference was one penny."[13] Those well-to-do towel buyers in New York are atypical: Ethical business is a market niche rather than a market-shaper.

Moreover, CSR tempts companies to lose one of their most valuable assets: focus. Old-fashioned shareholder capitalism provides a clean and simple way of measuring a company's performance, but CSR introduces all sorts of variables—particularly if you follow Novo Nordisk, a healthcare company, and introduce a "triple bottom line,'" or if you listen to CSR consultants and introduce several dozen measures of your contribution to society. If companies lose their focus, capitalism loses its crunchiness, and if capitalism loses its crunchiness it becomes more difficult to make decisions that, however painful, eventually benefit society as a whole. .

Which leads to the most stinging criticism of CSR: that it can end up harming the very people it is supposed to help. Companies may think twice about investing in the developing world if they have to pay more for their labor and raw materials. Low-paying jobs may turn into no jobs. New companies may find it harder to challenge deep-pocketed incumbents. The worry is that CSR is dominated by a soft conspiracy between Western NGOs (who have little understanding of the sort of choices that poor people confront), Western trade unions (who are intent on stifling global competition), Western media companies (who make a living out of selling moral outrage), and global multinationals (who are delighted to be able to make it harder for new companies to get a start in life).

Far from providing companies with insurance, CSR reinforces the case against them. CSR may buy a little good publicity for business in the short term, but it does so only at the expense of reinforcing antibusiness prejudices in the long term. It institutionalizes the belief that business can earn a license to operate only by paying a penance to society, whereas in fact the justification for business is business itself. It also creates an army of antibusiness pressure groups. The more business participates in CSR conferences and the like, the more it finds itself paying for the rope that will hang it.

Why put up with all this moral blackmail? Free-marketers point out that the best way for business to help the poor is not to sign up to grand-sounding declarations but rather to do what comes naturally—and treat poor people as customers. The late C. K. Prahalad famously argued that people at the "bottom of the pyramid" represent a vast underserved market. The markets in the rich world are bound to shrink due to low birth rates and slow economic growth. The developing world, on the other hand, is producing a benign combination of high birth rates and rapid economic growth. In the free-marketers' view, companies should devote their energies to dreaming up new products that are suited to the developing world and new ways of getting those products to poorer consumers, rather than to preening themselves over how responsible they are.

An Idea Whose Time Is Passing

For the first decade of this century, CSR carried all before it: companies rushed to sign up to it and critics were widely dismissed as cranks or curmudgeons. But over the past two years or so the wind has been taken out of its sails. Many companies responded to the 2007–08 recession by focusing on the old-fashioned single bottom line. Citigroup's charitable foundation reduced its grant budget from $90 million in 2008 to about $60 million in 2009. (Taxpayers might well wonder why the company was giving money away rather than using it to repay government loans.) Ford's philanthropic arm reduced its spending by 40 percent. Companies also embraced harsher management techniques. Bain's annual survey of management techniques discovered that three techniques long associated with (sometimes brutal) cost-cutting crept back to the top of the management pops—benchmarking (at number one), outsourcing (at number five), and, yes, business process reengineering (at number eight).[14]

BP's oil spill in the Gulf of Mexico arguably played an equally important role in CSR's problems. BP had been a world leader of CSR. In 2000, the company that was then known as British Petroleum launched a multimillion-dollar advertising campaign to rebrand itself as the jolly green giant of the oil world, with a new motto, "Beyond Petroleum"; a new logo, a green-and-yellow sunburst; and a mountain of bumph about "corporate sustainability."[15]

The company's brand awareness jumped from 4 percent in 2000 to 67 percent in 2007, and BP was regarded as the world's most "environmentally conscious" company.

At the same time, John Browne, the company's chief executive from 1995 to 2007, seized the crown as the corporate world's most "socially responsible" businessman. He wrote florid introductions to BP's corporate social responsibility report, gave speeches on how companies needed to be good citizens as well as successful businesses, and threw his arms around Tony Blair and the New Labor project. But none of this came at the expense of his business success, or so it seemed. Browne presided over BP's rapid expansion—most notably with the acquisition of Amoco—and boosted the company's market capitalization tenfold. He won Britain's "most admired leader" award four times in a row.

The disaster in the Gulf was thus a calamity for CSR as well as for BP. In fact, Lord Browne had been forced to retire in 2007, as a result of a sex scandal, and Tony Hayward, his successor, had tried to focus the company back on the basics. But as far as the public was concerned, BP was CSR incarnate. "Beyond Petroleum" provided the material for a dozen disparaging plays on words, and the green-and-yellow sunburst became synonymous with corporate hypocrisy.

The disaster strengthened the left's argument that CSR was nothing more than greenwashing. Examine the jolly green giant for a moment and you discovered that it was one of the most unscrupulous oil companies in the business. It demonized health and safety rules as "over-regulation" in congressional hearings and focused almost exclusively on fossil fuels: in the first quarter of 2010, BP brought in $73 billion in revenue from fossil fuels and only $700 million from alternative energy. The disaster in the Gulf was only the biggest of a succession of disasters, which included an explosion in a Texas City refinery that killed fifteen workers and injured 170 others.

Fury at BP's hypocrisy had an immediate effect on the CSR-inspired alliance between NGOs and companies. NGOs that had collaborated with BP in various ways—by receiving its largesse or advising it on green policies—were bombarded with complaints. These included some of the biggest in the business, such as the Nature Conservancy and the Environmental Defense Fund. NGOs that had refused to dine with the devil, such as Greenpeace, were praised for their farsightedness. A huge swathe of the "NGO community" concluded from the debacle that they needed to put more distance between themselves and the corporate world, partly because they did not want to be caught in bed with the next corporate villain, but mainly because they calculated that the "win-win" formula had lost its shine.

At the same time the disaster also strengthened the right's argument: far from protecting BP from criticisms, it actually made those criticisms all the more stinging. Conservatives pointed out that their insurance policy had turned into a charge sheet. They also complained that CSR had been a costly distraction from real business: if the company had invested the money that it spent rebranding itself on improving its operations, it might never have got itself into trouble in the first place. One of the ironies of the entire episode was that this is exactly what Tony Hayward, Lord Browne's unfortunate successor, felt: "BP makes its money by someone, somewhere, every day putting on boots, overalls, a hard hat and glasses, and going out and turning valves," he argued shortly after taking over the company. "And we'd sort of lost track of that."[16]

The Balanced Scorecard

CSR clearly lacks the wonder-working powers that many of its advocates imagine: the tedious need to make trade-offs cannot be wished away by waving CSR's win-win wand. Still, CSR is unlikely to disappear entirely, however loud the critics bay and however deep the economy shrinks.

Western companies will continue to find CSR a useful tool in one of their most important "wars," the war for talent. Many of the most desirable job-seekers, particularly in the millennial generation, are motivated by "meaning" as well as money. They want to make a good living, to be sure, but they also want to help to improve the world. (David Brooks has coined the phrase "bourgeois bohemians" to capture the mixture of capitalist and countercultural values that are common in professional circles.)[17] An imaginative CSR program can be a deal-maker for some people. Stony indifference to CSR can be deal-breaker.

Emerging-market companies will find CSR a useful tool in an even more vital war: the war against chaos. The emerging world is marked by "institutional voids" (to borrow a phrase from Tarun Khanna, of the Harvard Business School): governments that don't work properly, markets that are full of holes, chaos that threatens to envelop everything that you do. Officials are frequently corrupt or incompetent. Roads are potholed. Schools fail to impart the basics. So companies have no choice but to fill the voids—sometimes by forming "charitable" divisions and sometimes by striking alliances with charities. In the first half of the century these companies dubbed what they were doing "corporate philanthropy"; today they are much more likely to call it CSR. But in both cases their behavior is dictated by the hard logic of market and government failure. Thus, Tata Steel has built a town in the middle of the jungle, Jamshedpur, to house a workforce that would otherwise be living in huts; Hindustan Unilever has formed an alliance with various NGOs to teach 133 million peasants the importance of washing their hands; and Infosys has forged alliances with over three hundred engineering colleges across the country, sponsoring students and helping to design the curriculum.

The world has also seen the rise of a new sort of hybrid organization: entrepreneurial startups that straddle the gap between business and charity. These hybrids flourish in the emerging world. Vinod Kapur has built a successful for-profit company with the express purpose of feeding India's rural poor. He invested $1 million and many years of his life in pursuit of his dream of breeding a "perfect" chicken. The result was the Kuroiler: multicolored for camouflage, resistant to disease, happy with farmyard scraps, strong and wily enough to fight off predators, and capable of producing twice as much meat and five times as many eggs as common or garden chickens. Kapur has built an entire supply chain around the Kuroiler, including farms that specialize in breeding the chickens and vendors who sell them across rural India.[18]

Shane Immelman has pulled off a similar trick with school desks in South Africa. Appalled that four million children did not even have desks, let alone schoolrooms, he invented a "lapdesk" that sits on the child's lap and provides students with a stable surface. Immelman gives away the desks free, paying for them by allowing companies to cover them with ads. The desks have proved so popular that affluent people have started to buy them, and Immelman is exporting them to other developing countries.[19]

Social entrepreneurs have popped up in the rich world, too. A new breed of "philanthrocapitalists," to borrow a phrase from my colleague Matthew Bishop, has taken to applying business theory to charity, seeding charities with startup money in much the same way you would seed tech startups and measuring them according to their performance.[20] The Robin Hood Foundation, created by a group of successful young philanthropists in New York City, "invests" in local poverty-fighting organizations, and favors the most successful and innovative. Nancy Lublin has become the charitable version of a serial entrepreneur: so far she has founded Dress for Success, which provides clothes for poor women looking for work, and DoSomething.org, which helps young people link up with good causes.

Nor is the traffic all one-way: philanthropists have plenty to teach as well as to learn. Voluntary organizations have mastered the art of getting by on a shoestring. Habitat for Humanity, which builds cheap homes, and Make a Wish, which help terminally ill people, have turned themselves into global brand names without spending any money on advertising. They have outperformed for-profit companies when it comes to the art of getting people (particularly millennials) to work for peanuts. Mozilla and Wikipedia do not even pay their contributors a penny.[21] Voluntary organizations have also pioneered the use of social media: the Red Cross raised more than $30 million via text messages in the days following the 2010 Haiti earthquake.[22]

So CSR is turning into a classic business fad: promising to change the world and rewrite the rules of business, initially sweeping all before it, eventually losing its momentum, but, in the end, yielding one or two valuable insights. Which brings us to our starting point: that the biggest management fad of the noughties has much more in common with the biggest management fad of the nineties than you might think. Reengineering is now regaining some of its lost ground (sometimes in different guises) just as CSR is fading. But in reality, both ideas are gaining in realism what they are losing in luster—and becoming just two useful but imperfect management techniques among many.

2

The Management Theory Industry

As the United States sank into the Great Depression, a young lawyer in one of Cleveland's poshest law firms kept running across the same problem. Marvin Bower regularly served as the secretary of committees of bondholders who were forced to seize control of failed companies. The committees were stuffed full of bankers and lawyers who knew how to put the firms' financial and legal affairs in order. Yet nobody seemed to know how to do the same thing with their management affairs—despite the fact that, as Bower saw it, it was poor management that, as often as not, had gotten the firms into trouble in the first place.

Bower already knew something about business—he had an MBA from Harvard Business School as well as a JD from Harvard Law School—and he became fascinated by the idea of creating a firm that could do for management advice what his law firm did for legal advice. In 1933 he met James O. McKinsey, a former professor at the University of Chicago who had founded a firm of accountants and engineers in Chicago a few years earlier, and decided to go into business with him, adding management to the firm's areas of expertise and setting up an office in New

York. The relationship with the Chicago company did not last, but Bower continued to chase his dream, serving as the guiding spirit of McKinsey & Co. until his death in 2001.

Bower is an unlikely founding father for an industry that many people associate with hucksters who merrily appear on the cover of their books dressed in their underpants, as Tom Peters, a sometime McKinseyite, once did. He was punctilious to a fault. McKinsey was a "firm" rather than a company (even today insiders refer to it simply as The Firm). Jobs were "engagements"; business units were "practices." Bower expected McKinsey men to wear hats until the early 1960s, personally ending the tradition by coming to work bareheaded. Noticing that too many ellipses and dashes were making their way into company reports, he issued a memo banning them. He repeatedly turned down jobs that he thought might not play to the firm's strengths, refusing to help the American government restructure General Motors, for example. A quick buck today meant nothing compared with an unsullied reputation for excellence.

Yet Bower put into place most of the building blocks of today's management theory industry. He insisted on hiring brainboxes from business schools—particularly from his old alma mater, HBS—rather than veteran managers. He urged The Firm to invest heavily in intellectual capital, and obsessively searched books and articles for new management ideas. He forged close, almost confessional, relations with many of the world's leading companies.

Today, consultancies, business schools, and management gurus are all part of a single prosperous industry. Everybody involved in the industry is making money out of management ideas in one way or another, sometimes sotto voce, like McKinsey's firm, sometimes con brio, like Tony Robbins. Indeed, the "management theory industry" seems destined to thrive come hell or high water: consultancies take on more staff as their clients employ fewer, and business schools become more ornate as the universities around them crumble.

The management theory industry's success is largely driven by the seemingly limitless demand for its products. Management theory has always appealed to thousands of people who want to get ahead; now it has tapped into the market of the millions who are scared of being left behind. The industry's relentless appetite for new ideas to process, print, sell, and regurgitate has helped to make it a peculiarly faddish discipline where ideas are grabbed at rather than matured. And the industry's huge vested interest in selling its products means that self-criticism of the type that Marvin Bower championed is often lacking. In Bower's day, theory was a guide to practice; today, theory is increasingly in the driver's seat.

The Breadth of the Industry

Like Gaul, the management industry can be divided into three parts. The first part, the one that makes the other two possible, consists of business schools. Business schools are the glittering success stories of modern academia, the cauldrons of capitalism, the boot camps of CEOs and "global leaders." Every year a quarter of a million people from one hundred countries take the GMAT in the hope of winning a place in one of them. Harvard Business School has an endowment of $2.3 billion, a professoriate of more than two hundred, a campus of more than forty-four plush acres, research offices in Hong Kong, Paris, Tokyo, Mumbai, and Buenos Aires, and a $100 million-a-year Harvard Business School Publishing arm. Chicago Business School recently changed its name to the Booth School when an alumnus handed it $300 million. Even less prestigious schools are islands of luxury compared with their surrounding universities.

These schools are teeming with academics who are desperate to make their name as theorists in their own right: the 2009 meeting of the American Academy of Management, the discipline's annual jamboree, attracted no fewer than 4,500 budding gurus. They are also homes to publications such as the *Harvard Business Review*, the *Sloan Management Review* (the Massachusetts Institute of Technology), and the *California Management Review* (Haas Business School, University of California, Berkeley) that have an influence and an audience far beyond the universities that spawned them. (Walter Kiechel, one of the powers behind the Harvard Business Publishing brand in the 1990s, recalls hearing a guru who regularly charged $20,000 or more a day for consulting, explaining his "business model": "you can get a year's worth of business, maybe two, on the strength of one [*Harvard Business Review*] article."[1])

The second part of the industry is the management consulting business, which raked in revenues of about $300 billion in 2007 and which has been growing twice as fast as the overall economy for three decades. McKinsey employs 17,000 consultants in fifty countries and, according to *Forbes*, enjoyed revenues of about $5.35 billion in 2007. Its clients include 90 percent of the world's hundred biggest companies and government departments in thirty-five countries. Big IT consultancies such as Accenture and Capgemini enjoy even bigger revenues (although they make less per head than McKinsey and other strategy consultancies such as the Boston Consulting Group and Bain) and clients that include governments as well as companies.

Business schools and consultancies have replaced Oxbridge and the Ivy League as nurseries of the powerful. Indeed, students from the latter jostle to get into the former, and with good reason. The list of companies headed by ex-McKinseyites includes such giants as General Electric (Jeff Immelt), PepsiCo (Indra Nooyi),

Volkswagen (Wolfgang Bernhard), and Boeing (James McNerney). Politicians with MBAs include William Hague, the British foreign secretary; Mitt Romney, a former governor of Massachusetts and possibly the next Republican candidate for the presidency; Wim Kok, a former Dutch prime minister; Jan Kees de Jager, the Dutch finance minister; Vladimir Gurgenidze, a former prime minister of Georgia; Wong Kan Seng, the deputy prime minister of Singapore; Jusuf Kalla, the vice-president of Indonesia; and a raft of Indian politicians such as P. Chidambaram, Mukul Wasnik, Mallipudi Raju Pallam Mangapati, Jyotiraditya Scindia, Jitin Prasada, and Sachin Pilot.[2] Benjamin Netanyahu, the Israeli prime minister, and Bobby Jindal, the governor of Louisiana, both started their careers in consulting. Why obsess about the membership of Bilderberg Group or the Trilateral Commission when you can simply get hold of a list of McKinsey's alumni and identify the members of the real world government?

The third and least well-defined part of the industry is the guru business—the whirligig of book-writing and lecture-giving that is associated with names like Gary Hamel and Jim Collins. The most famous business school professors regularly blur the boundaries between teaching and consulting. Michael Porter, Harvard Business School's most famous guru, was one of eight founders of the Monitor Group, one of the most successful startups of recent years, but one that has recently been sullied by its links to the Gaddafi regime in Libya. John Kotter and Clay Christensen, two of Porter's colleagues at Harvard, have also founded consultancies: Kotter International dispenses advice on change management ("because change is essential"), and Christensen's Innosight helps companies become more innovative.

These superstar professors have been joined by an army of other gurus. There are lean and hungry people from other professions such as journalism and mainstream academia who are desperate to jump on the guru bandwagon. There is also a hard core of full-time gurus who do nothing but dispense management wisdom. Keith Ferrazzi left Deloitte (where he was the youngest-ever partner) to devote himself full time to advising people on how to be better net-workers and marketers. (A clue to his theory is provided in the title of his most famous book: *Never Eat Alone*.)[3] Seth Godin has turned himself into one of the world's most revered experts on marketing by putting his own principles into practice. Godin believes that you need to get people's permission to command their attention rather than forcing yourself on them in the way of classic television adver-tisements. He has used this idea to engineer a succession of brilliant public-relations coups: by giving one of his books, *Unleashing the Idea-virus*, away for free, he stirred up enough interest to strike publishing deals in forty-one countries and launch a public-speaking career.

To a striking degree, business books remain the passports into the profession. Gurus launch all sorts of other "devices" from their lofty "platforms," from DVDs to webinars and from podcasts to ideacasts. But ever since Tom Peters and Robert Waterman trans-formed management books from an exotic species into a main-stream cash cow, books have defined the industry. Books give you a stamp of legitimacy. They also open the door to a speaking circuit that regularly pays top-rank gurus $50,000 or more per speech. This suggests that there may be a fourth division to the management-theory industry: the publishing industry.

Overpaid and Over Here

These rough divisions—into consultancies, business schools, and gurus—imply that the management industry is a much more struc-tured affair than it really is. How can you classify psychometrists who specialize in evaluating potential CEOs or psychologists who help to counsel outsourced workers? What should you make of outward-bound companies that take executives to the African bush to hone their leadership skills? And where should you put *What I Didn't Learn in Business School: How Strategy Works in the Real World*, a novel by Jay Barney and Trish Gorman Clifford, that tells the story of a young consultant's struggle to apply his "strategy toolkit" to the real world of business, and that ends each chapter with "reflection questions" such as "How should the strategy team leverage Bill?" "Why is synergy often promised, seldom realized?" and "Why didn't Justin get more value out of his orientation training with the consulting firm?"[4] Apart from in the dustbin, that is.

Adding to the complexity of the management industry is the fact that it is now a global enterprise. Not that long ago anyone who wanted to understand management went to an American business school, studied American gurus, argued about American corporations, and probably joined an American consultancy. The great debates on the subject—such as the one about the relative merits of scientific and humanistic management—were conducted primarily among American thinkers. You could probably discover all you needed to know about the subject without venturing too far away from Harvard's Baker Library.

The United States is still the epicenter of the industry, with more than seven hundred business schools. But the rest of the world is catching up fast. In 1998–2007, the proportion of non-Americans taking the GMAT rose from one-quarter to 42 percent, with 21 percent of that 42 percent coming from India.[5] Non-Americans are building their own businesses schools, such as the Indian Business School in Hyderabad and the Chinese European Business School (CEIBS) in Shanghai. And they are producing their own management gurus: lists of the world's best-known gurus are rapidly being taken over by Indian names. Gurus of all sorts, American and non-American alike, focus on the likes of Infosys and Huawei as well as old stalwarts such as IBM and General Electric.

Europe is producing a lengthening list of first-class business schools, such as the London Business School; INSEAD, just outside Paris; IMD (the Institute for Management Development), in Switzerland; and IESE, in Spain. In the mid-1990s, Oxbridge dons choked on their port at the very thought of their universities providing a home to business schools. Now, Oxford's Said School and Cambridge's Judge School are butting heads with America's best schools.

Europe is also warming to the guru business. Some Europeans, notably the French, remain snooty about management theory, but most are acquiring a taste for it. The works of Tom Friedman and Malcolm Gladwell sell across the continent. Gary Hamel spends part of the year at the London Business School. German businesses are some of the world's most eager consumers of management consulting. Europe is also producing gurus of its own. There may be only one European guru who has been admitted to the global first division, Britain's Charles Handy (I am classifying Austrian-born Peter Drucker, who once described Handy as "the most interesting management writer today," as an American rather than a European). But a cluster of other petitioners, including John Kay, a former head of Oxford Business School, Yves Doz of Insead, and Hermann Simon of Simon-Kucher & Partners, are knocking on the door.

European business schools have one big advantage over their American rivals—an advantage that translates into the management ideas that they produce. They are much more global. In 2008, 85 percent of students in Europe's fifty-five top MBA programs and 46 percent of professors were "international." The comparable figures in America were 34 percent and 26 percent, respectively.[6] INSEAD has a twin campus in Singapore and research outposts in Israel and Argentina. The majority of INSEAD students spend some time on the other side of the world, either as "swingers" (hopping from one location to another) or "switchers."[7] (Wharton and Chicago's Booth School have also built campuses in Singapore, but only for their executive education programs.) IESE has helped to found schools in fifteen other countries, including Argentina, Brazil, China, Guatemala, Kenya, Mexico, Nigeria, Peru, and the Philippines. This international orientation gives both professors and students a more global perspective: it is difficult to see the world as Franco- or British-centric when the vast majority of the people in the classroom come from somewhere else. It is noteworthy that Pankaj Ghemawat, one of the world's leading experts on globalization, has abandoned Harvard Business School, which nurtured him and gave him tenure, for IESE.

With Western Europe firmly under its thumb, the management industry is advancing east and south. In the wake of the Soviet Union's collapse, Western governments and philanthropists, and of course business schools, made a concerted attempt to export management theory to the former Communist world, on the assumption that better management was vital to the region's prosperity. George Soros started the trend in 1988 when he helped to found CEU Business School in Budapest. Since then, Western European business schools have been busy setting up satellites in the East, while local universities have been expanding into the business school market. The management theory industry has even received the imprimatur of Russia's most powerful man, Vladimir Putin: in 2005 he ordered the establishment of two new schools of management, one in Moscow and one in St. Petersburg, to address Russia's shortage of high-class managers (only three in every

100,000 Russians have MBAs, compared with seventy in every 100,000 Americans).

Management gurus have duly added the former Communist bloc to their ever-expanding itineraries. Tom Peters begins his forward to the 2009 edition of *Re-imagine! Business Excellence in a Disruptive Age* by telling a story about giving a one-day seminar on management in Novobrisk, in a far-flung bit of Siberia (naturally enough, the foreword was written in Golden Bay on New Zealand's South Island, which is as far away from Novobrisk as heaven is from hell).[8]

But the biggest growth in the industry by far is in Asia. The region has long sent its brightest young people to American business schools, much as it once sent them to Oxbridge colleges. The governments of Taiwan and Singapore are stuffed with people with American MBAs. Now the region is producing business schools of its own: local universities are expanding aggressively into the business school market, while Western universities are establishing satellite campuses in the East.

The rise of Asian-based business schools has already shaken up the global pecking order. The *Financial Times* ranked Shanghai's CEIBS number nine in the world in its 2009 business school rankings, placing it above such American powerhouses as MIT's Sloan School of Management and New York University's Stern School. But it is likely to shake it up much farther in the future as the region's brightest people set their hearts on a business career. The Indian Institute of Management in Ahmadabad has 681 applicants for every place, compared with Stanford Business School's pitiful seventeen. FasTracKids, a booster program patronized by ambitious Chinese parents, calls itself a "junior MBA program" and accepts children as young as four.[9]

The consulting business has made impressive inroads in Asia, despite the fact that many Asian companies are family-run. The skylines of Shanghai and Delhi are punctured by the same neon signs as the skylines of London and New York, for Accenture as well as HSBC, PriceWaterhouseCoopers as well as Citi. McKinsey's Mumbai office is its fastest-growing branch. As the younger business school–educated generation of Asians takes over from their school-of-hard-knocks fathers, the consultants can expect a bonanza.

So has the guru business. Step into a bookshop in Beijing or Shanghai and you are immediately confronted with piles of management books. Venture farther into the business sections and you find crowds of students religiously taking notes. Some Western gurus have taken to adding a couple of Asian cities to their speaking tours in much the same way that aging rock stars do the same thing: the money is good, the audience is large and polite, and you can use an Asian anecdote to spice up your performances back home. But other gurus are taking the challenge more seriously. John Quelch and George Yip have both moved to CEIBS (from HBS and Rotterdam Business School, respectively).

The Heat of the Kitchen

The management theory industry is being reshaped by explosive growth and intensifying competition as well as globalization. The business school business has exploded since the Second World War: in the United States, the global trendsetter, the number of MBAs awarded every year has increased from 3,200 in the mid-1950s to about 150,000 today. "Sometime in the next decade, the population of living MBAs will exceed the population of Chicago," notes Matthew Stewart.[10] Competition between business schools is ever more intense, encouraged by the parent universities, which treat business schools as cash cows, and supercharged by the annual MBA rankings produced by the likes of the *Financial Times*, the *Wall Street Journal*, *U.S. News & World Report*, and *The Economist*. Brand-name schools such as Harvard and Wharton have to keep blowing their own trumpets to retain their places in the top ten. And new business schools are always coming up with new ideas to try to attract the attention of potential customers: Henry Mintzberg's International Masters in Practicing Management has dispensed with both spotty youngsters (it admits only practicing managers) and a home campus (it takes place on five continents).

Business schools have shown an astonishing ability to survive both savage criticism and economic downturns. The financial crisis hit them with a one-two punch—blackening their reputations (all that talk of "agents of the apocalypse") while also devastating the market for their products (Wall Street laid off 240,000 people in the eighteen months following the middle of 2007),[11] yet business continued to boom. More than three-quarters of full-time MBA programs received more applications in 2009 than in 2008, their best performance for five years, according to the Graduate Management Admission Council (GMAC), a business school association. Business schools were able to raise their tuition and increase the number of courses they offered. To cynics, this almost looked like a conspiracy: first you create a storm and then you offer students a safe port until the storm blows over.

The obvious reason for the schools' continuing popularity is that they sell something worth having: an MBA is the equivalent of a union card for the corporate elite, a card that, at best, can get you the top job, and at the very least, boosts your earnings power. Employers pay MBAs twice as much, on average, as people with undergraduate degrees, and 30 to 35 percent more than people with lower-level management degrees, such as master's of finance.

Some 98 percent of corporate employers report that they are sat-isfied with their MBA hires, a figure that has not changed since 1998, suggesting that they will continue to fish in the same pond.

The schools have proved strikingly adept at adjusting to criticism. They began to prepare for a potential downturn in the market even before the crisis struck, worried about overexpansion and stung by criticisms from the business world about the practical relevance of their courses. In 2005–06, Stanford Business School introduced the most radical changes since its foundation and increased its faculty by more than 10 percent. The Yale School of Management replaced tra-ditional subject-based courses such as marketing with "integrated" courses based on various constitutiencies (investors, customers, em-ployees). The University of Michigan's Ross Business School gave students a chance to work on "projects" with, say, hospitals in India and energy companies in Mozambique. Lower-ranked business schools were arguably the most innovative. A growing number of American business schools followed the European example and offered one-year MBAs. Others offered more specialized courses: Manchester Business School offers twenty courses in subjects like marketing and finance.

The ferocity of the backlash against the "agents of the apoc-alypse" only intensified the schools' commitment to change. A striking number of the world's leading schools appointed new deans in the wake of the crisis: the London Business School, the Judge School, and INSEAD in Europe, and the Kellogg School, the Booth School, and the Harvard Business School in the United States. HBS's decision to appoint Nitin Nohria in 2010 was partic-ularly significant: Nohria is the first HBS dean to be born outside North America and the first to come to office proclaiming that business faces a "crisis of legitimacy" and that business education is at an "inflection point."

Nohria considers his first task to be to restore faith in business schools. This means improving two things that have been neglected: "competence" and "character." He wants the faculty to focus more on the risks of clever financial techniques; they will have plenty of case studies to choose from. He also wants HBS to renew its commitment to shaping its students' characters as well as their intellects. Nohria has long argued that business people should regard themselves as members of an honorable profession. He also supports the idea of students taking the equivalent of the Hippocratic oath.

At the same time he also adds a generous dose of optimism to his message: HBS is on the cusp of "a period of extraordinary innovation." Nohria wants to make the school more global: one of his first acts as dean was to embark on a whistle-stop tour of the world's business hot spots. He also wants to rethink the school's hallowed teaching methods. Since the 1920s, HBS students have pored over case studies of business decisions. The new dean wants them to take part in live case studies as well—to take themselves to the Midwest or Mumbai and spend time working for real companies.

The same process of growth and reform is sweeping through the consulting profession. In the days when Bower's boys always wore a hat, consulting was a comfortable and cozy business. Today corporate giants, including accounting firms such as PriceWaterhouseCoopers and Accenture and technology companies such as Electronic Data Systems (EDS) and Infosys, are pouring resources into the area. Cisco, a technology giant, snapped up 20 percent of KPMG Consulting. Altran, a French technology company, gobbled up Arthur D. Little, the world's oldest management consultancy, when overexpansion plunged it into bankruptcy. But, despite the invasion of these giants, smaller firms keep multiplying.

The up-or-out system adopted by most consultancies leaves many middle-aged consultants with nothing to do but start their own consultancies. And the size of the market means that there are plenty of bright young MBAs who are looking for a lucrative niche.

The Importance of Theory

The thing that provides this disparate industry with both its glue and its vim is management theory. Take away management theory and you just have a collection of lackluster functionaries (professors, consultants, and book writers). Add management theory and you have a collection of people who promise to reimagine industries and reshape the world.

Consultancies have been making money out of business ideas since they were first launched. Bower turned McKinsey into the world's most successful consultancy by investing in ideas as much as cultivating relations. Then, in the 1960s, the Boston Consulting Group threatened to knock the Bower boys off their perch by producing not one but two "big ideas." The "experience curve" taught companies that they could reduce their costs as they expanded their market share, thanks to the accumulation of know-how. The "matrix" encouraged companies to view themselves not as an undifferentiated whole but as a portfolio of businesses that make different contributions to the bottom line ("cash cows" versus "dogs," for example).

Major consultancies are investing more heavily than ever in producing and promoting ideas. McKinsey spends $400 million a year on management theory. It also supports the McKinsey Global Institute to conduct cutting-edge research and the *McKinsey Quarterly*, and more important, the *McKinsey Quarterly*'s website, to disseminate its findings. BCG continues to challenge McKinsey's fiercely for preeminence: its annual reports on "emerging market giants" are particularly impressive. And other consultancies are on the march. Deloitte supports a growing number of research centers: the Center for the Edge provides a perch for two of the most interesting gurus in the business, John Seely Brown and John Hagel, for example. Booz Allen Hamilton supports one of the most successful business magazines around, *Strategy & Business*.

Most consultancies will go out of their way to nurture a best-selling business book, encouraging authors to turn an idea into a book and spending heavily on advertising and promotion. A successful business book can burnish the reputations of blue-chip consultancies for thought leadership. BCG burnished its reputation for thought leadership on emerging markets with *Globality*, by Harold Sirkin, James Hemerling, and Arindam Bhattacharya.[12] Booz & Company strengthened its position in the cutthroat Chinese market with *The China Strategy*, by Edward Tse. And Bain increased its ability to profit from its core strength, in strategic management, with *Profit from the Core* by Chris Zook.[13] McKinsey men and women have produced more than fifty books since 1980, compared with only two between 1960 and 1980; Lowell Bryan, who is a McKinsey man to his fingertips, has written six.

For less elevated consultancies a successful business book can be a money-spinning franchise. The Gallup Organization has been squeezing the idea of "strength assessment" (which might be crudely summarized as playing to your strengths rather than obsessing about your weaknesses) until the pips squeak. It has launched a succession of best-sellers such as *Strengths Finder 2.0* (by Tom Rath), *Strengths Based Leadership* (Tom Rath and Barry Conchie), and various books about filling your bucket. It has also created a highly successful training program on the back of the books.

Still the relationship between consultancies and business ideas is not quite as simple as this makes it seem. Top-flight consultancies frequently dump gurus if they get too big for their boots (as McKinsey famously did with Tom Peters and Robert Waterman). At the same time, famous gurus frequently dump their employers if they think that they are not getting enough out of them. Marcus Buckingham left Gallup in 2006, after spending two decades with the organization and co-writing two best-selling books, *First Break All the Rules* (1999) and *Now Discover Your Strengths* (2001), to found his own consultancy, The Marcus Buckingham Company (TMBC), because he thought that he was putting in more than he was getting out. John Hagel left McKinsey after sixteen years to join Deloitte (after a spell as an independent consultant) because he thought that the less well-known consultancy would provide him with more independence.

Academics have always been in the business of thinking up striking new ideas (or so one would hope). But for many business school academics, marketing those ideas seems to be as important as generating them. In the early days of business schools such a brazen taste for publicity might have provoked academic ostracism, but today it is mainstream. Business school deans are engaged in such a desperate competition for buzz that they will do almost anything to attract a big name. And house prices are so steep in most university towns that even the most austere scholars end up compromising their standards. One moment they are having a quiet drink with a publisher to discuss a little idea; the next moment they are selling the latest "breakthrough idea," complete with press kits, book signings, and endorsements from leading businessmen.

Many of the executives who offer these endorsements also harbor dreams of becoming business gurus once they retire. Here, Jack Welch is the gold standard: he has published a succession of best-selling books, including *Winning*, which he co-wrote with his wife, Suzy Welch, a former editor of the *Harvard Business Review* (who lost her job when it emerged that her research for a profile of Mr. Welch for the magazine had become a little too thorough), and even established an eponymous school of management, the Jack Welch Management Institute at the Chancellor University in Ohio, which offers an MBA based on the great man's ideas. But there are plenty of former and current CEOs with similar dreams.

It is tempting to damn chief executives for spending so much time chasing will-o'-the-wisp theories when they should be looking after their shareholders. In many cases, however, the chief beneficiary is the company they head. A taste for management theory can allow companies to brand themselves as "go-ahead" and "cutting edge." The likes of W. R. Grace, Whole Foods, and Best Buy devote a great deal of effort to wooing management writers and presenting themselves as centers of managerial excellence. Many companies, including Merck, 3M, Procter & Gamble, and even McDonald's, go so far as to brand their internal training programs as "universities" or "business schools," in the hope that some of the magic of the management theory industry will rub off.

If these three guru-breeding grounds provide a constant supply of fresh new gurus, there is nevertheless more to the guru industry than just supply. The business world is constantly throwing up new problems that do as much as anything to reorder the guru market—promoting this guru or downgrading that one, sprinkling gold on this corner of the management theory industry and throwing another corner into the dark. There are no prizes for guessing the two market-shaping trends of recent years: the rise of emerging markets and the advance of the Internet.

The rise of emerging markets has reordered the world of management theory as thoroughly as it has reordered the business world in general. Many of today's most influential business gurus hail either from emerging markets or emerging-market diasporas. India has always punched above its weight in the management theory business (perhaps there is something about living amidst constant chaos that turns your mind to management theory), but recently it has threatened to take over the subject entirely. A partial list of first-division Indian gurus would include the following: Nirmalya Kumar (London Business School), Timur Kuran (Harvard Business School), Vijay Govindarajan (Tuck Business School), Jaideep Prabhu (Judge Business School), Pankaj Ghemawat (IESE), Anil Gupta (University of Maryland at College Park), Arindam Chaudhuri (Indian Institute of Planning and Management, New Delhi), Ram Charan (no particular abode). India has even produced one of the few CEOs who has found the time to produce a book for the Harvard Business Press, which is rather more demanding than many more commercial presses: Vineet Nayar, the boss of HCL Technologies, an outsourcing firm, and author of *Employees First, Customers Second.*

The Indians are supplemented by a handful of people from other emerging markets. South Korea has W. Chan Kim; Bangladesh, Muhammad Yunus; Lebanon, Nassim Taleb; and Greece, Costas Markides. There are even a few people from the Old World who have produced some valuable insights into the new world. John Hagel has astonished his fellow inhabitants of the Bay Area by arguing that the emerging world is taking over from Silicon Valley as the new hotbed of innovation.

The rise of the Internet has shaken the management theory industry equally thoroughly. Most of the leading high-tech gurus made their careers in high-tech companies or technology journalism rather than in business schools. Don Tapscott (*Wikinomics* and *Macrowikinomics*) started out in enterprise collaboration. Chris Anderson (*The Long Tail*) is a long-standing technology journalist, most recently as editor of *Wired*. Jeff Jarvis (*What Would Google Do?*) made his reputation blogging about new media at Buzzmachine.com. Clay Shirky (*Here Comes Everybody* and *Cognitive Surplus*) is a jack-of-all-trades (including theater director, lecturer, and consultant) who happens to have a lot of clever ideas about the new media.

Thriving on Anxiety

The management theory industry is clearly a formidable business, broad enough to draw on the brainpower of everybody from professors to CEOs and flexible enough to respond to sudden changes in the business climate. But that does not entirely explain why it is so successful. Why are so many people so eager to throw themselves under its wheels? Why do so many business people who are already working themselves into an early grave pick up yet another book on organizational transformation? And why do so many companies that have sworn never to have any more truck with consultancies decide to give them just one more go?

Andrzej Huczynski, a student of management gurus, argues that some of the answer lies in managers' anxiety about their status.[14] Business schools were initially created so that business people could look lawyers and doctors in the eye (even today, Nitin Nohria and Rakesh Khurana long for a world in which managers embrace the same professional standards as other respectable people). Scientific management initially took off, in the days of Frederick Taylor, because managers thought that anybody who was anybody needed a branch of science to support them. These days managers have lots of different sub-specialisms to boost their status (or at least defend their turf): general managers have "management by objectives," production chiefs have

TQM, and human resource managers, the perennial losers in the status competition, have the "war for talent."[15]

Some of the most successful gurus have been shameless flatterers of managerial egos. Peter Drucker subtitled his classic *The Practice of Management* "A Study of the Most Important Function in American Society." "The manager is the dynamic, life-giving element in every business," he cooed; scientific management is "the most powerful as well as the most lasting contribution America has made to Western thought since the Federalist Papers." What mid-level manager could fail to feel the cockles of his heart warm at these words? Gary Hamel has one-upped Drucker in a sentence that is worth savoring: "The machinery of management—which encompasses variance analysis, capital budgeting, project management, pay-for-performance, strategic planning and the like—amounts to one of humanity's greatest inventions."[16] Tom Peters lays on the flattery with a different trowel: rather than telling managers that they are the last best hope of humanity, he tells them that they are wacky and exciting. Their children may call them squares. Their wives may yawn at their every utterance. They may worry that they are turning into their fathers, working stiffs on the conveyor belt to retirement and death. But, listening to Peters, they become crazy guys who dream impossible dreams and make unbelievable things happen.

The average struggling journalist or liberal arts professor might be surprised to discover that managers are so insecure. The well-scrubbed buildings and carefully manicured lawns of business schools; the rising salaries and generous expense accounts of successful executives; the ever-proliferating multinational companies and global banks—all these things bespeak the arrogance of power rather than the anxiety of the status starved. But in fact these masters of the universe are no more confident than the rest of us.

Today's managers are well aware that they are not always respected or liked. A 2009 survey for *Management Today* discovered that one-third of respondents had either no trust in their managers or very little.[17] Managers are also terrified of the future. Three-quarters of managers quizzed by Bain for its 2009 survey of management tools believed that today's market leaders will have faded in five years' time.[18]

As well as worrying about losing their jobs, managers also suffer from more existential fears. What on earth does their job mean? What are they actually supposed to do when they "manage"? Are they strategy-setters, or just hand-holders? Are they sergeant majors in business suits, or amateur psychotherapists? In the old days of steep hierarchies and deferential workers, such heretical questions never arose. But now that the Internet is putting information in the hands of more employees, and decision-making is being devolved to front-line workers, the traditional sources of managerial authority are disappearing. The result is not only confusion but widespread angst: it turns out that the top dogs of the management world are nothing more than trembling Chihuahuas.

Often, the gurus offer the illusion that, for all the complexities of the world, the answers are really rather straightforward, provided the guru is one's guide. Gurus of every stripe have tried to reduce the world's complexities to simple phrases ("core competencies") or to lists of "must-do's" (the five forces and six trends). These days alliterative formulas are so rampant that a reader does not know whether the "three Cs" refers to commitment, creativity, and competition, as Kenichi Ohmae preaches, or competence, connections, and concepts, as Rosabeth Moss Kanter would have it.

When these snake charmers are not soothing managers' fears, they are firing their ambitions. They are past masters at turning bad news into good. A posse of management writers presented the 2008 credit crunch as a blessing in disguise: see, for example, *The Upside of Turbulence* (by Donald Sull) and *The Silver Lining: An Innovation Playbook for Uncertain Times* (by Scott B. Anthony). They are also purveyors of privilege. They not only promise to teach managers the secret language that is spoken by the powerful; they hold out invitations to secret conclaves such as meetings in Davos. Being sent for an MBA course means that a young manager is being singled out for the fast track to the top. Being elected a Global Leader of Tomorrow by the World Economic Forum means that you might get to rub shoulders with Angelina Jolie.

If management gurus are virtuosos at exploiting this combination of fear and greed, they also have something more admirable on offer: intellectual stimulation. Back in the 1950s, in the days of "the organization man," most business people were affable types, pleasant and easy to get along with but hardly rocket scientists. The intellectual gap between Harvard Business School and Harvard Law School was a chasm. Today managers are better educated than they have ever been before, the gap between HBS and Harvard Law School has been obliterated, and a growing number of rocket scientists are looking for jobs in business. The graduates of today's business schools and consultancies are not content to just ship product and pore over balance books. They crave clever ideas and cutting-edge theories.

The Importance of Being Faddish

Why do managers flit from theory to theory rather than settling for just one, or, as their disappointment mounts, rejecting the whole guru business entirely? And why do management gurus keep tearing up the sacred texts and starting from scratch? The glimmer of an answer should already be apparent. The sheer number of would-be gurus means that there are always numerous ideas in the market-place. The prevalence of fear and ambition among the consumers of management ideas means that the market is always unstable. And the instability of the business world means that businesses are always confronting new problems and looking for new solutions.

The groundwork for the current frenzy of management fads was prepared by the professionalization of management in America in the wake of the Second World War. The premise behind this change was that a set of general concepts and generic principles could be applied in all circumstances. Belief in these universal ideas weaned managers from their earlier reliance on improvised in-house management practices and prepared them to become consumers of mass-produced and mass-marketed managerial techniques.

This regimented system, which allowed for fads but was not built around them, lasted only until the 1980s. Then, most of the fixed points in the business world were called into question. The mass-production model no longer seemed to be working. The paragons of good management—companies such as General Motors and IBM—were slipping. Ideas that had been invented outside the system—foreign notions such as "lean production" and "customer–supplier" partnerships—appeared to have the edge. American companies now had to consult Tom Peters and Toyota as well as Harvard Business School and McKinsey. The velocity of management fads has increased ever since, as the global economy has become more unstable, Indian and Chinese management techniques have been added to the Japanese ones, and ever more gurus have jumped on the management theory bandwagon.

Yet for all these changes, one man continues to tower over the industry: Peter Drucker.

PART II

THE PROPHET AND THE EVANGELISTS

3

Peter Drucker: The Guru's Guru

When he died on November 11, 2005, a few days short of his ninety-sixth birthday, Peter Drucker was rightly celebrated as the alpha male of the management world. He was one of only a handful of management theorists who continued to churn out influential work for decade upon decade. He was also one of the few thinkers from any discipline who can claim to have changed the world: he was the inventor of privatization, the apostle of a new class of knowledge workers, the champion of management as a serious intellectual discipline, and a confidante to the world's corporate elite—not just in his native Europe and his adoptive America, but also in Japan and the developing world. Wherever people grapple with tricky management problems, from big organizations to small ones, from the public sector to the private, and increasingly in the voluntary sector, you can find Drucker's fingerprints.

The range of his influence was extraordinary. He changed the course of thousands of businesses, including America's most revered conglomerate, General Electric, where he spawned not one but two revolutions, first in the 1950s when GE followed his concept of radical decentralization, and second in the 1980s when Jack

Welch rebuilt the company around Drucker's belief that it should be first or second in a line of business or get out.

George W. Bush, America's first president with an MBA, was a devotee of Drucker's idea of "management by objectives." ("I had read Peter Drucker," Karl Rove once told the *Atlantic Monthly*, "but I'd never seen Drucker until I saw Bush in action.") Newt Gingrich mentions him in almost every speech. Rick Warren, America's leading mega-preacher, claims that Drucker helped to inspire his idea of "the purpose-driven church." One South Korean businessman has even gone so far as to adopt Drucker as his Christian name, in deference to the great man. Drucker is the one management theorist whose writings every reasonably well-educated person, however contemptuous of business or infuriated by jargon, really ought to read.

Drucker's influence has not only survived his death, it has continued to grow. The Drucker Institute in Claremont, California, keeps the flame burning with the help of hundreds of Drucker societies around the world. A celebration of his hundredth birthday in China attracted ten thousand fans. Drucker's oeuvre continues to expand despite his death, much as Isaiah Berlin's and Hugh Trevor-Roper's have. Drucker's last book, *The Effective Executive in Action*, was published a few months after he died, and books about his ideas continue to come out, either rejigging his writings or summarizing what he might have said about this or that problem.[1]

This is not to say that Drucker was invariably right—or even always sensible. He gave some silly advice (such as when he advised the *Los Angeles Times* to lower the Chinese wall between reporting and advertising) and produced some foolish generalizations (such as his insistence that America's research universities were "failures" that would soon become "relics"). But the quality of his intellect shone through everything he said, even the foolish stuff.

Though Drucker hated the word "guru," thinking it synonymous with charlatan, he remains, in truth, the one management
thinker who genuinely deserves the accolade.

The Road to Drucker

Tom Peters argues that "no true discipline of management" existed
before Drucker.[2] That is a stretch. Nevertheless, Drucker, partly
because of his own talents and partly because of the time when he
stumbled upon management, was the first great systematizer in a
diffuse and disorganized discipline. Like his biblical namesake, he
is the rock on which the current church is founded, as the voices
crying in the wilderness who preceded him will confirm.

In one sense, management is as old as humans: building the
pyramids or establishing the Roman Empire required management skills of a high order. Business-builders such as the Medicis
relied on theories of business (albeit ones that were seldom written
down) as well as gut feelings. Adam Smith devoted pages to the
organization of businesses. Robert Owen sketched out the first
theory of corporate social responsibility (he refused to employ
children under ten, for example). But it was not until the introduction of mass production in the late nineteenth century that
business demanded, as a matter of survival, the creation of a new
elite of managers and a new body of formal management theory.

The principal inspiration for this new science, in America at
least, was Frederick Winslow Taylor, an engineer who invented
carbon-steel machine tools. "It is fashionable today to look down
on Taylor for his outdated psychology," Peter Drucker noted, "but
Taylor was the fist person in history who did not take work for
granted, but looked at it and studied it."[3] Taylor believed that there
was a single best method of organizing work, and that this method

could be discovered through a detailed study of the time and motion involved in doing each job. The stopwatch, the motion picture camera, the slide rule, and psycho-physiological tests— these were the tools of the trade of Taylor and his acolytes. The principles at the heart of scientific management were crystal clear: break jobs down into their simplest parts; select the most suitable workers to fit the available jobs; turn those workers into specialists, each an expert in his own appointed task; arrange these special- ized jobs along an assembly line; and design the right package of incentives (including bonuses and prizes) to ensure that the work- ers exerted themselves to the maximum.

Taylor was as starry-eyed about managers as he was cynical about workers. To them, he assigned the job of turning factories into smoothly running machines. They coordinated the various specialized tasks (the workers themselves could hardly be expected to understand how their specialty fit into the larger enterprise), and they monitored and motivated the workers (who might easily weary of their tedious routine). The lower rung of the manage- ment hierarchy was dominated by specialists (accountants, recruit- ers, etc.). At the top of the pyramid sat Taylor's version of Plato's guardians—the people whose job it was to design and regulate the entire system, to monitor the behavior of competitors, and, above all, to plan ahead.

Taylor's ideas were put into practice remarkably quickly, partic- ularly by Henry Ford, a self-made mechanic just like Taylor, who organized his new factory in Highland Park, a suburb of Detroit, along Taylorist lines. Taylor's ideas helped shape the curriculum at a new sort of educational institution, the business school, which began to appear on the scene with the foundation of the Whar- ton Business School, by the University of Pennsylvania, in 1886 and then began to pop up everywhere at the turn of the century.

(Harvard Business School's decision to use his work as the basis of the first year of its MBA program gave Taylor particular pleasure, because he had dropped out of the university without a degree, but not so much pleasure that he was willing to accept the offer of a job there.) His ideas also helped to shape the practice of a new sort of institution, the management consultancy. Arthur D. Little, which had started life as an engineering firm, added management advice to its services after the Great War, and James McKinsey founded his eponymous consulting firm in 1925.

Taylor's ideas were soon everywhere. Henry Ford's great rival, Alfred Sloan, applied them to General Motors (rather more successfully than Ford, it turned out: Sloan was a professional manager, detached from the hurly-burly of the shop floor, whereas Ford was an inveterate meddler). Many of Taylor's disciples found their way into state and local government and tried to apply scientific management to places like the schoolroom and the operating theater.[4] Congress held hearings on the subject as early as 1912, giving publicity to the new idea. Herbert Hoover, an engineer by training, tried to use scientific management to make government more efficient.

Still, the apostles of scientific management did not have it all their own way. A rival group of theorists, who became known as the human-relations school, wanted to see workers involved in managerial decisions. Mary Parker Follett, a lonely woman among these macho management pioneers, stressed that "we can never wholly separate the human from the mechanical side."[5] Elton Mayo, a psychologist based at the Harvard Business School, emphasized noneconomic rewards for productivity: "So long as commerce specializes in business methods which take no account of human nature and social motives, so long may we expect strikes and sabotage to be the ordinary accompaniment of industry."

This humanistic school was at its most influential in Europe, particularly in Britain, where the powerful craft unions faced off with Taylorism and leading businessmen sought a gentler approach. Quaker businessmen such as the Cadburys and the Rowntrees urged other employers to treat their workers like human beings rather than machines. William Richard Morris, the father of Britain's automobile industry, was so dismayed by the difficulties of introducing the new system that he christened it "mess production."[6] C. S. Myers, a psychologist, criticized scientific management for taking a simplistic view of human motives. Elliott Jaques, another psychologist, focused on the social dynamics of group behavior and, after the Second World War, turned Tavistock Institute in London into the headquarters of humanistic management.

A fair number of Europe's leading intellectuals were caught up in the struggle between scientific and humanistic management. In Germany, avant-garde thinkers were mesmerized by the cult of scientific management. Bauhaus architects like Walter Gropius and Ludwig Hilberseimer tried to marry design with scientific management. Bertolt Brecht and Fritz Lang briefly sang the praises of the new craze. In Britain, intellectuals usually sided with the humanists. Aldous Huxley in his book *Brave New World* (1932), English-born Charlie Chaplin in his film *Modern Times* (1936), George Orwell in his essay "James Burnham and the Managerial Revolution" (1946) and his novel *Nineteen Eighty-Four* (1949)—all expressed their fear of mass production, scientific management, and the reduction of the individual to a cog in a vast industrial machine.

An Intellectual Refugee

This was the slightly schizophrenic discipline that Peter Drucker stumbled upon on the eve of the Second World War. Drucker scorned the idea that he was the man who invented management (though there is a book about him with that title). Instead, he argued that, by the mid-1930s, "nothing had come together." Nobody had asked the question, "What is management?" It fell to Drucker to do the asking and preside over the coming together.

Drucker was born in 1909 into the Austrian upper middle class. His father, a cosmopolitan government official, introduced his young son to Sigmund Freud when he was eight or nine years old. As a student, he got to know such illustrious figures as the historian Karl Polanyi and the military strategist Fritz Kraemer. He earned a doctorate in international and public law from Frankfurt University in 1931 and published articles in German economics journals.

The events that led this Viennese intellectual to write about something as far removed from the mainstream as management were complicated and largely accidental. Drucker spent his twenties trying to avoid Adolf Hitler and drifted from job to job, including banking, consultancy, academic law, and journalism. (His journalistic training included a spell as the acting editor of a women's page.) He finally found a home in an American university, teaching politics, philosophy, and economics. His first book, *The End of Economic Man* (1939), concentrated on politics and economics and warned about the Holocaust. His second book, *The Future of Industrial Man* (1942), annoyed academic critics because it mixed economics with various social sciences. In it, Drucker argued that companies had a social dimension as well as an economic purpose. This unorthodox idea attracted the attention of General Motors.

The American car giant, then the biggest company in the world, invited Drucker to draw its portrait and gave him unrestricted access to GMers, from Alfred Sloan down. The result, *The Concept of the Corporation*, sealed Drucker's fate. The book immediately became a best-seller, in Japan as well as in America, and has been in print ever since. However, it further alienated turf-minded American academics: economists regarded it as vulgar sociology while sociologists dismissed it as economics gone mad. One reviewer hoped that "this promising young scholar will now devote his considerable talents to a more respectable subject."[7] Shunned by the rest of academia, Drucker had no choice but to throw in his lot with management theory.

Over the following decades Drucker either invented or influenced virtually every part of management theory (his name will thus crop up in this book with infuriating frequency). Many of the themes that have dominated his work were already present in *The Concept of the Corporation*. Like all Drucker's books, *The Concept of the Corporation* is a roaming narrative: it begins with a story from China and, at different times, worries about the percentage of Victorian Englishmen who were gentlemen (a minute fraction, in Drucker's view) and the efficiency of Russian industrial management. The book's central purpose was to treat a company as a social system as well as an economic organization. The two longest sections are titled "The Corporation as Human Effort" and "The Corporation as a Social Institution." Companies were intricate social mechanisms rather than just machines for making profits, in Drucker's view, and all the more interesting for that.

All the same, the subject that gripped most of Drucker's readers, particularly the CEOs among them, was decentralization. Drucker showed how GM's decentralized structure enabled it to respond to the difficult challenges that faced it, such as the transition from war to peace.[8] And other organizations such as Ford and General Electric rushed to copy it, blithely ignoring Drucker's warning that he had doubts about the general applicability of the idea. By the 1980s, Drucker was credited with "moving 75–80 percent of the Fortune 500 to radical decentralization."[9]

Drucker's People

As well as being a somewhat academic treatise on decentraliza-tion, *The Concept of the Corporation* was an unashamedly passion-ate plea for GM to treat labor as a resource rather than just as a cost. Drucker insisted that industrial relations ought to be based on people's desire to be engaged in their job and proud of their prod-uct. He was also a stern critic of the assembly line, even though at the time it was regarded as the most advanced form of manufactur-ing. In "the assembly-line mentality," he said, "the more efficient a worker is, the more machine-like and the less human he is."[10] Drucker charged that the monotony of assembly-line production actually made it an inefficient process—partly because the line had to adjust to the speed of the slowest member and partly because workers never got any job satisfaction from seeing the finished product.

This enthusiasm for self-management was ahead of its time. Nowadays, team-manufacturing techniques are commonplace, and many companies are handing more power to their workers. When Japanese carmakers set up shop in Britain in the 1980s and told Geordie factory workers that they were supposed to think as well as rivet, weld, and hammer, many of Britain's car bosses scoffed at the foreigners' naïveté. Today, every car factory in Europe imitates their methods. The tragedy for GM was that it rejected Drucker's advice about using teams in the 1940s—only to have the same lesson rammed down its throat by the Japanese in the 1970s.

Drucker's enthusiasm for empowerment was reinforced by his belief that the old industrial proletariat was being replaced by knowledge workers. He believed that the advanced world was moving from "an economy of goods" to "a knowledge economy," and that management was changing as a result: managers needed to learn how to engage the minds, rather than simply control the hands, of their workers. This softer approach was a direct challenge to Taylor's stopwatch theories and their fans in business. But the idea of a "knowledge worker" (a term that Drucker coined in 1959) also posed questions for politicians. It suggested that rather than defending dying industries against cheaper, less "knowledgeable" workers abroad, governments should concentrate on improving the country's stock of knowledge, but otherwise keep well out of the way.

Drucker did not confine himself to the question of how managers and governments ought to handle these new knowledge workers. He spent much of his career looking at how the knowledge workers themselves could come to terms with this new world in which they were neither workers nor bosses. Knowledge workers have much more freedom than old-fashioned workers because they control the most important productive asset of modern society: their brainpower. Brainworkers are free, or, in the jargon that Drucker did not invent but unfortunately helped to legitimize, "empowered" to shape their own careers, hopping from firm to firm in pursuit of the highest salary or the most interesting job. But freedom could be destabilizing as well as liberating: knowledge workers needed more training and different pension arrangements, for example. Drucker knew whereof he spoke: an itinerant Mittel-European who had dabbled in banking and journalism and always remained ambivalent about America's hyperspecialized academic system, he was an archetypal knowledge worker.

But he was a knowledge worker with a growing number of acolytes in the real world. The younger Henry Ford took *The Concept of the Corporation* as his text when he tried to rebuild his company after the war. As Drucker himself has boasted, the book "had an immediate impact on American business, on public service institutions, on government agencies—and none at all on General Motors." (If a GM manager was found with a copy of the book, Drucker noted, his career was over.) Institutions as diverse as Michigan University and the Archdiocese of New York have used the book to restructure themselves. It was the first book to be prescribed for students entering Charles de Gaulle's elite École Nationale d'Administration. *The Concept of the Corporation* also set the Japanese thinking about devolving power to their workers.

The Rational Temptation

All this sounds as if Drucker was an exponent of the airy-fairy human-relations school of management. In fact there was also a "hard" side to his work. Drucker invented one of the rational school of management's most successful products, "management by objectives," an approach that dominated "strategic thinking" in the postwar decades. *The Practice of Management* (1954) emphasized clear objectives, both for the corporation and the manager, and urged managers to translate long-term strategy into short-term goals. The structure of the firm should follow its strategy, he argued: "Organization is not an end in itself, but a means to the end of business performance and business results. . . . Organization structure must be designed so as to make possible the achievement of the objectives of the business five, ten, fifteen years hence."

Management by objectives has been under a cloud since the early 1980s. The best modern companies, such as Google and IBM, allow ideas—including ideas for long-term strategies—to bubble up from the bottom of the organization rather than being dictated from on high. Those companies that have stuck with the system of command and control—notably General Motors—have looked hopelessly inflexible. The problem is that command-and-control management cuts senior management off from the people who know both their markets and their products best: the ordinary workers.

Why did the apostle of empowerment embrace such a rigid approach to management? The most generous answer to this question is that Drucker wanted to reconcile the best of the humanist and rationalist schools. At its best, management by objectives supplemented rather than subverted empowerment: senior managers should set general goals for their subordinates but allow them to decide how to reach those goals. There is something in Drucker's instinct to have it both ways. It is impossible to remain an uncritical supporter of empowerment when you recall the collapse of Britain's Barings Bank. But simply restoring the old command-and-control system risks alienating the knowledge workers, on whom the success of most companies depends.

New Worlds to Management

Drucker was one of the first people to realize that good management is not restricted to the United States. In the 1950s, when most people dismissed Japan as synonymous with shoddy goods, Drucker became fascinated by that nation's idiosyncratic approach to management. As his fame grew, he extended his interest to the rest of Asia. Drucker also helped to free management from its corporate cage. He was emphatically a management thinker, not just a business one. He believed that management is "the defining organ of all modern institutions," not just business corporations—of universities, churches, hospitals, charities, and what you will.

In his later years he was arguably more interested in the voluntary sector than in the business sector (indeed, George Bush singled out his contribution to civil institutions when he awarded him the presidential medal of freedom in 2002). He thought "the large pastoral church" took over from the company as the most significant organizational phenomenon in the second half of the twentieth century because churches were second-to-none in motivating volunteers and creating social bonds.

Drucker's respect for these remarkable institutions was not just one-way. Many of the leading mega-preachers consulted him regularly. Rick Warren gave a stirring address to a conference in Vienna to celebrate what would have been Drucker's hundredth birthday. Bill Hybels, the founder of Willow Creek, in Barrington, Illinois, has a quotation from Peter Drucker hanging outside his office: "What is your business? Who is your customer? What does the customer consider value?" Hybels had got to know Drucker well and regards him as "a wisdom figure."[11] It is fitting that the management school Claremont College in California founded in his honor recruits about a third of its students from outside the business world.

Drucker's enthusiasm for applying management theory to civil society should not be confused with enthusiasm for government. Drucker had a typically Austrian disdain for government. He constantly complained about government's inability to run anything and was one of the earliest exponents of privatization. Richard Nixon once began a pep talk to the Department of Health, Education and Welfare with a side-swipe at his minimalist views of government: "Mr. Drucker says that modern government can do only two things well: wage war and inflate the currency. It's the aim of my administration to prove Mr. Drucker wrong." Drucker arguably got the better of the argument.

Does He Still Matter?

It is hard to find anybody who has a bad word to say about Drucker. Modern gurus have an almost superstitious fear of criticizing him—as if badmouthing the one guru who has won widespread admiration might bring the whole structure crashing down. Corporate figures routinely doff the cap to him: asked which management thinkers he has paid attention to, Bill Gates replies, "Well, Drucker, of course," before citing lesser mortals.

Yet, even around the management industry's great totem, doubts swirl. Drucker has never enjoyed quite as much adulation from academia as he has from either guru-land or his public. ("I have never been quite respectable in the eyes of academia," he confessed.)[12] There is no single area of academic management theory that he has made his own, as Michael Porter did with strategy and Theodore Levitt did with marketing. Some academics regard him as a journalist rather than a scholar, and, twisting the knife, as a glib generalizer rather than a first-class reporter. Tom Peters recalls that he never saw Drucker's name on any reading list when he was a student at Stanford Business School.

The least persuasive criticism is that Drucker does little more than state the obvious, that his persistent themes—about the rise of the knowledge worker, the importance of clear objectives, the fact that firms are social as well as economic institutions—are all too obvious to bear mentioning, let alone repeating over and over. The trouble with this argument is that most of his observations are obvious only because Drucker has made them so. Drucker is a victim of his own success in popularizing a way of looking at the world. And obvious or not, some of his insights do not seem to have gotten through to the managerial elite just yet. Would America's bosses be sacking their workers with one hand, while awarding themselves huge pay raises with the other, if they understood Drucker's arguments about the social nature of firms?

Other criticisms have more force. Drucker sometimes manages to be both simplistic and obscure at the same time. He repeatedly states that humans live in a society of organizations but fails to make clear what this means. In *Post-Capitalist Society*, he complains that the United States has embraced pension-fund socialism, but his comments are presented more as a play on words than a deep analysis of American society. In a broad sense, he is right: the real bosses are not the likes of John D. Rockefeller and J. P. Morgan, but the workers themselves. They are the ones who own most of society's capital, through their pension rights, and who receive most of society's rewards, through their wages and social benefits. But would it not be better to call this popular capitalism?

Drucker's work can also be criticized for its unevenness. Whereas *The Concept of the Corporation* is a model monograph, tightly argued and based on original research, some of his later books can be rambling and repetitive, full of recycled examples. His voice has also become less distinctive. Although it is true that as early as 1954 he was arguing that an "organization structure should contain the least possible number of management levels," his enthusiasm in the 1980s for "information-based organizations" and for stripping out layers of management seemed not much different from the voices of the baying pack following Tom Peters.

In general, he was not as good on small firms as big ones, particularly on the entrepreneurial startups that have redefined capitalism since the 1970s. In *The Concept of the Corporation*, he asserted, flatly, "We know today that in modern industrial production, particularly in modern mass production, the small unit is not only inefficient, it cannot produce at all."[13] Indeed, the book helped to launch the "big organization boom" that lasted for the next twenty years. Drucker later recanted: he argued that "the Fortune 500 is over" and wrote an increasing amount about the importance of entrepreneurship, as in his 1985 book, *Innovation and Entrepreneurship*. (Anybody who accuses Drucker in print of being a fan of big companies is in for a long letter, chronicling his enthusiasm for decentralization.)

All the same, Drucker seemed more at home with the giant corporations that dominated the United States under Dwight Eisenhower than with the small to medium-size businesses that regalvanized the country under Ronald Reagan. He wrote nothing as good as *The Concept of the Corporation* about a small company. This is odd, given his history and personality. This prophet of the "age of organizations" was a quintessential individualist who was happiest ploughing his own furrow (one of his favorite sayings was "one either meets or one works"). He was also an adoptive Southern Californian who lived in the hotbed of America's entrepreneurial revolution. But Drucker was no more capable than the rest of us of shaking off his early intellectual experiences as a young man starting out in a new profession.

On the other hand, the charge that Drucker is a jack-of-all-trades rather than a master of one reveals more about the limitations of academia than it does about Drucker's shortcomings. Remember that Drucker was expelled from the ivory towers of economics and political science because his work would not fit into their narrow classifications. As for charges that he resorts to the dark art of journalism, that may be just another way of saying that he is readable. Drucker was too idiosyncratic a figure to fit in with the turf-conscious conformists who make up modern academia.

In a business that is dominated by American business school specialists with nanosecond memories, Drucker was happy to range across the centuries and use a reference to China of the Tang dynasty, or seventh-century Byzantium, or eighteenth-century France. His historical knowledge allowed him to throw a shaft of light on contemporary debates. Commenting on globalization, for example, he pointed out that a larger share of manufacturing was "multinational" before the First World War than it is today. Companies such as Fiat (founded in 1899) and Siemens (founded in 1847) produced more abroad than at home almost as soon as they got off the ground. Henry Ford, although a notorious xenophobe, started his English subsidiary before he began to expand his original automobile plant in Detroit.[14]

In writing about business alliances, Drucker usually threw in a reference to his heroine, Jane Austen, and her obsession with dynastic alliances; in commenting on the latest bout of speculative fever on Wall Street, he soon regurgitated bits of Charles Dickens's *Little Dorrit*; most surprisingly of all, he illustrated an article on the rise of the knowledge-based organization with a reference to the civil service in British India. What is more, this was not garden-variety erudition. He quoted from Volume 3 rather than Volume 1 of Marx's *Das Kapital*, from Harrington rather than Locke. Among other activities, he wrote two novels and held a chair in Oriental Art at Claremont Graduate School.

Drucker's was not the sort of history that can be found in the textbooks: his interest lay neither in the kings and queens of the old history nor in the capitalists and proletarians of the new, but in managers and organization. His heroes were the likes of Jean Bodin, who (according to Drucker at least) invented the nation-state, and August Borsig, who invented the German apprenticeship system. His trademark was his ability to cut between panoramic views and striking close-ups. One moment he was churning out broad generalizations about the rise of the car industry; the next he was relating an anecdote about Henry Ford's forgotten partner.

He was not afraid to predict the future as well as to generalize about the past. If he had his share of failures, his batting average was higher than most (notably in the case of privatization and the collapse of the Soviet Union).

The Last Encyclopedist

Arguably, Drucker was not a management theorist at all, but a cosmopolitan intellectual in the great European tradition. Drucker was one of the last of the encyclopedists, contemptuous of the hyperspecialization of modern academia and determined to know everything about everything. He illustrated his writings with a wide range of references, from psychoanalysis and musicology to economics and sociology, from real-life case studies to academic literature.

Why, one might well ask, did this polymath concentrate so much of his energy on management? The glib answer, "because it is important," is probably the truthful one. Discovering management had much the same effect on Drucker as discovering God (or Marx) had on lesser mortals. "Management is the organ of institutions," he hymned, in one of his most famous quotations, "the organ that converts a mob into an organization, and human efforts into performance."[15]

If there is a core theme running through Drucker's writings, it is this: at best, good management will bring economic progress and social harmony in its wake. Marx based his prediction of the imminent demise of capitalism on the "inexorable law of the diminishing productivity of capital"; and it is because managers have succeeded in outfoxing this law, by realizing that the key to improved productivity lies in working smarter rather than working longer, that the modern economy goes from success to success.

The real reason, Drucker argued, that some countries made the breakthrough into sustained growth is not because they discovered new technologies but because they invented new organizations. Thus, Alfred Sloan's General Motors is a more awesome creation than the combustion engine, and the hospital is a more important medical breakthrough than any newfangled medicine.

Drucker had no illusions about how difficult management is. In *Managing in a Time of Great Change*, a collection of essays published in 1995, he focused on three problems that are making the modern manager's life hell. The first is the sheer scale of contemporary managerial change, as vertically integrated companies give way to networked organizations. The second is the frequency of managerial failure. Most managers, he points out, have failed to understand what it means to manage in revolutionary times, and they spend their time tinkering with their business when they should really be rethinking the whole theory on which it is based. The third is the growing tension between business and its environment: between business's need for perpetual innovation and the community's need for stability; between the rapidly changing nature of knowledge and the limited capacity of the human mind; and between business's need to compete internationally and society's interest in the common good.

Good management means doing the decent thing by both workers and consumers, not just amassing profits for bosses. "An organization is a human, a social, indeed a moral phenomenon," Drucker noted. He argued that the best managers are driven by the desire to create value for customers, and that the best way to do this is to treat workers not just as costs of production, but as resources, capable of making a sustained and valued contribution. This enthusiasm for the well-being of workers led Rosabeth Moss Kanter, a professor at Harvard Business School, to compare

Drucker to Robert Owen, the nineteenth-century Scotsman who ordered his factory managers to show the same due care to their vital human machines as they did to the new iron and steel that they so lovingly burnished.

Was Drucker right? Moss Kanter classifies Drucker as "a management utopian." Perhaps he is, but then there are worse sorts of dreamers.

4

Tom Peters: Management for the Masses

The man who has done more than anybody else to market management theory to the masses is Tom Peters. His first book, *In Search of Excellence* (1982), co-written with Robert Waterman, was for twenty years the best-selling management book ever, selling a million copies on its first printing and more than five million to date. More books have followed—as have a torrent of DVDs, podcasts, articles, and blog postings. Peters has delivered an estimated 2,500 speeches before two to three million people in sixty-three countries, and the numbers continue to mount: month in and month out thousands of middle managers gape in awe as Peters, arms flailing, brow sweating, voice hoarse with preaching, urges them to nuke hierarchy and learn to thrive on chaos.[1]

Peters is the Mick Jagger of the management business, one of a handful of Vietnam-era gurus who can still fill an arena. His staying power owes something to luck: blogging might well have been invented for him. The medium not only gives him a chance to rattle off his opinions about everything from service on Air India (outstanding) to the latest management fad; it has also allowed him to reinvent the management book as a sort of extended blog. His recent book *Re-Imagine!: Business Excellence in a Disruptive Age* reads more like a collection of blog postings than a traditional book: every chapter begins with a "rant" and then proceeds by way of a series of bite-sized entries in a wide assortment of typefaces.

But it owes even more to Peters's extraordinary energy. He has never lost his appetite for discovering examples of managerial excellence or idiocy and then using these examples to fuel high-octane lectures. Even after all these years a Tom Peters seminar remains an event. Against a backdrop of slides with messages such as "The Most Important Sentence in the English Language!?" and "May I Clean Your Glasses, Sir," he orders the befuddled young watchers in suits—some of whom are less than half his age—to make mistakes and have fun.[2] One moment Peters is unpacking the management lessons contained in a complimentary sewing kit in London's Four Seasons hotel, the next he is praising a car dealer who put flowers rather than automobiles in his showroom. Questions about practicalities only push him to new extremes. "I see no reason why you need to spend more than six minutes every three months in your office," he tells the head of the Eurostar London–Paris train service. "Get on that railroad."

Slow Down, You Move Too Fast

Peters's prominence is a mixed blessing for his profession. People have only to read his blog or catch sight of him on television to have their prejudices about management theory redoubled. How can a man in his sixties behave like a whirling dervish? How can a former McKinsey consultant appear on the cover of one of his books (*The Tom Peters Seminar: Crazy Times Call for Crazy Organizations*) dressed in his boxer shorts? Peters's books are littered with phrases like "wow," "yikes," and "ho-hum." And then there are all those infuriating exclamation points! "Prosewise, he is no Edward Gibbon," as he himself might put it.

There is, however, more to Peters than his peculiarities. True, he has contradicted himself spectacularly over the past decade. But then the corporate world has changed, too. True, he has a penchant for dashing off flimsy blog posts. But he also wrote an admirably obscure PhD dissertation. True, he is given to ranting and raving. But then he has also persuaded more managers to question their assumptions than almost anyone else alive.

Even Peters's harshest critics should be willing to concede two things in his favor. First, he has a remarkable talent for making a dull subject like management sound interesting. What is noticeable about all the titles of his books—*Liberation Management*, *A Passion for Excellence*, *Thriving on Chaos*, *Re-imagine!*—is that they convey his fascination with his subject. Second, he has an intimate knowledge of corporate life, not just in the United States but also in Asia, Europe, and the former Soviet empire (he even has an honorary doctorate from Moscow's State University of Management); not just in the boardroom but also in the marketing department and in the machine shop; not just the giants like 3M and IBM, but also in countless small companies that nobody else seems able to track down. He cannot book into a hotel, fly in an aircraft, or park his car without finding an interesting management angle. Other management writers fill their pages with stories about overexposed companies such as Whole Foods and Best Buy. Peters writes about Valerio's, an eccentric Italian restaurant he stumbled across in New Zealand that refuses to post menus outside and frames complaints from disappointed customers.

Peters's early life took him to both Vietnam (to serve in a war he later despised) and Washington, DC (where he worked in the Pentagon, the Office of Management and Budget, and the White

House). He also picked up an MBA from Stanford Business School. But the two most important parts of his training were the time spent earning his undergraduate degree in engineering and the subsequent time he spent as a consultant with McKinsey. Peters has always retained a consultant's ability to inveigle his way into hundreds of companies and an engineer's curiosity about how things actually work.

Peters is clearly a more complicated and accomplished figure than he first seems, but the verdict on his achievements is mixed. For it is increasingly clear that what he has done—launching, leading, and defining the guru boom—is more significant than what he has actually said, much of which has either been proved wrong or been contradicted by Peters himself. That judgment contains a fairly damning criticism of Peters, which I will try to substantiate later in this chapter. But it also contains a compliment. Few of the business heroes Peters worships have changed their industry as much as Peters has changed his. Insofar as the current management theory boom has a starting date, it is with the publication of *In Search of Excellence*; and insofar as it has a presiding genius who keeps the arguments rolling and the pretenders coming, it is Tom Peters.

An Excellent Beginning

In the late 1970s McKinsey was rightly worried that it was losing intellectual leadership to young upstarts such as the Boston Consulting Group and Bain, so it decided to pour a significant amount of money into research, including a research project on the "excellent company." Peters and various colleagues were chosen to review the existing literature on "organizational effectiveness." They soon concluded that the emphasis that theorists had traditionally placed

on strategy and structure had gone beyond the point of diminishing returns, and that other, softer factors, such as management style
and "culture," were also crucial to success. This was controversial
stuff given that most McKinsey men were steeped in the lore of
strategy and structure. Peters teamed up with a senior colleague,
Robert Waterman, to turn the project into a book—and the management guru revolution was launched.

Why did *In Search of Excellence* do so well? For one thing, it was
based on an impressive amount of evidence (at least by the far-
from-exacting standards of management science). But it also acted
as a showcase for the four basic ingredients of what might be called
the "Peters phenomenon": an uncanny sense of timing, an extraordinary ability to articulate the mood of the moment, the skill to
dispense advice that sounds practical, and a breathtaking talent for
marketing. The book appeared in October 1982, the month that
American unemployment hit 10 percent and the first time it had
broken the double-digit barrier since the Great Depression. It also
followed a glut of books on the wonders of Japanese management.

Indeed, the book seemed perfectly designed to appeal to an
America that was worried about its declining competitiveness but
tired of being told about the Japanese miracle. Like many other
pundits, Peters and Waterman agreed that American managers
bore much of the blame for their country's plight, thanks to their
obsession with the short term and their indifference to quality
and service.[3] However, they argued that Americans did not have
to look all the way to Japan for models of how to run excellent
companies and revive national competitiveness. America possessed
more than its share of companies that were producing new products, pioneering new processes, and working overtime to satisfy
all their constituents—customers, employees, shareholders, and
the public at large.[4] Peters and Waterman sounded the "morning

in America" theme two years before Ronald Reagan used it to seal his reelection. And, like "the great communicator," they argued that there was nothing wrong with America that could not be cured by what was right with America. Management theory had met American patriotism.

Peters also made the case for humanistic management: the good news that they had discovered across the country all resulted from treating people decently and asking them to shine, rather than treating them as merely factors of production; from producing things that people actually wanted, rather than just hitting the numbers. Efficiencies of scale and scope were giving way to small units led by dedicated champions. A numbing focus on cost was giving way to an enhancing focus on quality. Fat rule books were being shredded, hierarchies flattened, formalities abandoned.[5] Bourgeois America had met bohemian America and discovered that the two could forge an alliance in pursuit of the greatest of American passions—business.

The book had another virtue: simplicity. For all the research that went into it, *In Search* sometimes reads like a popular how-to book. Peters and Waterman list eight easily identifiable (and memorably expressed) characteristics of excellent companies, such as "sticking to the knitting" (i.e., concentrating on what the firm does best and contracting out everything else to other specialists), creating loose–tight control systems (i.e., centralizing core values but decentralizing the way they are achieved), and staying close to the customer. As Peter Drucker put it, slightly bitchily, *In Search* made management sound "incredibly easy": put the book under your pillow and you would wake up a great manager.[6]

The result was a democratization of management theory: Peters and Waterman took something that had traditionally been focused on chief executives and their boards—particularly if it came with the McKinsey name attached—and opened it up to junior managers and indeed the general public. It is significant that the book was full of examples from all levels of corporate life, not just the boardroom and strategy departments, and that it dealt with small companies as well as big ones. As Drucker conceded: "When Aunt Mary has to give that nephew of hers a high school graduation present and she gives him *In Search of Excellence*, you know that management has become part of the general culture."[7]

Peters also brought marketing pizzazz to the management theory industry. No conference was left unaddressed, no commission to write an article unsatisfied, no talk show untalked. He treated "excellence" as a crusade and his closest followers as crusaders. The truest believers were "skunks"—innovative outsiders who worked on the fringes of companies (the name came from a famously inventive part of Lockheed, called the Skunk Works). In September 1984, he held his first annual Skunk Camp: "40 brave souls who have been going their own way met in California and swapped tales about the battles fought, the scars accumulated, and the personal and soul-satisfying experiences that have come from watching their people become winners." Three years later he calculated that more than three thousand people had been through "excellence seminars" of one sort or another.

In the next few years he produced a succession of books that pushed the conclusions of *In Search* much further. In *A Passion for Excellence* (co-written with Nancy Austin), Peters argued that companies needed to hand decisions to the people who operated the machines or stocked the shelves. The pressure of competition and the pace of innovation meant that companies could no longer afford elaborate hierarchies and hit-or-miss planning departments. "If you aren't reorganizing, pretty substantially, once every six to twelve months," Peters warned bosses, "you're probably out of step with the times." In *Thriving on Chaos* he urged companies to turn chaos into a competitive advantage.

Peters's more recent books, such as *Liberation Management* and *Re-Imagine!*, pushed the anti-rationalist message of *Thriving on Chaos* still further. The layers of management that need to be eradicated now seem to include everything between the chief executive and the cleaning staff. *Liberation Management* touts a list of maxims for modern management that includes "get fired," "take off your shoes," and "race yaks."[8] He concludes *Crazy Times* with nine "beyonds," among them, "beyond change: towards the abandonment of everything" and "beyond TQM: towards wow!" The former McKinseyite now preaches "the sublime pleasures of modestly organized anarchy."

Some of Peters's writing can be read as a long hymn of praise to California's Silicon Valley ("through luck I ended up in Santa Clara county," he once wrote, "a big god-awful mess populated by failures").[9] California's computer industry has generated an extraordinary entrepreneurial, freewheeling, convention-busting management style. Schumpeter's phrase "creative destruction" might have been minted to describe the area, with more than three hundred companies founded every year and almost as many going out of business. If a company succeeds, it is relatively easy to attract people and capital; if it fails, bankruptcy is a badge of honor rather than, as it is in many countries, a permanent black mark; the result is that people and capital are recycled quickly and efficiently to take advantage of changes in fashion or breakthroughs in technology.

The inhabitants of Silicon Valley are happier in sneakers and jeans than in suits and ties, and appalled at the idea of people spending their entire lives working for the same organization. They like to work in companies that are structured around projects and are as free from bureaucracy as possible. Even a fairly large company, such as Intel, is a free-flowing collection of "chip squads"—a series of ever-changing teams working on different generations of microprocessors. They hop not just from job to job but also from career to career, with scientists becoming entrepreneurs, entrepreneurs becoming managers, and managers becoming venture capitalists. In other words, they thrive on chaos.

The Point of Peters

All this explains why Peters is a perennial guru. But is he any good? Even if he knows a huge amount about companies, two serious flaws mar his work. The first is that he got it wrong too often for comfort. Two years after the publication of *In Search*, *Business Week* produced an article, titled "Who's Excellent Now?," that pointed out that half of the supposedly excellent companies were in serious trouble.[10] By the book's fifth anniversary, two-thirds had underperformed the market. The second is that he has contradicted himself even more often than the average politician. Add these two problems together and the canon of Peters's work looks worryingly insubstantial and ephemeral—hence the suspicion that what he has done is more interesting than what he has said.

This charge can partly be answered by saying that Peters writes his books for the real world, for people to use, and that the real world changes fairly quickly. Although he has not quite stooped to writing get-rich-quick books, he has always made it clear that, far from being exercises in academic analysis, his books are intended to help people prosper, or at least survive. *Thriving on Chaos* is subtitled *Handbook for a Management Revolution*. From this perspective—from the perspective of the manager (one is tempted to say the skunk) in the field—an unfailing nose for business trends is one of Peters's strengths rather than one of his weaknesses, even if those trends often do not last long.

Peters's modus operandi is to sense where the corporate world is heading, usually correctly, and then shout it from the rooftops. *Liberation Management* is, among other things, a feisty guide to the latest management fads, each amply illustrated with case studies, such as flexible organizations (CNN virtually reinvents itself at the start of every news day), learning organizations (Quad/Graphics insists that its employees keep on educating themselves), and a relentless focus on customers (in Britain, Joshua Tetley's pub chain offers prizes to bar staff who can recite the names and drinking habits of one hundred customers). The list could go on for pages. One of the faults of *Liberation Management*, and some of Peters's later books, is that it does. Criticizing Peters for giving out advice that was relevant for, say, only five years, or for idolizing a company like CNN, which now seems slow and tired, misses the point. In the world of just-in-time management we need just-in-time management advice.

This may get Peters off the most common charge against him: that he has been disproved by events. But what of a second charge: that even by the standards of one-minute managers, Peters's books taken as a whole are full of contradictions? Peters certainly has a higher tolerance for self-contradiction than most authors: this is a man who, having launched the "excellence movement" in 1982, began *Thriving on Chaos*, published five years later, by claiming that "there are no excellent companies." All the same, the charges against him are often exaggerated. One of the most frequently voiced objections is that, having started his career genuflecting before big companies, Peters now preaches that small is beautiful. Though *In Search* is devoted to giant companies—which, incidentally, were the only companies that could afford to pay McKinsey's exorbitant fees—it is, on closer reading, remarkably sensitive to the ills of gigantism and the advantages of staying small:

> The message from the excellent companies we reviewed was invariably the same. Small, independent new venture teams at 3M (by the hundred); small divisions at Johnson & Johnson (over 150 in a $5 billion firm); ninety PCCs at TI; the product champion-led teams at IBM; "bootlegging" teams at GE; small, ever-shifting segments at Digital; new boutiques monthly at Bloomingdale's . . . Small is beautiful.[11]
>
> Such decentralization cut down on the need for layer upon layer of middle managers. It also ensured that companies were committed to innovation and that they focused on their customers.[12]

Still Crazy After All These Years

Indeed, there is a deeper consistency to Peters's work. Everything he has written, from *In Search of Excellence* to his latest *The Little Big Things* ramblings, can be read as an extended critique of scientific management. One of his most characteristic phrases, about creating a "technology of foolishness," came from his first book.[13] Peters is the Michel Foucault of the management world: a scourge of the rationalist tradition and a celebrant of the creative necessity of chaos and craziness.

When Peters went to business school, management was still dominated by numbers: "The only facts that many of us considered 'real data' were the ones we could put numbers on."[14] Management education celebrated the virtues of quantitative analysis, pooh-poohed "soft-headed humanism" and unscientific intuition, and sought detached, analytical, rigorous justifications for all decisions. In short, it made damn sure that the "technical jocks" were in charge.

The rationalist model found its most influential exponents in "the whiz kids," a group of strategic analysts who helped mastermind America's victory in the Second World War and then went on to reshape the Ford Motor Company.[15] For Peters and his generation, the horrific weaknesses of this approach to management were demonstrated not just in America's ailing industries but in its hopeless foreign policy: the brightest whiz kid of them all, Robert McNamara, whom Peters once cheekily dubbed "the Peter Drucker of the Pentagon," left the chairmanship of Ford to become Secretary of Defense, and then tried to win the Vietnam War by escalating enemy kills. The rationalist model "is right enough to be dangerously wrong," Peters and Waterman mused in 1982, "and it has arguably led us seriously astray."

In Search advances three arguments against the rationalist model. First, the model puts too much emphasis on financial analysis and too little on motivating workers or satisfying customers. The obsession with cost persuades firms to undervalue quality and value, to patch up old products rather than invent new ones, and to treat workers as costs of production rather than sources of value. The authors quote their colleague Anthony Athos approvingly: "Good managers make meanings for people, as well as money."

Second, the rationalist model encouraged bureaucratic conformity at the expense of entrepreneurial innovation. Rationalist managers believe that big is best, because it brings economies of scale; that messiness is disastrous, because it means waste and confusion; and that planning is essential, because it allows firms to control the future. For Peters and Waterman, the best firms, such as 3M, an office products giant, were almost exactly the opposite: they were hotbeds of experimentation, happy with irrationality and chaos.

Third, the rationalist model rests on a misunderstanding of human nature. "The central problem with the rationalist view of organizing people is that people are not very rational," the authors argue. "To fit Taylor's old model, or today's organizational charts, man is simply designed wrong."[16] Scientific managers overestimate the importance of financial rewards in motivating workers: people are much more interested in intangible things, such as winning the praise of colleagues or working for an organization they admire. "All the companies we interviewed," the authors note, "from Boeing to McDonald's, were quite simply rich tapestries of anecdote, myth, and fairy tale."[17]

Peters and Waterman were hardly the first people (and certainly not the last) to draw attention to the limitations of the rationalist model of management. There is a long tradition of bashing scientific management stretching back to the human-relations school of management; indeed, it is reasonable to argue that the critique of scientific management is as old as scientific management itself. In *The Human Side of Enterprise*, published in 1960, Douglas McGregor argued that management theory paid too much attention to "theory X," which holds that workers are lazy and need to be driven by financial incentives, and not enough to "theory Y," which holds that, on the contrary, workers are creative and need to be given responsibility.

Even so, Peters has taken his anti-rationalist campaign to extremes hardly dreamed of by his predecessors. It is no longer enough for managers to pay attention to the intuitive as well as the rational side of their jobs. They must go bonkers: throw away their spreadsheets, forget about climbing the career ladder, and turn themselves into zany entrepreneurs. It is no longer enough for companies to slim their headquarters and thin the ranks of middle management. Firms should use internal markets to turn their employees into mini-entrepreneurs, and external markets to make sure that they are not wasting their time doing things that could be done better elsewhere. For Peters, "crazy" organizations are more efficient as well as more fun than their sane rivals.

But is this really true? Peters has had plenty of reason over the years to congratulate himself on his influence. Zappos, America's most successful online shoe and clothing store, has borrowed many of Peters's principles: the company's number-one core value is to "deliver WOW through service." He has even more reasons to relish the failures of scientific managers, with their complex mathematical formulae. In *Re-imagine!* he boasts that he tried, without success, to persuade Stanford University to retract his MBA when he saw one of his old accounting professors, Robert Jaedicke, on television explaining (away) his role in the Enron fiasco. Jaedicke had not only been a member of Enron's board, he had also been chairman of the compensation committee. Yet he claimed that he did not have a clue about the bizarre accounting that brought the company down. Peters concluded that this meant his MBA was worthless.

His craziness mantra is nevertheless overdone. Peters is indifferent to old-hat subjects such as oversight and due diligence, but the corporate world would be a better place if it had put more emphasis on oversight and due diligence and less on creativity. Enron, after all, was widely celebrated for its willingness to stretch traditional management structures to the breaking point in pursuit of the next big idea. Peters is blind to such humdrum virtues as stability and continuity. Yet in the real world, middle managers are often the people who hold organizations together, and schedules are the framework around which most people build their days. In short, Peters fatally underestimates the need, in even the craziest organizations and wackiest people, for some stability if they are to thrive.

Peters's beloved Silicon Valley is fortunate to possess two islands of stability in the forms of Stanford University and Hewlett-Packard, both of which have trained entrepreneurs and provided them with a network of contacts. The relentless reconfiguration of companies that Peters celebrates can come at a terrible cost. Hypermobility can produce waste and despair, as business plans are torn up, intellectual capital is destroyed, and careers are disrupted. The Israeli authorities are currently worried that their country is too committed to the here-today, gone-tomorrow startup model. Israel's poor record at turning "tomato seeds into tomatoes" (the country has 3,800 high-tech startups but only four high-tech companies with sales of over a billion dollars a year) means that the high-tech miracle is in danger of becoming a mirage. The industry is benefitting only a tiny slither of the population: Israel has a higher level of structural unemployment than other rich countries. It is also looking for easy money—all those IPOs—rather than making big bets on the future.

Far Enough Out to Be Interesting

The world may never go as "crazy" as Peters predicts, but it may well be moving in his direction, as product cycle times collapse, command-and-control systems buckle, and the pace of innovation increases. The most successful company of the past decade—Google—often gives the impression that it has drunk deep from Tom Peters's Kool-Aid. For years Larry Page and Sergey Brin shared an office and eschewed assistants and secretaries, keeping their own schedules and answering (or rather, not answering) their own phones. They give their employees extraordinary degrees of freedom, but also intervene in seemingly trivial questions such as the number of people that the cafeteria can seat.[18] Peters's ambition is to be an agent of change: "far enough out to be interesting, close enough in to be plausible."[19] Though he has sometimes been a little too far out, he has largely succeeded in his ambition to be a provocateur with a plausible message.

5

Flat Worlds, Tipping Points, and Long Tails

Ever since Tom Peters succeeded in marketing management to the masses, the guru business has been in a state of permanent priapism. Management books have become fixtures on bestseller lists. Management writers have turned into the star attractions of corporate conferences. Conference organizers would no more dream of leaving out these practiced performers than circus entertainers would dream of leaving out the performing seals.

Many of these gurus are business professors with a talent for popularization. Rosabeth Moss Kanter, of Harvard Business School, has written or co-written eighteen books, including *When Giants Learn to Dance*, earning her the sobriquet "the thinking woman's Tom Peters." Others are management consultants with the gift of gab or a taste for self-promotion. Most top-rank consultancies employ at least one "thought leader" who regularly writes business books: George Stalk at BCG (who has written or co-written four) and Lowell Bryan at McKinsey (who has written or co-written six) are prominent examples.

A few brave spirits have become more-or-less full-time gurus. Stephen Covey has sold 30 million copies of *The Seven Habits of*

Highly Effective People. Jim Collins has become one of the world's most influential business thinkers, thanks to *Built to Last: Successful Habits of Visionary Companies* (1994), co-written with Jerry Porras; *Good to Great* (2001), and, most recently, *When the Mighty Fall* (2009), which focuses on the understudied subject of failure rather than success. These full-time gurus come closest to the popular conception of a guru as a combination of a seer and an eccentric. Covey looks like a character from the Cone Heads and regularly mixes management advice with spiritual wisdom. Collins lives an ascetic life in Boulder, Colorado, where he has a private management "laboratory" staffed by five assistants and spends as much time as he can spare climbing mountains.[1] But even these professional gurus were conceived in the womb of the management theory industry. Covey has an MBA from Harvard Business School and a PhD in business studies; Collins started his life as a professor at Stanford Business School.

However, since the turn of the century we have seen a striking new development in the world of business gurus: the rise of a subspecies of guru who have no background in either business schools or consultancies. In 2008, Thomas Davenport, a management professor at Babson College, compiled a list of the world's most influential management thinkers for the *Wall Street Journal* on the basis of Google hits, media mentions, and academic citations. Only one member of the top five was a certified management guru with a PhD in business and a perch in a business school: Gary Hamel (who was ranked number one). The other four were journalists (Thomas Friedman and Malcolm Gladwell), a retired CEO (Bill Gates), and an academic from a department of education rather than business (Howard Gardner).[2]

Bill Gates's position on the list is hardly surprising: he is arguably the world's most thoughtful businessman as well as one of its most successful entrepreneurs. It is impossible to listen to him talk about one of his many passions—healthcare, say, or energy—without being impressed by his combination of expertise and originality. But what about Tom Friedman and Howard Gardner? And what about people lower down the list, such as Robert Reich and Richard Florida?

Since 2000, the management theory business has been revolutionized by the arrival of two new kinds of practitioners: journo-gurus from the world of "big media" and academic entrepreneurs from what business school professors might well regard as the wrong side of the tracks (or, in the case of Harvard, the river Charles). If Tom Peters discovered that it is possible to sell management theory to the masses, Tom Friedman and company discovered that it is possible to reach the lucrative business market through bypassing the conventional suppliers, the business schools, and consultancies. To mimic the language of the industry itself: first Tom Peters turned a B-to-B business into a B-to-C one, then a new generation of entrepreneurs disintermediated the established suppliers and went straight to the consumers.

The Rise of the Journo-Gurus

The most eye-catching change in the guru business is the rise of the journo-gurus. These are the locust years for the journalistic profession as a whole. Newspapers from the *New York Times* down are sacking journalists by the hundred. The surviving hacks are being forced to work ever harder for their stagnant salaries—to produce blogs and podcasts, Twitter feeds and video diaries, as well as old-fashioned reporting (which now has to be updated several times a day), and all in an atmosphere of tedious sobriety. There is no end to the misery in sight: circulation is slumping and advertising sales (which traditionally made up 80 percent of newspapers' revenues) have imploded. "I wish I'd gone to law school" is now the most commonly heard refrain in the world's newsrooms.

But amidst the wreckage, the journo-gurus are thriving. These are the first-class passengers of the journalistic world—sitting on upholstered thrones, surrounded by adoring hostesses, feasting on champagne and canapés, while the rest of their profession is crowded into cattle class or waiting to be hurled off the airplane because their publisher bought the cheapest ticket imaginable. Malcolm Gladwell, who lives in Greenwich Village, seldom deigns to visit *The New Yorker*'s head office on the grounds that he has a strong "aversion to mid-town."[3] The magazine deals with him by courier instead. Tom Friedman has boasted, to a *New Yorker* journalist who was writing an article about Carlos Slim, the Mexican billionaire who has been helping the *New York Times* out of its financial difficulties, that he essentially has a blank check when it comes to travel: his publisher, Arthur Sulzberger, has never asked him what he is planning to write or how high his travel expenses will be.[4]

The journo-gurus have also posed a powerful challenge to traditional management gurus—the professors and consultants who once had a monopoly on producing books and then turning them into business fads. They have outshone their more entrenched competitors by the simple expedient of writing better—weaving words into jargon-free narratives and enlivening them with powerful images. Poor Michael Porter has spent his entire life building a reputation as a management guru, but suddenly he has been driven out of the *Wall Street Journal*'s top five by people who have not even gotten an MBA! The *New Yorker* is now a more fecund mother of management ideas than the *Harvard Business Review* (which, incidentally, is now edited by a former journalist, Adi Ignatius, who worked for *Time* and the *Wall Street Journal*).

Three Kings

The king of the great journo-gurus is Tom Friedman, a *New York Times* op-ed columnist and, by common consent, the most influential opinion journalist in the United States.[5] Friedman spent the first half of his career as a conventional, if highly successful, journalist: he was broken in at one of the salt mines of the profession, the United Press International (UPI), before moving to the *New York Times*, and specialized in the most explosive area of old-fashioned political and diplomatic news, the Middle East. His reporting on the Middle East, particularly the Israeli invasion of Lebanon, in 1982, and the first intifada, earned him two Pulitzer prizes and provided him with the material for his first, and in many ways still his best, book, *From Beirut to Jerusalem* (1989). In 1995 he was offered the most desirable perch in the *Times*'s aviary—that of the paper's foreign affairs columnist. "Being the foreign affairs columnist for the *New York Times* is actually the best job in the world," he purred. "I get to be a tourist with an attitude."

In fact, Friedman was not content to be just a tourist with an attitude. He could easily have spent the rest of his days warbling, from his golden perch, about the minutiae of international relations. A lifetime of off-the-record briefings and lunches with the high-and-mighty in Washington, DC's highly agreeable Metropolitan Club stood waiting. He chose to do something far more interesting instead—he reinvented his job. He noticed that, as the 1990s wore on, the big story was changing dramatically. The end of the Cold War had ushered in if not the end of history, then a radically new era, defined not by the relations between the two superpowers but by globalization. Globalization was not a freak or a fad, Friedman argued; it was a system, just like the Cold War system that it was replacing, a system with its own rules and logic, its own heroes and villains, a system that was shaping the political and social lives of everybody on the planet.

The people who were making history in the age of globalization were not statesmen but business people. The relations that mattered most were not international relations but business relations. Bill Clinton might be an engaging character, in his way, but he was doing far less to change the world than Bill Gates. Friedman decisively broke the mold of *New York Times* foreign-affairs columnists by spending as much time interviewing business leaders as heads of state, and devoting as many column inches to the capital markets as to diplomatic maneuvers. In doing so he introduced his readers to a succession of people who had never had so much as a walk-on part in an international relations column before—bankers and buccaneers, dotcom billionaires and hedge fund managers, computer geeks and mobile-phone entrepreneurs. Given the American newspaper world's institutional conservatism, this was journalistic innovation of a high order.

The book that turned Friedman into America's founding journo-guru was *The Lexus and the Olive Tree* (1999). Friedman argued that globalization was being driven by a combination of technological innovation (which was killing distance) and financial deregulation (which was making it easy to shift vast sums of money hither and thither). But globalization could not banish the need for roots: the olive trees that people squabble over on the West Bank are shaping the modern world as surely as the Lexuses that the Japanese factories churn out.

Several other writers had made similar points, not least Benjamin Barber in *Jihad versus McWorld*, a 1995 book that was based on a 1992 article in the *Atlantic Monthly*. But Friedman illustrated his arguments with dozens of vivid examples culled from his extensive travels. He filled his pages with descriptions of factories in far-flung corners of the world and with anecdotes about rising business people. He also had a gift for memorable phrases: "the electronic herd" for currency traders, the "golden straightjacket" for the market-friendly rules that governments must wear if they want to thrive in a borderless world. He morphed *Das Kapital* into "DOS Capital" and propounded the "golden arches theory"—that no two countries lucky enough to have McDonald's restaurants will go to war with each other.

Friedman returned to his first calling, the Middle East, in the wake of September 11, when, as it were, the Lexus and the Olive Tree collided with each other with horrific consequences, becoming one of America's leading "liberal hawks" and providing powerful support for preemptive action to reorder the Middle East. However, as the Iraq War turned into a disaster, he distanced himself from the neoconservatives and returned to the subject of globalization with *The World Is Flat* (2005), which sold even more copies than *Lexus*.

Friedman argued that the trends that he had analyzed in *Lexus* had accelerated dramatically in the ensuing years. The Internet had introduced a new phase of globalization: services were being denationalized and brainworkers were joining the global labor market as computer programmers in Bangalore competed head to head with computer programmers in Boston.

Once again, Friedman did not pull any rabbits out of a hat: America had been abuzz with talk of the outsourcing of service jobs long before he published his book. But once again he produced compelling reporting and vivid phrases (though the trope about the flattening of the world became a little tiresome). He was one of the first Western journalists to write extensively about companies such as Infosys (he came up with the book's title during a brainstorming session with one of the company's founders, Nandan Nilekani)

He grasped the importance of global supply chains as well as global communications—and produced fascinating accounts of the internal operations of companies such as Walmart and UPS to illustrate his point. And once again Friedman acted like an enthusiastic tour guide to the future, introducing us to the companies that are inventing the future and giving us a few minutes of face time with the new masters of the universe.

If Friedman is the king of the journo-gurus, then Malcolm Gladwell is the crown prince, more glamorous than his elder competitor and arguably even more popular. Gladwell received a million-dollar advance for his first book, *The Tipping Point* (2000), and amply repaid his publisher's confidence, selling two million copies of the book and reserving a permanent spot on the best-seller list for his subsequent publications. By the time he came up with the idea for his third book, *Outliers* (2008), his advance had grown to $4 million. *Fast Company* calls him "a rock star, a spiritual leader, a stud."[6] *New York* magazine calls him a "Geek pop star."[7] Stephen Gaghan, the screenwriter of *Traffic* and *Syriana*, is writing a film based on his second book, *Blink* (2005).

Gladwell followed a more circuitous route into journalism than Friedman. The sprig of a liberal academic family—he was born in Britain and brought up in Canada—Gladwell was a rebel-in-reverse: he embraced conservatism as a teenager and even put up a poster of Ronald Reagan on his wall at the University of Toronto, a gesture that must have required considerable courage. His first job in journalism was with the Clinton-bashing *American Spectator*. He could easily have become lost in the echo chamber of right-wing journalism, perhaps joining the *National Review*, the ultimate journalistic dead end, and devoting himself to defending the true religion from various apostates. Instead he moved to the *Washington Post*, where he discovered that he had a talent for explaining business and science to the layman, using gripping narratives and astute examples to capture his readers' attention. By 1996 he had acquired enough of a reputation to be snapped up by *The New Yorker*, where he has remained ever since, growing more famous with every article.

If Friedman's talent is making sense of the most momentous development of our time, globalization, Gladwell's is for forcing us to take a fresh look at some of the commonplaces of our daily lives. Why do trends suddenly become unstoppable? How can we make complicated judgments in the fraction of a second? Why are some people much more successful than others? In answering these questions, Gladwell takes you on an enjoyable journey—perhaps too enjoyable given the underlying complexity of his subject matter—that makes the commonplace look not only exotic but fascinating.

The Tipping Point focuses on the moment when a trend becomes an avalanche or, to vary the metaphor, when an outbreak of a dis ease becomes an epidemic. We have all seen sudden enthusiasms for obscure books and pop songs spreading mysteriously from a hard core of zealots to the mass market. Gladwell tries to show how this happens and why. He is particularly interesting on the handful of people who precipitate the avalanche: on the "connectors" (who have a "special gift for bringing the world together"), on the "mavens" (who have the ability to plug us into new information about new markets), and on the "persuaders" (who possess enough charisma to persuade people to buy their products, which often means buying into their worldview). *The Tipping Point* quickly became a prime example of the very trend that it tried to analyze: the connectors, mavens, and persuaders all worked together to turn the book into a publishing phenomenon.

Gladwell capitalized on the success of *The Tipping Point* with a book on first impressions, which he variously calls "thinking without thinking" and "thin slicing," *Blink*. First impressions have got a bad rap as another name for prejudice: who would defend judging people by the color of their skin or the cut of their jib? But, without ignoring the dark side of "thin slicing," Gladwell was more interested in the bright side. Snap judgments are not always blind judgments, he argued; on the contrary, they can embody the wisdom of subtle unconscious calculations. Human beings are hard-wired to make complicated judgments about people they meet by reading their facial expressions, or to react in an instant to accidents and emergencies, often heroically, by relying on pure instinct. Gladwell even argued that activities that are normally taken slowly, such as looking for a potential mate or formulating a business strategy, can be done better by relying on intuition rather than engaging in endless ratiocination. Blind dating can be more productive than endless agonizing.

Gladwell's third book, *Outliers*, was also his most political, a cri de coeur against meritocracy, at least in its crude form. Gladwell argued that there is more to "genius" than a simple gift from the gods, and more to meritocracy than the allocation of fair rewards for individual ability. He insisted that successful people are "invariably the beneficiaries of hidden advantages and extraordinary opportunities and cultural legacies that allow them to learn and work hard and make sense of the world in ways that others cannot."

Gladwell deconstructed what he regards as the naïve popular idea of merit in two stages. He pointed out that success depends as much on hard work as on God-given talent. He even introduced, with the dubious precision beloved of management gurus, something called the 10,000-hour rule—the idea that you have to put in 10,000 hours of practice to excel at your calling. Mozart did nothing but practice music as a child. The Beatles played endless sets in

Hamburg strip clubs. Gladwell's emphasis on practice was part of a bigger point: that success depends on social circumstances as much as on anything else, not least natural talent. Canada's best hockey players were all born at a certain time of the year. Bill Gates went to a private school that gave him the opportunity, denied to his less privileged contemporaries, to work on a mainframe computer.

Gladwell's extraordinary success has produced an epidemic of imitators—young journalists (or more often ex-journalists these days) who fill their books with interviews of out-of-the-way heroes and give them titles like *Bunk* or *The Wisdom of Idiocy*. Most of this is tedious stuff that even the most slap-dash publishers are forced to reject. But one journo-guru has succeeded where thousands of others failed: Christopher Anderson. Anderson is the Malcolm Gladwell of the digital world—similar enough to the young master to attract the same readers but different enough not to be written off as a crass imitator.

Anderson shares Gladwell's talent for spotting and then unpacking big business trends. He also shares his talent for eye-catching titles. But he belongs to a different world from Gladwell: the world of West Coast high tech rather than East Coast marketing. Anderson has been writing about high tech for decades (full disclosure: Anderson was a colleague of mine for several years at *The Economist*, and we even shared an office for a couple of agreeable years). He is now the editor of *Wired*, the bible of the hard-core digitari, and a fixture on the high-tech lecture circuit. There is nobody in the tech world who does not know Chris Anderson or respect his opinions.

Anderson made his name with *The Long Tail: How the Future of Business Lies in Selling More of Less* (2006). *The Long Tail* is the product of a melding of the new business culture and the old one. The book started life as a blog in which Anderson conducted a sort of online seminar with his readers. It ended up as an old-fashioned business best-seller: a carefully packaged "big idea" that was supposed to reveal the secret of prospering in the new economy and that also includes a business tool that managers can apply to their businesses, the "long tail" of the title. This was Silicon Valley repackaged for the business traveler class.

Anderson's big idea was that we are moving from a world of big hits to a world of niche products. Technological innovation (particularly the Internet) is removing bottlenecks in distribution that forced companies to focus on a few products. Readers can quickly search amazon.com and have a book on Peruvian penis gourds delivered to their door by the next day. Technological innovation is also making it easier to gather information on your pet interests. Google will suggest several different books on penis gourds. Various online reviewers will give their opinions on the merits of each penis-gourd study. Pretty soon you have books on penis gourds inundating your postbox.

Niche markets have always existed, of course. Raymond Williams, a British cultural critic, once noted that "there are no masses. There are only ways of seeing people as masses." At the same time, the demand for hits is eternal: being social animals, people want to become part of a crowd of fans. Anderson's point was that the balance of power between the two is changing inexorably. Companies are finding it easier to reach those niche markets, making them ever more attractive. And hits have to compete with an infinite number of niche markets, making them ever harder to produce and even harder to sustain. With consumers favoring organizations that can provide them with the maximum amount of choice, business organizations must adjust or die. "The era of one-size-fits-all is ending," Anderson argued, "and in its place is something new, a market of multitudes."[8]

There are plenty of people who lament the rise of these micro-markets. Those of us of a certain age agonize about what sort of culture our children are absorbing clicking around on the Web, and not just because it contains so many weird and murky corners. We also lament the loss of a common culture that had everybody gathering around the watercooler to discuss last night's television show. Remember how we all talked about *Seinfeld* when it first hit the small screen, or how we all discussed *The Office*? Part of the pleasure of these two mold-breaking programs was that we all watched the mold being broken together. For his part, Anderson preferred to see fragmentation as an example of the rise of diversity, and a symptom of a tectonic cultural shift away from wanting to be normal to wanting to be special. He pointed out that the rise of micro-markets is shifting the balance of power away from the old bosses of culture to ordinary people, quoting Rupert Murdoch, perhaps not the best witness for his case, saying that "young people don't want to rely on a Godlike figure from above to tell them what's important. They want control over their media, instead of being controlled by it."[9]

To clinch his argument, Anderson added that the new technology is democratizing production as well as consumption. The average PC or Mac now contains everything from a printing press to a recording studio, giving your average smelly teenager access to tools that were once the monopoly of professionals. Blogs and YouTube allow people to share their creations with one of Anderson's micro-markets or, if they are lucky, with millions of strangers. Craigslist and eBay allow them to trade everything from quirky memorabilia to exotic information.

This blurring of the distinction between producers and consumers, between professionals and amateurs, between "them" and "us," is massively increasing the world's supply of talent. *Wikipedia* has outperformed the venerable *Encyclopaedia Britannica*, and Microsoft's generously funded *Encarta*, by the simple expedient of drawing on the talents of more people: anybody, from an acknowledged expert to a knowledgeable amateur, can contribute to the wiki. "Fluid, fast, fixable, and free" is more powerful than authoritative, slow, and inflexible. YouTube, which adds twenty hours' worth of new video every minute, throws up a few unmissable videos every day, funny, tragic, or riveting, among all the dross. "Talent is not universal," Anderson argued, "but it's widely spread. Give enough people the capacity to create, and inevitably gems will emerge."[10]

Whatever you think of the cultural impact of the long tail, there is no doubt that it is producing a new economy, with new giants emerging to take advantage of the world of micro-markets. eBay, which was born as recently as 1996, is now worth in excess of $35 billion, with more than 200 million registered users shifting more than $40 billion of merchandise every year. The new economy is also creating new marketing opportunities (and new marketing nightmares). Top-down messaging is losing influence while bottom-up buzz is gaining power. People are less and less likely to trust traditional advertisers and more and more likely to trust people who write online reviews or generate links on social networks. Dell spends hundreds of millions of dollars each year in promoting its quality and customer service, but Google quickly directs you to "Dell hell."

Anderson followed *The Long Tail* with *Free: The Future of a Radical Price* (2009). *Free* is essentially an extended meditation on an idea that has long been popular in tech circles—that "information wants to be free"; that digital technology is making it ever easier to store and distribute anything that is "made out of ideas," smashing barriers to entry, destroying business empires, and driving the price of information down toward zero. Anderson's take on "free" is a mixture of fatalism and techno-utopianism. His advice to people who worry about piracy is brutal: get over it. Stop fighting the inevitable and start reconceptualizing piracy as a marketing opportunity rather than a threat. To a large extent that is also his take on the entire "free" economy. Wonderful things will happen if we just allow prices to fall to their natural level, he argues: wonderful things for consumers, who will gain access to a cornucopia of books and music, but also wonderful things for companies, if they can learn how to use free things as a "hook" to get people to spend money on other things. Google was the trendsetter here, becoming a billion-dollar company by giving away search and email but charging for advertising—by hooking consumers with free services, Google can make billions selling information about those consumers to advertisers—but other behemoths such as Facebook are following fast on its heels.

Professors as Prophets

In his occasionally amusing autobiography, Bill Clinton tells a story about his arrival at University College, Oxford, with three other Americans. The college porter, Bill Mullins, greeted them by saying that he'd been expecting four Yanks but they sent him only three-and-a-half.[11] The half was Robert Reich, a fellow Rhodes Scholar and close friend of Mr. Clinton who, because of a genetic disease, is less than five feet tall.

Reich is the closest thing the modern American left has to John Kenneth Galbraith (who, by a strange twist of fate, was at the opposite end of the height spectrum, at six foot seven). Reich has regularly come near the top of various lists of management gurus for years. In a list produced by Accenture in 2002 he claimed third place (Michael Porter was number one, Tom Peters number two, and Peter Drucker number four). In the *Wall Street Journal*'s 2008 list he ranked number seven.

Reich started his career as a pundit by mouthing liberal boilerplate. In *The Next American Frontier* (1983) he blamed America's economic woes on its "paper entrepreneurialism"—its preference for financial gamesmanship over making and improving things—and called for more protectionism. But then he produced a series of articles and books that challenged the left to rethink some of its basic assumptions. In "Who Are We?" he demolished the case for protectionism in a world of global supply chains. What does it mean to protect the "American" car industry when the components of the average car are made all around the world? In *The Work of Nations* (1991) he argued that a country's competitiveness depends on its human capital—on the education and skills of its population—rather than on the profitability of the companies that happen to have their headquarters within its borders. The United States had embraced a "new economy" based on high value rather than high volume and on customization rather than standardization, he argued, in phrases that have resounded through his later work, and companies had been transformed from nation-bound pyramids into world-spanning networks. In this new world, the only "industrial policy" worth bothering with is to invest in education and training: countries with the highest-quality human capital will act as magnets to the highest-value-added jobs.

Reich never achieved as much success as a policymaker as he did as a policy-dreamer: during his five years as Bill Clinton's labor secretary he was repeatedly outmaneuvered by deficit hawks such as Robert Rubin and Larry Summers. But since leaving the Clinton administration in 1996 he has gone from strength to strength as a guru, propelled in part by the fame that attaches to people who have served in high office, but also by his impressive appetite for hard work and his keen eye for trends. I once spent an evening debating Mr. Reich at the Kennedy School of Government at Harvard; returning to my hotel room after a few post-debate drinks I turned on the late-night news only to discover my sparring partner sounding off on quite a different subject.

In *The Future of Success* (2001)—a perfectly titled book for a business market that is obsessed, above all, with success and the future—Reich argued that we live in the age of the terrific deal.[12] Choices are almost limitless and a better deal is always waiting around the corner, a wonderful situation for the consumer but a much more problematic one for the producer. Workers are always in danger of losing their jobs, companies of losing their markets, and society of losing the glue that holds it together. The terrific deal has replaced the ethic of loyalty with the "logic of disloyalty."[13] Workers have to market themselves in order to secure the next job. Companies have to slim themselves in order to avoid obsolescence by elephantiasis. And communities have to market themselves— and, in effect, commoditize themselves—in order to attract residents and businesses. In the age of the terrific deal, economies of attention replace economies of scale as the currency of business success. What matters is the ability to attract people's attention and then to create the "stickiness" that is the closest thing the modern world has to loyalty. If "attention must be paid," as Willy Loman said, the price of commanding it is endless self-publicity.

In *Supercapitalism*, Reich argued that today's turbo-charged capitalism is at the same time both generating profound social problems and using its political muscle to prevent those problems from being solved.[14] Again he went beyond liberal boilerplate. He argued that the people who are driving supercapitalism—who are giving the system its remorseless logic—are not greedy CEOs or faceless apparatchiks but you and me. Consumers are putting relentless pressure on companies to improve their quality and cut their costs. Investors are equally relentless in their pursuit of better returns (some of the most demanding investors are the pension funds that look after the life savings of government workers and bleeding-heart academics).

Reich was at his cutting best on the subject of corporate social responsibility. He described it as nothing more than a public relations ploy—advertising with a bit of Sociology 101 thrown in, something that companies embrace when it suits their interests but drop as soon as it threatens them. For Reich the former secretary of labor, it was clear that governments rather than companies should be in the business of protecting public goods. Governments are the only people who can represent the democratic will; governments are the only people who can be trusted to put the general interest above the profit motive.

Reich is clearly no business booster. In his memoir, *Locked in the Cabinet*, he recalls giving a lunchtime speech to the National Association of Manufacturers only to be howled at by a bunch of all-male cigar-smoking bigots. The memory was in fact a revealing fantasy: when the book was published, Jonathan Rauch pointed out that the speech took place at breakfast, that the Association has a no-smoking policy, and that a third of the delegates were women.[15] But Reich's antibusiness venom has not prevented business people from listening to what he has to say. And rightly so. Business people applaud Reich's critique of the protectionist wing of his party. They also share his enthusiasm for education and training: a succession of blue-ribbon business panels has echoed the basic argument of *The Work of Nations*.

The Florida Option

The most irritating thing about Reich is not his tendency to turn his nose up at business but his willingness to prostrate himself before what he calls "symbolic analysts." Yet Reich is restrained about these *übermensch* compared with Richard Florida, a specialist on urban studies who currently teaches at the University of Toronto. Florida has gone two better than Reich. He has given the symbolic analysts a sexier name—the creative class—and he has given them the starring role in everything he writes.

Florida's career-making book, *The Rise of the Creative Class: And How It's Transforming Work, Leisure and Everyday Life* (2002), is an odd mixture of Michael Young's *Rise of the Meritocracy* (1957) and Candace Bushnell's *Sex in the City*. Florida argues that the creative class is at the heart of the post-industrial economy. In 1900, fewer than 10 percent of Americans were doing creative work. Most broke their backs in farms or factories. Today the figure is 30 percent.[16] He also provides a portrait of how "creatives" live, chronicling the casual-dress revolution ("The No-collar Workplace"), the fashion for binge working ("The time warp"), and the fuzzy boundaries between work and leisure. Just as William Whyte's managerial class set the "American temper" in the 1950s, he argues, so the creative class sets the American temper today.[17]

It is not difficult to pick holes in Florida's use of the term "creative class." He uses the term to mean everything from street buskers to IT professionals, expanding and contracting it at will. In fact, the defining characteristic of most members of Florida's creative class is their willingness to play by the rules—to excel at school and university and to get professional qualifications—rather than their predilection for tuning in, turning on, and dropping out. They are primarily knowledge workers (to borrow Drucker's term) or members of the professional managerial class (to borrow Erik Olin Wright's) rather than bohemians. Florida's argument nevertheless contains a sensible point wrapped up in a deceptive package. The knowledge workers who are at the heart of the modern economy combine a liberal cultural sensibility with a reverence for brainpower.

For Florida, catering to this creative class is the key to success in the modern economy. The defining thing about "creatives" is that they are mobile. Manual workers had no choice but to live where there was coal to dig or steel to smelt. Creatives can live wherever they can get access to the Internet. In Florida's view, cities should forget about wooing companies with promises of light taxes and good roads; instead, they should focus on luring creative people. This means building lots of "creative districts" with lofts and blues clubs (and lots of bike paths so that you can get from one creative hub to another without adding to the world's carbon footprint). It also means embracing liberal values. For it is a fact demonstrated by a dozen indexes—gay indexes, bohemian indexes, and creativity indexes at the very least—that creative people will congregate only where tolerance is cherished.

The Rise of the Creative Class has been good to Florida. Born in the heart of Tony Soprano's America—he grew up in an Italian neighborhood of Newark, New Jersey, the son of a factory worker—he worked his way through the Ivy League and eventually landed a slot in academia. A lifetime laboring on obscure articles lay ahead of him. Then his discovery of the "creative class" turned him into a superstar. Publishers came knocking. His lecture fees mounted. Toronto University offered him his own institute, the Martin Prosperity Institute, and $346,000 a year to move north of the border. What streetwise New Jersey boy could refuse such an offer?

Florida has a legion of fans in the business world. Urban developers regard him as a one-man green light for lots of their projects. Human-resource managers love the way he emphasizes the importance of "experiences" (rewarding jobs and sabbaticals) rather than pay.[18] Nevertheless, Florida has also attracted an army of critics. The right dislikes him for downplaying the importance of cutting taxes and instead urging politicians to spend public money on lofts and bike paths.[19] The hard left is even more vitriolic, accusing him, in effect, of ignoring the working class, into which he was born, and instead fawning over the new elite. Where is the angst about inequality in Florida's work? Or the paeans of praise to "socially affordable housing" for the service class? Leftists in his adopted city of Toronto have even created an anti-Florida website—the Creative Class Struggle—and taken to disrupting his lectures.

Florida has responded to this criticism in the best way possible: by wading deeper into the fray. In his latest book, *The Great Reset*, he argues that the "great crash" of 2007–08 will reinforce the power of the creative class. Just as the Great Depression of the 1930s led to the rise of the suburbs, and the great malaise of the 1970s led to the rise of the sun belt, the crash of 2007–08 will hasten the rise of high-density cities. "Every phase or epoch of capitalism has its own distinct geography," he argues, "and the next phase will have the geography of the inner city." The housing crash will persuade people to stop driving themselves into debt to buy McMansions and the SUVs that go with them; instead they will start renting lofts and getting on their bicycles, helping to produce a general civilizational shift of shrinking suburbs and expanding urban cores.

But what exactly does creativity mean? Why do some people have it and others not? How can you encourage people to be more creative, and how can you build creativity into the DNA of your company? To answer these questions, a growing number of business people have been turning to the third member of my trio of academic entrepreneurs, Howard Gardner.

Gardner is the closest of the trio to a stereotypical ivory-tower intellectual. Howard Gardner has been a professor at Harvard University for forty years. His high-minded liberalism has never been diluted by contact with high politics (like Reich) or relentless self-promotion (like Florida). He eschews junkets of all kinds, shuns the corporate lecture circuit, and has never capitalized on the thousands of educational programs that his ideas have generated.[20]

Gardner is best known for his theory of multiple intelligences. For most of the twentieth century, his fellow psychologists had been trying to rank people on a linear scale on the basis of their general intelligence. In the early 1980s Gardner challenged this orthodoxy (and delighted the many people who disliked IQ tests) with his theory of multiple intelligences. He argued that intelligence could be subdivided into several different types (including linguistic, logical-mathematical, and musical), and that people who did poorly in one activity might excel in another.

As *Multiple Intelligences* turned him into an academic star, Gardner became preoccupied with two of its manifestations, creativity and persuasion. In *Creating Minds* (1993), he profiled various people who exemplified different creative styles. In *Leading Minds* (1995), he used the same technique to discuss people who had been geniuses at changing other people's minds. These books were written for his fellow academics, but it so happened that business thinkers were increasingly interested in the same subjects. In 1996 the World Economic Forum invited Gardner to Davos, where he was surprised by how comfortable he felt talking to business people, and subsequently Harvard Business School Press began to pump him for ideas for books.

Five Minds for the Future was one product of this pumping. The classification-obsessed Gardner argued that there are five different types of cognitive abilities—"minds," in his phrase—that are essential for success (the five mind-types are disciplined, synthesizing, creative, respectful, and ethical). These minds are not the distinct mental abilities that he discussed in *Frames of Mind*; rather they are mental attitudes that can be cultivated in school and work. The synthesizing mind seeks order in disorder. The creative mind seeks uncertainty and surprise. But these virtues are useless without discipline (which allows us to draw on the achievements of our predecessors), respect (which allows us to collaborate with others), or ethics (which are central to any functioning civilization).

Gardner argued that people who lack a command of one or more of these mental disciplines will have a hard time of it. People who cannot synthesize will be overwhelmed by information. People who cannot create will be replaced by machines. People who lack ethics will destroy their organizations and eventually themselves. People who refuse to respect others will poison their surroundings.[21] Gardner was particularly passionate about ethics and respect. Ethics need to be inculcated through tight codes of professional conduct in order to avoid greed and anarchy (Gardner's influence can be seen in the move by business schools and economics faculties to embrace codes of conduct). Respect needs to be instilled in everybody who claims to be a professional. Here the tone of his book is personal: Gardner was one of the leaders of the campaign to oust Larry Summers from the presidency of Harvard on the grounds that he showed too little respect for his colleagues (though Summers might well retort, rightly in my view, that Cornel West showed too little respect for his prestigious Harvard chair by frittering his time away on rap songs and failing to produce a serious work of scholarship).

A second product of the pumping was *Changing Minds* (2004). Changing minds (your own as well as other people's) is a skill that we lose as we get older. Young children are natural mind-changers, but age brings stubbornness. Mental arteries harden. Neural networks become hard-wired. Emotions become vested. Gardner argued that the best way to overcome this resistance to change is "representational redescription." It is not enough to repeat a message over and over. You need to repeat it in lots of different ways that appeal to different sorts of intelligence.

Though Gardner has diluted his criticisms of business a little as he has acquired a business audience, he still thinks that it is wrong for people to amass "excessive wealth" and worries that markets are "fundamentally amoral." He argues that business needs to adopt a code of ethics in order to elevate it to the level of a proper profession like teaching or doctoring. When he deigns to descend from grand abstractions, he produces some woefully shop-worn examples from the business world. To illustrate his belief in "respect," he repeated the old saw about the way that Xerox's Palo Alto Research Center (Parc) failed to exploit its brilliant technological innovations because different teams of researchers had little respect for each other. He wrote this at a time when the banking industry in general and Lehman Brothers in particular were being torn apart by the internal battle between investment bankers and traders.

Still, his lack of familiarity with the business world did little to deter his business audiences. The notion of the synthesizing mind was voted one of the "breakthrough ideas" in management theory for 2007, for example. Gardner had the good luck to be a distinguished psychologist at a time when psychology was in vogue. Many with-it managers are more interested in discovering people's psychological secrets than they are in understanding competitive advantage and strategic design. He also had the good sense to focus on a topic that excites business audiences, creativity. Why do some people come up with business-changing ideas while others are stuck on the treadmill? How can we synthesize ideas from lots of different areas? How can we fix creativity into the heart of our business DNA? Gardner's popularity is a sign not so much of his ability to answer these questions (which is open to doubt) as of business's desperation to find somebody who is at least willing to ask them.

The Lessons of the Insurgents

The success of these outsiders provides an interesting commentary on the nature of the management theory industry. Study a list of the world's top economists and you quickly discover that they all have one thing in common. They may be conservatives or liberals. They may regard Keynes as an angel or an apostate. But they are all . . . economists: members in good standing of an academic guild with their MPhils, PhDs, and lists of refereed articles to prove it. Study a list of the top gurus and you discover a different picture. Not only have some of the most influential management theorists never taken an MBA or a PhD in business studies, but the imposters are arguably becoming more prominent as the profession grows older.

What does this tell us? You could certainly argue that it is yet another sign of the profession's immaturity. The economics profession is not open to people without PhDs in economics for the simple reason that economists need to master a demanding but agreed-upon body of knowledge: Keynesians and monetarists are as one when it comes to the importance of mastering differential equations. But you can equally validly argue that it is a sign of the

profession's vitality—its openness to outside ideas and its willingness to allow a thousand flowers to bloom.

I am inclined to the second school of thought. Academic economics sometimes gives the impression that it has degenerated into
a glass bead game played, however skillfully, by tenured insiders. The economics profession did an abysmal job of predicting
the worst economic crisis since the Second World War—a failure of foresight that is made all the worse by the fact that several
economists designed the fancy financial techniques that helped to
produce the disaster. The management theory industry's openness
to outsiders has protected it from this sort of sclerosis. It has also
kept it fizzing with new ideas. Given the huge challenges that face
the industry—the collapse of corporate giants such as Enron and
the rise of alternative organizational forms such as public-private
hybrids—it can only be a good thing that it is looking for solutions in lots of different places. The most interesting question is
not whether openness is a good thing in principle, but whether the
new class of gurus has brought light as well as heat to its calling.

Entrepreneurs who shake up businesses and blur boundaries inevitably arouse hostility from incumbents. The journo-gurus have
annoyed both journalists and management writers. Some of this
can be put down to professional jealousy. Few profiles of Thomas
Friedman neglect to mention his 11,400-square-foot house set in
seven-and-a-half acres of land and his generous travel budget. Some
can be put down to questions of taste. Friedman's folksy prose
annoys some people even more than his generous accommodation.
Walter Russell Mead, of the Council on Foreign Relations, describes his style as being "an occasionally flat Midwestern demotic
punctuated by gee-whiz exclamations about just how doggone irresistible globalization is." (Mead gets it exactly wrong when he
says that this style is best "taken in small doses": analyzed sentence

by sentence, Friedman's style can grate; taken in rapidly, preferably on an airplane, it can carry you along.) Gregg Easterbrook complains of *Hot, Flat, and Crowded*, Friedman's green-tinged follow-up to *The World Is Flat*, that "there are so many buzz phrases in Thomas Friedman's new book that it practically vibrates in your hand."

Malcolm Gladwell's style also grates on some of his critics. Joseph Epstein has produced an uncannily accurate parody of Gladwell's signature pen portraits: "Tall, wearing earrings and a metal plate in his head, availing himself of profanity of a kind that would make an Algerian camel driver blush, Zack Zipperman, PhD, has for the past 26 years, in his windowless laboratory at MIT, been teaching white mice to dance the cha-cha-chaa, with interesting results for those who can't comprehend why men born after 1942 never carry handkerchiefs."

But some of these criticisms have more bite. The journo-gurus are certainly guilty of the oldest journalistic sin in the book—simplifying and exaggerating. I will have plenty of occasion to expose this in future chapters, particularly those on globalization and talent, where I think they have simplified and exaggerated more than is helpful. And the academic entrepreneurs are also guilty of what might be called overleveraging their expertise. Richard Florida responds to justifiable criticisms by repeating rather than refining his argument. Howard Gardner offers his business readers sloppy seconds—*Five Minds* is a decidedly substandard book compared with the books that he writes for his fellow psychologists.

Still, in general these outsiders have been a force for good. They have brought fruitful new perspectives to bear on management theory (from other subjects in the case of the academic entrepreneurs, and from "the university of life" in the case of the journo-gurus). They have helped to make management theory more accessible to ordinary people. Friedman has a knack for illuminating the globalization debate with clever phrases. Gladwell's storytelling skills can enliven even the most tedious areas of psychology. At the very least the journo-gurus have raised the bar for business writing in general, forcing many gurus to untangle some of their metaphors and add a bit of color in the form of anecdotes and pen portraits.

If the interlopers have been good for management theory, management theory has also been good for the interlopers. The journo-gurus—and here Friedman was clearly the pioneer—have enriched journalism by focusing on big business trends rather than just political and diplomatic events (the stuff of mainstream journalism) or individual industries (the stuff of the business pages). The academic entrepreneurs have also grown intellectually as a result of their encounter with management theory. Reich questioned old-fashioned protectionism in part because he learned about the complexities of today's supply chains. Florida enriched urban geography by thinking about "no-collar workers" and new work habits. Our various imposters have grasped that management theorists have been writing about some of the most interesting subjects around today—from the dramatic change in the nature of work to the integration of the global economy—and have sensibly decided that they want to get in on the act.

This fashion for intellectual miscegenation will only become more pronounced in the future. There is a growing army of journalists and academics who want nothing more than to become gurus in their own right. Reich and Florida are the models for many a young academic who craves to be able to afford a house in Berkeley or Boston. Friedman and Gladwell have replaced Woodward and Bernstein as the models for young journalists. Joshua

Cooper Ramo, a former foreign editor of *Time* magazine, presents Hezbollah as one of the world's great "learning organizations"; wields experts such as Bill Browder, a successful fund manager who also happens to be the grandson of Earl Browder, a former head of the American Communist Party; and even talks at length about the way a sand pile can be destabilized by the addition of a single grain of sand. We will be reading a lot more of this sort of thing before this particular fad has run out of steam.

PART III

THREE MANAGEMENT REVOLUTIONS

6

Rethinking the Company

The Shell Center, in the heart of London, is a striking monument to corporate self-confidence. Solid and imposing, it serenely surveys all that surrounds it, including the Palace of Westminster, a dozen Whitehall departments, and—a recent addition—the London Eye. With its labyrinthine corridors, hundreds of meeting rooms, and all-pervasive sense of bureaucratic permanence, the building has been a perfect habitat for Shell Man, as the company's employees were once mockingly known the world over.

By tradition, Shell Man was a bureaucrat in all but name, differing from the government paper pushers who accompanied him on the daily commute from the shires or the suburbs to Waterloo Station in only one thing—the size of his paycheck. He looked forward to a lifetime of secure employment and an index-linked pension at the end of it. The company provided country-club membership not just for him but for his children. When he was posted to Asia and Africa—as he routinely was as part of his stately progression up the company ranks—he competed in pomp and circumstance with the British ambassador and was not above doing a little spying on the side for his friends in the British Secret Service.

The headquarters of Google in Mountain View, California, not far from Stanford University, could hardly be more different. The Googleplex looks more like a with-it university campus than a company. It flaunts all the clichés of creative workspaces: high ceilings, bright colors, open spaces, Ping-Pong tables and, outside, picnic tables, park benches, a vegetable garden, and walkways busy with people and bicycles. There are power outlets in all sorts of unusual places, as well as the usual ones, in case one of the company's crazily brilliant employees is seized with an idea as he walks upstairs.

The atmosphere is thoroughly informal and egalitarian: all first names and casual clothes, wide-ranging discussions and freedom to fail. Informality goes hand in hand with paternalism. The company provides everything the workers need to keep their lives in order—dry cleaners, day care, dog care, dentists, doctors, gym instructors, masseurs, and, on Thursdays, car washes and oil changes. You can grow fat without ever leaving the Googleplex. Eleven restaurants serve $70 million of free food every year. Free snacks and cappuccinos are an arm's reach away. Company vehicles, equipped with Wi-Fi and powered by biodiesel, transport workers from as far away as San Francisco from early in the morning to late at night. Women get five months of maternity leave on full salary; men get seven weeks.[1]

None of this should be mistaken for softness, however. Google is skilled at putting limits on its workers as well as giving them freedom to fail. Shona Brown, a former McKinsey consultant who wrote a book on organized chaos, *Competing on the Edge: Strategy as Structured Chaos*,[2] before being snapped up by Google, describes the company's approach as "to determine precisely the amount of management it needs—and then use a little bit less."

Two principles provide the protean company with structure:

meritocracy and the bottom line. Google accepts only 1 percent of applicants and judges them on the basis of their brainpower, as manifested in their SAT results and college grades, rather than character or connections.[3] Google's annual revenues grew from nothing in 1998 to $20 billion four hundred weeks later. Today the company bestrides the information superhighway like a Godzilla: Googlezilla controls 80 percent of all searches online, two-thirds of all video traffic, and 40 percent of all advertising revenue. Look almost anywhere in the world of information, from libraries to advertising to television, and you can see the new boy forcing older companies to march to its tune.

To the casual observer of the business world, Shell probably looks like a "normal" firm and Google like an outlier; indeed, in a note to prospective shareholders just before the company went public in 2004, Larry Page proclaimed, "Google is not a conventional company. We do not intend to become one."[4] But in many ways it is the other way around. Management gurus are producing books with titles such as *What Would Google Do?* (by Jeff Jarvis), and established companies are behaving like middle-aged men in the throes of a midlife crisis. Shell has appointed a chairman from the high-tech sector, Jorma Ollila, the former boss of Nokia, and created a Silicon Valley–style incubator, called Gamechanger, with a staff of twenty-five and an annual budget of $40 million, which is charged with encouraging all Shell employees to come up with ideas for new businesses (successful entrepreneurs are given as much as $500,000 in initial funding).

Management theory is currently trying to understand the seismic shift in corporate organization that has driven Shell and Co. to become more like Google. I will explore the complexities of this transformation in later chapters on knowledge, learning and innovation, strategy and vision, and leadership. But in this chapter I will focus on the way that a mighty threesome—technology, capital, and globalization—have forced companies to question their old assumptions about size, strength, and structure.

The End of Certainty

Companies have arguably been the world's most important organizations since the midnineteenth century, the engines of global prosperity and the building blocks of most people's social lives. But they are remarkably fluid organizations. Over the past couple of decades they have been forced to rethink almost every tenet of managerial wisdom. Once companies prided themselves on "vertical integration" and were run like self-contained empires, with as little recourse to outsiders as possible. Now they are "sticking to their knitting," focusing on their core businesses and contracting everything else out to independent specialists. Once companies had a clear line of command and control, starting with the chairman at the top and stretching to the lowliest menial. Now they are turning themselves into "inverted pyramids," encouraging workplace democracy and handing power to front-line workers.

Radical change has become a constant backdrop of business life (and Niccolò Machiavelli's maxim, "Whoever desires constant success must change his conduct with the times," has become a favorite corporate motto). Business cycles can play themselves out in months rather than decades. Companies can be reduced from exemplars to has-beens in the blink of an eye (remember how we used to admire Nokia and AOL?). Many new-economy companies are no more than glowworms: brilliant for a few hours but soon dead. Yossi Vardi, an Israeli entrepreneur, compiled a list of thirty-four technology companies that were ranked as "premier growth stocks" in 1980. Two decades later, twenty-three had disappeared and only one, Intel, had produced a consistent record of growth.

A dozen business gurus have tried to capture what is going on in the titles of their books: *Faster, Blur, Out of Control, Blown to Bits, Fast Forward, Speed of Thought, Wake Up!, The Age of Unreason . . .* But John Chambers, Cisco's boss, has expressed it as well as anyone in a prosaic yet deadly accurate phrase: we live in an era of "unusual uncertainty."

What forces have unleashed this maelstrom? Three stand out: the Internet, the capital markets, and globalization. Each one of these is a world-shaking force in its own right. Taken together, they are producing unprecedented turmoil and change.

The Internet has rewritten the rules of business in less than two decades. No previous world-changing innovation has spread so far and evolved so fast. "It took telephones 71 years to penetrate 50 per cent of American homes, electricity 52 years, and TV three decades," Ken Auletta reminds us in his study of Google. "The Internet reached more than 50 per cent of Americans in a mere decade . . ."[5]

The Internet has already evolved from an asocial medium into a social and interactive one. Almost 10 percent of the world's population has clambered onto one social-media platform or another, and the enthusiasm for clambering aboard is only increasing: it took Facebook five years to attract its first 100 million users and five months to attract its second 100 million.[6] Now it is beginning to embrace things as well as people: soon you (or your electricity company) will be able to control your fridge and radiators over the Internet. The speed of evolution is set to increase. Google is experimenting with super-high-speed networks, in various locations in the United States, that will operate more than a hundred times faster than regular broadband.[7] Cisco claims that its latest router can deliver the entire printed collection of the U.S. Library of Congress in just over a second.

The Internet has made it easier for Davids to take on Goliaths. Small startups can quickly acquire both a professional infrastructure and a global reach. Ponoko, a New Zealand–based company, will arrange to have your ideas turned into products and then delivered to your customers wherever they might be in the world. Amateurs can shake up long-established professional guilds. Blogs have rewritten the rules of journalism: teenage scribblers in Washington basements and law professors in the wilds of Tennessee have repeatedly out-scooped and out-analyzed the *New York Times* and the *Washington Post*.

All this has forced established Goliaths to improve their game. They can no longer hide behind old-fashioned barriers such as huge factories and elaborate distribution networks. Nor can they rely on softer barriers such as deference or loyalty. Technorati determines the "authority" of a blog by the number of people who link to it rather than the institutional connections of the bloggers. Old-fashioned intermediaries such as dealers and brokers are being disintermediated regardless of how much loyalty they have built up over the years. Established companies must keep running in order to stay in the same place.

The capital markets are also giving companies a shaking. The markets control vastly more money than ever before: the U.S. Investment Company Institute calculates that the volume of money controlled by American mutual funds increased from $135 billion in 1980 to $12 trillion in 2007. Financial institutions not only put pressure on companies to perform from quarter to quarter; they also cajole them to organize themselves in certain ways: the "conglomerate discount" means that companies have a huge incentive to focus on their core businesses. The power of finance capital has

dramatically changed the way that most Americans (and a growing number of people in other countries) think of businesses. They
increasingly see them as sources of dividends as well as jobs. They
are constantly gauging the relative performance of different companies by studying stock market quotations (which float along the
bottom of our television screens) and listening to financial news.

The lords of finance have also introduced a far more unwel-
come element into the management mix, uncertainty, frequently
of an extreme variety. Financial markets have always been unstable: the world has seen at least one big financial panic every decade
for the past century. But financial earthquakes seem to be getting more frequent and more far-reaching. In 2007–08, problems
with arcane securities traded by often obscure financial institutions
shook "real" companies to their foundations and threw millions of
people out of work.

The most famous analyst of the growing uncertainty is Nassim
Taleb, whose impeccably timed *The Black Swan: The Impact of the
Highly Improbable* (2007) has become a global best-seller, translated
into thirty-one languages, turning its author into the prophet-
cum-rock star of the global economic meltdown.[8] The product of a prominent and polyglot Lebanese family, Taleb began
his career in finance, as a Wall Street trader, including a spell at
Lehman Brothers, and as a hedge fund manager. But once he had
made enough money to be "free from authority," as he put it, he
turned to academia—he is now a professor at both the Polytechnic
Institute of New York University and Oxford University—and to
the wider world of punditry.

The Black Swan was a quirkily learned polemic against humanity's hubris about its ability to predict the future. Taleb argued
that our minds are wired to deceive us. We like to think that we
can predict and control the world. But most of the greatest events,

from scientific breakthroughs to global upheavals, are black swans. This tendency is particularly dangerous when it is allied to arrogant bankers and a globalized financial system. Before the global meltdown, the lords of finance liked to boast that the combination of global integration and the development of sophisticated financial models had dramatically reduced volatility. Nonsense, said Taleb: while volatility might have declined in the short term, giving the appearance of stability, the world was on the verge of a "Black Swan" of devastating proportions. No sooner had the book hit the bookstores than the black swan flapped its wings.

The Internet and the capital markets have both reinforced the third revolutionary force: globalization. Globalization is speeding ahead at a faster pace than at any time since the late nineteenth century. This is changing the "old" economy as well as the new. Every day tens of thousands of ships, flagged in Panama, registered in Malta, insured in London, and staffed by sailors from every corner of the world, carry goods from one corner of the world to another. In general, this is making knowledge ever more important: as the death of distance brings millions of cheap hands and brains into competition with more expensive ones, the only sustainable source of advantage becomes the ability to outthink your rivals.

Reasons to Panic

What does all this mean for the heroes of this chapter—everyday companies and the company men and women who run them? One of the most popular answers is that it is leading to the "demise of size," as yesterday's behemoths give way to today's nimble champions. The most enthusiastic advocates of this argument (who include gurus such as Tom Peters and magazines such as *Fast Company*) argue that the future lies with "virtual" companies—tiny amoeba-like organizations that come together to get a job done and then break apart, only to reconfigure in a different form around another project. The more moderate advocates argue that size is being converted from an advantage (which you boast about) to a hindrance (which you either conceal or try to get rid of). Peter Drucker once announced that "The Fortune 500 is over." Tom Peters argues that "smaller firms are gaining in almost every market."[9] *The Economist* has frequently praised small startups and cautioned governments against protecting dying giants.

The demise-of-size crowd certainly has some arguments on its side. "Lean manufacturing" and "just-in-time production" have shifted the emphasis from size to timeliness. And a host of technological advances—most recently the development of "cloud computing"—have given small companies command over resources that used to be reserved for their big brothers. As the advantages brought by economies of scale have shrunk, the disadvantages have grown. Giant companies generate bureaucratic bloat; giant factories create shop-floor alienation; and many giant corporations fail to attract creative workers, or to make good use of them if they do get hold of them. The result has been an epidemic of downsizing and pseudo-downsizing: big companies have been reducing layers of management, subdividing themselves into smaller units, and moving their operations from swanky skyscrapers in the middle of cities to dismal office parks in the suburbs.

Yet the argument is easy to exaggerate. Big companies remain enormously powerful in every sector from retail to information technology. Walmart has more employees than Iceland has citizens.[10] Mega-churches are driving mom-and-pop churches out of business. Successful new-economy startups such as Microsoft and Google have done what all successful startups throughout history have done and grown into giants. The financial crisis has been good for big companies. The government has intervened to rescue too-big-to-fail companies such as General Motors and Citibank (the financial services sector is now more concentrated than ever). And the rise of the emerging world has projected a new set of giant conglomerates onto the global stage.

In many ways the argument about size depends on a false antithesis: big and small companies are potentially allies rather than alternatives. Cloud computing could not provide startups with access to huge amounts of computer power if big companies had not created giant servers. Biotech startups could not survive if they were not given work by biotech giants. The most successful economic ecosystems contain a variety of big and small companies: Silicon Valley boasts long-established giants such as Hewlett-Packard as well as an ever-changing array of startups. The reason why the American economy has been more dynamic than the European economy over the past few decades is not just because it is better at producing startups, but also because it is better at allowing startups to grow into Microsoft and Google.

Who Killed Alfred Sloan?

The real explanation of the ongoing corporate revolution is much deeper than the debatable demise of size. A growing band of management thinkers believes that companies of all sizes are living through a transition from one corporate model based on control to another based on entrepreneurialism. The founders of the school were Christopher Bartlett, of Harvard Business School, and the late Sumantra Ghoshal, of the London Business School, but its members also include Yves Doz and Chan Kim of INSEAD, Gary Hamel of the London Business School, and, of course, the late C. K. Prahalad of the Ross Business School at the University of Michigan.

The departing ideology is Sloanism, a managerial philosophy named after Alfred Sloan, who took over as president of General Motors in 1923. Sloan's great achievement was to do for management what Henry Ford had done for labor—to turn it into a reliable, efficient, machine-like process. Indeed, to a large extent, Sloan's system was supposed to be an antidote to temperamental pioneers like Ford, whose irrational dislike of producing anything other than the Model T (he once kicked to pieces a slightly modified version) nearly bankrupted his company.

Sloan wanted to invent a company that could run itself. His solution to the problem was the modern multidivisional firm, in which businesses are divided into a set of semiautonomous operating units, each responsible for maintaining the market share and profits of a single business or market and each having its division heads reporting to a group headquarters in charge of setting long-term strategy and allocating capital. On the top of the pile sat a class of professional managers—the people that sociologists once dismissed as "organization men" and that some commentators remember with growing nostalgia.[11]

Sloanism was responsible for some of American capitalism's greatest achievements. General Motors increased its share of the American market from 18 percent in the early 1920s, when Sloan took over, to upward of 45 percent by the late 1970s, making it by far the largest car company in the world. And most other American companies, from DuPont in chemicals to General Electric in engineering, adopted their own variations of the same theme. Yet from the 1970s onward, Sloanism came under attack on four fronts. The Japanese opened the first front by inundating Western markets with better, cheaper, more reliable goods through "lean" production based on teamwork, which avoided both the alienation and the waste of Sloan's system. Michael Milken, the junk bond king, and Michael Jensen, the leading theoretician of shareholder value, opened the second front, demonstrating that Sloanism had allowed many American firms to be hijacked by managers more interested in their pay and perks than in shareholder value. Steve Jobs and other Silicon Valley entrepreneurs opened the third front, demonstrating that you can succeed in business without growing a giant bureaucracy. The reengineers opened the final front, ripping apart all the old Sloanist functional departments such as "marketing," "production," and "research" and pushing workers into cross-functional teams, forcing them to use computers to bridge the gaps.

All of these changes—and a hundred smaller ones—can be traced back to two mighty forces: growing uncertainty about the future, as markets became less predictable, and the rising importance of knowledge. Buffeted by these forces, the Sloanist system gradually collapsed—or, more accurately, an extreme version of one of Sloan's beliefs, decentralization, triumphed over two of his other tenets: his emphasis on formal controls and self-sufficiency.

Consider, first, Sloan's enthusiasm for a steep corporate hierarchy, in which the most senior managers concentrated on long-term planning, like latter-day Platonic guardians, and the most junior focused on day-to-day problem-solving. The hierarchy was a slowly moving conveyor belt, relaying information (ground into statistics and reinterpreted by middle managers) to the strategy-makers at the top. The problem with this arrangement, in Jack Welch's punchy expression, is that the company ends up with its "face toward the CEO and its ass toward the customer." But today's best modern companies are customer- rather than boss-facing: Craig Newmark even calls himself the founder and chief customer-service representative of Craigslist.

As for the data conveyor belt, markets today are so like quicksilver that information that arrives late is worse than useless. Rather than worrying about rationality and the importance of being "an objective organization, as distinguished from the type that gets lost in the subjectivity of personalities," as Sloan once put it, modern business has a craving for the instinctive. Richard Branson, for example, had the idea of setting up his airline when he spent three days trying to get through to People Express and found the phone permanently engaged. There had to be a severe shortage of any product for which there was so much demand, he reasoned, and so he founded Virgin Airlines.

Inside the Walls

The next casualty is the idea that each company is a more or less self-sufficient organization. Sloanist firms were fortresses, making many of their own raw materials. Henry Ford's car company even owned the sheep that provided the wool for the car seats. Now, managers are smashing down barriers—not only with suppliers but even with competitors. Marks & Spencer, a British retailer, has been encouraging its suppliers to come up with ideas for new products. Procter & Gamble and Walmart have invested in a joint information system in a bid to coordinate production with sales. IBM and Cisco claim to have more than 100,000 "business partnerships" apiece.[12] Many of the world's largest firms derive more than one-fifth of their revenues from alliances. The basic assumption behind such "connected corporations" is that, far from being the property of a particular company, products and services are the products of an entire chain of firms, starting with suppliers and ending with distributors.

Some of today's most interesting companies are radically redefining the relationship between producers and consumers—and in the process redefining the borders of the corporation. Zipcar and

Netflix are harnessing a combination of new technology and the zeitgeist ("Sharing is clean, crisp, urbane, postmodern," says the *New York Times*'s Mark Levine. "Owning is dull, selfish, timid, backward.") to pioneer a new model of collaborative consumption.[13] Zipcar made $130 million in profits in 2009, a year in which car sales fell by 40 percent, and Netflix made $359.6 million. Bag Borrow or Steal allows you to rent a glamorous purse. TechShop, in Menlo Park, California, rents "tinkering space" and equipment to thousands of inventors, hobbyists, and fanatics.

Other pioneers of "collaborative consumption" have gone further, dispensing with the idea of buying inventories of their own and contenting themselves with the role of brokers. CouchSurfing connects people who have a spare couch with people who are willing to pay for the privilege of using it. There are 1.7 million registered couchsurfers in 70,000 cities worldwide. Others operate in a barter or even a communist economy. ThredUP specializes in exchanging children's clothes. There are versions of thredUP for everything from makeup to video games. Freecycle helps people give things away. The website has 5.7 million members around the world and processes 12,000 items a day.

The moguls who run Zipcar clearly have different motives from the crypto-communists who run Freecycle, but both are driven by the same two insights: that access is increasingly trumping ownership, and that a company is more a network of renewable relationships than a mighty engine churning out stuff.

"Collaborative production" takes these insights even further, and turn Sloan on his head.

They don't just look outside the company every now and again; they do so as a matter of course. For them, companies are little more than the junction points of networks. In *Remix: Making Art and Commerce Thrive in the Hybrid Economy*, Lawrence Lessig, of

Stanford University, argues that a host of new companies such as Flickr, Twitter, and Linux specialize in taking the shared efforts of thousands or even millions of people and then using them to create communities. If the Sloanist company's core competency lay in vertical integration, the "hybrid" company's core competency lies in organizing "communities of meaning," tapping into the enthusiasm of thousands of people and then converting their ideas into a coherent product or service.

Even those managers who are unfashionable enough to try to defend the old Sloanist fortress find that they are fighting a losing battle. Customers have learned how to turn blogs and tweets into irresistible weapons of siege warfare. In 2005, word got out that New Line Cinema was filming *Snakes on a Plane* with Samuel L. Jackson. Fans embraced the film even before it came out, with blogs such as Snakes on a Blog and hundreds of unofficial T-shirt designs at cafepress.com. But they also exacted a price: they insisted that Samuel L. Jackson should utter the line "I have had it with these mother-fucking snakes on this mother-fucking plane." New Line was eventually forced to include the line—and lost the film's PG–13 status as a result.[14]

From Decentralization to Empowerment

Inviting lots of suppliers and rivals inside Sloan's fortress is a blatant attack on everything that the great man held most dear, yet another way in which modern management has turned against Sloan is perhaps the most cruel. Critics of Sloan have accepted one of his ideas, "federal decentralization," and then taken it to extremes that he would never have countenanced.

Sloan divided General Motors into separate arms, such as Buick, Pontiac, and Chevrolet. Today, some big companies are trying to break themselves into thousands of small units— thereby hoping to "empower" the workers in the front line. Whole Foods, America's most profitable food retailer when judged by profit per square foot, is organized into self-governing teams. Team members control everything from the company's workforce to its stock: they vote on whether to allow a potential new hire to join the team and collectively decide what to put on the shelves. For some management theorists, even this level of decentralization is inadequate: never willing to be outdone Tom Peters thinks that companies should treat each worker as a small company in his or her own right.

The problem with decentralization on this scale is that it may seem only a step away from anarchy. The natural reply of some Peters acolytes might be: "Fine. Step on the gas!" On the other hand, a whole range of big companies, such as Procter & Gamble and McDonald's, seem just as capable of thriving in the new chaotic world as virtual companies. And even trendy companies like Google are not so much disorganized as organized in a different way. Such firms may be flat and flexible, but they are also more than just a collection of individuals. There is something holding them together. It is a new collection of building blocks.

The New Building Blocks: 1. Core Competencies

With the collapse of the Sloanist system, the natural inclination is to look for another structure to replace it—a new set of departments, divisions, and teams. Unfortunately, there is no universal answer of that sort. Rather, management theory has tended to focus on management techniques that a horizontally organized company can use to give structure and direction to its various component parts. These include network building and entrepreneurialism. But the starting point for every company is one of management theory's ugliest but most important buzzwords: "core competencies."

The idea of core competencies' was dreamed up by Gary Hamel and C. K. Prahalad in the 1990s. Core competencies are essentially the skills and capabilities, formal and informal, that give a company its peculiar flavor and unique competitive edge, the secret sauce that cannot be copied by a rival. Sony's core competency in miniaturization, for example, allows the company to make everything from video cameras to notebook computers; Tata's core competencies in frugal innovation allows the conglomerate to produce value-packed products in everything from cars (the Nano) to water purifiers (the Swatch).

However, the whole point of core competencies is not so much what a firm does as what it decides not to do (which it then contracts out to specialists). Often, selecting a core competency means excluding itself from parts of the production process it performs poorly. Nike designs and sells sports shoes but does not assemble anything itself. In the semiconductor industry, "fabless" (or fabricationless) firms, such as America's Cirrus Logic, have stuck to design; that has left room for companies such as Taiwan Semiconductor Manufacturing Company to sell their services as "foundries"—manufacturers who will work to order.

One problem with core competencies is that they can be interpreted to mean almost anything. In South Korea, when the government tried to restrict companies to a few core businesses in the 1990s, the *chaebol* (as the country's conglomerates are called) responded by choosing broad areas such as technology, industry, and energy. In France, water companies persuaded themselves that media is a natural business for them to be in, because, like water, it involves pipes and has a complicated billing system. The result was the disaster at Vivendi.

Another problem with core competencies, as Hamel and

Prahalad admitted, is that if the market changes and managers get stuck in a rut, they can easily degenerate into "core rigidities." The relentless focus that allows startups to succeed can often turn into blinders. Sony's skill in churning out endless variations on its products eventually exhausted its customers. The engineering-dominated culture that is at the heart of Google's success may also blind it to worries about "softer" questions, such as privacy, that may ultimately undermine it.

The New Building Blocks: 2. Renewal

It is dangerous, therefore, to treat core competencies as though they are set in stone. That is why modern management theorists are always looking for ways to keep a company on its toes—or to practice "renewal," in the jargon. The impetus for a serious exercise in renewal must come from the top. Sometimes CEOs feel that they have no choice but to "blow up" their companies from within: Jack Welch was perhaps the best practitioner of this style of management. But usually they settle for something less drastic. In early 2010, Google was entering a midlife crisis, left behind by Apple's iPhones and iPads and denounced by the technorati as a Googlezilla, huge and insensitive. The company skillfully used the introduction of the Android phone to reinvigorate itself.

For Google, the Android was not simply a best-selling gizmo (by mid-2010 it was outselling the iPhone, though producing much lower profit margins); it was also a key to the company's renewal. The company recognized that its famed search box was becoming dated. The Android phone—and a legion of other smart hand-held devices—offered it a way of keeping its grip on Web advertising. The trouble with the search box is that is simply responds to your needs. But how about a device that knows what you want before you know you want it? That suggests a great new place to have dinner on your way home, or that tells you that, just around the corner, you can find a first edition that you have been seeking for years? Google believes that the power of search is only just beginning to be exploited—and that mobile devices, rather than personal computers, are best positioned to expand that power.[15]

The New Building Blocks: 3. Networking

There is no better way to regalvanize yourself than to produce a new "platform." But companies have also come up with a more mundane way of keeping themselves on their toes: incessant internal networking. IBM has conducted two company-wide electronic brainstorming exercises, involving more than 150,000 people, that have encouraged it to put more emphasis, for example, on green computing. Cisco Systems is pioneering the use of its own video technology to improve communications between its employees.

Electronic meetings are no substitute for physical meetings. It is not uncommon for senior managers to spend three out of every four weeks on business trips—managing by walking around has turned into managing by flying around. But sensible companies also throw lower-level people together in the hope that they will generate electricity. Walmart uses its private air force to ferry store managers to its headquarters in Bentonville, Arkansas. Almost everybody has regular retreats for senior managers and global get-togethers for the marketing department.

The New Building Blocks: 4. Culture

Core competencies, renewal, and networking—a cynic might say that this sounds like a fairly vague list around which to build a company. The cynic might be just as unimpressed by the final item in the list: corporate culture. Management theorists argue that "culture" is the glue that holds the gelatinous mass together: the X-factor that inspires employees to be self-disciplined and allows managers and workers (to use two outdated terms) to trust each other. But isn't "culture" a hopelessly vague term? And aren't many arguments about the power of corporate culture circular? Management theorists like to point to companies such as Procter & Gamble and GE as evidence of the power of corporate culture. But are these companies successful because they have strong cultures, or do they have strong cultures because they are successful?

The proponents of corporate culture hardly strengthen their case by putting so much emphasis on mission statements, which usually read like lists of buzzwords strung together in no particular order (there is even an automatic "mission statement generator" that does the stringing together for you). Google has successfully mocked the mission statement industry by adopting the simple formula "don't be evil." Instead of a hefty rule book, Nordstrom's employees are issued a single piece of paper that reads "Use your good judgment in all situations."

Still, there is no doubt that the best companies are guided by a core set of values, values that they work hard at refining and instilling into their employees. Jim Collins has written a succession of books arguing that the one thing successful companies have in common is a set of "core values," a sort of cultural version of core competencies. Hewlett-Packard has the "HP way." Johnson & Johnson has a "credo" (which is credited with having guided the company through the Tylenol crisis, when a lunatic laced some of the company's Tylenol tablets with cyanide). The HP way has never been captured in a rule book. Disney's sprawling empire of TV stations and theme parks is held together by its commitment to wholesomeness and happiness. IBM recovered when it refocused its attention on its core value (IT solutions) rather than on a mere business strategy (dominating mainframe computers).

The best companies work hard at creating a common culture. Camden Property Trust, an American property company, designates "ambassadors of the culture" to guide new employees. J. M. Smucker Company, an American food-products giant, holds a refresher course, called "back to basics," for all employees who have been with the company for five years or more. Senior employees are encouraged to share "tribal stories" about the company's values and how they have helped them to overcome adversity.[16] eBay uses the design of its campus in San Jose to both express and reinforce its culture. Each building represents a category of goods sold on the site (jewelry, cars, toys, etc.), and within each building each conference room is named after items within that category (ruby, diamond, etc.). And there's more: each room is given a budget, and employees are encouraged to shop on eBay for appropriate decorations: the ruby room is decorated with ruby slippers, and the "Sweet Caroline Room" doubles as a shrine to Neil Diamond.[17]

It is noticeable how many of today's business heroes—Richard Branson of Virgin, Oprah Winfrey at Harpo, Inc., or Herb Kelleher of Southwest Airlines, for examples—are impresarios of enthusiasm. Yet even the most inspirational leadership requires perspiration. Winfrey spends much of her time meeting, berating, and praising her employees. Larry Page and Sergey Brin have been appearing at their company's informal get-togethers on Friday afternoons for years. Employees sit in chairs arranged in semicircles or tune in electronically while the founders share corporate news and answer whatever questions are thrown at them. Senior managers everywhere are spending more time on what might be called "human engineering": getting to know workers.

The heart of human engineering is recruitment and training. One aim of modern corporate education is to encourage self-discipline (which, in the ideal post-Sloanist organization, is supposed to replace authority from above). P&G looks for a particular type of person. At Google, Page and Brin get involved in the nitty-gritty of recruiting. A growing number of companies are promoting the heads of their once-despised human resources departments to seats on the board. The more human and less machine-like companies become, the more they have to make sure they recruit the right sort of people.

But Is It Stable?

Today's business school academics are perhaps a little hard on Alfred Sloan. Sloan was not quite the advocate of machine-like obedience that people now imagine. He also anticipated that his ideas might well be abused, as indeed they were, by bores and bureaucrats. He argued that managers should see themselves as workers' servants rather than their masters, and he tried to encourage intellectual independence. On being told that one of GM's top committees was in complete agreement on a subject, he interjected, "I propose we postpone further discussion of this matter until the next meeting to give ourselves time to develop disagreement, and perhaps gain some understanding of what the decision is all about."[18]

What would Sloan have made of the post-Sloanist company that has replaced his? He might well have pointed to three protruding fault lines in the new model. The first is the enormous importance the model ascribes to charismatic leaders. The modern boss is seriously overextended. Companies are also having to confront problems that Sloanism banished: the risk that an all-powerful boss will gently go off the rails, and the difficulty of finding an equally charismatic successor. ABB was thrown into chaos when its charismatic boss, Percy Barnevik, tried to furnish himself with an over-generous retirement package. The fact that powerful leaders have a habit of grooming second-rate people to succeed them means that succession crises are likely to be a recurring problem.

The second problem is that, as companies grow more complicated, the job of managers becomes more ill defined. Once, managers could simply tell their subordinates what to do. Now, people have to report laterally as well as vertically, downward as well as upward, across borders as well as within countries, and they have to do so in conditions of mounting ambiguity, where competitors are suddenly allies and where the supplier the manager used to boot around is now given a bigger office than the manager's, in the same factory. One newly minted boss ruefully complained that "it's not as lonely at the top as I had hoped."

However, Sloan's biggest worries would have been about command and control. Companies are finding that the shift from formal to informal management structures is rife with risks. The Baring family lost its bank because the management overempowered one individual, Nick Leeson. Enron's embrace of the post-Sloanist mantras of de-layering and empowerment allowed it to cover up a financial Ponzi scheme. In theory, all these external sources of control are supposed to be replaced by "trust" and "self-discipline." But the power of trust and self-discipline is constantly being undermined by all the other things modern management is up to. The system that has replaced Sloanism is fraught with contradictions.

The post-Sloanist company is supposedly built on trust. But the fluidity of alliances means that friends may be rapidly transformed into enemies, the emphasis on speed means that long-term relationships are hard to create, and the arrival of multicultural companies means that people can no longer rely on shared backgrounds and tacit understanding to bind them together. The post–Sloanist company is supposedly built on empowerment. But the destruction of hierarchy often leads to powerlessness rather than empowerment: local bosses have to transform themselves from local barons into loyal lieutenants, and middle managers are forced to develop systems that will make middle management unnecessary.

These contradictions are encouraging some gurus to think again about the revolt against command and control. Harold Leavitt, of Stanford University, has argued forcefully that hierarchies are both inevitable and productive: inevitable because they help people to cope with complexity, and productive because they act as "psychological magnets" to attract achievement-driven men and women.[19] Who wants to join a company if he is going to be stuck in the same place in ten years' time? It is notable that the creative industries that Sloan's critics celebrate are neither as flat nor as anarchic as these critics imagine. Park your car in somebody else's space in a Hollywood studio parking lot and you soon discover that all the Armani casual wear disguises a rigid class system. Try to get through to Keith or Mick when they are on tour and you discover that the Rolling Stones have seventeen grades of security pass.

At the same time, some businesses are reembracing aspects of Sloanism. Vertical integration is back in fashion in some quarters. Boeing is taking more of its manufacturing in-house because so many of its suppliers failed to hit their targets for timeliness and quality. Tata Steel and other steel companies are buying up raw materials because they are worried about impending shortages of resources, driven by China's appetite for raw materials. The Sarbanes–Oxley rules that were introduced in the wake of the collapse of Enron are obliging companies to put a greater emphasis on traditional reporting.

Still, all this is a correcting impulse rather than a reversal. The forces that have changed corporate life over the past couple of decades—notably the rise of the Internet and the growing sophistication of capital markets—are simply too all-consuming to allow for a return to the old corporate model. The Sloanist company was based on the assumption that its most precious resource was capital, and all it needed was a small elite to allocate that capital and boss around workers. Now firms realize that their most important asset is knowledge. The trouble with knowledge is that it is so much more difficult to manage than capital: not only is it fixed in the heads of pesky employees rather than stored in the bank, but it is infuriatingly volatile as well. Like it or not, the corporate world will look more like the Googleplex than the Shell Center.

7

Entrepreneurs Unbound

The greatest of the journo-gurus, by some distance, was a man of whom few readers will have heard. He was in his disheveled pomp when today's journo-gurus were holding forth in their playpens. He also worked for a publication that cherishes its tradition of anonymity.

Norman Macrae was a stalwart of *The Economist* for half a century: he joined the paper in 1946 and worked as deputy editor for twenty-three years, starting in 1965. Macrae kept the flame of free-market thinking burning during the long night of collectivism. He constantly enlivened editorial meetings with proposals to allow Disneyworld to run Paris or move the British government from London to New York. Roy Jenkins rightly described him as the "epitome of the internal spirit of *The Economist*, Willie Whitelaw to the Conservative Party, Gubby Allen to the MCC."

Macrae predicted almost all the great revolutions that changed the world in the second half of the twentieth century and beyond: the collapse of the Soviet Union (when the CIA was obsessed by Russia's growing strength), the rise of Japan (when businessmen dismissed it as nothing more than a source of knickknacks and

knockoffs), and so on. Reluctant to use the telephone and incapable of operating a photocopier, he even foresaw the rise of the
Internet: in 1984 he wrote a long article on how life was about to
be transformed by "terminals" that would allow us to access giant
databases.

One of Macrae's central themes, which he kept returning to
from the 1950s onward, was that capitalism was destined to be
transformed by an entrepreneurial revolution. He predicted the
privatization of industry at a time when the likes of Roy Jenkins
and J. K. Galbraith were celebrating the triumph of the "mixed
economy." But he was just as hard on big private-sector companies
as he was on lumbering government bureaucracies. In a special
report on "the coming entrepreneurial revolution," published in
1976, he argued that big business was as doomed as big government.[1] Hierarchical management sitting in their skyscrapers could
no longer determine how brainworkers could best use their imaginations. The future lay with small firms that could exploit individual creativity and with bigger firms that could split themselves
into small centers and encourage internal competition between
these profit centers. "Jesus Christ tried 12," Macrae argued in one
of the telltale phrases that made his work so readable, "and that
proved one too many."

This was heresy at the time. In 1942, Joseph Schumpeter had
warned, in *Capitalism, Socialism and Democracy*, that the bureaucra-
tization of capitalism was killing the spirit of entrepreneurship.
Why should governments risk the turmoil of "creative destruction" when Keynesian economists, working hand in glove with
big business and big government, could provide orderly prosperity?
And why should individuals take their fates in their hands—and
risk humiliating defeat—when they could burrow into a comfortable Hobbit hole in the ever-expanding welfare state? A few years

later the architects of the postwar consensus—the Butskellites, in Macrae's immortal phrase—took up Schumpeter's theme but without any of his sense of loss. J. K. Galbraith confidently argued that the modern bureaucratic corporation had replaced "the entrepreneur as the directing force of the enterprise with management," and Galbraith's acolytes poured money into British Steel and the Project Concord.

Macrae had no time for this conventional wisdom. His unusual childhood had left him with clear-eyed contempt not only for Soviet totalitarianism but for the West's more modest version of central planning as well. His father was a British consul in Moscow in 1935–38, and he had summer holidays from school at the height of Stalin's purges. He saw members of the embassy staff—including fellow teenagers, like some of the maids—disappearing, almost certainly to be shot. He went to Cambridge University after the war only to hear state-worshipping intellectuals like Joan Robinson lauding Soviet-central planning and rubbishing American capitalism. Yet he knew in his bones that they were not just wrong but murderously wrong. And he spent his next fifty years at *The Economist* predicting, championing, and analyzing the rise (or perhaps re-rise) of a new form of entrepreneurial capitalism.

Riding the Tiger

The rise of entrepreneurialism is the second great management revolution of the past thirty years. Governments of almost every ideological stripe have embraced entrepreneurship. The Chinese Communist Party praises "red entrepreneurs." The European Union hopes that entrepreneurs will rescue its sclerotic economy. The World Bank suggests that unleashing entrepreneurship is the best way to cure poverty. The likes of Bill Gates and Richard

Branson are treated as heroes wherever they go. The cult of entrepreneurship is so widespread that Aravind Adiga has devoted an entire novel, *The White Tiger*, to mocking it. Listen to me, the leading character says, and "you will know everything there is to know about how entrepreneurship is born, nurtured, and developed in this, the glorious twenty-first century of man."[2]

The cult of entrepreneurship was subjected to its toughest test since it was born, in the Reagan–Thatcher revolution, by the global economic crisis of 2008–09. Customers disappeared. Investors fled risk. Capital dried up (venture capital investment fell by 31 percent between 2007 and 2008). The United States suspended its free-market principles to bail out banks and prop up General Motors.

Yet the entrepreneurial phoenix did not perish in the flames of the financial crisis. This is partly because downturns release capital and labor from dying sectors and allow newcomers to recombine in imaginative new ways (Microsoft, Genentech, Southwest Airlines, The Gap, The Limited, and Home Depot were founded during recessions; Hewlett-Packard, Texas Instruments, United Technologies, Polaroid, and Revlon were started during the Great Depression).

But there is a deeper reason why the damage done by the crisis was short-lived: the world has seen a structural shift from "managerial" to "entrepreneurial" capitalism. Schumpeter once observed that all established businesses are "standing on ground that is crumbling beneath their feet." Today the ground is far less solid than it was in Schumpeter's time. The information revolution is blowing established business models to pieces. Growth is being driven by industries, such as computing and telecommunications, where innovation is preeminent. Service firms, which are increasingly important in advanced economies, are more open to disruption than manufacturing firms. And, above all, people are increasingly taking their economic fate into their own hands. Capgemini, a consultancy, calculates that in 2010, nearly half (47 percent) of the world's wealthy people were entrepreneurs. The result is that the American model of entrepreneurial capitalism is spreading rapidly around the world.

The United States of Entrepreneurs

For all its recent economic woes, the United States remains a global beacon of entrepreneurialism—a shining entrepreneurial city on a hill calling the rest of the world to learn its ways. America is strikingly fecund when it comes to giving birth to small businesses. In 1996–2004 it created an average of 55,000 of them every month. It is even more fecund when it comes to giving birth to new businesses that sprout into big businesses. America's biggest company, Walmart, was founded in 1962 and went public only a decade later; multibillion-dollar companies such as Google and Facebook did not exist a decade ago.

In *Good Capitalism, Bad Capitalism*, William Baumol, Bob Litan, and Carl Schramm, the three wise men of entrepreneurial studies, have shown how America was the first country to ditch managerial capitalism for the entrepreneurial variety.[3] In the wake of the Second World War, managerial capitalism swept all before it: big business and big labor worked hand in hand with big government to deliver predictable economic growth. This changed dramatically in the late 1970s, as predictable growth turned into stagflation, and an army of innovators, particularly in the computer and finance industries, undermined the logic of the old industrial corporation and unleashed a wave of entrepreneurship.

The United States found the transition to a more entrepreneurial economy easier than any of its competitors because entrepreneurialism is deeply rooted in its history. The very word "innovation" made Dr. Johnson, the archetypical British Tory, shudder. By contrast, America was founded and then settled by innovators and risk-takers who were willing to sacrifice old certainties for new opportunities. American schoolchildren are raised on stories about inventors such as Benjamin Franklin and Thomas Edison. The American landscape is littered with monuments to entrepreneurs such as Andrew Carnegie and Henry Ford. One of the country's most popular television programs features the *USS Enterprise* going where no man had gone before.

Americans are currently even more infatuated with entrepreneurs than ever. The likes of Bill Gates and Steve Jobs have all the upsides of Carnegie and Ford without the downsides—the useful products and open-handed philanthropy without the sweatshops and bloody massacres. Universities set up special dorms for entrepreneurs. Preachers style themselves as pastorpreneurs. Business books sell in the millions. "When I was in college, guys usually pretended they were in a band," one observer has commented. "Now they pretend they are in a startup."

Americans are unusually comfortable with the risk-taking that is at the heart of entrepreneurialism. The rewards for success can be huge—Facebook's Mark Zuckerberg was a billionaire before he was thirty—while the punishments for failure are often trivial. In some countries bankruptcy spells social death. In the United States, particularly in Silicon Valley, it is a badge of honor. Monitor, a consultancy, discovered that 96 percent of Americans who responded to its survey said that it was common for people who had failed in business to try again, compared with just 16 percent in Austria.[4]

The United States also has several structural advantages when it comes to entrepreneurship. The first is the world's most mature venture-capital industry. The nation's first venture fund, American

Research and Development, was founded in 1946 and has been gathering momentum ever since. Highland Capital Partners receives about 10,000 plausible business plans a year, conducts about a thousand meetings followed by four hundred company visits, and ends up making about ten to twenty investments a year, all of which are guaranteed to receive an enormous amount of time and expertise. Global Insight, a consultancy, calculates that companies that were once backed by venture capitalists now account for nearly 18 percent of America's GDP and 9 percent of private-sector employment.

The second is close relations between universities and industry. America's universities are economic engines rather than ivory towers, with proliferating science parks, technology offices, business incubators, and venture funds. Stanford University, which has so far made more than $200 million from its investments in Google alone, is so keen on promoting entrepreneurship that it has created a Monopoly-like game to teach its professors how to become entrepreneurs. About half of the startups in Silicon Valley have their roots in the university. The Massachusetts Institute of Technology (MIT) has produced so many successful spin-offs that, if they were turned into a nation, they would have the 28th-largest GDP in the world.

The third is a historically open immigration policy. Vivek Wadhwa, of the University of California, Berkeley, notes that 52 percent of Silicon Valley startups were founded by immigrants, up from 25 percent a few years ago, with Indian immigrants founding 26 percent of them. In all, one-quarter of America's science and technology startups, generating $52 billion and employing 450,000 people, numbered somebody born abroad as either their CEO or their chief technology officer. In 2008, foreign nationals were named as inventors or co-inventors in a quarter of American patent applications, up from 7.6 percent in 1998.

Amar Bhide, of Columbia University, suggests a fourth reason for the country's entrepreneurial success, "venturesome consumers."[5] Americans are unusually willing to try new products of all sorts, even if it means teaching themselves new skills and scrimping on their savings; they are also unusually willing to pester producers to improve their products. Half a million people lined up all night to buy the new iPhone on the day that it was released.

America's advantages are particularly marked when you compare it with the world's next two biggest economies—the European Union and Japan. Europeans are much less keen on establishing startups than Americans: only 4 percent of German residents are "opportunity-driven" entrepreneurs compared with 11 percent of Americans, according to the Global Entrepreneurship Monitor (GEM), a joint venture between the London Business School and Babson College that monitors entrepreneurship. And far fewer of those European startups become big businesses. Janez Potocnik, the EU commissioner for science and research, points out that only 5 percent of European companies that were created from scratch since 1980 are in the top thousand EU companies as defined by market capitalization. The figure for the United States is 22 percent.

This reflects cultural attitudes. Europeans have less to gain from taking business risks, thanks to higher taxation rates, and more to lose, thanks to more punitive attitudes toward bankruptcy (Germans are prevented by law from becoming CEOs if they have ever been bankrupt, for example). When Denis Payre was thinking about leaving a safe job at Oracle to start up a company, back in the early 1990s, his French friends habitually gave him ten reasons to stay put while his American friends gave him ten reasons to get on his bike. In January 2008, Payre sold his startup, Business Objects, to Germany's SAP for €4.8 billion.

European egalitarianism militates against entrepreneurialism: the European Union is much keener on promoting small businesses in general than it is on fostering high-growth companies. So does Europe's growing aversion to work. In the late 1960s, Europeans worked more weeks a year than Americans; today they work thirty-five to forty weeks a year compared with America's forty-six weeks. Europeans are also much more suspicious of business. According to a Flash Eurobarometer poll, 42 percent of Europeans agree that entrepreneurs exploit other people's work, compared with 26 percent of Americans.

These cultural problems are reinforced by structural ones. The European market remains fragmented compared with the American one: entrepreneurs have to grapple with a patchwork of legal codes and an expensive and time-consuming patent system. In many countries the tax system and labor laws discourage companies from growing above a certain size. A depressing number of European universities remain suspicious of industry, subsisting on declining state subsidies but still unwilling to embrace the vulgar private sector. The European venture capital industry is much less developed than the American one (significantly, in many countries it is called "risk" rather than "venture" capital). The United States has at least fifty times as many angel investors as Europe, thanks, not least, to the taxman's greater willingness to allow money to fructify in the pockets of the people.

Japan suffers from an even bigger dose of enterprise-killing problems than Europe. The latest GEM global report gives Japan the lowest score for entreprencurship of any major country, putting it on a par with Greece. The brightest people want to work for big companies or the government (and, if they are lucky, are rewarded not just with lifetime employment but company housing). The big banks work hand in glove with big companies. Risk capital is rare. Bankruptcy is severely punished. The small business sector is wrapped in cotton wool, encouraging businesses to set up "me-too" operations rather than to offer anything new. Over the past quarter century, business formation in Japan has been one-third to half of that in the United States.

So America has a huge head start over the rest of the world when it comes to entrepreneurship. But two things are beginning to erode its lead—one negative and one positive. The negative is that the United States is currently facing a striking number of threats to its remarkable entrepreneurial ecology. The legal system can be burdensome or even destructive. One of the biggest new problems comes from "patent trolls"—trial lawyers who bring cases against companies for violating this or that trumped-up patent. The tax system is so complicated that many companies devote time and ingenuity to filling out tax forms that would be better spent on business. And, thanks to a combination of the "war on terrorism" and rising xenophobia, the American immigration system has turned into a nightmare: rather than trying to attract the world's best and brightest, the United States forces them to run an obstacle course. This might have made sense when everybody was desperate to work in the United States. You could even justify it on the Darwinian grounds that only the fittest got through the system. It is a serious threat to the nation's competitiveness now that so many opportunities are opening up elsewhere.

The positive change is the global spread of the entrepreneurial revolution. The European Union is far more entrepreneurial than it was a few decades ago. Europe has produced some notable startups. Skype, which pioneered Internet-based telephone calls, exemplified the continent's potential strengths: it was founded by a Swede and a Dane who based the company in London, contracted out much of their work to computer programmers in Estonia, and eventually sold their creation off to an American company, Microsoft, for more than $8 billion.

More importantly, it has begun to create an entrepreneurial ecosystem. European venture capital investment grew by 23 percent a year in 2003–06, compared with just 0.3 percent a year in America. Indeed, three European countries, Denmark, Sweden, and Great Britain, have bigger venture capital industries, relative to the size of their populations, than the United States. Venture-backed startups produced more than one hundred "exits" (stock market flotations or sales to established companies) worth more than $100 million in 2004–08, most notably the sale of Tele Atlas, a Dutch mapping outfit, to TomTom for $4.3 billion.

European universities have begun to shake off their ancestral contempt for "business." The Cambridge high-tech hub, the most successful of a growing breed, has given birth to more than three thousand companies and produced more than two hundred millionaires. European governments have also begun to recognize the importance of high-growth companies. The Danish government has established a network of "growth houses"—office hotels that provide startups with many of the advantages of large companies, such as consulting advice, legal services, and conference rooms. It has also created a public venture fund, the Vaexsfonden, which tries to leverage private investment in the high-tech sector.

Outside Europe, two very different countries—an embattled sliver of land in the Middle East and an autocratic city-state in Southeast Asia—have both embraced the entrepreneurial revolution with unusual fervor. In 1992, Israel's leading exports were diamonds and citrus fruits; today it exports more than $3 billion worth of software a year. Israel is the world's greatest Start-up Nation, to borrow the title of an excellent book on the subject, home to 4,500 high-tech companies; more than three hundred venture capital funds, which collectively invested more than a billion dollars in the nation in 2007; and a growing healthcare industry.[6] A partial list of the innovations developed in Israel includes the Pentium chip (Intel), voice-mail (Comverse), instant messaging (ICQ, Ubique), firewalls (Check Point), and the "video pill," which allows doctors to study your insides without the need for invasive surgery. Israelis like to joke that the ubiquitous "Intel inside" logo should be replaced by "Israel inside."

Israel partly has America to thank for sparking its entrepreneurial revolution. A brigade of American high-tech companies, including Intel and Microsoft, have established research arms in the country. And an army of Israeli émigrés, who once fled to the United States in search of education and opportunity, have returned home, bringing American assumptions with them. Many Israeli entrepreneurs ricochet between Silicon Valley and Tel Aviv; more than seventy Israeli companies are traded on the NASDAQ.

The Israeli government also acted as a catalyst, by providing a ready supply of both human and physical capital. Israel has the highest ratio of PhD's per capita in the world, the highest ratio of engineers and scientists, and some of the world's best research universities, notably Technicon. Israel's native talent was also supplemented by the arrival of 100,000 well-educated Jewish refugees from the former Soviet empire. In 1993, with high-tech talent flooding into the country, the government kick-started a domestic venture capital industry by establishing a $100 million venture capital fund, Yozma, which matched private money with public.

But Israel's biggest advantage in embracing entrepreneurialism was more idiosyncratic: its status as an embattled Jewish state in a sea of Arab hostility. The Israeli Defense Forces (IDF) not only help to keep the country on the cutting edge of technology; they also train young Israelis (who are conscripted at age eighteen) in the virtues of both teamwork and improvisation. It is strikingly common for young Israelis to form businesses with friends that they met in the army. Add to that a high tolerance of risk, born of both a long history and an ever-present threat of attack, and you have the makings of an entrepreneurial colossus.

Singapore's approach to turning itself into an entrepreneurial giant was, predictably, more top-down. The government sees entrepreneurialism as the next step that that must be taken if the city-state is to continue to thrive. Having spent the postwar era climbing up the "value chain," from manufacturing to services and from trade to finance, the government thinks that it is confronted with perhaps its biggest test yet—creating knowledge industries and producing companies that can commercialize intellectual breakthroughs. Singapore has invested heavily in digital media, bioengineering, clean tech, and water purification, creating huge incubators and "kidnapping" foreign scientists with huge pay packets. It has also, like both Israel and Denmark, created a public venture capital fund that has in turn brought in lots of private venture capital. More than 5 percent of Singapore-based companies are backed by venture capital.

Singapore has also done everything in its power to make life easy for entrepreneurs. The World Bank ranks it number one in the world when it comes to ease of doing business. It is also engaged in a trickier enterprise—encouraging a traditionally passive population to be more entrepreneurial. Schools teach the virtues of entrepreneurialism and offer prizes to children who come up with the best ideas. (In one example, a group of schoolchildren sold $15,000 worth of customized action figures to American collectors on the Internet despite never having left Singapore.) The universities put a heavy emphasis on business education and on links with industry. The Nanyand Technological University offers a degree in technopreneurship and innovation (50 of the 150 people who graduated from the course in 2002–06 have gone on to start businesses).

Yet the transition to a more entrepreneurial form of capitalism will not be easy for the city-state. The best and the brightest want to be Platonic guardians rather than risk-taking entrepreneurs. Eighty-nine percent of people say that declaring bankruptcy has "excessive" consequences, according to Monitor. The Singaporeans are also the very opposite of "venturesome" consumers: for all the island's cultural diversity, they remain obsessed by Western brand names. The country has already paid a heavy price for this latter-day version of the colonial cringe. A Singapore-based company, Creative Technology, invented a digital music player, the Nomad Jukebox, two years before Apple invented the iPod. But Creative designed the Jukebox to look like a clunky CD player rather than a miniature fashion accessory. The $100 million it received from Apple for patent infringement did not make up for its loss of a mass market. It is perhaps instructive that the quintessential corporate state—a country obsessed with top-down planning and command and control—should recognize that it needs to embrace entrepreneurialism in order to prosper.

You do not need to be one of Singapore's mandarin bosses to tell which way the wind is blowing: the world's two most populous nations, India and China—nations which, incidentally, provide Singapore with many of its citizens—are going entrepreneur crazy.

Entrepreneurs by the Million

Gurcharan Das, an Indian venture capitalist, consultant, and author, tells a story about stopping at a roadside café in southern India and chatting with a fourteen-year-old boy who was waiting tables. The boy said that he was waiting tables in order to pay for computer lessons. His ultimate ambition was to run a computer company just like his hero, the richest man in the world, "Bilgay."[7]

Over the past couple of decades, India has dismantled its licensed Raj in order to take part in the global entrepreneurial revolution. I will discuss India's thriving high-tech sector in the next chapter. But the revolution is not confined to software. Bollywood produces 1,100 films a year for an audience of 3.6 billion people (Hollywood produces 600 for 2.6 billion). Internal flights in India are some of the best in the world. Indian beers are selling wherever spicy curries are eaten. Everywhere you go in India you are confronted by would-be Bilgays: budding entrepreneurs who have swapped the country's traditional fatalism for can-do optimism.

India has drawn heavily on its expat population, particularly the 250,000 Indians who live in California and 500,000 who live in the United States as a whole, to kick-start its entrepreneurial economy. Rajiv Gupta, a former head of McKinsey, helped to create the Indian Business School in Hyderabad. Ravi Deshpande, who sold his company, Cascade Communications, to Ascend for $3.7 billion, is a ubiquitous cheerleader for entrepreneurialism. Draper International, which became, in 1995, the first foreign venture fund to invest in India, relied on money from Silicon Valley's Indian community. Hundreds of thousands of Indians are returning home, drawn by India's growing dynamism, to participate in what many see as their country's second founding.

Communist China's conversion to entrepreneurialism is even more surprising than Fabian India's. The vice-premier, Wu Yi, took more than two hundred entrepreneurs with him when he visited the United States in 2006, in a public demonstration of where his priorities lie. Over sixty-five Chinese companies are now traded on the NASDAQ. In 2006, 112 Chinese startups received venture finance, double the number in 2005. The Communist Party school even offers special courses for entrepreneurs (aka "red capitalists").

In some ways China has had a more difficult task than India. The Cultural Revolution destroyed the country's intellectual and managerial capital. Few Chinese speak good English. The state is more interested in grand projects—from state-owned companies to giant infrastructure schemes—than in letting a thousand flowers bloom. Still, China shared one important advantage with India—the army of overseas Chinese who have made their home in America, particularly in Silicon Valley. The Chinese authorities have long been acutely aware of the role that the overseas Chinese played in Taiwan's economic takeoff. And, from the late 1990s onward, they did everything they could to tempt expats back, setting up science parks and research triangles and putting out a welcome mat for foreign companies. The flood of returnees has become so strong in the past few years that it has acquired its own Valley slang, B2C (back to China).

Many of China's most successful entrepreneurs have done little more than produce knockoffs of American companies, mostly ones that they studied when they were based in the United States. Baidu is a Chinese Google; Dangdang is a Chinese Amazon; Taobao is a Chinese eBay; Oak Pacific Interactive is a mishmash of MySpace, YouTube, Facebook, and craigslist; ChinaCars is a Chinese American Automobile Association.

But even producing knockoffs takes skill, particularly when the original companies are determined to colonize the Chinese market (Baidu's outmaneuvering of Google was particularly impressive). And Chinese imitative entrepreneurs are also bringing innovative management methods to China. Baidu's founder, Robin Li, raised funds from American venture capitalists and offered his earliest employees stock options. At the same time China is also producing some genuinely innovative entrepreneurs. The most famous of these, Jack Ma, uses a website, Alibaba, to sell goods from China's thousands of mom-and-pop stores to the world's consumers. (Ma has also created a college for entrepreneurs, Alibaba College.) Jeff Chen has developed an Internet browser that has attracted venture capital from Denmark and users in twenty countries. Many of the country's leading innovators are working with mobile telephony, which is even more important in China than in the West. Liu Yingkui is selling insurance, mutual funds, and bank services over the mobile Internet. Charles Wang is busy getting subscribers addicted to his free text-messaging service, PingCo, so that he can start signing them up for premium services such as backing up address books, selling astrological charts, and providing weather updates.

Both India and China have a hard road to travel. The Indian government is a lumbering elephant that leaves 40 percent of the population illiterate and is riven with favoritism and corruption (when one ministry created a $20 million venture capital fund, the press immediately dubbed it the "nephews and nieces fund"). The law courts can make Jardine versus Jardine, the interminable legal case at the heart of Charles Dickens's *Bleak House*, look like an example of speediness. Much of the infrastructure is a mess.

Yasheng Huang, of the Massachusetts Institute of Technology, has detailed how Chinese capitalism is being badly distorted by the influence of politics (some 40 percent of entrepreneurs are members of the Communist Party). State-backed businesses receive a disproportionate share of capital. Even sound businesses are frequently opaque: the Chinese reportedly maintain three sets of books, for their bankers, their accountants, and the government. Businessmen often short-change their businesses because they have to spend so much time cultivating political connections.

Still, these obstacles should not be allowed to blind us to the huge distances both societies have already traveled. Harvard Business School's Tarun Khanna points out that the entrepreneurial spirit is beginning to breathe new life into India's public sector: New Delhi now boasts a brand-new metro, thanks to private money, and Bangalore has a splendid new airport. Even China's many critics admit that the red capitalists are changing the Communist Party as much as the Communist Party is distorting entrepreneurialism. The result of this revolution has already been dramatic: millions of new entrepreneurs are entering the world economy, entrepreneurs who have already demonstrated their ability not just to translate Western ideas into their local idioms but also to drive technological advances.

Entrepreneurs from Everywhere

The globalization of entrepreneurialism means that successful entrepreneurs can come from every corner of the world, the developing world as well as the developed, distant countries as well as proximate ones, resource-poor countries as well as resource-rich ones, complicating the corporate battlefield immeasurably. New Zealand has turned itself into an entrepreneurial powerhouse, leading the world in the creation of small and medium enterprises, despite the fact that it is an enormous distance from many of its main markets. The country that brought the world *Lord of the Rings* is also bringing it fancy new underwear, made from Merino sheep, thanks to Iceberg. Bento Koike, a Brazilian, has created one of the world's most successful wind-turbine companies in his home country, despite the fact that his company's raw materials and its customers come from Europe and America and that the blades, which are almost forty feet long and weigh six tons, are extremely hard to transport.

Daniel Isenberg, of Babson College, points out that today's entrepreneurs are pioneering a new business model. In the old days globalization was incremental. Companies established themselves in their local markets and then expanded abroad slowly, starting in their own regions. Johnson & Johnson did not start its first foreign subsidiary until thirty-three years after it was founded in 1886. Today's entrepreneurs—or the smart ones, anyway—are born global. They search for materials, talents, and opportunities the world over, and define their competitive environment, in terms of defense as well as offense, globally rather than locally.[8]

EyeView is a perfect example of what Isenberg is talking about, a global citizen from the day that it first blinked. The company uses "rich media"—a combination of videos and audios—to teach people how to use websites (for example, how to trade goods on eBay or foreign currency on eToro). Most of the company's customers are big multinationals, so the videos are produced in numerous languages and then watched the world over. EyeView currently occupies the second floor of a nondescript building in Tel Aviv, but in its earliest years it lived on three continents. Two of the company's founders were based in Boston, the third in Sydney, and the fourth in Tel Aviv. The company made its first videos in Australia and found its first customers on the West Coast. The impecunious founders were able to make this arrangement work because of the cost-destroying wonders of Skype and the Internet.

Born-global entrepreneurs are forming some surprising cross-border collaborations. Shai Agassi, an American businessman based in Palo Alto, California, is promising to revolutionize the car industry in alliance with politicians, entrepreneurs, and corporations in Israel, Denmark, Japan, and France. Israel and Denmark are both building networks of recharging stations. Danish entrepreneurs are working on technology that will prolong the life of batteries. Renault and Nissan are building electric cars. The future of the car industry is more likely to be forged in Denmark and Israel, with their relentless focus on the future, than in subsidy-guzzling Detroit.

An Idea Whose Time Has Come

There is always a chance that the entrepreneurial revolution will fizzle out, or go into reverse. The Chinese boom may bust. The Indian state may rediscover the joys of the License Raj. Further financial crises may relegitimize interventionism. But at the moment, this looks unlikely; the entrepreneurial revolution is being driven by profound forces. Entrepreneurship is what Victor Hugo once termed, speaking of the French Revolution, an idea whose time has come.

The Internet is a perfect technology for entrepreneurs. It can provide people with the wherewithal to truck, barter, and exchange without ever meeting each other. It can allow upstarts to take on long-established and well-capitalized businesses. News aggregators such as RealClearPolitics and Memeorandum have become part of every news junkie's toolkit despite having almost no money (Memeorandum is little more than an algorithm). "Cloud" computing is shifting the playing field still further in favor of challengers: entrepreneurs can use their personal computers or laptops, whether they are in the office or a hotel halfway around the world, to gain access to sophisticated business services, such as tools for managing their relations with their customers.

The mobile phone has been almost as revolutionary. The mobile has allowed entrepreneurs to break into what was once one of the world's most regulated markets, telecoms. It has also linked some three billion people to the world market. Iqbal Quadir, a Bangladeshi who immigrated to America to become an investment banker and then a business academic, eventually became obsessed by the dream of an interconnected world. He struck up a relationship with Muhammad Yunus, the founder of Grameen Bank, a micro-financer, to turn the dream into a reality. If the bank was willing to lend women money to buy cows, why not lend them money to buy mobile phones as well? Grameen is now Bangladesh's largest telecom provider, with annual revenues of more than $1 billion; and Bangladesh boasts 250,000 phone ladies who borrow money to buy specially designed cell phone kits, each equipped with long-lasting batteries, and sell time on their phones to local villagers, who now have a chance to plug themselves into the global economy.

Entrepreneurialism is becoming more respectable as well as more democratic. Consider my old university, Oxford. Oxford boasts one of the world's longest traditions of anti-entrepreneurial prejudice. The dons valued "gentlemanly" subjects such as classics or philosophy over anything that smacked of utility ("He gets degrees in making jam/In Liverpool and Birmingham" went one popular ditty). The students dreamed of careers in the civil service or the law rather than business or, still less, entrepreneurship. "How I hate that man" was C. S. Lewis's tart comment on Lord Nuffield, his city's greatest entrepreneur and one of his university's most generous benefactors. When I went up to Oxford in the late 1970s, the one thing that the left and right could agree on was that entrepreneurs were lesser breeds without the law, a consensus that seemed to be amply confirmed when it turned out that the most prominent entrepreneur in the city at the time, Robert Maxwell, was nothing more than a common criminal.

Today all that has changed. Oxford has a thriving business school, the Said School, which boasts a center for entrepreneurship and innovation, and a growing business park, which tries to mix the university's scientists with entrepreneurs. Oxford Entrepreneurs is one of the university's most popular societies, with 3,500 members and a record of creating about six startups a year. Auctomatic, a company founded by members, recently "exited" for $5 million.

The story of Oxford's conversion to entrepreneurship is being repeated the world over as entrepreneurialism goes mainstream. One reason for this is intellectual: a growing number of respectable economists have now realized, as Schumpeter realized a century ago, that in a knowledge-based economy, entrepreneurs play a central role in creating new companies, commercializing new ideas, and, just as importantly, engaging in sustained experiments in what works and what does not. William Baumol has put entrepreneurs at the center of his theory of growth. Paul Romer argues that "economic growth occurs whenever people take resources and rearrange them in ways that are more valuable . . . It springs from better recipes, not just more cooking." Edmund Phelps, a Nobel Prize winner, argues that attitudes toward entrepreneurship have a big impact on economic growth.[9]

A second reason is the breaking of the old-fashioned social contract between employers and employed. In the 1960s, the average person had four different employers by the time he or she was sixty-five. Today the average person has eight by the time he or she is thirty. At its most brutal, this has forced many "outplaced" workers to set up their own companies. More generally, it has changed people's attitudes about the balance between security and risk. Why take a job in a big organization when that job can easily be taken away from you? Why not make your own job—or work just long enough to accumulate enough capital or contacts to branch out on your own? Today the majority of HBS graduates expect to be entrepreneurs at some point in their lives.

The third reason for the mainstreaming is that many powerful institutions have lent their support to entrepreneurialism. In 1998, HBS replaced general management with entrepreneurship as the foundation stone of business education. The school's center for entrepreneurship now employs forty professors. The Kauffman Foundation spends about $90 million a year, from assets of about $2.1 billion, to make the case for entrepreneurialism, supporting academic research, training would-be entrepreneurs, and sponsoring "world entrepreneur week," which involves eighty countries. (Kauffman has even partnered with Walt Disney to produce a board game that celebrates entrepreneurialism.) Goldman Sachs is spending $100 million over the next five years to promote entrepreneurialism among women in the developing world, particularly through management education. *Dragon's Den*, a television program that features entrepreneurs pitching their ideas to business people ("dragons") in order to attract venture capital, is shown, in various forms, in twelve countries, including Nigeria and Afghanistan. *The Apprentice*, which features Donald Trump looking for a protégé, has produced numerous spin-offs, including *Apprentice Africa*, which is seen in twelve African countries. Even China's state-owned Central Television has a show about entrepreneurs pitching ideas to try to win $1.3 million in seed money, *Win in China*.

The fourth reason for the mainstreaming is that the world's governments are competing to see who can create the most pro-business environment. In 2004 the World Bank began to rate countries in terms of their business friendliness (criteria including business regulations, property rights, and access to credit) in its annual *Doing Business* report. The results were striking. *Doing Business* demonstrated with a wealth of data that economic prosperity is closely correlated with a pro-business environment. Most

wealthy countries make it easy to start businesses and enforce contracts. Most poor ones make it difficult. In 2009, for example, New
Zealand had the highest rate of new business startups in the world
(27 percent) as well as the highest ranking for ease of starting a
business. The country with the lowest rate of new business startups, Haiti, ranked 176 out of 181 countries for ease of starting a
business.

This might sound obvious. But *Doing Business* did two things
that were not quite so obvious: it put precise numbers to problems that people had known about only vaguely; and it allowed
citizens and investors to compare their country with 180 others.
It is remarkable to learn, for example, that in the Republic of
Congo, where women require the permission of their menfolk
before starting a business, only 18 percent of businesses are run by
women, whereas in neighboring Rwanda, where no such permission is required, the figure for female-run businesses is 41 percent.

The result of this "naming and shaming" was a fierce competition between countries to improve their positions in the World
Bank's rankings. Since 2004, various countries have implemented
more than a thousand reforms. Eastern Europe and Central Asia
have accounted for more than one-third of this total. Three of
the top reformers have been African—Senegal, Burkina Faso, and
Botswana. Saudi Arabia has also made a dramatic leap forward.
Doing Business has persuaded countries to institutionalize reform:
in Canada, for example, it is now possible to start a business with
just one procedure. It has also institutionalized learning: Angola
has asked for legal and technical help from Portugal. Azerbaijan
reformers visited Georgia and Latvia. Kauffman's Robert Litan
suggests that the World Bank may have done more good by compiling *Doing Business* than by lending all the money that has flown
from its coffers.

The Secrets of Success

Policymakers almost everywhere are obsessed with discovering the secrets of entrepreneurialism. How do you uncage the animal spirits of entrepreneurs? And how do you use those animal spirits to power broader economic growth? It is heartening that policymakers are asking such questions. Less heartening is the fact that so many of them produce such lousy answers. The road to the entrepreneurial Jerusalem is littered with failed government schemes. Malaysia's massive BioValley complex, which opened in 2005 at a cost of $150 million, is now known as the "Valley of the Bio-Ghosts." Dubai's entrepreneurial hub is awash in a sea of red ink, many of its buildings empty and its parking lots full of abandoned Mercedes.

The errors start at the very beginning—with a failure to understand the meaning of the term "entrepreneurship."

For most people, an "entrepreneur" is simply anybody who starts a small business. But this lumps together all sorts of very different companies, from the local corner shop to the next Google. It is more illuminating to use the term to describe anybody who offers an innovative solution to a (frequently unrecognized) problem. Not all startups are innovative: most new corner shops sell exactly the same range of sweets and girlie mags as old corner shops. And not all entrepreneurial companies are either new or small. Google is constantly innovating despite being, in Silicon Valley terms, a gray-beard. The defining characteristic of entrepreneurship is not the size of the company but the act of innovation.

This narrower definition of entrepreneurship has an impressive intellectual pedigree dating right back to Schumpeter. Peter Drucker defined the entrepreneur as somebody who "upsets and disorganizes." "Entrepreneurs innovate," he said. "Innovation is the specific instrument of entrepreneurship." William Baumol defines the entrepreneur as "the bold and imaginative deviator from established business patterns and practices." Howard Stephenson, the man who did more than anybody else to champion the study of entrepreneurship at Harvard Business School, defined it as "the pursuit of opportunity beyond resources currently controlled." The Kauffman Foundation makes a fundamental distinction between "replicative" and "innovative" entrepreneurship.[10]

Innovative entrepreneurs are not only more interesting than replicative entrepreneurs; they also carry more economic weight. They create more jobs. Just 5 percent of startups create 75 percent of all the jobs created by small and medium enterprises. And they operate in all sorts of arenas other than just small businesses. Some of the world's most impressive entrepreneurs are at work in big companies and charitable organizations. Jorma Ollila transformed Nokia, a long-established Finnish firm, from a maker of rubber boots and cables into a mobile-phone giant that is still, for all its current troubles, the world's biggest producer of handsets. It would be perverse to exclude such men from the pantheon of entrepreneurs.

The subject of entrepreneurship is befuddled by myths as well as befogged by linguistic confusion. One myth is that entrepreneurs are "orphans and outcasts," to borrow George Gilder's phrase: lonely Atlases battling a hostile world or antisocial geeks inventing world-changing gizmos in their fetid garrets. In fact, entrepreneurship, like all business, is a social activity. Entrepreneurs may be more inner-directed and self-obsessed than the usual corporate types, but they almost always require business partners and social networks in order to succeed.

The history of high-tech startups is largely a history of business partnerships: Steve Jobs and Stephen Wozniak (Apple), Bill

Gates and Steven Balmer (Microsoft), Sergey Brin and Larry Page (Google). Ben & Jerry's was formed when two childhood friends, Ben Cohen and Jerry Greenfield, got together to start a business (they wanted to go into the bagel business but could not raise the cash). Richard Branson relied heavily on his cousin, Simon Draper, as well as several other partners. The Rolling Stones would not have been the Rolling Stones without Mick Jagger *and* Keith Richards, nor the Beatles the Beatles without Lennon *and* McCartney.

Entrepreneurship also flourishes in certain clusters. One-third of American venture capital flows into two places, Silicon Valley and Boston, and two-thirds into just six places, New York, Los Angeles, San Diego, and Austin as well as the Valley and Boston. This is partly because entrepreneurship is encouraged as a way of life—coffeehouses in Silicon Valley are full of young people loudly talking about their business plans—and partly because the infrastructure is already in place, radically reducing the cost of starting a business.

A second myth is that most entrepreneurs are twenty-somethings, or even adolescents. Some of today's most celebrated figures have certainly been astonishingly young: Bill Gates, Steve Jobs, and Michael Dell all dropped out of college to start their businesses, and the founders of Google and Facebook were still in college when they started theirs. Ben Casnocha started his first company at age twelve, was named entrepreneur of the year by *Inc.* magazine at seventeen, and published a guide to running startups at nineteen. But there is no biological law against elderly entrepreneurs. Harlan Sanders founded Kentucky Fried Chicken when he was sixty-five. Gary Burrell was fifty-one when he left Allied Signal to help start Garmin, the GPS giant. Geoffrey Roux was forty-six when he left a successful career at L'Oréal to start Phonehouse, one of France's most successful mobile phone companies.

A survey by the Kauffman Foundation of 652 U.S.–born bosses of technology companies founded in 1995–2005 discovered that the average boss was thirty-nine when he established his company. Twice as many founders were over fifty than were younger than twenty-five. It is never too late to become an entrepreneur.

A third myth is that entrepreneurship is primarily driven by venture capital. Venture capital certainly matters in capital-intensive industries, such as high tech and biotechnology; it can also be vital when it comes to supercharging the growth of start-ups. Venture capitalists bring "smarts" as well as money, providing entrepreneurs with advice, contacts, and management skills, sometimes in the form of outside managers. But venture capital is focused on a sliver of business: in the United States, 80 percent of all venture capital is devoted to computer hardware and software, semiconductors, telecommunications, and biotechnology. Venture capitalists fund less than one-half of 1 percent of all startups. In fact, most startups are funded either by personal debt or by the three "f's"—friends, fools, and families. Google is often quoted as a triumph of the venture capital industry, but Messrs. Brin and Page founded the company without any money at all and launched it with about $1 million raised from friends and connections.

Monitor, a management consultancy that has conducted an extensive survey of entrepreneurs, emphasizes the importance of angel investors. Angel investors operate in a world somewhere between the two poles of friends and family, on the one hand, and venture capitalists on the other: they usually have some personal connection with their chosen entrepreneurs, often through an alumni network, and they are more likely than venture capitalists to invest in a business when it is little more than a budding idea.

A fourth myth is that entrepreneurs need to produce some world-changing new product. In fact, some of the most successful entrepreneurs focus on processes rather than products. Michael Dell applied just-in-time customization to the PC business. Richard Branson made flying a lot less tedious by providing his customers with entertainment. Fred Smith built a billion-dollar business by improving the delivery of packages.

We have already alluded to the fifth myth: that entrepreneurialism is incompatible with big companies. This is not entirely misguided. Successful entrepreneurs have a different mindset from company men. Startups are often more innovative than established players because their incentives are sharper: startups need to innovate in order to break into the market, and owner-entrepreneurs can win much bigger prizes than even the most innovative company man. But many big companies work hard to keep the entrepreneurial flame burning. Johnson & Johnson operates like a holding company that provides financial muscle and marketing skills to internal entrepreneurs. Jack Welch tried to transform General Electric from a Goliath into a collection of entrepreneurial Davids. Just as importantly, big firms often provide startups with their bread and butter. In many industries, especially pharmaceuticals and telecoms, the giants have contracted out innovation to smaller companies. Microsoft has a network of 750,000 small companies around the world with which it works closely. As many as 3,500 companies have grown up in Nokia's shadow. Far from being sworn enemies, startups and established companies usually exist in a codependent symbiosis.

Many of the silliest government policies are driven by what might be called "Siliconitis": the conviction that encouraging entrepreneurialism is synonymous with creating your own version of Silicon Valley—hence Silicon Alley, in New York; Silicon Glen, in Scotland; and even, depressingly, Silicon Roundabout, in London. But most Silicon knockoffs are failures. There is no point in trying to create the next Silicon Valley if you lack the Valley's remarkable resources: two world-class universities, Stanford and Berkeley, and a major financial center, San Francisco. Instead, you are much better off focusing on your own strengths, whatever they might be. Monitor argues that there are two models of successful entrepreneurial ecologies other than the "classic" Silicon Valley model.

One is the anchor-firm model. Alfred Marshall, one of the first economists to write about entrepreneurship, said that successful entrepreneurs are like large trees in a forest, towering over their neighbors and depriving them of light and air. In fact, the big trees usually produce lots of little ones. They spin off subsidiaries, produce experienced employees who decide to go it alone, and conjure up dozens of suppliers. When Earl Bakken founded Medtronic in Minneapolis, in 1949, he was creating a local industry as well as a company. After developing the world's first pacemaker, Medtronic grew into the largest medical technology company in the world, giving birth to a gigantic litter of smaller medical technology firms.

A second model is the crisis-driven model. People turn to entrepreneurship when the economy delivers a cold shower. This happened in the San Diego region in the 1990s when the end of the Cold War threw hundreds of highly trained military scientists out of work. Local startups such as Qualcomm thrived by hoovering up the talent and putting it to new uses. Let's hope this model works again given the economic record in recent years.

Then Think Seriously About the Rules

Two further things complicate the search for the secrets of success. One is the role of chance. The Indian Institutes of Technology were designed to create technocrats rather than entrepreneurs. It was more a matter of luck than planning that they were churning out exactly the sort of people that the Indian software industry required. The second is the importance of culture. "If we learn anything from the history of economic development," David Landes, one of the deans of economic history, has argued, "it is that culture makes all the difference." You can throw as much money as you like at the economy but if you hand all the country's leading jobs to members of the royal family, and if you exclude half the population from meaningful employment, as Saudi Arabia does, then your civilization is destined to crumble back into the sand.

Though this complicates the work of policymakers, it should not be treated as a council of despair. Economic policies can trump culture: look at the way that the overseas Indians and Chinese thrived abroad in the 1950s and 1960s when their culturally similar brother and sisters were stagnating at home. And culture can be changed. The Thatcher government shook Britain out of its antibusiness sloth in the 1980s. More recently, India and China have become the second and third most pro-business countries in the world, trailing only the United States, according to Monitor's polls. Accident will always play a role in human affairs, but you can increase your chances of promoting entrepreneurialism by doing the right thing.

And what exactly is the right thing? At the very minimum, countries need to implement the policies that the World Bank lays down in *Doing Business* (such as transparency, convenience, and rule of law). At best, they need to embrace three qualities that can be found in the world's most successful entrepreneurial clusters. The first is a vibrant higher education system. Even if competing with Silicon Valley is a pipe dream, business is increasingly dependent upon knowledge, particularly technical knowledge. Eighty-five percent of all the high-growth businesses created in the United States in the past twenty-five years were established by people with college degrees, engineering being the most important. University research departments have helped to drive innovation in everything from design to entertainment.

The second is openness to outsiders. Émigrés have always been more entrepreneurial than their stick-in-the-mud cousins: the three most entrepreneurial "countries" in modern history have been the ones inhabited by the Jewish, Chinese, and Indian diasporas. In today's knowledge economy, educated émigrés are at the cutting edge of innovation. They create more firms than other people, as Silicon Valley demonstrates; circulate ideas, money, and skills; fill skills gaps; and mix and match knowledge from different parts of the world.

A third thing that policymakers need to do is free their mind of one of Schumpeter's most bewitching phrases: creative destruction. Creative destruction implies that the destructive part of entrepreneurship is just as weighty as the creative part. This is unnecessarily harsh. Amar Bhide points out that a great deal of creation is of the nondestructive variety. Rather than displacing existing products and services, many innovations promote and satisfy new demands. William Nordhaus, an economist at Yale University, points out that about 70 percent of the goods and services consumed in 1991 bore little relationship to the goods and services consumed in 1891. Today's teenagers live in a different world from the previous generation of teenagers, cocooned by Facebook and Google and surgically attached to their mobile phones and Game Boys. There are entire worlds of nondestructive creation yet to be conquered—new cures for diseases, for example, or innovations that will improve the lives of elderly people.

And when we do have to endure "creative destruction," it normally involves more of the latter than the former. Most innovations increase productivity and thereby improve the general standard of living. Carl Schramm also points to a paradox at the heart of entrepreneurial capitalism: "the less secure we are economically, the more secure we are economically." The more we allow "fit" companies to replace the "unfit," the sounder the general economy becomes and the more secure we are in the long run.

Entrepreneurialism promotes individual creativity as well as economic dynamism. William H. Whyte called one of the most chilling chapters of *The Organization Man* (1957), his study of corporate America at the height of managed capitalism, "The Fight Against Genius." "Well rounded team players would be more valuable than brilliant men," the thinking went, "and a very brilliant man would probably be disruptive." Entrepreneurial capitalism has brought the rehabilitation of the "very brilliant man" who, thanks to their enthusiasm for disruption, can turn maverick insights into industry-changing organizations.

"Every generation needs a new revolution," Thomas Jefferson wrote toward the end of his life. The new revolution of our generation is the entrepreneurial revolution, a revolution that has spread around the world, from America and Britain outward, and from the private sector to the public one. It is a revolution that is bringing a great deal of disruption in its wake, disruption that is being exaggerated by the current downturn. But it is a revolution that is doing something remarkable: applying more brainpower, in more countries and in more creative ways, to the art of raising productivity and solving social problems. The "gale" that Schumpeter celebrated is blowing us, a little roughly, to a better place.

8

The World Turned Upside Down

In 1980, American car executives were so shaken to find that Japan had replaced the United States as the world's leading carmaker that they decided to go there to find out what was going on. How did these upstarts beat the Americans in both price *and* reliability? And how did they manage to produce new models so quickly? The visitors discovered that the answer was not industrial policy or state subsidies, as they had expected, but business innovation. The Japanese had invented a new system of making things that was quickly dubbed "lean manufacturing."

Something comparable is happening today but on a far larger scale. Developing countries are becoming hotbeds of business innovation in much the same way that Japan did from the 1950s onward. And they are threatening to upend the world even more completely than the Japanese did in the 1970s and 1980s.

These countries are coming up with new products and services that are dramatically cheaper than their Western equivalents: $3,000 cars, $300 computers, and $30 mobile phones that provide nationwide service for just two cents a minute. They are reinventing systems of production, distribution, and exchange. And they are experimenting with entirely new business models. All the elements of modern business, from supply-chain management to recruitment and retention, are being rejigged or reinvented in one emerging market or another.

Why are countries that were until recently associated with cheap labor now becoming leaders in innovation? Most obviously because local companies are dreaming bigger dreams. Driven by a mixture of ambition and fear—ambition to bestride the world stage and fear of even cheaper competitors in, say, Vietnam or Cambodia—they are doggedly climbing the value chain. Emerging-market champions have not only proved highly competitive in their own backyards, they are also going global. The United Nations World Investment Report calculates that there are now about 21,500 multinationals based in the emerging world. The best of these, such as India's Bharat Forge in forging, China's BYD in batteries, Mexico's Bimbo in baked goods, and Brazil's Embraer in jet aircraft, are as good as anybody's in the world. The number of companies from Brazil, India, China, or Russia on the Financial Times 500 list more than quadrupled in 2006–08, from fifteen to sixty-two. Brazil's top twenty multinationals more than doubled their foreign assets in a single year, 2006.

At the same time, Western multinationals are investing ever bigger hopes in emerging markets. They regard them as sources of economic growth and high-quality brainpower, both of which they think are in short supply, at least at the right price, in the West. Multinationals expect about 70 percent of the world's growth over the next few years to come from emerging markets, with 40 percent coming from just two countries, China and India. General Electric expects 80 percent of demand to come from emerging markets in a few years' time compared with just 20 percent a decade ago. They have also noted that China and, to a lesser extent, India have been pouring resources into education over the past couple of decades. China produces 75,000 people with higher degrees in engineering or computer science and India, 60,000 every year.

The world's biggest multinationals are relocating more of their research and development to emerging markets. Companies in the Fortune 500 list have ninety-eight research-and-development facilities in China and sixty-three in India. Some have more than one. General Electric's healthcare arm has spent more than $50 million in the past few years to build a vast R&D center in Bangalore, its biggest anywhere in the world. Cisco has spent more than $1 billion on a second global headquarters—Cisco East—in Bangalore. Microsoft's R&D center in Beijing is its largest outside its American headquarters in Redmond. Knowledge-intensive companies are hiring workers form the emerging world: a quarter of Accenture's workforce is in India.

Both Western and emerging-country companies have realized that they need to try harder if they are to prosper in these booming markets. It is not enough to concentrate on the Gucci and Mercedes crowd; they have to learn how to appeal to the billions of people who live outside Shanghai and Bangalore, from the rising middle classes in second-tier cities to the farmers in isolated villages. That means rethinking everything from products to distribution systems.

Anil Gupta, of the University of Maryland at College Park, points out that these markets are among the toughest in the world.[1] Distribution systems can be hopeless. Income streams can be unpredictable. Pollution can be lung-searing. Governments can be infuriating, alternately meddling and neglectful. The 2010 *Doing Business* report ranked India 133rd out of 183 for ease of doing business. Pirating can squeeze profit margins, and poverty is ubiquitous. The islands of success are surrounded by a sea of problems, which have defeated some doughty companies. Yahoo! and eBay retreated from China with their tails between their legs; Google moved its server to Hong Kong. Black & Decker, America's biggest toolmaker, is almost invisible in India and China, the world's two biggest construction sites.

But the opportunities are equally extraordinary. Rapid economic growth is set to continue for decades. Millions of people will be marching into the middle class in the coming decades. Few companies suffer from the costly "legacy systems" that are common in the West. Brainpower is relatively cheap and abundant: in China more than five million people graduate from college every year and in India about three million, respectively quadruple and triple the numbers a decade ago.

This combination of challenges and opportunities is producing a fizzing cocktail of creativity. Because so many consumers are poor, companies have to go for volume. But because piracy is so commonplace, they also have to keep upgrading their products. Again, the similarities with Japan in the 1980s are striking. Toyota and Honda took to "just-in-time" inventories and quality management because land and raw materials were expensive. In the same way, emerging-market companies are turning problems into advantages.

Until now it had been widely assumed that globalization was driven by the West and imposed on the rest. Bosses in New York, London, and Paris would control the process from their glass towers, and Western consumers would reap most of the benefits. This is changing fast. Muscular emerging-market champions such as India's ArcelorMittal in steel and Mexico's Bimbo in baked goods are gobbling up Western companies. Brainy ones such as Infosys and Wipro are taking over office work. And consumers in developing countries are getting richer faster than their equivalents in the West. In some cases the traditional global supply chain is being reversed: Embraer buys many of its component parts from the West and does the high-value-added work in Brazil.

Old assumptions about innovation are also being challenged. People in the West like to believe that their companies cook up new ideas in their laboratories at home and then export them to the developing world, which makes it easier to accept job losses in manufacturing. This is proving less true by the day. Western companies are embracing "polycentric innovation" as they spread their R&D centers around the world. And non-Western companies are becoming powerhouses of innovation in everything from telecoms to computers. A UNESCO report on innovation argues that the proportion of global R&D that is being done in the emerging world increased from 30 percent to 37 percent in 2003–07.

The emerging world has already leapfrogged ahead of the West in areas such as mobile money (using mobile phones to make payments) and online games. Microsoft's research laboratory in Beijing has produced clever programs that allow computers to recognize handwriting or turn photographs into cartoons. Huawei, a Chinese telecom giant, has become the world's fourth-largest patent applicant. But the most exciting innovations going on in the emerging world are of the Henry Ford variety: smarter ways of designing products and organizing processes to reach the billions of consumers who are just entering the global market.

Growth is breeding optimism. Large majorities of people in China and India say their country's current economic situation is good, expect conditions to improve further, and think their children will be better off than they are. This is a region that, to echo Churchill's phrase, sees opportunities in every difficulty rather than difficulties in every opportunity. This has huge implications for the future. Optimism is breeding self-confidence, and self-confidence is breeding a distinctive approach to business. In the past, emerging economic leviathans tended to embrace new management systems as they tried to consolidate their progress. America adopted Henry Ford's production line and Alfred Sloan's multidivisional firm and swept all before it until the 1960s. Japan invented lean production and almost destroyed the American car and electronics industries. Now the emerging markets are developing their own distinctive management ideas, and Western companies will increasingly find themselves learning from their rivals. People who used to think of the emerging world as a source of cheap labor must now recognize that it can be a source of disruptive innovation as well.

The Charms of Frugal Innovation

General Electric's healthcare laboratory in Bangalore contains some of the company's most sophisticated products—from giant body scanners that can accommodate the bulkiest American football players to state-of-the-art intensive-care units that can nurse the tiniest premature babies. But the device that has captured the heart of the center's boss, Ashish Shah, is much less fancy: a handheld electrocardiogram called the Mac 400.

The device is a masterpiece of simplification. The multiple buttons on conventional ECGs have been reduced to just four. The bulky printer has been replaced by one of those tiny gadgets used in portable ticket machines. The whole thing is small enough to fit into a small backpack and can run on batteries as well as on the mains. This miracle of compression sells for $800, instead of $2,000 for a conventional ECG, and has reduced the cost of an electrocardiogram to just $1 per patient.

In Chennai, 202 miles farther east, Ananth Krishnan, chief technology officer of Tata Consultancy Services (TCS), is equally excited about an even lower-tech device: a water filter. It uses rice husks (which are among the country's most common waste products) to purify water. The device is not only robust and portable but also relatively inexpensive, giving a large family an abundant supply of bacteria-free water for an initial investment of about $24 and a recurring expense of about $4 for a new filter every few months. Tata Chemicals, which is making the devices, hopes for an eventual market of 100 million.

These innovations are aimed at two of India's most pressing health problems: heart disease and contaminated water. Some five million Indians die of cardiovascular diseases every year, more than one-quarter of them under the age of sixty-five. About two million die from drinking contaminated water. The two companies are already at work on "new and improved"—by which they mean simpler and less expensive—versions of these two devices.

There is nothing new about companies adapting their products to the pockets and preferences of emerging-market consumers. Unilever and Procter & Gamble started selling shampoo and washing powder in small sachets more than two decades ago to cater to customers with cramped living spaces and even more cramped budgets. Nike produces an all-enveloping athletic uniform to protect the modesty of Muslim female athletes. Mercedes-Benz puts air-conditioning controls in the back as well as the front of its cars because people who can afford a Mercedes can also afford a driver.

But GE and TCS are doing something more exciting than fiddling with existing products: they are taking the needs of poor consumers as a starting point and working backward. They are producing radically simpler products in order to reduce costs: instead of adding ever more bells and whistles, they strip the products down to their bare essentials. But there is more to frugality than simply cutting costs to the bone. Frugal products need to be highly adaptable.

Anurag Gupta, a telecom entrepreneur, has reduced a bank branch to its essence—a smartphone and a fingerprint scanner—so that banks can take ATMs to rural customers. These products also need to be tough and easy to use. Nokia's cheapest mobile handsets come equipped with flashlights (because of frequent power cuts), multiple phone books (because they often have several different users), rubberized key pads, and menus in several different languages. Nor does frugal mean second-rate: emerging-market consumers are obsessed by both value-for-money and the latest trends. GE's Mac 400 ECG incorporates the latest technology. Many inexpensive mobile handsets allow users to play video games and surf the net.

Frugal innovation is not just about redesigning products; it involves rethinking entire production processes and business models. Companies need to squeeze costs so they can reach more customers, and accept thin profit margins to gain volume. Three ways of reducing costs are proving particularly successful.

The first is to contract out ever more work. Bharti Airtel, an Indian mobile-phone company that charges some of the lowest fees in the business but is worth $30 billion, has contracted out everything except its core business of selling phone calls, handing over network operations to Ericsson, business support to IBM, and the management of its transmission towers to an independent company. To make this work, Bharti had to persuade its business partners to rethink their business models, too. For example, Ericsson had to agree to be paid by the minute rather than for selling and installing the equipment, and rival mobile-phone companies to rent their towers rather than own them outright.

The second money-saver is to use existing technology in imaginative new ways. TCS is looking at using mobile phones to connect television sets to the Internet. Personal computers are still relatively rare in India, but televisions are ubiquitous. TCS has designed a box that connects the television to the Internet via a mobile phone. It has also devised a remote control that allows people who have never used keyboards to surf the Web. This idea is elegant as well as frugal: by reconfiguring existing technology it can potentially connect millions of people to the Internet.

The third way to cut costs is to apply mass-production techniques in new and unexpected areas. India's software companies blazed the trail. Wipro applied the Toyota manufacturing system, with its emphasis on continuous improvement, to software development. Other entrepreneurs are extending it to new areas such as healthcare. Devi Shetty is India's most celebrated heart surgeon, having performed the country's first neonatal heart surgery on a nine-day-old baby, and numbered Mother Teresa among his patients. Yet his most important contribution to medicine is not his surgical skill but his determination to make this huge industry more efficient by applying Henry Ford's management principles. He believes that a combination of economies of scale and specialization can radically reduce the cost of heart surgery. His flagship Narayana Hrudayalaya Hospital in the "Electronics City" district of Bangalore, not far from GE, Infosys, and Wipro, has one thousand beds (against an average of 160 beds in American heart hospitals), and Dr. Shetty and his team of forty-odd cardiologists perform about six hundred operations a week.

The sheer number of patients allows surgeons to acquire world-class expertise in particular operations, and the generous backup facilities allow them to concentrate on their specialty rather than wasting their time on administration. Dr. Shetty has performed more than 15,000 heart operations and other members of his team more than 10,000. The hospital charges an average of $2,000 for open-heart surgery, compared with $20,000 to $100,000 in the United States, but its success rates are as good as in the best American hospitals.

Dr. Shetty has devoted much of his energy to boosting his customer base, largely for humanitarian reasons but also because he believes that higher volumes lead to better quality. He has established video and Internet links with hospitals in India, Africa, and Malaysia so that his surgeons can give expert advice to less experienced colleagues. He also sends "clinics on wheels" to nearby rural hospitals to test for heart disease. He has created a health insurance scheme, working with various local self-help groups, which covers 2.5 million people for a premium of about eleven cents a month each. About one-third of the hospital's patients are now enrolled in the scheme. A sliding scale of fees is used for operations so that richer customers subsidize poorer ones. The entire enterprise is surprisingly profitable given how many poor people it treats. Dr. Shetty's family-owned hospital group reports a 7.7 percent profit after taxes, compared with an average of 6.9 percent in American private hospitals.

The group has recently built three other hospitals next to the heart clinic—a trauma center, a 1,400-bed cancer hospital, and a 300-bed eye hospital. They all share central facilities such as laboratories and a blood bank. Dr. Shetty is also setting up "medical cities" in other parts of the country. Over the next five years his company plans to increase its number of beds to 30,000, making it the largest private hospital group in India and giving it more bargaining power when it negotiates with suppliers, thus driving down costs further.

Bamboo Bandits

Indians like to think of frugal innovation as their distinctive contribution to management thinking. Many of them even prefer the adjective "Gandhian" to "frugal." They point to the national tradition of *jugaad*—meaning, roughly, making do with what you have and never giving up—and cite many examples of ordinary Indians solving seemingly insoluble problems. But China is giving India a run for its money. Mindray, for example, specializes in inexpensive medical products such as ECG devices, and BYD has radically reduced the price of expensive lithium-ion batteries by using less costly raw materials and learning how to make them at ambient temperatures rather than in expensively heated "dry rooms." This has reduced their price from $40 to $12 apiece and made them competitive with less powerful nickel-cadmium batteries.

The Chinese have made two distinctive contributions to frugal innovation. The first is the use of flexible networks—powered by *guanxi*, or personal connections—to reduce costs and increase flexibility. Li & Fung, a Hong Kong–based company, has long been a pioneer, working closely with a network of about 12,000 companies operating in more than forty countries. It puts together customized supply chains from its vast network of associates and keeps an eye on quality and order fulfillment. Similarly, Dachangjiang, a motorcycle-maker in China's Guangdong province, works with hundreds of parts suppliers.

These postmodern *guanxi* have several powerful qualities. They can contract or expand with demand. Li & Fung and Dachangjiang seldom have problems with excess capacity when times are hard or with waiting lists when times are flush. The companies can also be turned into engines of innovation. Li & Fung relies on its partners to help solve problems, not just fulfill orders. Dachangjiang provides its suppliers with rough sketches rather than detailed blueprints and encourages them to innovate. And they tap into centuries of tradition in the Chinese business diaspora.

A second area where the Chinese excel is in "bandit" or

"guerrilla" innovation, known as *shanzhai*. The original bandits lived in isolated villages and carried out raids on upright citizens. Today's bandits live at the margins of official society but are much in evidence: in Shanghai's People's Square you will be offered a cheap watch or phone at every step, as well as sundry other services. These bandits are parasites who profit from China's weak property rights, but they are also talented innovators, quickly producing copies of high-tech gadgets that are cheap enough for migrant workers to be able to afford but also fashionable enough for young professionals to covet. Some of the more exotic phones are designed to look like watches or packets of cigarettes (they even have room for a few real ones) and often have striking new features, such as solar chargers, superloud speakers, telephoto lenses, or ultraviolet lights that make it easier to detect forged currency. In their own way, the bandits deploy as much innovation and ingenuity as their legitimate counterparts.

Frugal innovation is the most distinctive form of innovation coming from the emerging world. But there are plenty of other types of innovation coming out of these hotbeds: innovations designed to deal with the complexities of distribution in difficult markets and innovations designed to deal with the problems of pell-mell growth.

Easier Said Than Done

Unilever's Concept Center in midtown Shanghai attracts hundreds of human guinea pigs every day, ranging from housewives with time on their hands to migrant laborers looking for easy work. The center is a consumer's paradise. There are salons where people can get their hair done. There is a living room and a bedroom—called "the chatting room"—where they can make themselves at home. There is a shop where they can browse the company's latest products. Researchers discreetly monitor consumers' reactions from behind one-way mirrors.

The Concept Center is just a small part of Unilever's growing R&D effort in China, where it has struggled in the past and where it is now determined to catch up with its perennial rival, Procter & Gamble. Half an hour's drive away, in one of the city's sprawling office parks, the company has a huge new R&D center where it does everything from conducting basic research to producing three-dimensional mock-ups of new packaging.

Consumers in emerging markets are far more difficult to reach than their counterparts in developed markets. There is little spare money around: the average income per person in China is about $3,500 and in India, $1,000. Cultural complexities are confounding. Tastes are fluid; people who are not used to brands flit easily from one to another.

This has turned great metropolises such as Shanghai into vast laboratories of consumer research. Companies are always coming up with new products, or tweaking old ones, to suit local tastes and meet idiosyncratic preferences. Unilever makes its soaps and shampoos foamier than their Western equivalents. P&G produces toothpaste in herbal and green-tea flavors. PepsiCo adds spice to its potato chips. Adidas has created two kinds of shops—"local" ones that specialize in sportswear designed for Asian bodies and "global" ones that sell the same products as in the West. The shopping mall beneath the company's regional headquarters in Shanghai has one of each kind.

Innovation extends to changing entire business models. Yum! Brands, which owns KFC and Pizza Hut, has repositioned itself as an upmarket company in China, offering comfortable dining for middle-class families rather than fast food for the masses. It has also launched a new chain of restaurants, East Dawning, serving Chinese dishes. Levi Strauss has introduced a pay-as-you-wear model for its most fashionable jeans in India to preserve an upmarket status while broadening its customer base. Dell sells its PCs in China through shops as well as to order.

Because of the lack of brand loyalty, companies have to put even more thought into marketing than they do in the West. Shanghai is plastered with advertisements on everything from airport trolleys to lavatory walls. Companies project giant logos onto the sides of skyscrapers. Many elevators and cabs have televisions that pour out a constant—and infuriating—stream of commercials. Mobile phones are bombarded with texts advertising vacations, massages, and much more. Emerging-market companies are particularly adept at adding the human touch. Most consumer goods firms, and a growing number of electronics ones, use sales representatives to demonstrate their products to customers. Unilever employs an army of "Pond Girls" who show department store customers how to use the eponymous face cream.

As companies work their way down the income pyramid, the problems proliferate. Distribution is tricky: modern retail chains account for only one-third of consumer goods sold in China and one-fifth in India. Branding can have pitfalls: the locals may be suspicious of foreign products. Companies may find themselves up against feisty rivals that they have never heard of, not to mention unscrupulous pirates. And China's rural areas account for 54 percent of its population but produce a much lower share of its gross domestic product.

Companies in search of the much-vaunted fortune at the bottom of the pyramid have to start not with consumers but with nonconsumers. They need to get inside poor people's heads to develop new markets, shaping people's tastes and establishing habits. The techniques they use include "embedding" employees with local families in order to study their day-to-day behavior. P&G sends young marketing people to live with Chinese peasants for months on end. They hand out their products free (sometimes through local NGOs) to see what people make of them. GE donates medical equipment to rural healthcare centers and keeps a careful watch on how it is used.

Heavy investment in education is also essential. Unilever has teamed up with various NGOs to teach people about the importance of personal hygiene (and of buying Unilever's products). Metro Cash and Carry, a German wholesaler that sells to hotels and restaurants, trains farmers in looking after their crops, encouraging them to store their vegetables in boxes rather than leaving them to spoil on the ground.

Yet it is no use educating consumers unless they can get hold of the products. Even the most sophisticated companies have to fall back on established distribution systems. That might mean working with local mom and pop shops. P&G puts products into packages small enough to fit on crowded shelves and uses a network of local representatives to keep the shops stocked. Or it might mean using local women to sell things to their friends and neighbors. In Brazil, Nestlé sends its comestibles to local entrepreneurs who sell them to their neighbors. Some companies provide locals with bicycles so they can cover a wider geographical range.

East African Breweries, a division of Diageo, launched a cut-price beer, Senator Keg, to help reduce demand for illicit alcohol, which is cheap but is frequently contaminated with methanol, fertilizers, and battery acid. The company reduced the cost of the beer by negotiating a tax waiver with the government and by distributing it in kegs rather than bottles. The company made use of the shadow economy to get the beer delivered to the outlets. It also trained bar staff to understand the importance of rotating kegs to make sure the beer was fresh, and of washing glasses. Senator Keg is now ubiquitous in Kenya, sold in every makeshift roadside bar, and is affectionately known as "Obama."

Dealing with distribution problems can lead to some surprising innovations and even generate entirely new businesses. Future Group, India's largest retailer, has introduced "organized chaos" into its shops to make consumers feel at home, breaking up long aisles with untidy-looking displays. Grupo Elektra, a Mexican retailer, started offering credit to consumers who did not have a bank account, and ended up holding so much financial information on its customers that it decided to take the next step and go into banking. The company now has one of the country's biggest network of bank branches as well as one of its most popular retail chains.

New technology can also work wonders for distribution. The Indian Tobacco Company, one of the country's biggest conglomerates, has created a network of more than five thousand Internet kiosks known as *e-choupals* to help farmers communicate with both the supply and the distribution chains. Farmers can bring their goods for sale and ITC will display their products. Tata Consultancy Services has installed sensors in some rural areas to gather information about local soil and weather conditions. Farmers can call helplines on their mobile phones and receive advice about the best products to use in those conditions, which in effect creates a market. And recall the Indian entrepreneur who distilled an ATM into a smartphone and a fingerprint scanner: local bank clerks now bicycle out to villages and set up shop under a tree, using the scanner to identify savers and taking in or handing out money. The transactions are recorded over the mobile phone and the banker-on-wheels returns to the local bank branch with the money.

The most difficult trick of all is what some call "straddling the pyramid" or "playing the piano": serving both the people at the bottom of the pyramid and those at the top. The acknowledged masters of this are consumer goods giants such as P&G and Unilever. These companies not only rigorously segment their markets by income level, they also lead consumers up the value chain as they become richer. A couple of decades ago Unilever noted that rural Indians were in the habit of washing their clothes with bars of soap, so it first offered detergents in bar form and then began to introduce its customers to washing powder. The company is now trying to pull off a similar trick with tea in the Middle East. Most people in the region prepare their tea from leaves, but Unilever has introduced tea bags that appeal to local tastes and has started selling them in trendy cafés.

China's Haier has proved particularly good at market segmentation. It produces a line of extremely robust washing machines for rural users, having discovered that older models frequently got clogged with mud because farmers were using them to clean vegetables as well as clothes. It also makes small washing machines that are just right for young urban professionals, many of whom live in tiny apartments.

The masters of pyramid-straddling are mobile-handset makers. Nokia produces phones for every market, from rural models designed to cope with monsoons to fashion accessories that will look cool in a Shanghai nightclub. The inexpensive phones are sold through a vast network of local outlets, such as mom-and-pop stores and rural markets, and the upmarket models through shops in fashionable city centers. The aim is to create a brand that is at once universal and aspirational.

Miracle Grow

The view from the 87th-floor lobby of Shanghai's Grand Hyatt hotel is a wonder to behold (if you can behold it through the ever-threatening smog). Lesser skyscrapers glow with the logos of global giants such as Citi and HSBC. The river carries ships loaded with the riches of the world's workshop. High-rise housing projects stretch into the distance: the city's population, already 19 million, is forecast to grow to 45 million by 2025.

The emerging world is enjoying the most spectacular growth in history. Its share of global GDP (at purchasing-power parity) increased from 36 percent in 1980 to 45 percent in 2008 and looks set to grow to 51 percent in 2014. This dynamism shows no signs of waning: many economists expect growth in emerging markets to be four percentage points higher than growth in the rich world for at least the next five years.

This dynamism has created an army of world-class companies. In 1990, Mittal was an unknown producer of steel in Indonesia. Today, as ArcelorMittal, it is the world's largest steel company, bigger than the next three combined. Lenovo, which did not exist in 1990, bought IBM's personal-computer business five years ago and is now the world's fourth-largest PC maker, after Hewlett-Packard and Dell. Goodbaby, which did not exist when many of today's leading politicians were children, now operates the world's largest complex of factories devoted to children's goods: a stroller factory, a car seat factory, a toy car factory, a wooden furniture factory, and a diaper factory, all located on its 12,000-acre industrial campus in Kunshan.

Dynamism has also shaped the culture of the corporate world. It has created a fearsome work ethic. The official motto of the Lishui Economic Development Zone is "each person does the work of two; two days' work is done in one." It has also created a buccaneering spirit, born from a mixture of optimism and arrogance. The business news buzzes with stories of acquisitions and startups. The corporate go-getters love to explain that if you can make it here, despite the poverty, the dismal infrastructure, and the unpredictable politicians, you can make it anywhere.

The growth is driven as much by companies' internal dynamics as by the abundance of opportunities. The importance of volume for frugal products means they have to keep expanding in order to justify their investments. The ambitions of their relatively youthful workforce push in the same direction. The companies' up-and-coming managers have never experienced anything but hyper-growth, and their lower ranks are staffed by young men in a hurry who expect to be given their way.

To flourish in this atmosphere, it helps to have the spirit of a frontier settler, not a corporate bureaucrat. Companies are obsessed with grabbing their share of the frontier, both geographical and technological, before somebody else does. This puts a premium on both speed and flexibility. But businesses also sometimes engage in lateral moves that make little sense to Western managers. A property company, say, might suddenly move into computers. Rather than worrying about synergies or core competencies, they see opportunities and seize them.

The pursuit of growth is forcing firms to engage in relentless innovation, nowhere more so than in two of the basic building blocks of corporate management: recruitment and retention (which we will look at in more detail in a later chapter) and mergers and acquisitions (M&A). Even as Western companies reeled from the recent recession, emerging-market giants went on a shopping spree. India's Tata Consultancy Services bought Citigroup Global Services, the outsourcing division of the American bank, for $512 million in October 2008. HCL, another Indian technology group, snapped up Britain's Axon Group for $672 million two months later. Bharti Airtel, yet another Indian company, gobbled up Zain, a leading African telecom company, for $9 billion.

Nirmalya Kumar, of the London Business School, says that two things are allowing emerging-market giants to rewrite the rules of M&A: money and flexibility.[2] The combination of rapid growth and extensive internal restructuring has left many companies with plenty of cash in their pockets. Profit margins of 10 percent are common, double the average in the West. Business families and founding entrepreneurs, with large shareholdings in their companies, are willing to make long-term bets on growth and do not have to worry about losing control of their companies if their stocks take a nosedive.

Kumar points out that emerging-market firms have a different approach to M&A from their Western counterparts. They are less interested in cutting costs—through synergies, greater efficiency, and lower head count—because they know that they can deal with those issues by plugging their acquisitions into their low-cost production machines at home. What is much more important to them is to acquire the skills, brands, and distribution channels that will enable them to join the club of world-class companies. In many ways this is "reverse M&A" to complement reverse innovation: instead of Western companies buying cheap manufacturing in the developing world, emerging-market companies are buying sophisticated corporate machinery in the West. Thus, India's Hindalco, an aluminum company, used a succession of well-planned acquisitions to turn itself into a global force, boosting its revenues from $500 million to $15 billion in seven years. It was not just trying to achieve rapid growth (which it already enjoyed) or deal with overcapacity (which was not an issue). Instead it identified internal weaknesses and systematically eliminated them.

Perhaps Kumar is being a tad bullish. Some emerging-market acquisitions are driven by a combination of hubris and frontier mentality. Emerging-market managers have got into the habit of overvaluing their own companies and underestimating the difficulties of expansion. Bharti Airtel bid for Zain because it was looking for virgin territory for its low-cost business model as the Indian market became saturated. One thing is certain, though: with emerging markets surging ahead, their local champions will be on the prowl for more acquisitions.

New Masters of Management

"Frugal innovation" is only the most eye-catching part of a much broader revolution that is going on in the emerging world: the wholesale reinvention of long-established business models.

Economies of scale have traditionally meant scaling up. Companies reduce unit costs by centralizing their manufacturing and producing long runs of standardized items. But centralized production has always had a big drawback—it adds expensive layers of bureaucracy—and it is hard to make it work in emerging markets, where populations are often widely scattered and distribution systems abysmal. The Boston Consulting Group notes that emerging-world entrepreneurs are using modern technology, particularly mobile phones, to replace scaling up with scaling out. The most successful examples of this are clinics on wheels, but there are plenty of others. Nutriset, a French manufacturer of fortified food for malnourished children, has outsourced production to local franchises in Africa. The company maintains quality control and the franchises are close enough to the children to make distribution quick and easy. Kenya's Child and Family Wellness Shops offer shares in the company to the nurses who operate the clinics, which encourages them to serve more children and helps stem the brain drain from rural areas.

A second business model takes an equally contrarian approach to production. John Hagel and John Seely Brown argue that Western companies have spent the past century perfecting "push" models of production that allocate resources to areas of expected demand.[3] But in emerging markets, particularly those where the Chinese have a strong influence, a very different "pull" model often prevails, designed to help companies mobilize resources when the need arises. Hong Kong's Li & Fung or China's Chongquing Lifan Group can use their huge supply chains to produce fashion items or motorcycles in response to demand. These pull models fundamentally change the nature of companies. Instead of fixed armies looking for opportunities, firms become loose networks that are forever reconfiguring themselves in response to a rapidly shifting landscape. Such models are not peculiar to emerging markets— Dell builds computers to its Western customers' specifications, for example—but they are being taken to new heights there.

The developing world's most innovative business model may be the application of mass-production techniques to sophisticated services. India's outsourcing firms demonstrated that economies of scale and scope could be reaped from services that used to be highly fragmented and geographically rooted. Dr. Shetty is only one of many Indians who are applying Henry Ford's principles to healthcare. LifeSpring has reduced the cost of giving birth in a private hospital to $40 by looking after many more mothers. Aravind, the world's biggest eye-hospital chain, performs some 200,000 eye operations a year. It takes the assembly-line principle literally: four operating tables are laid side by side and two doctors operate on adjacent tables. When the first operation is done, the second patient is already in place.

These three business innovations are remarkable. But something even more fundamental is going on: business innovation in the emerging world has arguably gotten to the point where all the individual advances add up to more than the sum of their parts. Just as Japan's quality circles and just-in-time delivery were part of a new system called "lean production," so the emerging world's reverse innovation and frugal production are part of a new approach to management.

This new management paradigm pushes two familiar ideas beyond their previous limits: that the customer is king, and that economies of scale can produce radical reductions in unit costs. Companies are starting with the needs of some of the world's poorest people and redesigning not just products but entire production processes to meet those needs. This can involve changing the definition of a customer to take in all sorts of people who were previously excluded from the market economy. It means cutting costs to the bone and eliminating all but the most essential features of a product or service. And it often stretches the idea of economies of scale beyond products to sophisticated services such as information management and even heart operations.

The evolution of this new paradigm is strikingly reminiscent of the emergence of earlier management paradigms, particularly the rise of mass production in the United States in the 1900s and lean production in Japan in the 1960s. Emerging-market companies are harnessing technologies such as mobile phones and the mobile Internet in much the same way that American companies harnessed the railroads and the telegraph. They are discovering new customers, much as American companies discovered their Everyman. They are turning disadvantages (such as poverty and dreadful distribution systems) into strengths, much as the Japanese invented just-in-time production to compensate for their lack of storage space. This new management system, like all successful ones that went before it, is self-reinforcing. New technology allows companies to bring their services to more customers and to apply economies of scale to new areas. Globalization allows them to cut costs by serving ever more customers.

The emerging markets' new management paradigm also has an army of proselytizing gurus and consultants, much as mass production did in the early twentieth century and lean production in the 1980s, led by an Indian elite, who are busy refining it, advising companies on how to exploit it, and selling it to companies anywhere in the world that want it. C. K. Prahalad was arguably the world's most creative management guru over the past two decades, and his *Fortune at the Bottom of the Pyramid* was arguably the most influential single book. Prahalad has been joined by a number of rising superstars such as Vijay Govindarajan, Tarun Khanna, Ranjay Gulati, Nirmalya Kumar, and Anil Gupta, who all possess an extraordinary ability to shape events as well as influence them. Asian management consultancies, such as Tata Consultancy Services, which operates in forty-two countries and had revenues of $6 billion in the 2009 tax year, are also vigorous advocates of frugal innovation. The emerging-market paradigm may have been a response to local deficiencies, but some of the world's best business brains are now turning it into a coherent management system that is just as applicable in rich as in poor countries.

The Power to Disrupt

During the long boom of the 1950s and 1960s the Marxist intelligentsia in the rich countries, furious at their proletariat's refusal to rise up in revolt, turned to the third world instead. Frantz Fanon celebrated anticolonial revolutionaries in *The Wretched of the Earth* (1961). A generation of student radicals wore Che Guevara T-shirts and chanted "Ho, Ho, Ho Chi Minh" at any passing university dean.

These days the third world is known as the emerging markets, the Che Guevara T-shirts are made in China, and the wretched of the earth are enjoying growth rates that are the envy of the former colonial powers. Moreover, these emerging markets are likely to shake things up not only in their own backyards but in rich countries, too. Clayton Christensen has coined the term "disruptive innovation" for new products that slash prices and new processes that radically change the way they are made and delivered. Today, many of the most disruptive innovations hail from emerging markets. They will make a bigger difference to life in the West than lean production, the previous great disruptive management innovation from the East.

There are four reasons why things will move faster and further this time. The first is that the markets for corporate control and for senior managerial talent are much more liquid than they were twenty years ago. The great Japanese and South Korean giants grew organically, whereas emerging-market champions are keen on mergers and acquisitions. They have access to highly developed capital markets, both public and private, and to armies of experienced investment bankers and consultants. Emerging-market giants are snapping up Western companies and employing Western managers.

The second factor is the sheer size of the emerging markets. The Japanese export machine was powered by a handful of engines, notably cars and electronics. By contrast, the emerging-market export machine has engines in almost every industry. Arcelor-Mittal is the world's biggest steel company. Infosys and TCS are among the world's biggest IT companies. Haier is the fourth-largest manufacturer of home appliances. ZTE, which started foreign operations only in 1997, looks set to become one of the world's top five mobile-handset makers. Just a decade ago not a single emerging-market company could be considered world-class. Today such companies are among the world's leaders in twenty-five big industries, according to the Boston Consulting Group.

The third reason to expect a big impact is the emphasis on volume. Emerging-market companies are obsessed with finding new markets to make up for their slim profit margins. Indian and Chinese mobile-phone companies have been adding eight to ten million new subscribers a month for the past few years. Emerging-world giants such as Infosys and ZTE have been growing at more than 40 percent a year.

Fourth, the West's best companies have grasped the potential of emerging markets. Henry Ford Jr., who ran the Ford Motor Company for decades after the Second World War, continued into the 1980s to dismiss Japanese cars as "those little shitboxes." By contrast, the best Western companies are now looking to emerging markets as sources of innovation and growth. Cisco expects 20 percent of its best people to work in its "Cisco East" center in the future.

Moreover, the West is ripe for frugal innovation. The West is entering an age of austerity, as consumers tighten their belts and governments struggle to balance their budgets. At the same time, the burden on the welfare state is growing, as medical innovations push up healthcare costs and baby boomers start drawing their pensions (by 2050, one in three people across the rich world will be drawing a pension). The only way to cope with all this will be to take a leaf out of the emerging world's value-for-money handbook. Peter Williamson, of the Judge Business School at the University of Cambridge, regards emerging markets as repositories of "value-for-money strategies for recessionary times."

Frugal innovation is already beginning to make itself felt in the West, particularly in healthcare. GE's inexpensive ultrasound device, originally developed for the Chinese market, has become the basis of a global business, with eager customers in the developed as well as the developing world. Dr. Shetty is building a 2,000-bed hospital in the Cayman Islands, a short flight from Miami, where he will offer surgery at half the price charged by American hospitals. But the trend is apparent in consumer goods, too. Haier has become the market leader in the West for cheap fridges. Most Western carmakers are producing small, inexpensive vehicles that have been influenced by the Nano. Mahindra & Mahindra's nifty little tractors are popular with hobby farmers and gardeners in America.

John Hagel and John Seely Brown have predicted that the emerging world's advance will lead to a serious "blowback" in the West: rich-world companies that exported capitalism to developing countries may soon find themselves humbled by more innovative companies from the East, and rich-world voters, who once regarded globalization as a plus, may eventually turn against it as they see one product market after another tuned upside down.[4]

Yet it is important to remember that disruption will bring benefits as well as problems to rich countries. Reengineered medical devices could slash healthcare costs without reducing the quality of care. Compact and fuel-efficient cars will allow people to keep driving but cause less damage to the environment. And the developed world still has some powerful weapons in its arsenal. The average Western company is much better managed than the average emerging-world company: for every Infosys and Haier there are plenty of poorly managed and uncompetitive firms in developing countries. Michael Gibbert, of Italy's Bocconi University, notes that the West also has a long tradition of inventiveness in hard

times, demonstrated during the Second World War. Williamson
points out that Western companies such as Walmart are already
making a success of value-for-money strategies. And some of the
most articulate promoters of reverse engineering and frugal innovation from emerging countries run Western companies or teach
in Western business schools.

The United States and other first-world countries quickly
learned the art of Japanese manufacturing. Americans rediscovered
Deming and turned him into a hero. American companies formed
joint ventures with Japanese companies, largely to learn the secrets
of lean production. Western companies also improved on what
they learned. There is no reason to think that this cannot happen
again, given time, with the frugal revolution.

Even so, the new management paradigm now taking shape in
the emerging world has big implications for the global balance of
power. The world's creative energy is shifting to the developing
countries, which are becoming innovators in their own right rather
than just talented imitators. A growing number of the world's
business innovations will in the future come not from "the West"
but "the rest." Anand Mahindra, vice-chairman of the eponymous
family firm, says that these days when Indians go to bed at night
their dreams about their country's future "are not just colorful but
steroidal." His compatriots are at last beginning to believe that
"the sandcastles we build in our minds are not going to be simply
washed away by the morning tide." The same is true across the
emerging world, whose "sandcastles" are now being built on the
solid foundations of business innovation. They will endure, changing not just emerging markets but the rest of the world as well.

PART IV

THE GREAT DEBATES

9

Knowledge, Learning, and Innovation

In his delightful autobiography, *Still Surprised*, Warren Bennis tells a story about Sigmund Freud's flight from Vienna in 1938. On arriving in London he asked Stefan Zweig, a fellow Viennese intellectual, what his new home was like. "London?" Zweig thundered. "How can you mention London and Vienna in the same breath? In Vienna there was sperm in the air."

Today there is no hotter topic in management theory than "sperm in the air." The fate of companies is increasingly determined by their ability to mobilize and motivate brainworkers—that is, their ability to turn themselves into the corporate equivalents of pre-war Vienna. How do you amass more brainworkers than your rivals? How do you unleash their creativity without risking anarchy? And how do you turn brilliant ideas into successful products? These are the problems at the heart of modern management theory.

Workers by Hand and Brain

Henry Ford once complained that brains are bothersome inconveniences when attached to members of the working class. Many of the 7,882 operations required to build a Model T did not require so much as a full complement of limbs, let alone a questioning intelligence, he argued: 2,637 of these operations could be performed by "one-legged men," 670 by "legless men," 715 by "one-armed men," two by "armless men," and ten by "blind men." "Why is it that when I ask for a pair of hands," he growled, perhaps forgetting those 715 one-armed men, "a brain comes attached?"

Today management is all about brains rather than limbs. Peter Drucker's knowledge workers have taken over from Karl Marx's proletarians as the drivers of economic growth. Knowledge-intensive companies such as Apple and Infosys have taken over from car companies such as General Motors and Ford as the symbols of modern times. And even old-fashioned companies have caught the knowledge bug: James Brian Quinn, of Dartmouth's Tuck School of Business, claims that even in the manufacturing sector, three-fourths of value-added comes from knowledge. Henry Ford's old company has improved its productivity enormously by treating its workers as sources of innovation rather than just as collections of limbs.

Management theorists are busy rethinking the basic tenets of their discipline in the light of this knowledge revolution. Gurus are falling over each other to offer advice on "breaking the mold," "unleashing creativity," and "thinking outside the box." Business schools are putting innovation at the heart of their teaching. And CEOs are forever waxing lyrical about turning their organizations into innovation machines.

This ferment of thinking has produced some of the best books on management in the past few years: witness Prahalad and Hammer's work on "core competencies" in *Competing for the Future*, Ikujiro Nonaka's work on "tacit knowledge" in *The Knowledge-Creating Company* (1995; revised 2008), and Clay Christensen's writing about "the innovator's dilemma" in his classic of the same title. But for all this impressive intellectual effort, the field remains a messy one. We are a long way from producing a "single best system" comparable to Frederick Taylor's theory of "scientific management" in the early decades of the twentieth century.

This is partly because the field is a magnet for airheads. Bright-House, an innovation consulting firm in Atlanta, Georgia, gives its employees five "your days" a year, when they are encouraged to "visit a spot conducive to reflection and letting their neurons rip." Craig Erlich, boss of Pulse220, an event marketing company, has had bottles of water relabeled "creativity juice."[1] Josh Linkner, the founder of ePrize, recommends that companies replace brainstorming with edgestorming.[2]

But there is a more fundamental reason for the messiness: motivating knowledge workers and inspiring innovation is far more difficult than organizing assembly lines. Companies like to measure everything they do. But how do you measure something that you cannot even define, such as knowledge? Companies like to plan for the future. But how to you plan a new discovery? Henry Ford got the world-changing idea for the assembly line by watching cows going to the slaughter at a local abattoir.[3] And how do you know when a new product will take off? 3M's Art Fry invented the weak glue that is the basis of Post-It notes by accident, kept the glue around on the off chance he would need it, and only reactivated the idea when a friend wanted sticky paper for his music notations. The theory is messy because the reality is.

Difficult People

Henry Fairlie was arguably the greatest journalist of his generation, a superstar on both sides of the Atlantic. He invented the modern political column and coined the term "the establishment," among many other contributions to Grub Street. But he was a nightmare to manage. Drunk every evening, hung over every morning, and given to seducing his colleagues' wives, his copy was often as wild as it was brilliant. He fled the United Kingdom, never to return, because of his unreciprocated belief that taxation was optional, and spent his later years living in the *New Republic*'s offices. He planned to call his never-written memoir *Bite the Hand that Feeds You*.[4]

Fairlie was a one-off even in the relatively louche world of old-fashioned journalism, but his story illustrates one of the biggest problems in modern management. Brainworkers are far more difficult to manage than manual workers. They are all ego and self-righteousness. Apply the bridle too harshly and they are likely to head off in the wrong direction. Apply the whip too vigorously and they will sit down and refuse to move.

Rob Goffee and Gareth Jones, of the London Business School, have been observing "clevers" for years, including, one suspects, some of their own colleagues, and have come up with some suggestions about how to apply the bridle and the whip.[5] First: apply a light touch. Point them in the right direction and allow them to decide on the route; or, better still, give them the illusion that they are choosing both the direction and the route themselves.

Second: massage their egos at every possible opportunity. Clevers have spent their lives showing off to various authority figures. The easiest way to get them to exert themselves is to hold out the possibility of another gold star. The promise of a chance to mix with others of their kind at PopTech or TED is a particularly powerful motivator.

Third: use a thief to catch a thief. Knowledge workers are much more likely to pay attention to their own kind than they are to "suits." Bill Gates waxed lyrical about the joys of programming when he was CEO of Microsoft. Richard Sykes styled himself as

Dr. Sykes when he ran GlaxoSmithKline.[6] Knowledge-intensive companies would be well advised to keep their managers (particularly their human-resources staff) permanently muzzled. Nothing infuriates "clevers" more than a memo that starts with the imprecation "team" before regurgitating a lot of gobbledygook. They would also be well advised to keep the spotlight on intellectual achievements: Nestlé has introduced open days at its research center in Lausanne, Switzerland, to give researchers a chance to show off their projects to friends and family, for example.

Perhaps the key to managing "clevers" is that, in many ways, they are still stuck in kindergarten. They crave adulation. They are quick to take a slight and slow to learn how to play with others. They spend meetings giggling like naughty schoolchildren or ostentatiously reading newspapers.[7] If the secret of managing manual workers, according to Taylor, was to treat men like machines, then the secret of managing knowledge workers is to treat them like precocious children.

Still, there is a limit to how much freedom companies can give to their "clevers" without degenerating into mere collections of individuals. Knowledge-intensive companies need to introduce systems for managing knowledge. Management consultancies have taken the lead in appointing knowledge officers and charging them with circulating ideas. Technology companies have appointed "gatekeepers" whose job is to keep their colleagues up to date with what is going on in the entire industry. Many companies have taken to appointing "mentors": senior workers whose job, like that of the prefects of old-fashioned British public schools, is to watch over the progress of younger workers.

Knowledge companies need to work particularly hard at becoming melting pots. They need to recruit different sorts of people and then mix those people together. Knowledge workers are as cliquish as any other groups of people, if not more so. Engineers look down on "creatives." "Creatives" make jokes about "geeks." McKinsey has been trying to recruit medical and arts graduates as well as identikit MBAs. Microsoft tries to throw together super-logical "bit heads" with artistically sensitive designers.

Pixar has probably done better than anybody at combining "hard" and "soft" management. The company has not only produced one animated hit after another, including *Toy Story* and *The Incredibles*; it has made a success of being taken over, revitalizing Disney rather than being crushed by it. Pixar has done this by upending Hollywood's conventional wisdom. Most studios buy scripts from independent script writers (the people you see hanging around cafés in West Hollywood and Venice Beach). Pixar creates all its own scripts. Most studios assemble temporary teams around projects. Pixar keeps a permanent staff of about 1,200 creative people. Pixar's people take a wide-ranging interest in the life of the company. Teams hold daily sessions to review works in progress. A Brains Trust of senior executive stands by to offer advice and to conduct formal reviews at various stages in the creative process. When a film is put in the can, Pixar holds a formal postmortem. In lesser hands this might degenerate into a predictable Hollywood frenzy of backslapping and air-kissing, but Pixar demands that each review identify at least five things that did not go well in the film, as well as five that did.

Pixar got the inspiration for this system from a surprising place—Toyota's system of lean production. For decades, Toyota has solicited constant feedback from workers on its production lines to minimize flaws. Pixar wants to do the same with producing cartoon characters. The system of constant feedback is designed to bring problems to the surface before they mutate into crises, and to provide creative teams with a source of inspiration. Directors are not obliged to act on the feedback they receive from others, but when they do, the results can be impressive. Peer review certainly lifted *Up*, a magical Pixar movie that became the studio's highest-grossing picture at the box office after *Finding Nemo*. It helped produce the quirky storyline of an old man and a boy who fly to South America in a house supported by a bunch of balloons.

The hardest thing for companies to do is also the most important: they need to be able to tolerate failure. It is impossible to come up with paradigm-breaking ideas without failing a few times in the process (Thomas Edison generated hundreds of versions of the light bulb before creating the one that changed the world). But most companies try to reduce waste and keep errors down to a minimum, and most successful people learn from an early age to please their masters by getting things right. Tata Motors has tried hard to give its employees the courage to fail. Ratan Tata even gives a prize for the best failed idea in the company's annual innovation competition. Josh Linkner has collected several examples of organizations that have tried to make people less risk averse: a medical company in Germany gives a "failure of the year" award; a software company in Boston gives its employees the equivalent of two "get out of jail free" cards a year; a math professor at an elite university awards 10 percent of his students' marks for making mistakes.[8]

The Innovation Machine

Managing knowledge may be the very devil, but it is relatively simple when compared with managing innovation. How do you turn clever ideas into successful products? How do you follow one successful product with another? And how do you make sure that your company seizes the next wave rather than being caught in the undertow of the last one?

The most fashionable approach to innovation at the moment might be dubbed the Linus Pauling approach, after the great man's advice that "the best way to have a good idea is to have lots of ideas." Companies are currently obsessed with stimulating the supply of ideas. No discussion of innovation is complete without a reference to Google's practice of allowing its workers to spend 30 percent of their time on their own projects (20 percent on ideas that extend the company's core business and 10 percent on fringe ideas). But many companies introduced this practice long before Google: 3M owes many of its 60,000 products, including Post-It notes, to its system of "bootlegging," and W. R. Grace ascribes its long record of innovation to "noodling."

Much newer is the fashion for looking outside the borders of the organization for your best ideas. There are lots of different buzzwords to describe this activity—co-creation (C. K. Prahalad), crowdsourcing (Jeff Howe), wikinomics (Don Tapscott), we-think (Charles Leadbeater)—but it rests on a simple insight: that "there are always more smart people outside your organization than in it," to quote Bill Joy, a former boss of Sun Microsystems.

The most surprising convert to this idea is Procter & Gamble, the consumer goods giant. P&G was traditionally one of the world's most inward-looking organizations, headquartered in one of America's most provincial cities, Cincinnati, and populated by some of its most buttoned-up company men, the "Proctoids." This model served it brilliantly for most of its history: Ivory, the "soap that floats"; Dreft, the first synthetic laundry detergent; Crest, the first fluoride toothpaste; Pampers, the first disposable diaper; Pert Plus, the first combined shampoo and conditioner—all were created deep within the bowels of the organization. But by 2000 the company was running out of steam. P&G lost half of its stock value between January and June of that year. *Ad Age* splashed "Does

P&G still matter?" on its front page. Dirk Jager left the CEO slot after a mere eighteen months on the job.

A. G. Lafley, P&G's new boss, was determined to let some sunshine into his company. He pledged to increase the proportion of products that came from outside the company from 15 percent to 50 percent, a revolutionary target. P&G forged closer relations with its suppliers. It charged seventy "technology entrepreneurs" with the job of acting as the company's "eyes and ears." It plugged itself into open networks such as Innocentive. Today the Proctoids boast about how they learned how to print trivia questions on Pringles by studying a small bakery in Bologna, Italy, and how they acquired the technology for producing wrinkle-free shirts from an academic who was working on polymers on behalf of the semiconductor industry.

Companies today routinely ask their suppliers and customers to supply them with ideas. Asda, a British subsidiary of Walmart, involves regular shoppers in developing and testing new products— "chosen by you," as the advertising jingle puts it. TCHO, a San Francisco–based chocolatier, hands out "beta editions" of its chocolate bars, in plain brown bags, to regular customers to see if they like them. Google puts ideas-in-progress online, such as Google City Tours and Google Mars, for customers to experiment with.

But why just get comments from your customers when you can go the whole way? Threadless, a T-shirt company, has outsourced most of its business to its customers. The company receives a thousand designs a week from volunteers. The 6,000-strong "Threadless community" votes on the designs. Minted does the same thing for high-end stationery. We can expect thousands of imitators in the future: the Threadless model is perfectly suited to an industry with low barriers to entry, large supplies of underemployed designers, and a limitless demand for nanosecond novelty.

Don Tapscott and Anthony Williams argue that "crowdsourcing" represents a new phase in business history: by radically reducing the costs of collaboration, the Internet is forcing companies to transform themselves from hierarchies (which point inward and upward) into networks (which point downward and outward). The Web reduces—and often obliterates—barriers to entry by giving amateurs access to world-class tools and worldwide markets; it makes it easy for large groups of people to collaborate; and it supercharges innovation: crowds of people can develop new ideas faster than isolated geniuses and disseminate new products faster than most companies.

The impact of wikinomics has been most extreme in the media industries. Why buy newspapers when you can get up-to-the-minute news on the Web? (America's remaining newspapers have lost one-quarter of their circulation since 2007.) And why buy the latest disc by Eminem when you can watch the great man perform on YouTube for free? The dominant model in both industries is changing dramatically, from one in which the elite produce content for passive consumers to one in which consumers expect to play a much more active role, as co-creators or active editors or ruthless commentators.

Wikinomics is also reaching some surprising industries The car industry is governed by the logic of scale and scope. But Jay Rogers, an Iraq War vet, has established a virtual company, Local Motors, that specializes in producing bespoke cars for enthusiasts. Local Motors "employs" a network of 4,500 designers (who compete to produce designs) and uses dozens of micro-factories (which purchase parts on the open market) to produce his roadsters. This could be a template for the future as 3-D printing—a technique that allows you to "print'" products by adding layer upon layer of materials—catches on.

Tapscott and Williams argue that companies need to rethink their business models if they are to take advantage of wikinomics. They need to adopt "open architecture"—that is, become platforms rather than walled gardens. They need to make their products "modular, reconfigurable and editable." And they need to abandon their hangups about intellectual property. Novartis, a Swiss drug maker, blazed a trail in 2007 when it posted its raw research data for type 2 diabetes on the Internet. The company grasped that it could speed up innovation and stimulate demand for its products by breaking with the industry's obsession with secrecy.

Though the Pauling approach has created a huge amount of excitement, some of it justified, it suffers from an obvious problem: you can end up with a mounting pile of undercooked ideas. Vijay Govindarajan and Chris Trimble point out that Google's policy of turning everybody into innovators can spread resources too thinly and indiscriminately. Companies dissolve into a thousand small initiatives rather than focusing on a few big problems. Crowdsourcing can be more trouble than it's worth. Managers have to spend weeks panning through the dirt in order to find a few grains of gold. They also discover that the crowds don't always have their best interests at heart: when Justin Bieber, a Canadian teenage pop star, asked his fans for suggestions as to what country he should visit next, the most popular answer was North Korea.[9]

One popular solution to the problem of oversupply is to use prizes to give crowdsourcing a focus and structure. The value of prizes being offered by corporations has more than tripled over the past decade, to $375 million.[10] Netflix offers a $1 million prize to anyone who can improve its film recommendation system by 10 percent. Frito-Lay offers prizes to people who can come up with new TV ads for its products. Indeed, prizes have become businesses in their own right: InnoCentive has created a network of

170,000 scientists who stand ready to solve R&D problems for a price. Regular users include some of the world's biggest companies, such as Eli Lilly, which helped to found the network in 2001; Boeing; DuPont; and P&G.

Another problem with the Pauling approach is more fundamental: companies can become a prisoner of their customers. Forging close relations with your customers might sound like an obvious business practice. But what if you want to change your customers? What if you want to move from low-value-added products to higher-value-added products? Companies that make a virtue of "co-creation" have discovered that customers can be a pain. Several companies, including Starbucks, Gap, and Tropicana, have been confronted with digital lynch mobs when they tried to change their logos. Lego cannot alter a minor feature of its sacred bricks without being vilified by Lego-heads.

The problem of relying on your customers for ideas is that customers are usually conservatives: they want more of the same for less money. The more you listen to your best customers, the more you are deaf to your noncustomers. You are pushed relentlessly into "mature" or niche markets and ignore the blue ocean that surrounds you. IBM ceded the personal computer to Microsoft because it was obsessed with its traditional customers. Detroit's big three were late entrants into the electric car market not because they ignored their customers but because they listened to them too much. Henry Ford would have spent his life producing ever more comfortable horse buggies if he had listened to the good burghers of Dearborn.

It is notable that Apple, perhaps the world's most successful high-tech company at the moment, and one that has kept ahead of every wave of innovation, has had no truck with open innovation. Steve Jobs is the closest thing Silicon Valley has to an imperial

CEO: egocentric, control-obsessed, and supremely self-confident. "A lot of times people don't know what they want until you show it to them," he says.[11] As well as solving problems that people don't know they have, Apple believes in doing as much as possible in-house. It is true that they have decided to allow outsiders to design apps for their iPhones and iPods, but they subject them to the strictest possible rules. Apple even adopts a top-down approach to PR, managing every detail of the news cycle and treating people who question the party line like heretics.

Big Is Beautiful

In 1942, Joseph Schumpeter performed one of the biggest about-turns in modern economics. The prophet of "creative destruction" had set the fashion for arguing that small companies are more innovative than big ones—indeed that they drive their triumphant chariots over the bodies of dead behemoths.[12] Then in *Capitalism, Socialism and Democracy* (1942), he announced that he had changed his mind and that big companies have the edge.[13] Big companies can use the resources from their cash cows to support new businesses. They can make long-term bets rather than constantly struggling to pay the bills. They can bring huge resources to bear on projects that they green-light. And they can bring the benefits of scale and scope to new ideas.

This about-turn is worth studying today. Hitherto, connoisseurs of innovation have been obsessed by scrappy startups—particularly by the scrappy startups that flock together in Silicon Valley and Israel. But a few brave souls are beginning to speak up for the big boys. In particular, Vijay Govindarajan and Chris Trimble have made the case in favor of big, established companies in some detail.

Govindarajan and Trimble argue that big companies have huge

advantages over small ones. They can invest more money in research and bring a wider range of skills together. This may be essential to solving huge problems, such as our overdependence on fossil fuels or shortages of clean drinking water. They can also bring new ideas to market much more quickly than small companies.

Govindarajan and Trimble argue that you can prevent big companies from losing their appetite for innovation so long as you recognize that innovation is unnatural. Established businesses are built for efficiency rather than innovation. Efficiency depends on predictability and repeatability—on breaking tasks down into their component parts and holding employees accountable for hitting their targets. By contrast, innovation is by definition unpredictable and uncertain. CEOs may sing a pretty song about innovation being the future, but in practice the heads of operational units will favor the known over the unknown.

Many would-be innovators deal with the tradeoff between efficiency and innovation by rejecting traditional management entirely. They repeat mantras about "breaking all the rules" and "asking for forgiveness rather than permission." They establish skunk works and mock the boring corporate types who write their paychecks. But again, this is counterproductive. Mocking the corporate establishment only encourages it to starve you of resources. And producing ideas in isolated skunk works ignores the basic reason for doing innovation inside big companies in the first place—using their superior resources to supercharge the process.

The best way to solve the problem, Govindarajan and Trimble argue, is to build dedicated innovation machines. These machines need to be free to recruit people from outside the company (by their nature, big companies tend to attract company men rather than rule-breakers). They also need to be free to adopt many of their own metrics. But they must avoid becoming isolated skunk works. Instead, these innovation machines need to be integrated with the rest of the company, able to draw on the wider company's resources and staff. And they need to be tightly managed according to customized rather than generic rules. For example, they should be held accountable for their ability to learn from mistakes rather than for their ability to hit their budgets.

There are plenty of examples of such innovation machines embedded in big companies. Harley-Davidson discovered that its storied brand loyalty could be a hindrance when it came to attracting new customers, so it established a new group to come up with ideas for attracting beginners, such as safety courses and rental programs. BMW realized that its established system for producing brakes might be a hindrance when it came to designing brakes for hybrid vehicles (which benefit from capturing wasted energy and putting it back to work), so it set up an innovation team in which battery specialists regularly talked to brake specialists. Allstate, an American insurance company, noted that insurers had come to accept widespread customer dissatisfaction as a fact of life, so it wondered what would happen if you asked marketers rather than risk adjustment specialists to design car insurance. They came up with industry-changing ideas such as accident forgiveness and cash rewards for good driving.

Govindarajan and Trimble ignore the fact that there are lots of different ways of becoming successful innovators. Buying can be more efficient than making: it is hard to imagine that Unilever would have come up with Chubby Hubby ice cream if it had not bought Ben & Jerry's. "Hobbyists" can generate industry-transforming ideas: George de Mestral invented Velcro after studying the burrs that he found stuck to his clothes after a hike. Linus Torvalds began Linux as a hobby. Some of the most successful modern "companies," such as Wikipedia, are little more than collections of hobbyists.

They also exaggerate the extent to which innovation can be planned and programmed. The essence of innovative ideas is that they are anarchic. They can take their creators by surprise in all sorts of ways—arriving by the back door rather than the front door, or turning up years after they said that they would. The idea of the tablet computer failed ignominiously in the 1990s with the Newton tablet, but was gloriously resurrected in 2010 with the iPad. Pixar started life making computer parts and only dabbled in animation as a sideline. Hewlett-Packard came up with the idea of pocket calculators only because Bill Hewlett wanted an "electronic slide rule" for his own use. Some inventions arrive by accident. Tea bags were first used as packaging for samples of loose tea. Microwaves were produced as the accidental by-products of radar systems.

Above all, Govindarajan and Trimble downplay the importance of what Clay Christensen, of Harvard Business School, has dubbed "the innovator's dilemma." In *The Innovator's Dilemma*, Christensen argues that innovation confronts established companies with an agonizing choice. If they defend their business models, they may be swept aside by the tides of change. If they embrace the new technology, they may saw off the branch that they are sitting on. In many ways, IBM was acting rationally when it tried to defend its established mainframe computer business against the PC. The same can be said for Xerox when it tried to defend its high-volume copying centers against the arrival of desktop copying machines—and, indeed, for old media companies as they try to defend their traditional profit centers—books in the case of the publishing industry and newspapers in the case of the journalism profession—against the Internet. The defensive strategy almost destroyed IBM and Xerox, and may have the same effect on media companies.

Dealing with Dilemmas

This is clearly a field that is destined to remain a mess and a muddle; there are too many exceptions to every rule and too many downsides to every upside. Still, there is arguably one clear principle emerging from the intellectual effort that is being devoted to the subject: that foxes beat hedgehogs. Innovation is coming from ever more places, from Shanghai as well as Silicon Valley and from the Red Cross as well as Red Bull. Innovation is also taking lots of different forms—from co-creation at Threadless to charismatic dictatorship at Apple and from expensive frippery at LMVH to frugal innovation at Tata. It is time to modify Linus Pauling a little: the best way to have a successful innovation strategy is to have lots of them.

10

Lords of Strategy

In the management gurus' world, one talent is prized above all others: the ability to predict and control the future. In the old days, witch doctors donned feathered headdresses, performed exotic gyrations, and sacrificed unfortunate animals. In return, tribal chiefs put luxurious huts and an inexhaustible supply of young virgins at their disposal. Naturally enough, the witch doctors did everything possible to protect the secrets of soothsaying from the curious gaze of outsiders or the critical questions of cynics.

Management gurus may not wear a feathered headdress or pore over the entrails of dead animals—at least not in public. But in their bid to predict and control the future, they have developed exotic-sounding techniques, such as SBUs, PIMs, PPBSs, and 3 × 3 matrices (to name only the most comprehensible); and they have kept those techniques as mysterious as possible, protected from the prying eyes of laymen by complicated mathematical formulas and labyrinthine diagrams.

Indeed, strategy has become an ever more confusing art. In the 1960s and 1970s, "strategic planning" was regarded as the very kernel of management science. Companies had entire departments devoted to it. "Strategic consultancies" made their living from it (and charged far more than the lowly "body shops" that offered merely operational advice). Since the 1980s, however, "strategy" has been in a state of constant flux. In uncertain times, when few businesses feel happy predicting their next month's profits, the idea of long-term planning strikes many managers as a little, well, socialist. Yet the appeal of having some goal to aim for—even a less attainable, more ephemeral one—remains. Strategy has thus been recast in new terms, most prominently as "vision." The question that will haunt this chapter is whether this is really an improvement.

Building the Planning Machine

The organization that was most susceptible to the claim that management theory can confer control over the future was the multidivisional firm that achieved its finest flowering in America in the 1960s and 1970s. Technically, the credit for putting planning at the center of corporate life should probably go to writers such as Igor Ansoff and Alfred Chandler, who both, in their different ways, spent the 1950s and 1960s insisting that all companies needed an overall corporate strategy. However, the trail had already been blazed by a familiar duo—Frederick Taylor and Alfred Sloan. By separating the performance of a task from its coordination, Taylor prepared the way for the arrival of a new class of professional strategic planners. At Sloan's General Motors, managers sitting in the corporate headquarters were responsible for crafting long-term strategy for the entire organization.[1]

Arguably, managers' fascination with planning goes even deeper than that of Sloan and Taylor. Managers have always fancied themselves as the officer class of the business world—the people who see the big picture and draw up the battle plans. Strategy is what separates them from the sergeants. Strategy departments are the closest thing that companies have to an officer's mess, and strategy consultancies like McKinsey and BCG are the closest thing that the business world has to cavalry regiments. There was often an explicit connection between the military and strategy. The American army embraced planning with a rare fervor in Vietnam: one of the architects of the U.S. policy of "strategic bombing" had been an architect of strategic planning at Ford in the 1950s, Robert McNamara. Meanwhile, in France, strategic planners tried to run the whole country, public as well as private.

Planning became an ever more complicated and time-consuming process as the theorists took over. Strategists spent months drawing up their plans and issued weighty manuals (such as GE's "blue books") to tell managers what to do. George Steiner (no relation to the equally verbose literary theorist) took almost eight hundred pages to explain the rudiments of planning in *Top Management Planning* (1969). Ten years later, in *Strategic Planning* (tellingly subtitled *What Every Manager Must Know*), Steiner even introduced a new phrase, the "plan to plan."[2]

The trouble with all this was that it produced diminishing returns. Planning degenerated into a pedantic annual ritual in which representatives of each department tried to grab as many resources as they could—and real strategic thinking flew out of the window. It also degenerated into a numbers game. The real substance of General Electric's round of meetings was about making the numbers add up rather than discussing the company's future. Elite opinion shifted decisively against strategic planning. Henry Mintzberg dismissed it as an oxymoron. Michael Porter complained that for the most part it had failed to contribute to strategic thinking. James Brian Quinn argued that a good deal of corporate planning was nothing more than a "ritual rain dance."[3]

From Planning to Strategy

Even as the old jalopy of strategic planning broke down in the mid-1960s, an altogether shinier new machine came roaring down the road—simply called "strategy." The difference between strategic planning and strategy is more than simply semantic. Strategists paid more attention to the overall competitive environment than did the planners. They worked for independent consultancies rather than for particular companies. And they used intellectual tools that were far more sophisticated than anything the planners would ever have dreamed of. Walter Kiechel describes strategy as the most powerful business idea of the past half century, and strategists as the shock troops of one of the great business revolutions, the intellectualization of business.[4]

The man who did more than anybody else to produce this shiny new machine was Bruce Henderson, an irascible contrarian who boasted that he was sacked from every job he held until he started his own company, the Boston Consulting Group. With Henderson at the helm, BCG invented a new form of consulting: rather than just cozying up to CEOs as McKinsey's had done, it focused on designing elegant intellectual models. The "experience curve" taught companies that they could reduce their costs as they expanded their market share, thanks to the accumulation of know-how. The "matrix" encouraged companies to view themselves not as an undifferentiated whole but as a portfolio of businesses that make varying contributions to the bottom line ("cash cows" versus "dogs," for example). A glance at the matrix could tell a manager whether to invest, harvest, or divest, depending on where his business fell on the chart.[5] Established consultancies cemented their relationships with their clients over a game of golf; BCG did it by sending them copies of *Perspectives*, a publication that explored the latest business ideas, or by holding business conferences.

This sort of thinking may be par for the course for business today, but it was revolutionary in the stagnant corporate world of the 1960s. Most American companies were complacent and inward-looking organizations, borne aloft by the great postwar boom and almost free from serious foreign competition. Two standard textbooks on strategy from the early 1970s had, respectively, two and four pages devoted to competition.[6] And most were resolutely anti-intellectual; these were still the days when big companies liked to hire "rounded" people who were more at home on the sports field than in the library.

BCG succeeded in putting the notion of competitiveness at the heart of business thinking. It also succeeded in persuading people that brains mattered: business was more than just the application of common sense and the glad hand. Henderson was a fierce evangelist for the twin causes of competition and brains. He divided BCG into two "teams" who were encouraged to go head to head against each other. He once took out an advertisement in a Harvard Business School newspaper proclaiming that BCG was interested in recruiting not "run of the mill" students but scholars—Rhodes Scholars, Baker Scholars, Marshall Scholars, the elite of the elite.[7] People who worked for BCG in its glory days recall it as being the most exciting place to be in the business world, a place where super-smart people were always debating the next big idea and looking for the next managerial breakthrough.

The 1980s and 1990s saw BCG's revolution institutionalized. McKinsey shook itself out of its intellectual torpor and began to make its own contribution to the strategic revolution. A group of young consultants and business professors began to take Bill

Henderson's ideas in new directions. Two children of the revolution deserve particular attention: Bill Bain and Michael Porter. Bill Bain, who left BCG and its increasingly irascible boss to form his own eponymous consultancy, changed the rules of consulting for the second time in a decade. He argued that, as well as applying brainpower to consulting work, consultants should form deeper relations with their clients, working closely with the managers for years, even taking a financial stake in the outcome of their advice.

Michael Porter, who has both an MBA from the business school and a PhD from the economics faculty across the river Charles, brought a rare degree of intellectual rigor to the study of strategy (alas, Porter's rigor was not accompanied by brevity). In his first book, *Competitive Strategy* (1980), he tried to plot a middle way between the very different philosophies that he had encountered at the economics faculty and the business school, arguing that there were both individual and general lessons to be learned about strategy. Thus, he studied individual companies but set them in the context of their relevant industries, and he outlined "generic strategies" but emphasized that different firms must choose different paths to success.

In his next book, *Competitive Advantage* (1985), Porter became more prescriptive, outlining generic strategies that firms could take. Before deciding on what strategy to pick, he argued, a firm needed to do a lot of homework. This included analyzing the "five competitive forces" that determine an industry's attractiveness (potential entrants, buyers, suppliers, substitutes, and competitors) and deciding what sort of industry it was (growing or declining, ripening or mature, and so on). Porter also argued that a company should think of itself not as a single unit but as a "value chain" of discrete activities (designing, producing, marketing, etc.).

This love of analysis explains why Porter became something of a god to strategists. Porter's work does not lend itself to one-line summaries; yet, underneath all his lists and copious examples, there is a fairly simple message. In essence, strategy is about making a choice between two ways of competing. One choice is market differentiation, competing on the basis of value added to customers, so that people will pay a premium to cover higher costs. The other choice is cost-based leadership, offering products or services at the lowest cost. Porter's data showed that firms with a clear strategy performed better than those that either lacked a clear strategy or that consciously tried to follow both paths and lead the way on price and quality.

The Importance of Science Fiction

The profusion of strategic thinking in the 1970s and 1980s inevitably brought intense scrutiny. Tom Peters and Robert Waterman argued forcefully that the obsession with strategy was leading managers to ignore the human side of their calling. Richard Pascale pointed out that the Japanese, who were then sweeping all before them, regarded the West's newfound passion for strategy as strange, much "as we might regard their enthusiasm for kabuki or sumo wrestling." Some gurus latched on to the rather tiresome metaphor of jazz improvisation (and, even more tiresomely, jazz musicians began to make appearances at management conferences). John Kao, a business professor and entrepreneur, argued that strategists should forget about modeling themselves on Herbert von Karajan and instead unleash their inner Charlie Parker. More importantly, an army of younger thinkers shifted attention to business processes (which could be reengineered) and "core competencies" (which needed to be cultivated).

Yet, in the end, this emphasis on "process" was unsatisfactory:

what is the point of tuning up your engine to perfection if you have no idea where you are headed? Even during the height of the reengineering craze, many companies continued to be committed to dreaming up "strategic visions"—grand views of the future that provided them with a general sense of mission without imposing the costs and constraints of central planning. Electronic Data Systems hired Disney alumni to help the company put together an exhibit demonstrating how information technology would reshape people's lives. Some leading businessmen, including Olivier Lecerf, former head of Lafarge, a large cement manufacturer, and Frank Carruba, the chief technology officer of Philips, took sabbaticals in order to reflect on the future. Shell continued to put great faith in "scenario planning," an elaborate exercise based on a simple question, "What if . . . ?" Even bosses who took the same dismissive attitude toward "the vision thing" as George Bush Senior have had to knuckle under. Lou Gerstner came into IBM declaring that the one thing that the computer giant did not need was another vision; by 1995, he had begun mumbling about "building a networked future."

The gurus who did more than anything else to give substance to this vague quest for vision were C. K. Prahalad and Gary Hamel, with *Competing for the Future*. The central claim of *Competing* is that the most important form of competition is the battle to create and dominate emerging opportunities. Traditional strategists looked on companies as collections of products and business units; Hamel and Prahalad argued that it is better to see them as collections of skills (or "competencies"). Traditional strategists tried to position their organization as cleverly as possible in existing markets; Hamel and Prahalad argued that a company should try to reinvent its whole industry by following a vision. Strategy is about disruption rather than adjustment, about changing the world rather than just understanding it.

In Hamel and Prahalad's view, the best way of dealing with an increasingly uncertain world is not to take refuge in short-termism but to imagine what the market will be like ten or more years hence and then try desperately to get there. The winners can reap benefits in numerous ways: by establishing a monopoly, however briefly, of a particular product (Chrysler with minivans, Sony with the Walkman); by setting standards or owning intellectual property rights (Matsushita with VCRs, Microsoft with DOS); or by establishing the rules of the game (Walmart with out-of-town hypermarkets). And the losers? The people who don't arrive at the future first? They are consigned to a perpetual cycle of downsizing.

Inventing the future is all very well (many of us do it every morning as we lie in bed). But how do you turn your inventions into reality? Prahalad and Hamel came up with two influential concepts. The first was "stretch"—trying to achieve huge gains without telling people how to get there. Traditional planning departments were preoccupied with engineering a tight fit between goals and resources; Hamel and Prahalad argued that strategy is about using a vision of the future to inspire workers to go that little bit further. This sort of ambition is most common in startups. (Tracy Kidder's gripping account of Data General, *The Soul of a New Machine*, shows how managers can happily impose eighty-hour workweeks and impossible deadlines if they can inspire their workers with a vision of greatness.) But big firms have also pulled off the same trick, especially in Japan. Toshiba told its employees to design a new VCR using half the number of parts and taking half the time at half the cost. A team was dispatched and the job was done.

Hamel and Prahalad's other concept was core competencies. For the strategy gurus, defining your core competencies is the first step in designing your strategy: Federal Express needs to under-stand what it is good at (logistics management) before choosing what it aims at (on-time delivery). Competencies also form the basis for the modern equivalent of portfolio management. If a firm knows what it is good at, it will venture only into new areas where its core skills can be applied to create new products, and it will buy only the companies that can add substantially to its portfolio of skills.

Prahalad and Hamel's view of strategy-as-vision and strategy-as-stretch has remained enormously influential. When Prahalad died prematurely in 2009, the obituaries rightly hailed him as probably the greatest management thinker of his generation. Nevertheless, critics quickly raised serious doubts about *Competing*. Take the idea of inventing the future. Have British high street banks improved their businesses by moving into high finance? Or French water companies by moving into multimedia? Hamel and Prahalad hardly strengthened their argument by focusing exclu-sively on companies that have bet on a possible future and won (Canon, Motorola, Microsoft, etc.). What about companies that had made the same bet and lost? As chairman of General Motors in 1981–90, Roger Smith, the inadvertent star of Michael Moore's *Roger and Me*, did everything right in Hamel and Prahalad's terms, dreaming of making GM "the car company of the twenty-first century" and spending billions to improve the company's techno-logical skills, but he still saw his company's share of the domestic market fall from 46 percent to 35 percent.

And are companies that invent the future really that much better off than the plodders who follow in their wake? Bill Gates did not invent many of the products that made him a billionaire; he simply packaged them brilliantly. Procter & Gamble did not invent the disposable diaper; that honor belongs to the inelegantly named and now defunct Chux. The Japanese did not invent the video re-corder; the real pioneer was an American firm called Ampex. Two academics, Gerard Tellis and Peter Golder, decided to study more than fifty consumer markets to compare the performance of pio-neers against imitators. They discovered that pioneers were leaders in only one in ten of the markets, and, on average, the current leaders entered the market thirteen years after the "first movers."[8]

Or take the idea of "strategy as stretch." Setting companies am-bitious goals sounds wonderful in theory: one imagines a team of cheery souls setting off together in search of their dream, watched over by a kindly servant-leader. But the reality could be very dif-ferent: exhausted workers, disoriented organizations, cut corners, and frazzled command-and-control systems. Gary Hamel did more than any of his critics to discredit *Competing* by choosing to celebrate Enron in the most extravagant terms possible in his next book, *Leading the Revolution*.

Through a Glass, Obliquely

The backlash against Enron's favorite management guru reinforced a broader backlash against the lords of strategy in general. How could gurus talk about "envisioning the future" when the Internet was compressing both time and space? And how could managers talk about planning for the future when their time on the job was shrinking? The "life expectancy" of American CEOs fell from ten years in 2000 to just over eight a decade later. Shareholders shifted in and out of stocks at five times the rate that they had in 1980.[9] Industries were becoming ever more turbulent even before the market crashed in 2007–08. The market crash turned turbulence into a tsunami. Jeff Immelt, General Electric's boss, likes to quote "the great philosopher" Mike Tyson on the subject of preparing for the future: "everybody has a plan till they get punched in the mouth."[10] The time between the punches has been getting progressively shorter since the 1960s, and the strength of the punches progressively greater.

Recently several management gurus have shaken up some of the basic categories of strategic thinking. John Kay, a British management writer, has argued that the best way to achieve our objectives is often the most indirect. The best way to achieve happiness, for example, is to set ourselves a demanding aim and achieve it (or as J. S. Mill put it in his autobiography: "Those only are happy who have their minds fixed on some object other than their own happiness . . . aiming thus at something else they find happiness by the way."). The indirect route is particularly valuable when the terrain is difficult or when human motivation is at a premium.

Kay argues that companies that set themselves oblique or indirect goals (such as looking after their workers) often outperform those that set themselves much more direct goals (such as boosting shareholder value). He has no shortage of independent studies to reinforce his point. In *Built to Last*, Jim Collins and Jerry Porras demonstrate that "visionary" companies that downplay profitability often turn out to be more profitable, in the long term, than those that put profitability at the heart of their priorities: look at HP versus Texas Instruments or Merck versus Pfizer. In *Firms of Endearment*, Raj Sisodia, David Wolfe, and Jag Sheth argue that companies that focus on adding value to society, such as Whole Foods, significantly outperform the S&P average. Indeed, Whole Foods' boss, John Mackey, specifically argues that profits are best pursued as a by-product of other things, such as service to customers and developing employees. Obliquity is particularly valuable when it comes to managing brainworkers. Tell a scientist that his work is aligned with the goal of shareholder value and you will be greeted with a shrug. Tell him that he can solve one of the most challenging problems in his field—and thereby win the esteem of his colleagues—and you will see his tail wag.

Other gurus have taken the opposite approach and tried to reduce strategy to a mere question of technology. Robert Kaplan and David Norton have argued that the crux of strategy is alignment (making sure that the parts fit together to support the whole). They have also produced a technology to advance alignment in the form of the balanced scorecard. The scorecard allows a company to measure how well it is doing from the point of view of its various constituencies (such as employees and shareholders) and then use those measurements to fine-tune the behavior of all the units that make up the organization.

There is no doubt that balanced scorecards are useful devices in the hands of skilled managers, just as maps are useful devices in the hands of good generals. But scorecards cannot produce grand strategies—or even good ones—any more than maps can. The good news is that there are lots of management thinkers who continue to operate on the mid-level between John Kay's philosophical games and Kaplan and Norton's technological reductionism. None of these gurus has captured the field in the way that Prahalad and Hamel did in the mid-1990s, but they are beginning to reorganize strategic thinking around three propositions.

The first proposition is that the most successful strategies are usually based on "platforms" rather than products. Look at the world's most successful companies and you soon discover that they have built platforms that provide two things: a launching pad for a succession of products and services, and a set of grappling hooks that attach them firmly to their customers. Google is using its mastery of search to provide everything from email (Gmail) to blogging (Blogger), and from Internet browsers (Google Crome) to mobile-phone operating systems (Android). (Robert Thomson, the editor-in-chief of the *Wall Street Journal*, has even compared Google to a tapeworm that feeds on "the intestines of the Internet.")[11] But the strategy is not confined to the IT business. Walmart and, on a smaller scale, Marks & Spencer weld their suppliers into their global supply chain. CVS and Walgreens are using their mastery of filling prescriptions (which demands knowledge of their customers' doctors and insurers) to expand into providing flu shots and other personal services.

Platform leaders are more difficult to dislodge than product leaders: Microsoft has been a much more consistent performer than Apple from the 1980s onward despite offering an inferior operating system. They can lock their clients into their orbits, making it expensive and inconvenient to shift to other platforms. They can benefit from network effects, growing more powerful with every new customer. And they can reap the rewards of innovations across an entire network of firms.

Platform-based strategies are subtly different from product-based ones. Managers need to think more about ecosystems than about products. This does not mean ignoring products entirely— companies that produce lousy products are unlikely to be able to tempt people to jump onto their platforms (and companies that produce a stream of excellent products, like Apple, can sometimes end up almost accidentally evolving into creators of platforms). But it means putting more emphasis on orchestrating relationships than on producing a constant stream of world-beating products.

The second proposition is that "pull" strategies can be as powerful as "push" strategies. Push strategies were at the heart of mass production: companies designed products, produced as many of them as they could on the basis of economies of scale, and then tried to sell them, sometimes going to extraordinary lengths to manufacture demand. Pull strategies are the very opposite of this: companies scan the market to see what is going on, adjusting their behavior accordingly. They put a premium on flexibility rather than forward planning, on listening to shop floor workers rather than kowtowing before the central staff, on Hayekian liberty rather than Fabian command and control.

Toyota introduced a version of pull in the 1970s: the company kept its inventories as low as possible and tried to produce cars just in time for the market. But pull strategies have become widespread with the spread of the Internet. Some companies mix pull and push strategies: many consumer product companies introduce prototypes into the market to see how they do before deciding whether to roll them out or roll them up. Other companies have gone much further in embracing pull: Li & Fung is essentially a network of ten thousand companies that can be brought on tap to respond to consumer demand.

The third proposition is that strategy needs to bubble up from the bottom rather than being imposed from the top down. This is hardly a new idea: in the 1990s, Nokia tried to make strategy a daily part of every manager's activity, and EDS involved over two thousand of its employees in its strategic-planning process. But it is gaining momentum. The Internet is making it imperative for even the lowliest workers to keep themselves plugged into the global market. The financial markets are putting constant pressure on companies to respond to changing circumstances. Eric Beinhocker, a senior fellow with the McKinsey Global Institute, argues that strategy is as much an evolutionary phenomenon as anything else: successful businesses, like successful species, emerge through a constant process of differentiation, selection, and amplification.[12] Agile companies, which constantly adapt their strategies to changing circumstances, are strikingly rare. General Electric is the only Forbes 100 company to have both survived and outperformed the market since 1917. Most existing businesses are far slower to adapt to their environment—to abandon old market niches and invade newer ones—than new businesses. "Companies don't innovate," says the erstwhile management consultant, "markets do."

It is not hard to think of objections to these three arguments. Platform strategies are undoubtedly attractive, but by their very nature only a handful of companies will be able to adopt them. Others will inevitably have to rely on coming up with winning products or colonizing unexpected niches. Push and emergent strategies clearly have their merits, but they share the same weakness: they are both about responding to the world rather than creating it. Henry Mintzberg, hardly a fan of strategic planning, pointed out that incrementalism could easily lead to paralysis: "organizations that reassess their strategies continuously are like individuals who reassess their jobs or their marriages continually—in both cases, people will drive themselves crazy or else reduce themselves to inaction." The greatest entrepreneurs do not simply respond to market signals; they create markets where none previously existed. The urge at the heart of strategic planning—the urge to survey the horizon and shape the future, to rise above the hubbub of daily business and push the world in a new direction—remains as powerful now as ever.

Down in the Engine Room

How much do all these theoretical gyrations affect flesh-and-blood business people? They certainly matter. Business people beat a path to BCG's door during the glory days of the experience curve. Two decades later they turned Prahalad and Hamel into business celebrities. But even as we follow the rise and fall of these business fashions we need to remember two things. The first is that the business of business goes on relentlessly: companies have to take a view of the future and allocate their resources accordingly, whatever the management gurus are saying. The second is that business people tend to be opportunists rather than slaves of the theoreticians: they take what they need from the gurus and then mix it according to their taste.

Alan Mulally has been one of the world's most successful CEOs since he moved into Ford's glass-walled headquarters in Dearborn, a suburb of Detroit, in 2006. He has not only succeeded in saving Ford from bankruptcy, the only one of the big three to claim the distinction; he has improved its reputation and boosted its profits. His approach to strategy-making is thoroughly eclectic—sometimes he sounds like one of George Steiner's old-fashioned strategic planners (though operating at warp speed) and sometimes he sounds like one of Eric Beinhocker's emergent strategists.

Mulally's signature management technique, one that he brought from his time at Boeing, is holding a weekly meeting that involves all the company's top brass, some sitting in the office in Dearborn, others joining by video conference, all of them relishing the war room atmosphere. The company's main operating data are projected on screens. Mulally painstakingly takes the executives through every line of figures. He interrogates them to make sure that the figures add up and debates with them about what they mean for the future. An engineer by training, Mulally likes to make his decisions on the basis of hard data rather than vague hunches. At the same time, he says that, in some ways, business people now take a longer view of the events than they used to. They try to peer far into the future—and to work out how demand for their products will change in the light of a complicated matrix of forces.

The lords of strategy will continue to flit from one idea to another. But demand for what they are selling—a chance not just to see the future but to shape it—will survive forever.

11

What Does Globalization Mean?

O f all the words in the management guru's lexicon, none is used with quite so much relish as "globalization." Step into any business conference and you hear it hanging on almost every sentence. Talk to the chairman of any big company and, before long, you find that it starts dominating the conversation. Since the turn of the century more than a thousand books on globalization have been published every single year, according to the Library of Congress, not a bad achievement for a word that was only coined in 1951.[1]

This obsession with globalization makes a lot of sense. Globalization is now the leading concern (some would say the raison d'être) of nearly every big multinational company: it affects where they have their offices and factories, what they make, and who they employ. It is also a growing concern for thousands of smaller firms. Today many startups are born global, and many humble mom-and-pop companies are becoming nodes in the global market.

The past decade has seen a succession of blows to global integration. The terrorist attacks of September 11, 2001, highlighted the dark side of integration. Osama bin Laden used one symbol of globalization—the jet airliner—to destroy another—the World Trade Center. The financial crisis of 2007–08 plunged the world into the worst recession since the 1930s. Banks collapsed, companies tottered, and the French president, Nicolas Sarkozy, pronounced the death rites of Anglo-Saxon capitalism.[2]

Yet, at this time of writing, it looks as if globalization is resuming its onward march, if a little unsteadily. Companies are more interested in emerging markets than ever. Rather than repeating the mistakes of the 1930s, Western governments intervened surgically and then retreated. Most ordinary people did not allow their disgust with the banking industry to spill over into fury with business in general. Indeed, the Pew Global Attitudes Survey for 2009 saw people in most of the world—including crisis-whipped countries such as Britain and the United States—becoming more positive about globalization rather than less.

It is possible that globalization has now become so much a part of the woof and weft of daily life that most people are loath to question it. Senior managers are as familiar with the business lounge of their local airports as with their own sitting room. Web surfers can communicate with people almost anywhere in the world at the press of a button. The world's ever-growing army of investors has its savings tied up with the global markets. (Remember Adam Smith's observation, in *The Wealth of Nations*, that, while "the proprietor of land is necessarily a citizen of the particular country in which his estate lies . . . the proprietor of stock is properly a citizen of the world, and is not necessarily attached to any particular country.") Shoppers expect to be able to buy fresh kiwi fruit in the depths of winter, regardless of environmental crisis or recession.

The idea that the world is getting smaller sounds like a simple one. Yet management theory has complicated it in two ways. The first problem is with definition. For all its ubiquity, "globalization" has no single meaning. One moment globalization can refer to a borderless advertising campaign and the next, to an organizational matrix that is supposed to draw attention to national differences. Globalization is not so much a coherent idea as a fuzzy feeling. This might matter less were the second problem not one of exaggeration. For the three ideas that people have most often plucked out of this cloud—that globalization would usher in an era of standardized global products; that big, global companies would sweep all before them; and that geography and politics would be rendered irrelevant—have all been shown to be myths.

Tom Friedman has stamped his brand onto the idea that "the world is flat." But, in fact, the best modern starting point for this debate is an article that was published almost thirty years ago by Theodore Levitt, "The Globalization of Markets."[3] Levitt, Harvard's most respected marketing guru, argued that technology was creating "a new commercial reality—the emergence of global markets on a previously unimagined scale of magnitude." The world would be dominated by standardized products and universally appealing brands such as Coca-Cola. Christians and Hindus might worship different gods, but they still have to wash their hair—and want the best product to do the job. Global companies that ignored "superficial" regional and national differences and exploited economies of scale by selling the same things in the same way everywhere would soon displace not only small local companies but also old-fashioned multinationals that spent all their time trying to be "respectful" of local peccadilloes. "The earth is round," argued Levitt, anticipating the title of Tom Friedman's best-seller, "but, for most purposes, it's sensible to treat it as flat."

This future—where gigantic firms bestrode Levitt's flattened world like so many colossi, run by global managers, organized according to global rules, and making a point of boasting about their global aims, such as putting a soft drink within arm's reach of every man, woman, and child on the planet—was exactly the sort of thing that many managers had dreamt about for years. After all, what was the point of being a big company if you could not defy geography? One of the first serious studies of multinationals, written by Raymond Vernon in 1971, was called *Sovereignty at Bay*. Carl Gerstacker, sometime chairman of Dow Chemical, confessed that "I have long dreamed of buying an island owned by no nation and of establishing the world headquarters of the Dow company on the truly neutral ground of such an island, beholden to no nation or society." Dr. Evil could not have put it better.

Levitt's argument has hardly stood the test of time (though this has not prevented lesser figures from repeating it). True, there are a few big-ticket items, such as jumbo jets, that are made for the world market. And true, there are a few niche products, such as Burberry raincoats and Cristal champagne, that appeal to rich people the world over. But they are the exceptions: in the broad consumer market a succession of surveys have shown that there are only a few truly global brands, such as Coca-Cola, McDonald's, and Marlboro, and that even this select handful do not mean the same thing in, say, Beijing (where they are all status symbols) that they do in Baltimore (where they are just part of the general detritus of life).

Those companies that adopted Levitt's "flat earth" strategy usually came to regret it. In the 1980s, Coca-Cola's boss, Roberto Goizueta, instituted an aggressive policy of centralization and standardization. Surely, Coca-Cola could ride triumphantly over local differences? And surely global economies of scale could be used to get that product down as many gullets as possible? The strategy proved to be a short-term success but a long-term failure. Coca-Cola grew dramatically under Goizueta, but it ran out of steam under his successors, who embraced localism with a vengeance.

In the mid-1990s, Ford launched an ambitious plan to build a one-size-fits-all company under the slogan "Ford 2000." The American carmaker abolished a score of separate national units in Europe and North America and replaced them with five product teams, some of them headquartered in Europe. But it soon turned out that the problem with producing world cars was that there was no archetypical world consumer to buy them: in particular, American consumers were much keener on buying big cars than Europeans—partly because they wanted more space for their big bodies, but partly because gas was 40 percent cheaper in the States than in Europe.

There are two simple reasons for the failure of this flat-earth strategy. The first is that reports of the death of distance are exaggerated. Pankaj Ghemawat, of IESE Business School in Barcelona, conjures up a series of striking figures to support his contention that we live in an era of semi-globalization rather than globalization. People who talk dismissively of "snail mail" might not be too surprised to learn that only 1 percent of the world's physical letters cross national boundaries. But what about telephone calls? Less than 2 percent of calling minutes are international. Or Internet traffic? Less than 20 percent of the most global form of communication the world has ever devised crosses national borders.[4] Or globe-trotting business people? Only 1 percent of U.S. companies have any foreign operations whatsoever.[5] Millward Brown, a market research company, has produced a database of 10,000 brands across thirty-one countries. Only 329 brands of the world's top 10,000—3 percent of the total—are recognized in more than seven countries, and only 16 percent are recognized in two or more countries. Or global citizens? Overseas students account for 2 percent of all students, and international tourists make up only 10 percent of all tourists. Global exports account for less than 20 percent of the world's gross domestic product. Foreign Direct Investment accounts for an average of 10 percent of all fixed investment over the past decade.[6] If these figures underestimate the impact of global markets—globalization works its magic by the mere threat of competition—they are striking nonetheless.

The second reason is that tastes continue to vary dramatically from place to place. Britons are almost alone in loving Marmite (Unilever, which owns the brand, markets it under the slogan "love it or hate it") and the French are unusual in their penchant for eating frogs and snails. Most of the world's population worship at the altar of soccer—but Americans persist in worshipping their own peculiar game. Western commentators were appalled by Michael Jackson's alleged habit of whitening his skin—but skin-whitening creams are a billion-dollar business across Africa and Asia.

It is striking how many of the world's great companies have abandoned the conceit that the world is flat. Two-thirds of Coca-Cola's products in Japan, its most profitable foreign market, are unknown elsewhere, including Real Gold, a hangover cure, and Love Body, a tea that is supposed to increase bust size. Walmart sells crocodiles and frogs in the food section of its stores in China. P&G produced a bikini version of its Pampers brand for the Indian market because it is more comfortable in the heat and humidity.[7] The humble and delicious Kit-Kat bar (which was invented by Rowntree in York, England, in the 1930s and is now owned by Nestlé) comes in different flavors to suit the palates of the Japanese, Germans, Australians, Canadians, and Americans.[8]

Companies have been furiously adapting themselves to local tastes. MTV started life as a global company believing that "A-lop-bop-a-doo-bob-alop-bamboom" means the same thing in every language. Today it puts the call to prayer on its Indonesian channel five times a day. Mattel tried to break into the Japanese toy market with the same big-breasted blondes that had proved so successful in America. Sales took off only when the doll's local distributor reduced the size of Barbie's breasts and replaced her blond hair with brown.

Companies that fail to adapt to local tastes can face ridicule as well as poor sales. Pepsi-Cola renamed 7-Up for the Shanghai market because it discovered that the phrase sounded like "death through drinking" in the local dialect. Electrolux raised guffaws in the United States when it sold its vacuum cleaners under the slogan "nothing sucks like an Electrolux." Kona Coffee did disastrously in Portugal when it first ventured into the market because *cona* is a vulgar name for a vagina.

McDonald's is every lazy academic's favorite example of an imperial multinational, smothering local cultures under an ooze of processed cheese and ketchup. In fact McDonald's has made numerous concessions to local culture. In Japan, the company stumbled until it allowed a local entrepreneur to set up small stores in places like Tokyo's Ginza, rather than the large suburban stores favored by the parent company; he also ensured that burgers were made with local meat, which is much fattier than that favored in America, and provided local condiments. McDonald's sells vegetarian McAloo Tikki Burgers in India (and even provides home delivery), spaghetti burgers in the Philippines, porridge burgers in Malaysia, rice burgers in Taiwan, and burgers with chile peppers and hot sauce in Mexico. Even New Zealand gets a Kiwiburger with beetroot. Ronald McDonald celebrates the Chinese New Year in Hong Kong, quaffs wine in France, and goes under the name Donald rather than Ronald in Japan, because the Japanese have difficulty in pronouncing "r"s. Marketers are becoming obsessed with segmenting customers into micro-markets, using the wealth of data provided by checkout scanners, credit card receipts, and loyalty programs. Companies can produce niche products for Asian Americans, for example. They can also sell the same products in different ways to different groups of consumers (Britain's *Viz* magazine, with its fat slags and foul-mouthed yobs, is sold as a comic magazine in the south of the country but as an upmarket style guide in the north). The West is relatively simple compared with, say, India, where there are seventeen major languages, 844 different dialects, and eight religions, or even China, where the citizens of Shanghai live in a different century from the peasants in the countryside.

The second major problem with Levitt's argument is that it is often small companies rather than global giants that have reaped the biggest rewards from globalization. The debate about the merits of size is a complicated one, but it is clear that globalization frequently makes it easer for small companies to spread their wings. Small companies are finding it easier to purchase computer power (thanks to Moore's law) or to borrow serious money (thanks to the deregulation of the banks) or to learn how to manage themselves better (thanks in part to the commoditization of management ideas). Big companies are finding some of their old defenses crumbling, such as their expensively cultivated relations with governments or their long-nurtured knowledge of local regulatory quirks. Ghemawat calculates that the level of concentration in eleven key industries, including the capital-intensive car industry, has actually fallen since the late 1990s.[9]

At the same time, closer inspection reveals that multinationals are often much less multinational than they seem. They recruit their top people from their home turf. In 2008 only 14 percent of the CEOs of *Fortune*'s five hundred's biggest global companies were born abroad, and only 7 percent of directors of America's S&P 500 companies were foreign nationals. A striking number of multinationals focus on their own back gardens. American firms invest in Central and South America, the Japanese in a handful of Asian countries, particularly China, and European firms in other European countries. Some modern management techniques are reinforcing regionalization: the fashion for minimizing stocks and delivering supplies on a need-to-use basis means that suppliers need to be located as close as possible to their clients.

How Much Does Politics Matter?

This brings us to another common misunderstanding about globalization: the idea that globalization is marginalizing the nation-state and consigning politicians to the trash can of history.

This idea has plenty of support among management gurus. Kenichi Ohmae has published a succession of books hammering home the argument, such as *The Borderless World* (1990) and *The End of the Nation State* (1995). (For all his celebration of "borderlessness," Ohmae's fame depended on his ability to explain America to Japan and Japan to America.) The left has also jumped on the "borderless" bandwagon. Naomi Klein and various "Kleinians" like Noreena Hertz have long argued that the world's biggest multinational companies are bigger than all but a handful of nation-states.[10] These multinational giants are the real masters of the universe, the argument goes; governments are mere playthings by comparison, constantly adjusting their policies to attract foreign investment and to prevent domestic companies from fleeing abroad.

These arguments have a superficial plausibility. Globalization is persuading some national governments to lower trade barriers and create regional trading blocks (most notably in the European Union). It is also teaching people more about one another. But superficial is the right word. The defeat of Communism has left us with plenty to argue about—whether it be Islamic radicalism or American imperialism. Nation-states are arguably on the march once again after a period of consolidation in the twentieth century.

There is more to this than just resistance to globalization. Michael Porter has demonstrated in rich detail that companies owe a great deal of what makes them tick to these national differences. In *The Competitive Advantage of Nations* (1990), he argued that different countries (and regions) have different competitive strengths: the Germans excel at high-quality engineering and chemicals, the Japanese at miniaturization and electronics, the British at pop music and publishing, the Americans at films and computers. A German engineering firm will not necessarily become any better at engineering if it becomes less Germanic and more global, or an English advertising company better at advertising if it becomes less English; indeed, a company needs to retain its local roots if it is to find good recruits and suppliers or, more importantly, to remain in daily contact with challenging competitors.

Geographical differences matter at a local as well as a national level. Alfred Marshall once remarked, in an analysis of steelmaking in Sheffield, that certain skills seemed to be "in the air" in some regions. Some of these centers of excellence are familiar: Silicon Valley in computing, the Prato region of northern Italy in fashion and design, Hollywood in filmmaking. Others will become familiar in coming years. In an increasingly mobile world, such places represent stubbornly immobile resources: their skills are too bound up with the local culture to be easily copied elsewhere. Nobody has yet tried to build a cheaper Hollywood.

Far from contemptuously ignoring these geographic irritations, multinationals now bow down before them. Witness the number of electronics firms from around the world that have an outpost in Silicon Valley. Witness the way firms that already have roots in centers

of excellence are digging deeper, supporting schools, funding charities, and so on. And witness the way that companies are moving
responsibility for particular product lines to particular centers of
excellence. DuPont has moved its electronics-related businesses to
Japan, Siemens has moved its air traffic management to Britain, and
Hyundai its personal computer business to the United States.

This brings us to the final myth about globalization: the idea
that politics is dead (or at least irrelevant from business's point of
view). Business people like to believe that they live in a rational
world of profit and loss and comparative advantage. They are also
reluctant to engage in "political" debates, because such debates
threaten to alienate potential customers. Better to mouth bland
banalities and let the cash registers ring than engage in serious argument and risk putting off a potential customer.

In fact, politics is an omnipresent force in business life. The
proportion of GDP consumed by the state, which remained huge
even during the supposed era of free-market dominance in the
1980s and 1990s, has been rising in the past few years: it exceeds 50
percent in Britain as well as several other European countries. Politicians continue to lord it over businessmen despite the liberating
impact of the Internet. In 2000, the French government successfully prevented Yahoo! from selling Nazi memorabilia. In 2006,
the U.S. government banned online gambling. In 2010, Google
closed its server in China, after years of squabbles with the Chinese
authorities, and diverted local traffic to another server in Hong
Kong. Technological advance has sometimes played into the hands
of national governments rather than freewheeling business people:
governments have become ever more adept at using technology to
build "cyber-walls" and to identify "miscreants."

Companies are arguably more vulnerable to political risk than
at any time since the Second World War. Dick Cheney once

remarked that "the Good Lord did not see fit to put oil and gas only where there are democratically elected regimes friendly to the United States." It might be added that the Good Lord did not see fit to put economic growth in equally desirable places. The Arab spring demonstrated that emerging markets are rife with political risks—weak legal systems, makeshift institutions, volatile cities, and fragile regimes.

A growing number of countries, including not just China but also Russia and the Gulf states, are using business as an instrument of state power. Some of the world's biggest companies, including most of the largest oil firms, are run by politicians and their lackeys rather than ordinary business people. China routinely uses state companies to snap up natural resources. It also uses the state-industrial complex to pursue political goals—sometimes quite spiteful ones, as when it imprisoned four Rio Tinto executives on the slimmest of excuses. China is not alone: BP's partnership with Rosneft, Russia's state-controlled oil giant, to develop Russia's Arctic region has been complicated, from the first, by murky political considerations.

Political risks can bite Western companies where it hurts most, at home, thanks to growing vigilance about corruption. The Obama administration is enforcing the Foreign Corrupt Practices Act with an evangelical zeal—and employing techniques once reserved for fighting organized crime. The British government has introduced even tougher anti-bribery measures. Executives who adopt what they regard as local rules in Thailand or Indonesia on the assumption that politics no longer matters could find themselves facing long prison sentences back home.

But we should beware of thinking of politics purely in terms of risks: the financial crisis taught us that governments can provide security as well. It was only the coordinated action of various governments that saved the financial system from complete collapse. And it was only the vigorous priming of the public spending pump that kept demand buoyant when businesses and consumers were too nervous to spend. Far from rendering governments irrelevant, globalization has reemphasized their importance, as the only organizations that can cope with the crises and contagions that have been raging through the global economy with increasing frequency.

The Transnational Corporation

By now it should be clear that globalization does not entail a lot of things that are popularly associated with it—the triumph of giant companies, the eclipse of local differences, or the omnipresence of global products. But this does not mean that globalization is meaningless. The forces that are driving it—falling trade barriers, the ability to move ideas, people, and money around the globe with ever-increasing speed—are real enough even if they are not manifesting themselves in quite the way grand simplificateurs imagine. Companies may have launched a legion of dumb business strategies in the name of globalization, but nothing is as dumb as ignoring the phenomenon in the first place.

The trick is to get the balance between global scale and local relevance right. A firm that can leverage global resources without losing sight of local differences, that can exploit economies of scale but also plug into local centers of excellence, that can put, say, Japanese experts in miniaturization with Italian designers with American money-men, will be a mighty force indeed.

How can you construct such a fabulous creature? Business gurus and practitioners have provided numerous answers to this question over the past two decades, but three answers stand out as particularly coherent.

One answer is the "the transnational corporation," a phrase coined jointly by Christopher Bartlett of Harvard Business School and Sumantra Ghoshal of the London Business School. The transnational corporation is a tidying-up process. For most of the twentieth century, big companies were loose affiliations of national firms that happened to share the same name. Companies such as Ford and Unilever originally dealt with the problems of high tariffs, prohibitive transport costs, and stringent local-content rules by making clones of themselves in all the countries where they operated, with their own head offices, design facilities, and production plants. This was extremely expensive at the best of times. At one point, Ford had two Escorts on the road, which had been designed and built entirely separately.

Transnational companies try to do two things: abolish unnecessary duplication and bring national resources to bear on local problems. TNCs fold old-fashioned national headquarters into regional or even global headquarters. They also give national subsidiaries responsibility for global products or global functions, partly to disperse decision making throughout the organization and partly to capture local expertise. For instance, Nestlé has put the headquarters of its pasta business in Italy; Johnson & Johnson has given its German subsidiary a worldwide mandate for tampons.

Many TNCs are engaged in a constant internal tug-of-war between the principles of globalism and localism (or, more precisely, between managers who see their future in expanding the power of the center and those who see their future in expanding the power of the periphery). These civil wars can be so bruising that it is tempting to ask, Why bother? Why continue with the pretense that firms are integrated units? Why not just break them up into their component parts?

The answer is that TNCs are usually more than the sum of their parts. TNCs can mix and match skills from around the world. They can also use their size to cut through the global hubbub and cut down on costs (OC&C, a London-based consultancy, calculates that it costs 36 percent less for a "recognized" brand to persuade a customer to try a new product than for an unfamiliar brand). McDonald's global team of construction specialists can erect a new restaurant out of modular parts in as little as eleven days—and for two-thirds the cost of standard construction. The company's global purchasing scheme can save hundreds of millions of dollars a year by driving a hard bargain with suppliers.

A second answer to the question of how to construct a winning company is "the globally integrated enterprise," a phrase coined by Samuel Palmisano, the boss of IBM. Palmisano says that globally integrated enterprises are as different from the multinationals of the 1970s as those multinationals were from the great trading companies of the seventeenth century. They are not mere tidying-up operations like TNCs but new kinds of organizations.

For Palmisano, the globally integrated enterprise is a company that fashions its strategy, its management, and its operations in pursuit of a radically new goal: the integration of production and value delivery worldwide. Sensible multinationals no longer see themselves as a federation of national firms that couple together in order to create economies of scale and scope. Instead, they see themselves as an array of specialized components—procurement, manufacturing, research, sales, and distribution—all of which are organized on a global scale.

The signs of this corporate evolution can be seen everywhere, he says. Look at emerging markets. Between 2000 and 2003, foreign firms built 60,000 manufacturing plants in China. Look at the ever-growing legion of companies, such as Industrial Light and Magic and International Flavors & Fragrances, that perform

highly specialized functions on a global scale. Or look at Palmisano's own company, IBM. A company that was once synonymous
with command-and-control has been devolving authority as well
as blurring boundaries. IBMers are expected to work with their
peers across the global organization rather than constantly referring their decisions to IBM's headquarters in Armonk, New York.

Palmisano has been a notably successful boss, but his argument
begs lots of questions. What about political risk? Companies that
think about nothing other than the "logic" of global production
blind themselves to political risk. And what about the human
side of business? Managers can easily get carried away with the
pure mathematics of designing global companies—with the formidable challenges of balancing products against geographies and
centralization against localization—but they will fail abysmally if
they forget the human side of management. Look at virtually any
failed globalization strategy and you will find a human drama at
its heart. People from London regard their Frankfurt counterparts
as second-rate oafs; people from São Paulo feel that New Yorkers
ignore their knowledge of local markets . . . these are the sorts of
human dramas that shape globalization as much as the logic of size
and scale.

These various global companies—from old-fashioned multi-
locals to newfangled one-world companies—all have one thing in
common: they were designed in the West by Western managers on
the basis of Western assumptions. But the age of Western imperialism is coming to a close, in multinational companies as in everything else. The emerging world is producing a growing number of
plucky multinationals. These multinationals are not only challenging Western incumbents for markets, talent, and capital; they are
also challenging some of their most cherished notions of how companies ought to organize themselves. They are far more diversified

than Western companies and far more deeply involved in the life of society. A decade or so ago, most management thinkers would have confidently argued that these "immature" multinationals would one day grow into "mature" multinationals on the Western model, but now it seems more reasonable to argue that they are likely to preserve many of their distinctive features. It is perhaps fitting to end a chapter on globalization with a detailed look at a company that, not that long ago, was assumed to be a "victim" of globalization rather than one of its greatest beneficiaries.

Tata for Now

Tata is one of the world's biggest companies—or rather, a collection of some of the world's biggest companies. Imagine if Ford, IBM, U. S. Steel, Coca-Cola, Dow Chemical, and Hilton Hotels were rolled into a single family business and you get an idea of the scope of the empire in India. Tata Consulting Services (TCS) is Asia's largest software company. Tata Steel is India's largest steelmaker and ranks number ten in the world. Tata Power is the country's largest private electricity company. Tata Global Beverages is the world's second-largest maker of branded tea. Overall, the group earned 3.2 trillion rupees, or $67.4 billion, in revenues in 2009–10, and 82 billion rupees in profits.

Ratan Tata has transformed Tata. When he became chairman in 1991, India was groaning under the License Raj and Tata seldom ventured outside its home market. Today, as he prepares to step down in late 2011 and the search for a successor speeds up, India is one of the world's most dynamic economies and Tata operates in more than eighty countries.

Ratan Tata's enthronement in Bombay House, the group's headquarters, took place just before the liberalization of India's economy, an event that Indian business people habitually call the country's second independence. He perceived liberalization as both an opportunity and a threat. It was an opportunity because it set the business free: the economy had been so tightly regulated that you could be fined or even imprisoned for exceeding your output quotas. It was a threat because Tata was vulnerable, its companies uncoordinated, overmanned, and undermanaged.

Tata set about streamlining with a vengeance. He focused the group on six industries that have provided most of the group's revenues since 2000: steel, motor vehicles, power, telecom, IT, and hotels. He reined in over-mighty barons, sold off marginal companies such as soap and cosmetics, and insisted that subsidiaries could use the Tata brand only if they conformed to the highest standards.

The group also embraced globalization. Tata acquired a succession of iconic Western brands—starting with Tetley Tea in 2000 for $450 million and including Tata Steel's purchase of Corus, Europe's second-largest steel company, for $12.1 billion in 2007 and Tata Motors' purchase of Jaguar Range Rover (JLR) for $2.3 billion a year later. In all, Tata spent some $20 billion buying foreign companies. Today it earns about three-fifths of its revenue abroad, employs more British manufacturing workers than any other company, and lists two of its biggest companies, Tata Motors and Tata Communications, on the New York Stock Exchange.

The changes have been dramatic. A group that used to be identified with secure employment ("for shoes there's Bata and for jobs there's Tata" goes an old Indian saying) has become obsessed with serving customers and matching international standards. Tata Steel has more than doubled its output since 1994 (from three million tons to 64 million) while cutting its workforce in India by more than half (from 78,000 to 30,000). A jaunty self-confidence has replaced the self-doubt of the early 1990s. Yet Tata's changes have gone only so far. That is partly because of caution and reverence for tradition, but also because there is a logic behind the group's diversity.

E Pluribus Plura

In Jamshedpur, men in thick denim shirts and hard hats watch as molten steel is poured from a gigantic ladle. In Mumbai, Bombabes in exquisite saris serve some of the best food in India. In Pune, PhDs from MIT and various IIT Indian Institutes of Technology feed data into one of the world's most powerful privately owned supercomputers. They are all part of the Tata Group's global workforce of more than 395,000 people.

For all the frantic restructuring, the group remains strikingly diversified by global standards: ninety-eight operating companies, twenty-eight of them listed on the Bombay Stock Exchange, work in a bewildering range of industries. It is bound together by complicated interlocking structures: various central bodies (such as the Tata trusts and Tata Sons) hold shares in the companies. But above all it is held together by a common culture. Employees love to talk of how Tata got the better of the British overlords. They also love to point out that Tata created many of India's greatest institutions, such as the Indian Institute of Science and the Tata Institute for Fundamental Research. The reverence for Jamsetji Tata, the company's founder, whose garlanded bust can be found in most offices, borders on ancestor worship.

Tata prides itself, above all, on its corporate social responsibility. Tata charitable trusts own two-thirds of the holding company, Tata Sons. Alan Rosling, a former Tata executive who spearheaded the company's globalization, liked to say that "we're making money so that our shareholders can give it away." But the commitment to CSR goes deeper than this.

Consider Jamshedpur, the home of Tata Steel and perhaps the world's most successful company town. Tata Steel runs almost all the city's institutions: a 980-bed hospital; a zoo; a giant sports stadium; academies for football, archery, and athletics; golf courses; and the local utility company, among many others. The company also employs 250 people to work with local tribespeople, to improve agriculture, healthcare, and education, and regularly sends a hospital train even farther into the hinterland. Tata Steel gently mocks all this corporate philanthropy with the slogan "We also make steel."

The Tata Group inevitably provoked criticism as it strode out onto the international stage. How can it make sense to own both luxury hotels and chemical plants? But Tata executives, who might once have been stung by such criticisms from the West, now swat them aside. They treat a visiting journalist from the stricken West to long lectures about India's extended families. But they also claim support from management thinkers such as Tarun Khanna of Harvard Business School and Jim Collins. Khanna points out that diversified companies make eminent sense in underdeveloped countries where markets are fragmented, skilled labor is in short supply, and trust is at a premium. The group's size not only improves its chances of grappling with bureaucracy and filling various institutional voids but also helps it wage two of the hottest wars in modern India, for talent and trust. Tata can compete with Western talent-magnets such as General Electric and McKinsey (a place in the Tata Administrative School is one of the most coveted prizes in a prize-obsessed nation). In the 2010 BrandFinance Global 500, a ranking of the world's most valuable brands, the Tata name was reckoned to be worth $11.2 billion. Even the twin strategy of advancing at both the bottom and the top end of the market makes sense: it is hard to dismiss Tata as a "cheap" company when it also owns luxury hotels and fancy consultancies.

Collins argues that "culture" is one of the corporate world's most valuable resources; many of the "great" Western companies that he studies have an equally marked propensity for ancestor worship. Tata's reputation for probity has helped to insulate it from India's endemic corruption. It has also guided its behavior when standards have slipped: when the company discovered widespread irregularities in Tata Finance in 2001–02, it blew the whistle on itself.

Tata's diversified structure has given it a valuable mixture of flexibility and deep pockets. Its companies have been able to seize opportunities, such as Tata Steel's takeover of Millennium Steel or Tata Motors' joint venture with Marcopolo, a Brazilian bus manufacturer. Bombay House provides Tata companies with clout when they want to make ambitious acquisitions (Tetley was twice the size of Tata Tea) or when the market turns against it (as it did shortly after the ambitious Corus and JLR purchases).

A profile in *Fortune* in 2002 characterized Tata as both "one of India's most beloved companies" and "a mess." The latter is clearly wrong. But Tata will be held to much higher standards as it competes with the world's best. Its future success will depend on its ability to answer two questions. Can it use its muscle to become a master of innovation? And can it become a truly global company rather than just an Indian company that does good business abroad?

Ratan Tata's mission in his final years as chairman has been to foster innovation. He is focusing innovation on two levels. At the high end, Tata Chemicals is conducting research in nanotechnology and food science, and TCS holds regular innovation conferences in Silicon Valley. But what has captured people's imaginations is the company's commitment to "frugal innovation"—new products that are designed to appeal to the poor and the emerging middle class.

When it comes to globalization, Tata continues to face serious problems. One is the parochialism that afflicts big countries (and companies): the upper management is still dominated by Indians who know life only within Tata. A second is hubris. Tata is more inclined to celebrate the great pruning of the 1990s than to ask whether another is due. Still, these problems are not likely to hold it back, particularly given its ability to learn from its mistakes. Tata has a better chance of negotiating Western markets than Western companies have of picking their way through India's convoluted business terrain. Tata has also crafted a strategy that could power it growth for years: producing a stream of innovative products that will both cater to the rising masses of the emerging world and shake up markets in richer places.

12

Storm in the Boardroom

For all the flannel about "empowerment," management theory remains obsessed with the boardroom. It is the people in the boardroom who decide which way the company should be headed, and it is the people in the boardroom who decide which pedals to push. The world's bosses have taken a disproportionate share of the productivity gains of recent years. They have also taken the lion's share of the blame for corporate disasters.

The boardroom is the focus of three of the sharpest debates in management theory. First: What are companies for? To enrich their shareholders, or to please all their stakeholders? Second: Is there a single best way of organizing companies, or are there lots of viable corporate models? And third: How much should bosses be paid for their efforts? Are they "grotesquely overpaid," as most people believe, or are we getting it just about right? The boardroom is also the focus of one of the fuzziest debates. What is leadership? Are leaders born or made? Can leadership be taught? Is the nature of leadership changing in our demotic age? Do companies need a leadership elite anymore, or are they democracies of equals?

The End of Jack Welch Capitalism?

The great financial storm of 2007–08 blew new life into the perennial debate about shareholder versus stakeholder capitalism. Since the midnineteenth century there has been a prolonged war—sometimes hot, sometimes cold, but always raging—between two different conceptions of the company: the stakeholder ideal that holds that the company is responsible to a wide range of social groups and the shareholder ideal that holds that, in the last analysis, it is responsible to its shareholders. In the first view, boards are in the business of balancing a wide range of interest groups. In the second, they are responsible for boosting shareholder value.

In 1980–2000, the forces of shareholder capitalism were on the march. Michael Jensen and William Meckling formulated the theoretical case for shareholder capitalism in their 1976 article "Theory of the Firm: Managerial Behavior, Agency Costs and Ownership Structure,"[1] the most widely cited article about business ever. Jack Welch demonstrated the merits of the shareholder-focused approach during his long tenure as head of GE. The relative performance of America (with its cult of the shareholder) compared with continental Europe (with its emphasis on stakeholders) suggested that shareholder value provided the key to "creative destruction" and long-term economic growth.

Even during the boom years, some important management theorists were skeptical. Charles Handy argued that "it is time we killed a myth that it is the shareholders who run the business, and that it is for them that we all work."[2] Peter Drucker complained that the fashionable talk of shareholder value encouraged the worst sort of short-termism: "Long-term results cannot be gained by piling short-term results on short-term results."[3] Robert Reich, the

U.S. Secretary of Labor in 1993–97, frequently berated companies for putting short-term gains above the interests of their employees and local communities. Still, so long as the Dow kept booming and America kept outperforming continental Europe, these were voices crying in the wilderness. Reich lost all the significant battles to more orthodox members of the Clinton administration, such as Robert Rubin and Larry Summers.

More recently, the balance of advantage in this debate has been shifting toward the stakeholder camp. America has been convulsed by a succession of corporate scandals. Its economic performance has begun to slip—not just in comparison with China but also in comparison with Germany. And the 2007–08 crisis has raised profound questions about Anglo-Saxon capitalism. Many defenders of the system recanted or partially recanted. Alan Greenspan mumbled that his models had failed to predict the crisis. Jack Welch was widely quoted as saying that "shareholder value is the dumbest idea on the planet." Many management gurus suggested alternative measures for corporate performance. The era of "Jack Welch capitalism" was drawing to a close, Richard Lambert, then head of the Confederation of British Industry (CBI), told a meeting of the Royal Society of Arts on March 30, 2010.[4]

One of the most comprehensive attacks on "Jack Welch capitalism" came from Roger Martin, the dean of the University of Toronto's Rotman School of Management, in the pages of the *Harvard Business Review*.[5] Martin dismissed the view that companies should focus on shareholder value as "tragically flawed" and argued that it was time to abandon it. Share prices are a crooked measuring stick. Shares frequently rise in value as a result of general economic conditions rather than the success of individual managers—thereby providing bosses with lavish rewards for doing nothing more than allowing the incoming tide to float their yachts. It is also a flexible measuring stick that has persuaded bosses to cut costs in order to boost their short-term income.

Martin argued that "shareholder capitalism" should give way to "customer-driven capitalism" in which customer satisfaction replaces shareholder value as the key metric. This customer-driven model provides managers with an incentive to work hard to squeeze the most out of their resources while also forcing them to keep their eye on the horizon. It also chimes with the experience of ordinary managers who are much more interested in getting their products into people's hands than the intricacies of stock options. Paul Polman, the boss of Unilever, puts the point simply: "I do not work for the shareholder, to be honest; I work for the consumer, the customer . . . I'm not driven and I don't drive this business model by driving shareholder value."[6] In brief, shops beat stocks.

Others have suggested different metrics. Vineet Nayar, the boss of HCL Technologies, a successful Indian outsourcing firm, and one of the few bosses to take the time to write a management book for a respectable publishing house, Harvard Business Press, argues the case for putting "employees first, customers second" in a vigorous book of the same title.[7] In Nayar's view, focusing too much on your customers locks you into short-termism, while focusing on your employees lays the foundation for long-term growth—an approach that certainly makes a good deal of sense in India's red-hot and talent-starved market. Many managers prefer to use as many metrics as possible. The more companies have to respond to a wide range of "stakeholders," the more they need to abandon their obsession with a single measuring stick and to start using multiple measures.

Is it really time to bury the shareholder-value model? It is certainly true that few people continue to support the crudest version of this model. There is a declining appetite for linking bosses' pay to short-term fluctuations in their firms' share price. There is even less appetite for loading companies with mountains of corporate debt that may end up crushing them rather than imposing the discipline that Michael Jensen so memorably celebrated. The critics were right to argue that focus on day-to-day shareholder value produces short-termism. Why not close down that plant or sell off that division if it meant a gigantic payday? They were also right that incentives have been distorted by a succession of bubbles that first inflated stock-market prices and eventually inflated markets for corporate debt as well. These bubbles meant that many bosses reaped obscene rewards for having the parcel in their laps when the music stopped.

That said, there is a vital difference between focusing on shareholder value in the short term and focusing on it in the longer term. Bosses may wreak carnage if their remuneration is linked to quarterly earnings. But will they wreak the same carnage if their remuneration is tied to more long-term measures? Bosses may be rewarded for being in the right place at the right time if their rewards are linked to six monthly shifts in the market, but they are unlikely to be so well remunerated if they are forced to take a more long-term stake in their companies.

Many of the critics of the shareholder-value model of capitalism are, in fact, quarrelling with short-termism rather than with shareholder value as such. Martin argues that focusing on customer satisfaction is the best way to boost long-term shareholder value. Nayar makes the same case for putting employees first. Most advocates of stakeholder capitalism argue that their model is good for shareholders as well as for everybody else. Contented workers deliver better services; contented customers make for a profitable company; put the two things together and you have a recipe for happy shareholders.

The problem with this argument is that it risks dispensing with one of the great virtues of capitalism, which is clarity. If companies try to satisfy everyone, they can end up satisfying no one; if they try to measure their performance against too many metrics, they can end up dodging the difficult decisions that secure their long-term survival. After all, the easiest way to satisfy your customers is to give your products away for nothing.

This suggests that there is a strong case for preserving the focus on shareholder value, so long as we avoid putting too much emphasis on short-term results. To do so, value-maximizing bosses need an additional system of checks and balances to keep them on the rails. These checks and balances are provided by three groups: shareholders, regulators, and boards.

One of the most striking results of the corporate world's growing fixation on shareholder value was the shareholder rights movement. Shareholders were not content to sit back and let bosses enrich themselves in their name. They wanted to take a more active role in governing companies and preventing corporate disasters. From the perspective of shareholder rights activists, the problem with shareholder capitalism was not that it shifted the focus of corporate governance from the managers to the owners. It was that it did not shift the focus enough.

The shareholder rights movement produced a new class of boardroom activists who started popping up at normally somnolent annual meetings and peppering bosses with difficult questions. These included Robert Monks, an American gentleman of the old school, and Ekkehard Wenger, a rather less gentlemanly German economist who defends his abrasive style with a quotation from Schiller: "One must tell the Germans the truth as coarsely as possible." The movement was given its heft by institutional investors—big pension funds and the like—who started putting pressure on companies to make better use of their assets. The most famous of these is the California Public Employees Retirement System (Calpers), the state workers' pension fund, which has taken a vigorous approach to its portfolio, building up big blocks of shares in companies and then trying to force them to change. Many other funds have joined the movement more recently.

The 2002 scandals, which engulfed Tyco, WorldCom, and Global Crossing as well as Enron, also led to tighter regulations of the corporate sector. Sarbanes-Oxley was one of the most unpopular pieces of legislation of the Bush era. Conservatives hated it because they thought it went too far in regulating companies. (Conservatives repeatedly argue that it helped to destroy the initial public offering market, whereas, in fact, America's share of the global IPO market began to decline in 1996, hit rock bottom in 2001, and began to rise again thereafter.) Liberals hated it because it did not go far enough. And business people hated it because it meant an awful lot of work. But there is good evidence that Sarbanes-Oxley helped to protect shareholders from malign managers. Francois Brochet, of the Harvard Business School, points out that Sarbox has a good record in protecting corporate investors from insider shenanigans.[8] The legislation forces corporate insiders and big shareholders to report changes in their ownership of company stock to the SEC within two business days of their transactions. This not only makes it easier for small investors to respond to insider purchases quickly, it also discourages the Martha Stewarts of this world from selling stock in anticipation of bad news.

Sarbanes-Oxley helped to speed up a revolution in corporate governance that would probably have triumphed, eventually, even without the scandals of 2002. From the 1990s onward, reformers such as Sir Adrian Cadbury in Britain and Nell Minnow in the United States have been trying to sweep away the cozy old world of long lunches and old-school ties in favor of a new regime based on checks and balances in the distribution of power and professionalism in its execution. Board meetings were once lackadaisical affairs. Many directors had little idea what they were doing, and the meetings were rushed through. Lunch was accompanied by generous quantities of decent claret. The standard view of boards was that they were nothing more than "the parsley on the fish."

This world has now disappeared. Booz & Company's annual survey of the world's biggest public companies suggests that most companies are highly professional (and rather boring) places. Companies now routinely separate the jobs of chairmen and CEOs: less than 12 percent of incoming CEOs in 2009 were also made chairmen, compared with 48 percent in 2002. They also take boards much more seriously than they have ever done before. They increasingly draw on a new class of professional and well-trained directors. Both the New York Stock Exchange and the NASDAQ now demand that a majority of directors be independent. Leading business schools now do a good business in giving bespoke courses for directors.

The result is that the balance of power between CEOs and their boards has changed dramatically. A few years ago, the likes of Carly Fiorina could ride roughshod over their boards despite making huge strategic blunders based on little knowledge of their industries. Today boards regularly haul CEOs over the coals and sack them if they fail to perform. The list of CEOs who have fallen foul of their boards includes some of the most powerful people in the business world: Jean-Marie Messier of Vivendi, Philip Purcell of Morgan Stanley, Franklin Raines at Fannie Mae, Michael Eisner at Disney, Harry Stonecipher at Boeing, Hank Greenberg of AIG, and, in a strange irony, given his cracking business performance, Mark Hurd, Fiorina's successor at Hewlett-Packard.

Paying the Piper

The debate about shareholder value is intertwined with an even more bad-tempered debate—about executive pay. For some people it is enough simply to state the incomes of some of the world's top executives and leave it at that. How can you justify paying James McNerney, the chief executive of Boeing, $14.8 million in 2008, the annus horribilis of recent capitalist history? Or paying Tom Glocer, the chief executive of Thomson Reuters, $36.6 million? And McNerney and Glocer were mere pikers compared with Lee Raymond, the former boss of Exxon, who received a parting gift of $400 million. And how can we justify giving these overpaid people princely perks such as the use of private jets and country club membership? The very companies that boast about being lean and mean tend to be the very opposite when it comes to looking after their top people.

The critics of top pay have some sophisticated arguments as well as outrage on their side. They argue that exceptional pay is not linked to exceptional performance. Bob Nardelli proved to be such a disaster as CEO of Home Depot that he was eventually forced out. Yet he was given a severance package of $210 million and soon found a new job as CEO of Chrysler, which then went bankrupt. Stan O'Neal was paid $145 million in 2003–06 for leading Merrill Lynch ever deeper into financial disaster. "As Merrill's losses mounted," Michael Lewis wrote about O'Neal's approach to crisis management: "We know exactly where chief executive officer Stan O'Neal was, what he was doing, and with whom. On a golf course. Golfing. By himself."[9] Failed CEOs also have an infuriating habit of popping up somewhere else. Daniel Mudd, who steered Fannie Mae onto the rocks, was appointed CEO of Fortress Investment Group, in 2009.

Just as galling as the absolute level of CEO pay is the trend. In 1980, the average American CEO earned forty-two times as much as the average blue-collar worker. Today the multiple has increased more than 25-fold to 531. The majority of people around the world—in capitalist America as well as socialist France—tell pollsters that they believe that CEOs are paid too much. But so what? In May 2009, almost 60 percent of shareholders at Royal Dutch Shell voted against the company's proposed pay packet for its top executives, in the largest shareholder revolt in British corporate history. To which the company's reply was, essentially, "screw you."

What explains this trend? Some critics of CEO pay argue that the explanation is simple: CEOs pay themselves a lot of money because they can, either directly, by setting their own pay, or indirectly, by stacking the remuneration committee. As J. K. Galbraith put it back in 1979, "The salary of the chief executive of the large corporation is not a market reward for achievement. It is frequently in the nature of a warm personal gesture by the individual to himself." Nell Minnow, one of the fiercest critics of executive pay, argues that companies spend a lot of money preserving bosses' rights to make these warm personal gestures. The financial services industry spends $600 million a year in lobbying in Washington, DC. The result of all this political manipulation is nothing less than a "hostile take-over of capitalism by company executives."

For those who find this explanation a little crude, there is a more ingenious one called "the Lake Wobegon effect." Rachel Hayes and Scott Schaefer, two economists, argue that companies want to signal that they have the best CEOs, so they raise their pay to impressive levels. More generally, companies want to make sure that they pay their CEOs above average in the business because they want to employ above-average people. So CEO pay is set on an inflationary spiral.

What should we make of all this? There is no doubt that there are lots of galling examples of CEOs who are paid too much or who are rewarded for poor performance. It would be hard to find anyone who would be willing to plead Bob Nardelli's case in the court of public opinion. But we should not allow a few extreme cases to distort our judgment. The average pay of American CEOs in 2010 was about $10 million—a lot of money to be sure, but hardly an extravagant amount measured against the pay of other top people or against the burden of running companies that employ thousands of people. CEOs do not earn as much as top hedge fund managers or A-list celebrities. Nor do they live a life of leisure and luxury. CEOs are under constant pressure to perform. Their job tenure is getting ever shorter. They can see their life's work destroyed and their reputation torn asunder in a matter of weeks—as happened to Tony Hayward, a loyal company man who spent his career working his way up through the ranks at BP, who put fixing the company's safety problems at the top of his list of priorities when he took over the company, but who saw his reputation turned to ashes thanks to his handling of the Deep Water drilling disaster.

Few people will shed any tears for a failed CEO (who has a perfectly adequate pension to live on), but there are several abstract arguments in favor of high CEO pay. The most basic argument is that you need to pay well in order to attract the best people. CEOs have enormous power to shape the destiny of the organizations that they run. Joseph Bower, of Harvard Business School, points out that, to a surprising degree, CEOs are like the ship captains of old: the absolute rulers of their own domain.[10] The quality of these captains can make the difference between a successful voyage and a shipwreck. Compare the fates of General Electric and Westinghouse in 1980–2000. In 1980, GE and Westinghouse were playing in the same league. By 2000, GE was a $150 billion behemoth but Westinghouse, a company that had first commercialized electricity, radio broadcasting, radar, and nuclear power, was to all intents and purposes finished. What was the difference between the two? GE chose a CEO—Jack Welch—who remodeled the company and boosted its market capitalization by 6,000 percent. Westinghouse burned through a succession of bosses who all failed.[11] Welch undoubtedly "deserved" his pay in the sense that he created a huge amount of value for shareholders.

Nor is Welch an isolated case. Three Harvard Business School academics, Noam Wasserman, Bharat Anand, and Nitin Nohria, calculate that, controlling for extraneous factors, the impact of a CEO on corporate performance is about 15 percent.[12] A glance at corporate history suggests that, if anything, they may be understating things. Michael Eisner and Frank Wells inherited a moribund Walt Disney company and boosted its share price by almost 30 percent annually over the next ten years. Lou Gerstner transformed IBM from a fading giant into a global competitor. Most people other than hardened socialists are willing to tolerate large rewards for entrepreneurs who create something from nothing. Why not extend the same tolerance to CEOs who transform established companies and save them from bankruptcy?

Critics of executive pay might retort that there is no evidence that you need to pay quite so much in order to secure a CEO's talents. The majority of CEOs (including Jack Welch) spend their lives working for the companies that they run. A significant number of them (though not Jack Welch) like to claim that they would have been willing to work for less than they were paid. Even if this argument were true in the short term—and I doubt that GE would be able to keep first-class people in its executive suite if it paid significantly less than its competitors—it is treacherous in the long term. Cutting the pay of CEOs will eventually dry up the talent pool. Ambitious people will choose to follow other professions where they can make fortunes, such as hedge funds or finance. Or they may decide to go into academia rather than endure the relentless pressure of the boardroom.

The second argument in favor of high CEO pay is that awarding it to CEOs helps to motivate the rest of the workforce. Why do high-flyers accept an onerous assignment in a hellhole like Dubai? Why do they work late at night? Why do they persevere even though their wives leave them? In part because they think that they might one day earn the huge rewards that come along with being a CEO. High pay at the top helps companies to attract the best people and to keep those people working hard. Edward Lazear and Sherwin Rosen, the economists who first came up with this argument, dubbed it the "tournament theory."[13] The CEO's pay plays the same role as prizes do in other tournaments: it produces general benefits for the organization as a whole, not just for the winners.

Unaccountable, Sexist, and Under Siege

The other heated debate is about the composition of senior management. I once published a book on the history of the company, the cover of which displayed a group of dour-looking white men sitting around a boardroom table. Society has changed dramatically since that photograph was taken. Women have left home for work, and ethnic minorities have made huge strides. But a striking number of boardrooms would still look like the one that illustrated the cover of my book.

This is undoubtedly a problem. Drawing senior managers from a narrow range of society can only undermine the corporate world's legitimacy, particularly if inequalities continue to grow and financial crises continue to rage. It also creates more practical problems. Inbred elites lack the range of experience necessary to deal with an increasingly multicultural home market, let alone to mastermind the conquest of world markets. France's identikit corporate elite—with their educations at the same elite institutions and hands in each other's pockets—may be good at certain types of management such as long-range planning or big infrastructure projects, but is hopelessly out of its depth in fast-moving industries such as computers. America's equally identikit, but even more shamefully, monoglot elite has found it hard to adjust to an increasingly globalized world.

One of the most striking things about the modern boardroom is how few women can be found in them. Women have certainly popped up in some striking places: Alcatel-Lucent (telecom), AREVA (nuclear energy), SNCF (railways), Anglo American (mining), Drax (electricity), and Archer Daniels Midland (agriculture) all have female bosses. But boards still remain much more male than the workforce as a whole. Women make up 17 percent of board members in the United States, 9 percent in Europe, and 2 percent in Asia. Only fourteen of the bosses of the S&P 500 companies and five of the bosses of the FTSE 100 companies are women. The British Equal Opportunities Commission calculates that, at the current rate of progress, it will take sixty years for women to gain equal representation on the boards of the FTSE 100.

The slow pace of women's progress has inevitably led to demands for affirmative action. But this should be used only as a weapon of last resort. It brings all sorts of problems in its wake, from promoting unqualified people (Sweden, which has introduced quotas, has been forced to recruit many female board members from academia and NGOs) to casting doubt on the merits of women who reach the top. And we are far from being at the last resort. The pace of women's progress in business has never been faster, and women are now significantly outperforming men in schools and universities. There is no doubt that women will make their way into the boardroom in the coming years, just as they will make their way into the upper branches of government.

These "hard" questions continue to divide well-intentioned people. You can quote respectable management thinkers on either side of the debates. But at least the questions—and some of the answers—have a certain degree of clarity. That clarity almost disappears when we move to the next subject—the nature of leadership in general, and the X factor that distinguishes successful leaders in particular.

A Riddle Wrapped in an Enigma

One thing all students of leadership seem to agree on is that the CEO's job is getting more difficult. There are lots of obvious reasons for this: the pressure to perform is becoming more intense, the tolerance for failure is diminishing, and CEOs can no longer resort to the old dodge of marking their own term papers. In 2000, about half of North American and European CEOs entering office were named chairman as well as CEO. In 2009, that number had fallen to 16.5 percent in North America and 7.1 percent in Europe. But there is a more fundamental reason why life at the top is so difficult: the collapse of the old mindset of command and control. When Alfred Sloan ruled the roost, bosses had a fairly clear agenda. They were supposed to set the strategy, design the structures, and impose the controls. The collapse of the Sloanist model has made everything fuzzier. Bosses are supposed to be much less bossy than they used to be—yet they are also held accountable when anything goes wrong. They are supposed to unleash other people's creativity—and they are also responsible for ensuring that such creativity is channeled in the right direction.

The result is that we are becoming ever vaguer about what leadership actually means. Is leadership still ultimately a matter of telling people what to do, or is it a matter of engaging people's enthusiasm? Are velvet gloves enough, or do we still need to reinforce them with iron fists? Anyone who spends time studying management theory develops a high tolerance for nonsense. But even for people who have developed such a tolerance, reading the literature on leadership can be a trying activity.

The obvious people to consult about leadership are leaders themselves—the people who are (or were) in charge of the lumbering organizations that are supposed to run the world.

Jack Welch produces regular ruminations on the subject with no-nonsense titles such as *Jack: Straight from the Gut* (with John Byrne) and *Winning* (with Suzy Welch). Lesser CEOs are keen to get in on the act. These books can be a corrective to some of the more airy-fairy management literature about teacher gurus. Lord Sheppard of Britain's Grand Metropolitan once described his own style as "management by a light grip on the throat." But few of these books are worth reading. Welch has been no more successful at capturing the secrets of leadership than the rest of us have been successful at capturing lightning in a bottle. Most of his leadership maxims—"Don't manage, lead," "Control your own destiny or somebody else will"—are punchy rather than profound. And Welch is a veritable Aristotle compared with most other authors. These "tips from the top" belong to the world of vanity publishing rather than serious business studies.

What about management theorists? Over the past decade, leadership has become one of the most fashionable subdisciplines of management theory. So fashionable, in fact, that Henry Mintzberg complains that we hear so much about the "grand successes and even grander failures of the great leaders" that it is hard to come to grips with "the simple realities of being a regular manager."[14] Old warriors such as John Kotter and, particularly, Warren Bennis, who have spent their lives writing about leadership, have seen their reputations skyrocket. Bennis's classic distinction between a leader and a manager is now one of the most quoted nostrums of management thinking: "The manager maintains; the leader develops. The manager focuses on systems and structure; the leader focuses on people. The manager relies on control; the leader inspires trust."

Leadership has also attracted a new generation of younger thinkers. Ronald Heifetz, a popular lecturer on leadership at Harvard's Kennedy School and author, most recently, of *The Practice of Adaptive Leadership*, argues that the new role of leaders is to "help people face reality and to mobilize them to make change."[15] Heifetz pooh-poohs the smiley-faced version of leadership that is popular in new-age circles; exercising leadership can generate resistance, and overcoming that resistance is a test of character as well as a precondition for progress ("conflict is the primary engine of creativity and innovation," he says).[16] But that does not mean that he harkens back to the old days of command and control: he says that leadership is about posing well-structured questions rather than delivering definitive answers, about providing direction rather than detailed maps.

Other leadership thinkers have homed in on narrower areas. Marshall Goldsmith, of Dartmouth's Tuck School, more or less invented executive coaching, one of the great boom areas of modern leadership education. He has mentored more than 120 CEOs and their leadership teams. He has also developed various techniques to help leaders get a better sense of what they are doing, including "360-degree feedback," a quasi-Leninist device whereby managers are forced to listen to other people's opinions of them. Goldsmith frequently warns about the inertia of success: the very qualities that help people climb to the top of the tree make it difficult for them to change their behavior once they get there.

Michael Watkins, the boss of Genesis Advisers, focuses on "onboarding," a flourishing area given that the pace of executive turnover is rising, and that promotions are one of life's more predictable surprises (somebody has to get them). He argues that the first ninety days after a new leader takes over, whether as the result of a promotion or a merger, can be career-shaping: early triumphs can lead to long-term successes, early failures can leave you bloodied and broken, and nobody can escape the minutest scrutiny as they try to get their bearings. He lays out a "standard framework" for handling leadership transitions based on "five fundamental propositions," "ten key challenges," and a "four-fold typology of leadership challenges." Watkins's focus on transition has allowed him to produce a stream of publications such as *The First 90 Days* (the "onboarding bible") and to become a fixture on the speaker's circuit. It has also allowed him to sell a huge range of more personal services such as workshops, seminars, and one-to-one coaching.

Much of this is useful stuff; some of it is even inspiring. But it is hard to argue that any of these gurus has produced a theory of leadership in the same way that, say, Michael Porter has produced a theory of strategy or Michael Jensen has produced a theory of finance. The most serious among them can be frustratingly vague. "Never have so many labored for so long to say so little," was Bennis's waspish verdict on the leadership literature. The more pragmatic risk is stumbling into the world of self-help hucksterism that is populated by peak performance coaches such as Anthony Robbins, the Superman look-alike who teaches people to walk on hot coals and unleash the giant within.

Looking for Mr. Good Leader

The confusion about the nature of leadership can be seen in the wild gyrations of corporate fashion when it comes to leadership. The 1990s saw a cult of supermen leaders. Gurus swooned over macho types like Jack Welch and Percy Barnevik, who restructured vast institutions. They waxed lyrical about visionaries such as Bill Gates and Steve Jobs, who reinvented entire industries. Or they celebrated mavericks such as Richard Branson, who broke all the rules (as a youthful entrepreneur he once spent a night in a police cell after smuggling some records into Britain from France) but ended up on top of the world.

The model of the superman CEO has recently fallen out of fashion. Some imperial CEOs, such as Enron's Jeff Skilling, Tyco's Dennis Kozlowski, and Hollinger's Conrad Black, ended up in prison. Others, such as Home Depot's Bob Nardelli and Hewlett-Packard's Carly Fiorina, paid themselves like superstars but delivered like also-rans. The model of the superman CEO also suffered from a much bigger problem—replicability. Peter Drucker once noted that "no institution can possibly survive if it needs geniuses or supermen to manage it. It must be organized in such a way as to be able to get along under the leadership of perfectly normal human beings." Warren Buffet made the same point more pithily: "I only invest in companies which any fool can run, because some day some fool will run it."

The first decade of the twenty-first century has seen a striking backlash against the cult of the superman CEO, with a growing number of companies embracing, if not fools, then "perfectly normal human beings." Some of the world's most powerful bosses are striking mainly for their blandness. Sam Palmisano at IBM, Terry Leahy at Tesco, Vittorio Colao at Vodafone—these men are at the head of a vast army of even more forgettable bosses. Facelessness is the height of fashion among management gurus. Jim Collins argues that the best CEOs are not flamboyant visionaries but "humble, self-effacing, diligent and resolute souls." Journalists have taken to producing glowing profiles of self-effacing and self-denying souls such as Haruka Nishimatsu, the boss of Japan Airlines, who travels to work on the bus and pays himself less than his pilots. You have to go back to the 1950s, when books such as *The Organization Man* and *The Man in the Gray Flannel Suit* topped the best-seller list, and when two of America's biggest companies, General Motors and General Electric, were both run by men named Charles Wilson, to find such a cult of facelessness. It can only be a matter of time before somebody writes *The Management Secrets of Uriah Heep*: be "'umble, be ever so 'umble."

Yet there is a danger of taking the reaction against the superman CEO too far. There is no shortage of "humble" CEOs who have plenty to be humble about: Olli-Pekka Kallasvuo, Nokia's boss in 2006–10, proved to be as disastrous as he was colorless. More generally, the corporate world needs its flamboyant visionaries and raging egomaniacs as well as its corporate civil servants. Think of the people who have shaped the modern business landscape, and "faceless" and "humble" are not the first words that come to mind. Henry Ford was as close as you can get to being deranged without losing your liberty. John H. Patterson, the founder of National Cash Register and one of the greatest businessmen of the gilded age, once notified an employee that he was sacked by setting fire to his desk. Thomas Watson, one of Patterson's protégés and the founder of IBM, turned his company into a cult and himself into the object of collective worship. Bill Gates and Steve Jobs are both tightly wound egomaniacs. These are people who have created the future, rather than merely managed change, through the force of their personalities and the appeal of their visions.

This is not to say that companies should cultivate egomaniacs simply because they are egomaniacs, but the current cult of humility is no more convincing than the cult of the superman CEO that it replaced. George Bernard Shaw's observation about the importance of being unreasonable—"the reasonable man adapts himself to the world; the unreasonable man persists in trying to adapt the world to himself. Therefore, all progress depends on the unreasonable man"—is as good an insight into the nature of leadership as anything produced by today's management thinkers.

13

Managing Leviathan

Margaret Thatcher liked to say that *Ginger and Pickles*, by Beatrix Potter, was the only business book worth reading. The BBC, hardly an organization that is naturally sympathetic to the iron lady, elaborated on this insight in a series on *The Beatrix Potter Guide to Business*. "Jemima Puddleduck" is a treatise on entrepreneurship. "Samuel Whiskers" is a parable about the importance of "rolling audits." And "Mrs. Tittlemouse"? It is a warning about the dangers of employing management consultants.

Mrs. Tittlemouse is "a most terribly tidy particular little mouse," forever cleaning her house and shooing away intruders. But one day a "fat-voiced" toad arrives and makes himself at home, lounging in the rocking chair and putting his feet on the fender. He not only refuses to leave, despite repeated requests; he searches the house for tasty morsels, spreading chaos wherever he goes. Mrs. Tittlemouse has to spend the day cleaning up after him, when he finally condescends to be on his way.

It is not surprising that a group of BBC journalists should have been struck by the similarities between a badly behaved toad and management consultants. Management consultants have been hopping all over the British Broadcasting Corporation for decades. McKinsey masterminded two huge reorganizations of the BBC when the organization's current stars were still in short trousers— in 1968 and then again in 1972, largely to correct the mistakes of the first reorganization. But the current plague of toads at the BBC dates from 1992, when John Birt became director-general.

Birt had had a long career in television before he assumed this position. But he cut his broadcasting teeth in the private sector rather than the BBC, and he was savvy enough to realize that a public broadcasting organization was threatened in a world where the number of channels was exploding. So he staked his career as boss on two fashionable management ideas—the internal market and producer choice. He asked individual departments to compete with each other for contracts and charge each other for services (the internal market). And he forced program producers to use outside suppliers if they were cheaper (producer choice).

There are, in fact, reasonable arguments for both ideas. Yet the implementation of "producer choice" unleashed a plague of management consultants on the BBC. Consultants took up permanent residence in the BBC's headquarters in West London. There were eventually so many of the creatures that consultants had to be brought in to clear up the messes created by other consultants. Dennis Potter, Britain's foremost television playwright, spoke for most people in the BBC when he labeled Birt a "croak-voiced Dalek," referring to the rather absurd robotic villains in the popular TV series, Dr Who. Tony Garnett, a veteran producer, claimed that he practiced "totalitarian micro-management." Private Eye, the country's leading satirical magazine, lambasted Birt's addiction to convoluted management jargon in a regular feature titled "Birtspeak," complete with a miniature Dalek caricature of the great language-mangler himself.

A Plague of Toads

Everywhere you go in the public sector these days, in the emerging world as well as the emerged, you can hear "Birtspeak" being spoken. Government departments are "reengineering" their "core processes," introducing "quality performance measures," and adopting "customer services standards." Civil service heads are "empowering their front-line workers," "managing by objectives," and "outsourcing their non-core functions." Even generals and admirals are "downsizing their human resources" and "benchmarking their competitors."

Enthusiasm for management is not confined to any particular political party or clique. Britain's new Conservative-led government waxes lyrical about businessmen and their methods. Indeed, William Hague, the foreign secretary, is a product of both INSEAD and McKinsey. But the Tories are unlikely to outclass New Labor. The architects of New Labor, Tony Blair and Gordon Brown, were happier talking about Michael Porter and Tom Peters than Keir Hardie and Nye Bevan. They invited consultants to crawl all over the government, including Downing Street, the Cabinet Office, and the Department of Health, and installed a revolving door between politics and consultancy at the heart of government, with sometimes shameful consequences. John Birt, who left the BBC to act as Tony Blair's personal advisor on "blue skies" thinking, even tried to combine a job in Downing Street with a part-time role at McKinsey until the public outcry proved too much (Birt now works for another consultancy, Capgemini).

You can see a similar pattern on the other side of the Atlantic. Barack Obama has appointed a management consultant, Jeffrey Zients, as his "chief performance officer" to try to "streamline processes, cut costs, and find best practices throughout the US government," and generally fulfill his pledge, in his inaugural address, to deliver pragmatic government reform ("the question that we ask today is not whether our government is too big or too small, but whether it works").[1] Several of Obama's would-be replacements in the Republican Party are equally keen on management ideas. Mitt Romney, a Harvard Business School graduate who had a highly successful career with Bain Capital, helping to found Staples, among other companies, once told the *Wall Street Journal* that, if elected president, he would "probably" hire McKinsey to tell him how to reorganize the government—he then quickly added a proviso that it might be another firm such as the Boston Consulting Group or his old employer, Bain.

Nor is enthusiasm for management theory confined to the rich world. Singapore runs itself like a giant corporation and sends its brightest to Harvard Business School. Malaysia has hired McKinsey. Muammar Gaddafi and his presumed heir, Saif, hired a succession of well-known gurus before the Libyan regime imploded, in a vain attempt to join the family of nations. Michael Porter drew up a plan to turn Libya into one of the world's most entrepreneurial societies, even visiting Tripoli to unveil his ideas in person. Monitor, the consultancy that Porter had founded, was paid $250,000 a month to provide the regime with sundry services, including helping Saif to write his PhD for the London School of Economics and trying to whitewash the regime's reputation.[2] Sir Howard Davies, the LSE director who was obliged to resign in disgrace over the school's ties with the dictatorship, traveled to Libya to advise the regime on financial reforms.

How the Gurus Met Government

The first guru to think seriously about public-sector management was, predictably enough, Peter Drucker. From the 1960s onward he argued vigorously that the next great management revolution would take place in the public and voluntary sectors, as they learned how to improve their productivity. Michael Porter was also quick to recognize the potential of applying management theory to the public sector. He first got interested in the subject when Ronald Reagan, confronted by mounting demands for an "industrial policy" to deal with America's supposed economic decline, asked him to sit on a presidential Commission on Industrial Competitiveness, and he was struck by the huge role that nation-states and national differences play in determining the success of the companies that he had spent his life studying.[3] The result of this conversion was a huge book, *The Competitive Advantage of Nations* (1990). Over eight hundred pages long, lavishly illustrated with charts, diagrams, and maps of successful industrial clusters, littered with details about British biscuit companies and Italian shoe-makers, supported by hundreds of footnotes, the book can be read on three levels: as a general inquiry into what makes national economies successful; a detailed study of eight of the most important economies in the world, South Korea, Italy, Sweden, Japan, Switzerland, Germany, Britain, and the United States; and a series of prescriptions about what governments should do to improve their country's competitiveness. Porter soon found himself writing reports on competitiveness for national governments, including those of New Zealand, Canada, and Portugal, and for regional governments, including Massachusetts. Libya is in good company.

Other even more unlikely gurus caught the public-sector bug. Tom Peters, who initially dismissed government as a bureaucratic swamp, having worked in the military-industrial complex in the 1970s, was so impressed by his fans in the public sector that he threw his weight behind government reform, even producing a film about "excellence in the public sector." Kenichi Ohmae, the man who had once announced the end of the nation-state, gave up a lucrative job as head of McKinsey's Tokyo office to devote himself to politics, even forming his own political party devoted to freeing Japan from the tentacles of the special interests.

This dialogue between the public and private sectors also produced a new breed of management gurus—people whose expertise lay primarily in the public rather than the private sector. The pathfinders here were David Osborne, a public-policy consultant, and Ted Gaebler, a former city manager, whose *Reinventing Government: How the Entrepreneurial Spirit Is Transforming the Public Sector* (1992) reached the top of the best-seller list; spawned an influential pressure group, the Alliance for Redesigning Government; and provided the Clinton administration with both a model and an inspiration. But many other figures hiked down the trail that they had blazed. Who could forget Michael Barber's *Instruction to Deliver: Tony Blair, Public Services and the Challenge of Achieving Targets*, for example?

And How Government Met the Gurus

In Europe the public sector's love affair with management theory started at the top, in the wake of the malaise of the 1970s. Margaret Thatcher championed a wide range of market-oriented reforms— ranging from privatization (a word that Peter Drucker supposedly invented) and contracting out services to competitive tender, at the easy end of the spectrum, to introducing an internal market into the National Health Service at the much tougher end. She also established a succession of powerful bodies, some of them staffed by businessmen and consultants, to improve the management of the public sector: the Efficiency Unit (under Lord Rayner, head of Marks & Spencer), the Financial Management Unit, the National Audit Office, and the Audit Commission.

Many of these ideas spread from Thatcher's Britain to other countries. What became known as "new public sector management" involved a host of market-friendly ideas such as outsourcing, public-private partnerships, performance-related pay, and internal markets. These ideas were taken furthest in New Zealand and Australia, where mandarins sometimes acted almost like independent executives, hired to produce specific results and charged with striking "performance deals" with their departments. But in more nuanced form they permeated throughout much of the public sector in the Organization for Cooperation and Economic Development.

In the United States, on the other hand, the love affair with management theory started with the lower ranks. Around the country government officials, frustrated by their organizations and impressed by the revival of the private sector, started to talk to business people and read management books. Bob Stone, who worked as a bureaucrat in the Department of Defense in the early 1980s and became increasingly furious at the way that bureaucratic regulations were getting in the way of providing services for the troops, described Tom Peters's *In Search of Excellence* as nothing less than a revelation and embarked on a long career of slashing red tape (condensing thick Pentagon manuals into one-page mission statements, for example).

Even more reformers seized on quality gurus such as W. Edwards Deming and James M. Juran, who had previously had such a profound impact on the Japanese private sector. In the 1980s, "total-quality management" (which meant anything from reorganizing workers into teams to taking notice of customers) became a quasi-religion among local government officials, with endless award ceremonies and reform programs. One of the first nationally known figures to pick up on the movement was Bill Clinton,

then governor of Arkansas, who took to making speeches praising Deming and attending conferences on TQM. (Indeed, it was
at one of these conferences that he allegedly asked Paula Jones to
perform oral sex on him.)

The federal government's conversion to these ideas was com-
pleted when Bill Clinton put Al Gore in charge of "reinventing
government." Gore loudly complained that America suffered "from
a quill-pen government in the age of Word Perfect"—it was typical of Gore's luck that he chose a doomed operating system for his
example—and made a habit of visiting such celebrated businesses
as Southwest Airlines and General Motors' (now defunct) Saturn
plant in search of inspiration. He held seminars with business lu-
minaries such as Vaughn Beals, chairman of Harley-Davidson,
and Jack Welch, chairman of General Electric. He enthusiastically
endorsed government reforms based on business models (Henry
Cisneros, secretary for Housing and Urban Development, restructured his department after studying a reorganization at PepsiCo,
for example) and once took a chain saw to a pile of government
documents, briefly earning himself the sobriquet Chainsaw Al.

What explains this growing obsession with management
theory? The most obvious thing is the idea that business is more
efficient than government. Margaret Thatcher never tried to hide
her belief that civil servants were simpering do-gooders who
went into public service because they were too unimaginative
or left wing to go into business. Tony Blair loved mixing with
"wealth creators" such as Virgin's Richard Branson and BP's John
Browne. Even Gordon Brown, who was much more emotion-
ally committed to the public sector than Blair, and who poured
money into the public sector when he became prime minister,
was unhappy with Whitehall's mandarin elite. He repeatedly
talked about reinventing government and "transforming" the

civil service, and relied heavily on outside advisors from management consulting and business.

The second reason for government's infatuation is the desire to
do "more with less": to continue to provide reasonable public services without spending a higher proportion of GDP on the state.
Politicians have learned from watchdogs like Britain's Audit Commission and America's Office of Management and Budget that the
public sector is plagued by gigantic inefficiencies. It is only natural
for them to conclude that they can put off making hard decisions
about raising taxes or cutting services by calling on the help of
management consultants.

The third, and most important, reason is the need to move with
the times. The public sector has been caught up in the revolution that had been sweeping through the private sector for more
than a decade and that is being driven by fundamental forces such
as the spread of information technology and the emergence of
much fussier, value-conscious consumers. Even such notoriously
customer-hostile organizations as America's Internal Revenue
Service and London's Underground adopted "customer service
standards."

The ever-closer relations between the public and private sectors
produced a stream of prominent politicians who tried to squeeze
management lessons from their years in public life, invariably in
return for hefty lecture fees, just as prominent business people tried
to squeeze management lessons from their years in private industry.
Al Gore became a management guru before he became a global-
warming sage: his report on reinventing government reached the
New York Times best-seller list. Colin Powell earned a fortune telling business people about the lessons that he has gleaned from his
career in the army and Washington, DC. William Bratton, who
helped revolutionize the NYPD before Rudolph Giuliani kicked

him out in a fit of pique and forced him to ply his trade in Los Angeles, became a popular speaker. The annual meeting of the Clinton Foundation in New York City became one of the highlights of the global social scene, with throngs of CEOs queuing up to kiss the former president's ring.

The God That Failed

The love affair between government and management inevitably produced a backlash. The backlash was limited in the United States. George Bush strained people's patience with the cult of business by appointing five former CEOs to cabinet positions who then proceeded to make a hash of managing things, spectacularly so in Donald Rumsfeld's case. Barack Obama quietly substituted the cult of businessmen with a cult of the best and the brightest, such as Larry Summers, his chief economic advisor throughout most of his first term, and Tim Geithner, his Treasury Secretary.

The reaction was much louder in Britain, where consultant bashing became one of the most popular national pastimes.

The list of charges against consultants was a long one: That they have frequently left devastation in their wake. That they have built overly elaborate management structures that make it harder for people to do their jobs. That they have treated the public sector as dumping grounds for airy-fairy ideas such as "transformation" that have been rejected by the private sector. That they have demotivated people who once prided themselves on working for the public good. Cultures that had nurtured hospitals and schools for decades had been destroyed with the click of a PowerPoint presentation.

The public sector's obsession with management produced several tragedies. In Stafford Hospital, between 400 and 1,200 more people died in 2005–08, more than actuarial science would have predicted because the managers were so obsessed with hitting predefined targets that they routinely neglected patients.[4] Across the country, police officers focused on harassing people for minor misdemeanors rather than catching thieves and muggers because it was an easier way to hit their targets, and headmasters shunted their charges into undemanding subjects like media studies because they thought that it would be easier to get them through O-levels.

It also ended up costing the Treasury a huge amount of money. Spending on consultancy increased by one-third between 2003–04 and 2005–06, an astonishing growth in such a short period and something that could never have happened in the private sector. Two-fifths of Deloitte's consulting business in 2005 came from the public sector. The bill for IT projects in 2000–2010 may have been as much as £26 billion. Some of the most expensive consultant-driven "transformations" turned out to be flops. A £12 billion project for introducing better information technology into the National Health Service was largely abandoned as unworkable.

The result was a rare consensus. The only thing that everybody in this quarrelsome country could agree on was the sheer awfulness of managers: the hideousness of their language, the foolishness of their methods, and the sheer second-rateness of their intellects. The big question was why governments had allowed themselves to be hoodwinked by such obvious chancers and frauds.

This pointed to the wisdom of a management guru who has made his career out of exposing the errors of his colleagues: Henry Mintzberg. Back in 1995, Mintzberg treated the annual meeting of the Academy of Management to a coruscating attack on the growing influence of management theory on the public sector. The *Harvard Business Review* should have a skull and cross-bones stamped on the cover with the warning "not to be taken by the public sector," he argued. Look at all the management theory industry's favorite medicines and you find that they do more harm than good in the public sector.

The customer is king? Mintzberg pointed out that we are not customers of governments but citizens. Governments have to decide more difficult questions than companies. They have to stop us from doing things we want to do—like building a skyscraper in our back garden—because they have to balance our desires against those of our fellow citizens. They also have to force us to do things we do not want to do. Criminals have to be punished and, in wartime, reluctant citizens sometimes have to be conscripted.

Measurement and accountability? Mintzberg pointed out that these can force first-rate people to be second rate. The professions have traditionally exercised control through shared values, inculcated through long training; but "measurement and accountability" replaces self-direction with command-and-control, reducing "empowered" professionals to the level of cogs in a government machine.

Performance-related pay? Mintzberg argued that the gradgrinds who now run the public sector ignore the fact that many people go into public service to make the world a better place. They also find that they have to pay people more than they used to because they can no longer call on the public spirit.

Mintzberg recalls that he once heard a business manager proclaim, in all seriousness, that "through control, we can prevent people from falling in love with their business"; and he thinks that something of the same spirit has entered into the souls of government ministers. The emphasis on measurement and accountability is often either pointless (because a lot of what professionals do cannot be measured) or counterproductive. An academic may be promoted for writing a lot of articles that are mere verbiage (check out any of the edited volumes of conference papers that clog up university libraries). A surgeon may be demoted because so many of his patients die despite the fact that his skills are attracting the most difficult cases. Professionals are professionals precisely because they exercise judgment and hold themselves to professional standards; imposing government rules on them destroys what is most valuable about them.

God Is Back

For all these failures and frustrations, the public sector's appetite for management theory is likely to increase in coming years. This is because the financial crisis of 2007–08 put the question of size and scope of the state back at the heart of politics. The crisis exposed the fact that the state has been growing like topsy despite all the rhetoric about "the end of big government." In Britain, the state's share of GDP rose from 37 percent in 2000 to over 50 percent in 2010. It also persuaded politicians to start thinking about the direction of public spending: without serious reform, the demand for government from a rapidly aging population would bankrupt the welfare state.

Governments across the rich world set about balancing their budgets, trimming spending, pruning services, and drawing up long-term plans for more serious reform. In Britain, David Cameron's Conservative-led government announced plans to slim Whitehall departments by one-fifth—more than Margaret Thatcher had ever dared. The result was predictable. Public-sector workers and their allies took to the streets. In France, millions of people of all ages protested against a minor adjustment to the age of retirement. In Britain, a quarter of a million public-sector workers marched through London (and a hard core of anarchists smashed upscale shops and hotels in the West End). In Wisconsin, thousands of public-sector workers occupied the State Capitol. The German Language Society's word of the year for 2010 was *Wurtburger* (irate citizen).

The rise of the Wurtburgers forced governments to confront a question that they had long danced around: the question of public-sector productivity. How can you do more with less? How can you make sure that all the billions devoted to the public sector produces better results? In the 1990s productivity in the private sector had more than doubled, but over the same period, productivity in the public sector had remained flat—or even declined in some vital sectors. In the United States, school expenditure per pupil, adjusted for inflation, doubled in 1980–2005 but achievement on standardized test scores remained flat. Governments recognized that they faced a stark choice: leave the system in place and face a future of rising taxes and declining services or start thinking seriously about public-sector productivity.

This realization is forcing governments back into the arms of the gurus. Politicians are continuing to listen to the Mr. Toads of this world about opportunities for incremental improvements and labor-saving technology (though the New Tories are unlikely to follow their Labor predecessors and pour billions into new computers). But they are also paying more attention to a new breed of gurus who are willing to ask much more fundamental questions about the nature of the state. Three sets of ideas are already arousing a lot of interest in the political world. They are likely to arouse a lot more in coming years as the fiscal squeeze tightens.

FixTheState.com

The first idea is "wikinomics." In *Macrowikinomics*, Don Tapscott and Anthony Williams have updated their work on *Wikinomics* for the public sector. They argue that the radical reduction in the cost of collaboration brought about by the Internet might transform the public sector even more radically than it is transforming the private sector: the state could become a platform upon which various collaborative endeavors could be practiced and upgrade citizens from subjects into "prosumers."

The Web is already handing power to ordinary people. Fed up with all those potholes? You can log onto fixmystreet.com and add your voice to the multitudes. Worried about infirm parents? There are dozens of self-help groups that offer you advice and steer you through the government bureaucracy.

Savvy politicians are using the Web to harness people's energies. The Estonian government green-lighted a remarkable attempt to rid the country of toxic junk: volunteers used GPS devices to locate over 10,000 illegal dumps and then unleashed an army of 50,000 people to clean them up. They are also using the Web to mobilize the energy of public servants—particularly public servants from the younger generation. Vivek Kundra, an Internet-savvy public servant, designed a suite of Web-based apps for the District of Columbia. He has now moved to the White House to bring the same problem-solving attitude to the national stage.

Tapscott and Williams think that we are only at the beginning of the revolution: macrowikinomics will rapidly hand power from bureaucrats to citizens. Douglas Jay, a British Labor politician, once wrote that "in the case of nutrition and health, just as in the case of education, the gentleman in Whitehall really does not know better what is good for people than the people know themselves," a view that most of the architects of the modern welfare state probably shared, though they were too wise to put it down on paper. The Internet will turn Jay's *de haut en bas* world upside down. Governments will increasingly become networks that intertwine themselves with civil society. Citizens will take a more active role in shaping public services and changing the way they operate.

Even governments that see all this citizen activism as a threat to be resisted rather than an opportunity to be seized will not be able to resist the power of the Web. The Web will make comparative information ubiquitous, and ordinary people will be unable to resist the temptation to ask difficult questions about their tax dollars. Why does the United States spend twice as much per patient as Sweden but have a shorter average life expectancy? Why do some American states perform so much worse than others when it comes to education? (McKinsey estimates that the achievement gap in education between low-performing states and the rest costs the country up to $700 billion a year, or 5 percent of GDP.[5]) Why do some nurses spend only 40 percent of their time with patients? People who are armed with these facts will put constant pressure on public services to explain and improve.

The second idea goes under the very ungentlemanly name of disruptive innovation. Clayton Christensen made his reputation looking at the way disruptive innovators have reconfigured markets and boosted productivity in the private sector. More recently, he has devoted a lot of his energy to the public sector, most provocatively to education. In *Disrupting Class: How Disruptive Innovation Will Change the Way the World Learns*, he argues that the education system was designed for a world where most students go on to do repetitive jobs and where teachers were confronted by large classes and confined by the technology of "chalk and talk."[6] But the information revolution is about to disrupt this model: the arrival of ever cheaper and ever more powerful computers is making it possible to customize courses for the needs of individual students. The market for computer-based classes is about to explode, he says, from under 5 percent of all high school classes today to more than half by 2020.

At the same time, Christensen argues that disruptive technology needs a helping hand from what he calls "mutants": new organisms that can be spun out of Leviathan's body. Charter schools, which enjoy more freedom to control their own affairs than classic public schools, will be in the forefront of spreading customized learning, just as they are in the forefront of other radical innovations in the education world.

The third idea is to make more use of the voluntary sector. David Cameron, Britain's Conservative prime minister, is blazing a trail here, trying to transform Britain's over-mighty state into a post-bureaucratic "big society." Cameron is giving parents the power to establish their own publicly funded schools on the model of Swedish "free" schools. He is urging public-sector workers to establish self-governing "cooperatives," on the model of John Lewis, a successful department store that is owned by its employees. He is also contracting out some welfare services to external providers (including voluntary organizations).

Some of the thinking behind this is simple, even cynical: with 50 percent of its GDP eaten up by the public sector, politicians are desperate to off-load their burdens onto somebody else. Some of it is more imaginative: Cameron realizes that governments do not possess a monopoly of wisdom. In particular, he realizes that charities and other voluntary organizations—what Edmund Burke memorably called "little platoons"—are much more innovative than governments. They are better than governments at doing more with less, and much better at coming up with new ideas. The little platoons are little think tanks as well.

One of the most interesting examples of "little platoons" at work comes from the United States, where the welfare state is smaller than that in Europe and civil society more vital. Teach For America (TFA) offers the pampered products of America's elite

universities the modern equivalent of blood, sweat, and tears—
two years teaching children in some of America's toughest schools.
The pay is low. The conditions are testing in the extreme: the
schools are protected by metal detectors (all those guns) and populated by hard-to-control children and adolescents. Accepting a job
means missing out on two years of big money at Goldman Sachs
or McKinsey. Yet competition is so intense that TFA rejects 90
percent of applicants.

TFA has reenergized America's school reform movement. It
has not only poured talent and energy into failing school districts
across the country; it has reconnected America's elite with "the
other America": the America populated by the poor and vulnerable. TFA alumni are now at the forefront of the school reform
movement. Michelle Rhee, the former chancellor of the District
of Columbia, was producing remarkable changes in the district's
unhappy schools before the teachers' unions succeeded in knee-
capping her. TFA has even produced a consultancy that tries to
distill its wisdom and sell it to other school districts. Not bad for
an idea that was dreamt up by a Princeton undergraduate, Wendy
Kopp, as part of her undergraduate dissertation.

The final idea would fit in better with Douglas Jay's view of the
world than the others. This is the idea that the government should
persuade rather than force people into improving their behavior.
This dispenses with the old heavy-handed view of state interven-
tion. Instead, it recommends that the state take advantage of the
power and flexibility of the market to shape people's behavior.
Advocates of this approach would no doubt argue that this is a
matter of encouraging people to listen to their better angels. But
in reality it preserves the mindset of old-fashioned paternalism, in
which people need to be guided from on high to follow their own
best interests.

The most prominent advocate of this position is Cass Sunstein, one of America's leading legal scholars and a long-standing professor at the University of Chicago. Sunstein is the author of *Nudge: Improving Decisions about Health, Wealth, and Happiness* (2008), which he co-wrote with Richard Thaler, a behavioral economist. The argument of *Nudge*, in a nutshell, is that people frequently make poor choices that they look back on with a mixture of regret and bafflement. They give in to short-term impulses or fail to calculate the long-term costs of what they do. But never fear: the government can use insights from behavioral economics to nudge them into behaving in a more sensible manner without ever having to resort to anything so crude as compulsion. Policymakers can "rig the system," as it were, so that people act more prudently—for example, by putting fruit at eye level in a school cafeteria to encourage healthy eating. Sunstein and Thaler have dubbed their approach a "real third way" between the Republicans obsessed with free markets and the Democratic belief in command-and-control.

Sunstein is admirably well placed to give force to his ideas. He holds a prominent job in the Obama administration, as head of the White House Office of Information and Regulatory Affairs. He is also married to another prominent White House insider, Samantha Power. But his influence is not confined to the United States: the British Tories have also caught the nudging bug. Both David Cameron and George Osborne, his chancellor of the exchequer, have lavishly praised Sunstein and Thaler, turning their book into a must-read in British policymaking circles. "Nudging" is well suited to Cameron's brand of post-Thatcherite conservatism because it mixes the paternalism of the shires with the libertarianism of the Notting Hill set. Nudges allow the Tories to make a show of dealing with Britain's manifold social problems—such as the highest rate of teenage pregnancy in Europe and an epidemic of binge drinking—without resorting to the nanny statism that made the previous Labor government so unpopular.

The first three of these new ideas are giving new life to an old idea that was at the heart of the first wave of public-sector reforms: the internal market. The internal market allows the state to function as a wiki-like platform for various providers. It also allows the state to work with voluntary organizations. Over the past two decades the internal market has brought important improvements, particularly in the British National Health Service, which is far more customer-focused than it once was: it has handed power from central governments to local public servants and institutionalized competition. But it has been hampered by the word "internal." These new ideas offer the chance of turning the state into a wiki-like platform. They also offer the chance to harness the energy of voluntary providers.

Reforming the state will be hard work. Governments are by their nature insulated from tooth-and-claw competition. They are also dominated by powerful trade unions that have proved that they can be ruthless in blocking reforms (36 percent of public-sector workers belong to trade unions in the United States, compared with 7 percent in the private sector). Nevertheless there are some reasons for optimism. The devolution of power to schools and hospitals is proving to be a self-reinforcing process: the more powers they get, the more they want. It is also proving to be increasingly popular: witness the American public's reaction to *Waiting for Superman*, a film about the way the educational establishment has tried to destroy charter schools.

The new gurus, then, could prove remarkably useful to public-sector reformers. But they will be useful only so long as these reformers keep two things in mind. The first is that Henry Mintzberg was on to something. Governments should be in the business of setting public servants free from micro-managers, not forcing them to spend their lives ticking boxes. The second is that you should never use the managerialism as an excuse to avoid asking more fundamental questions about the scope of the state. Peter Drucker once argued that if politicians were serious about "really reinventing government" they would go back to "first principles" and ask if large parts of government needed to be there in the first place. Tell Beatrix Potter's "fat-voiced toad" to follow Drucker's advice and he might yet produce value for money.

PART V

WORKERS OF THE WORLD

14

The Common Toad

Charles Handy has the air of an old-fashioned Oxford don rather than a conference-hopping management wizard. It is easier to imagine him giving a tutorial on Aeschylus—reclining in a comfortable leather armchair, taking an occasional puff on his pipe, chuckling at a learned joke—than delivering a PowerPoint presentation on value-chain management. But do not be deceived by appearances: Handy is Europe's most creative management thinker, and a man who, unlike the average Oxford don, deals in big ideas and provocative generalizations.

What makes Handy so striking is his choice of subject. Most gurus have chosen to view the world from the viewpoint of the boardroom. Where are companies heading? How can they reduce their costs and boost their profits? Who should be next for the axe? Handy adopts the viewpoint of the average working stiff. His subject is nothing less than the changing nature of work. In the late 1970s he noticed that work was being reinvented, as trade unions lost their power and companies slimmed down in order to deal with global competition. Managerial capitalism was being replaced by something very different—more entrepreneurial and

more unpredictable—and workers were having to adjust themselves in consequence. Handy chose a subject that affects everyone
other than the underclass and the playboy set. And he wrote about
his chosen subject with unique panache—mixing vivid images
with literate writing and broad themes with an acute eye for detail.

The flavor of Handy's writing can be got from two of his best
images—the "shamrock organization" and the "portfolio life."
He argues that today's organizations resemble nothing so much
as shamrocks—with the three leaves representing core employees,
subcontractors, and temporary workers. He also argues that today's
workers are destined to live "portfolio lives." As human life expectancies increase while organizational life expectancies contract,
workers are destined to pursue more than one career. They may
well shift from one vocation to another; they will certainly spend
some time as contract workers as well as core employees.

The two images fit together neatly. The heart of the shamrock will be staffed by a small squad of corporate heavies, and
governed by the "1/2 by 2 by 3" rule of corporate fitness: half as
many people will be paid twice as much for doing three times as
much work. Two sorts of people will try to sell their services to
this inner ring. The first will be the general, unskilled "somebodies" (as in "somebody can do that"). The second will be "portfolio
people"—independent workers who, through necessity or choice,
put together a packet of different jobs, clients, and types of work.
It will not be unusual for people to be portfolio workers in their
twenties, then join the core of an organization in their thirties,
then return to being a portfolio worker in their "troisième age."
One of Handy's recurring themes is that workers will carry on
working much longer (albeit on a part-time basis), partly to earn
more money and partly to give themselves something to do.

Handy knows whereof he speaks. He started his career as a

classic Shell Man, joining the company as one of fourteen graduates (the "golden boys") and soon being appointed to work as an
economist in charge of Southeast Asia (he had never so much as
opened an economics textbook, but the prevailing assumption, in
Shell as well as in the civil service, was that a man with a degree
in classics from Oxford could pick up economics in no time). But
he soon tired of the corporate life and flirted with a career as a
business professor before becoming a portfolio worker. Though
he enjoyed putting together a portfolio of jobs—writing articles,
giving lectures, delivering the BBC's "thought for the day"—he
also found that hopping from assignment to assignment could be
nerve-wracking. Projects are not as much fun as they might be if
you have nobody to share them with. The periods between one
project and another can be unsettling. And you sometimes end up
taking assignments from people you do not respect for purposes
you do not admire.[1]

Handy has had surprisingly few imitators among today's generation of management gurus: there is no Handy school of management thinking in the way that there is a Drucker school or a
Prahalad school. Most gurus prefer to study "hard" subjects like
strategy rather than "soft" ones like work. But Handy deserves to
be taken more seriously. He realized that work is undergoing a
profound revolution—the most profound since the industrial revolution. And he came closer than anyone before him to charting the
nature of that revolution. His shade will hover over this chapter.

The Workplace Revolution

The world of work is currently undergoing its biggest change since
the late nineteenth century. That era saw the triumph of big organizations. Big companies summoned the workers from the fields

and workshops and crowded them under a single roof. Big government extended its power over more and more areas of society. Big capital, big labor, and big government all embraced the same principle of command-and-control: they divided work into predictable components and divided the workforce into a steep hierarchy—the managers at the top and the "hands" at the bottom, executing their orders.

The current changes are more complicated than the ones in the late nineteenth century. Are organizations getting smaller or bigger? Are workers being empowered or displaced? Are careers being destroyed or reconfigured? There are no clear answers to any of these questions. But the changes are nevertheless driven by equally powerful forces.

The Internet gives people the power to reconfigure brainwork. Companies can slice and dice intellectual tasks and outsource them around the world. Office workers can skip their commutes and work from home but still summon up the most advanced computer resources in the world, thanks to the cloud. Solo workers can plug themselves into global networks, through various social media, or summon up the help of "virtual secretaries" or "cognitive assistants" that help to organize their work and filter their email and phone calls.

The pill has paved the way for the feminization of the workforce. Commentators have advanced many explanations for the rise of career women, from the force of ideas (writers such as Betty Friedan and Germaine Greer) to the power of example (leaders such as Margaret Thatcher and Hillary Clinton). The pill trumps them all. The spread of the pill has not only allowed women to get married later; it has also increased their incentives to invest in skills, particularly skills that are hard to learn and take time to pay off. The knowledge that they would not have to drop out of, say, law school to have a baby made law school more attractive.

Other advances on the biological front are also reshaping work. The declining popularity of smoking, the introduction of anti-cholesterol drugs, advancing knowledge about the links between obesity and illness—all are helping to prolong people's working lives. At the same time, governments, terrified of the rising cost of entitlements, are asking people to retire later. Today's graduates may find themselves working into their seventies and still enjoying two decades of retirement.

As biological life expectancy has increased, corporate life ex-pectancy has shrunk. The mighty fortresses that Alfred Sloan and his allies built have been replaced by much less substantial struc-tures: "virtual organizations," "corporate condominiums," and, the engines of most job growth: small entrepreneurial companies.

Virtually Abnormal

What do all these changes add up to? The most sweeping answer is that they add up to the rise of a new sort of economy—an econ-omy dominated by free agents rather than organizations. Compa-nies are dissolving into networks of contracts, the argument goes; governments are contracting out as much as possible; work is being deconstructed into a succession of projects, which can be done from home as easily as from the office; and careers are going the way of abstinence before marriage.

There is some evidence to support this argument. The average length of job tenure is shrinking (for American men aged fifty-five to sixty-four it fell from 15.3 years in 1983 to 10.2 years in 2000). Manpower has taken over from General Motors as America's biggest employer. The fashion for temporary work has even reached the boardroom. The Business Talent Group in Los Angeles or Epoch in Boston offer just-in-time CEOs.

Workers are also getting more footloose and fancy free. Knowledge workers have always owed their primary obligation to their professional guilds rather than their corporate masters. Now they are getting better at selling themselves on the market: witness all those star professors who ricochet from one university to another with the same enthusiasm as star footballers. Young people have always been reluctant to wear the company collar. Now they have common sense as well as animal spirits on their side: many of them grew up watching their parents being downsized in the 1980s and 1990s. They are also dab hands at using the Web to find out how well companies pay their workers and how well they treat them.

But there are lots of holes in this argument. Organizations still have powerful advantages over networks of free agents: they possess skills and competencies that cannot be easily replicated on the open market. Boris Groysberg, of Harvard Business School, conducted a fascinating study of Wall Street analysts. These analysts are ideal free agents. Their skills are highly portable and they can get another job by simply crossing the street. However, Groysberg discovered that star analysts saw immediate decline in their performance if they switched employers. This was most marked for those who moved from higher-rated companies to lower-rated ones, but it was also noticeable for people who moved between similar firms. Talented people may think that their brainpower allows them to walk upon water, but in reality many are walking on the stones that their employers have conveniently placed beneath them.

Organizations are also social institutions. Daniel Pink, the most prominent exponent of the free-agent school, likes to talk about Karl Marx's revenge—the workers now have the means of production in their hands in the form of laptops and Black-Berrys. But people are social animals. They enjoy the rituals of office life. They like working with their colleagues. The future of work will be dictated by the human need to belong as much as by the logic of technology.

What is happening at the moment is more complicated than the rise of "free agents." Rather than dissolving into atomized individuals, organizations are splitting into two groups: an inner core of full-time workers and a periphery—or perhaps a penumbra—of part-time and contract workers. It is this growing distinction between the core and the penumbra rather than the rise of the free agent that is the most distinctive change in the modern workforce.

The core of modern companies consists of company men and women who are repositories of the company's distinctive values and skills. Four-fifths of CEOs are appointed from the inside, according to a study of the world's top 2,500 public companies by Booz & Company, a practice that is amply justified by their relative performance.[2] Of the CEOs who have left office over the past decade, insiders have produced significantly superior results, with an average return of 2.5 percent a year compared with 1.8 percent for outsiders. They have also lasted longer in their jobs (7.9 years compared with 6.0 years) and have been less likely to be defenestrated.

The loyalists who form the heart of today's companies probably work harder than yesterday's company men. But they are better rewarded, too. By the time they reach their forties, high-flyers can expect to be rewarded with partnerships (if they are in the professional service sector) or bonuses and stock options (if they work for banks or companies). These loyalists are surrounded by an ever-growing cloud of associates. Some of these "associates" are former loyalists who have left to start a family or who have lost out in the race for promotion. Some are contract workers who have been brought in to work on a particular project—IT workers who are installing a computer system or proofreaders who are helping with a particularly heavy workload.

Though these associates are the closest things to Pink's free agents, they are much less free than they seem. They usually form close relations with particular companies, rather like small fish swimming along in the wake of bigger fish. They often crave social connections. Many freelancers are forming "virtual guilds" such as LawLink (for lawyers), Sermo (for physicians), NewDoc (for dentists), and H-Net (for social scientists). These guilds provide job-hoppers with a source of stability, allow them to cultivate their reputations with their peers, and provide them with a way of keeping their skills and knowledge up to date. Sermo allows physicians to exchange information and advice about the latest medical breakthroughs. It is also ingeniously self-policing: the community ranks members based on the quality of their answers.

Freelancers crave physical as well as intellectual connections. In 2005, Brad Neuberg got together with three friends to rent some space in a run-down part of San Francisco.[3] They furnished the space with wireless Internet, a few folding tables, and a trendy name, Spiral Muse—and were soon inundated with requests for a seat at the table. Since then, co-working "offices" (variously dubbed Hubs, Sandbox Suites, and Citizen Spaces) have mushroomed across the world. Many of them are much fancier than the original Spiral Muse: one of the most popular Hubs in London, near King's Cross Station, is housed in a huge converted warehouse and contains kitchens and lounges. But they appeal to the same basic desire: to enjoy the social benefits of office life without the tedious restrictions. And, whether fancy or basic, they often arouse passionate emotions in their users, who refer to them as "hubs of interaction" and "fraternities of mutual interest."[4]

Woman Power

Only a generation ago, working women performed menial jobs and were routinely subjected to casual sexism, as *Mad Men*, a program about advertising executives in the early 1960s, brilliantly demonstrates. Today, women make up almost half of the American workforce and 60 percent of university students. They constitute the majority of professional workers in many countries (51 percent in the United States, for example) and run some of the world's most successful companies, such as PepsiCo, Archer Daniels Midland, and W. R. Grace. In the European Union, women have filled six of the eight million new jobs created since 2000. In the United States, women make up more than two-thirds of the employees in ten out of the fifteen job categories that the U.S. Census department thinks will grow fastest in the next few years.

The growing demand for female labor is a function of economic progress. The landmark book in the rise of feminism was arguably not Betty Friedan's *The Feminine Mystique* but Daniel Bell's *The Rise of Post-Industrial Society*, an account of the decline of the manufacturing sector (where men had an advantage in terms of brute strength) and the rise of the service sector (where women can compete as well as men). What happened in the developed world over the past fifty years is now being repeated in the developing world.

The story of women's economic empowerment comes with some stings in the tail. Women are still underrepresented in the middle and upper rungs of the occupational ladder. Only fourteen of the bosses of the S&P 500 companies and five of the bosses of the FTSE 100 companies are women. Women make up 17 percent of board members in the United States, 9 percent in Europe, and 2 percent in Asia. The upper ranks of management consultancies and banks are dominated by men. The typical full-time female worker earns only about 80 percent as much as the typical male.

This no doubt owes something to sexism. But the biggest reason why women remain frustrated is more profound: many women are forced to choose between motherhood and careers. Childless women in corporate America earn almost as much as men. Mothers earn 15 percent less, and single mothers 40 percent less. The cost of motherhood is particularly steep for fast-track women. Traditional "female" jobs such as teaching mix well with motherhood because their hours are relatively generous. But successful companies have up-or-out promotion systems and relentless schedules. Companies expect future bosses to have worked in several departments and countries. Professional service firms reward lucrative partnerships only to the most dedicated. The reason for the income gap is arguably the very opposite of prejudice. It is precisely because women are judged by exactly the same standards as men that they have to choose between having children or staying on the treadmill.

The rise of women is part of a bigger process: the diversification of the workforce. Today's workers come in all sorts of shapes and sizes. They may include sixty-year-olds who grew up listening to vinyl LPs (and thinking they were very cool doing so) and twenty-year-olds who live in a virtual world. They may include hard-core company types and associates who have only just walked in through the virtual door. These diverse workers are often part of a global supply chain that keeps going twenty-four hours a day.

Students of "diversity" are usually hung up on race and sex, but in fact some of the most interesting management problems are posed by the aging of the workforce. Companies are flexing their work schedules to suit older people. Britain's Asda has introduced long winter breaks (known as Benidorm leave after a popular Spanish tourist destination) for older workers and given them time off to help out with their grandchildren. Some are going further and reengineering their production processes to make life easier for older people. BMW decided to staff one of its production lines with workers who reflected the age composition of the company in 2017. Though the production line was quickly dubbed "the pensioner's line," the company boosted the line's productivity by 7 percent over the year, bringing it in line with the rest of the plant, by introducing seventy relatively small changes, such as new chairs, weight-adapted footwear, magnifying lenses, and adjustable tables.

The Old Adam

"Work" has always aroused contradictory emotions. For some, work is "Adam's curse," the eternal punishment for man's original sin, and the essence of freedom is freedom from routine labor (in *The Communist Manifesto,* Marx and Engels envisioned Communist society as one where you can go hunting in the morning and be a literary critic in the afternoon). For others, work is the meaning of life. In *Paradise Lost,* Milton was careful to portray Adam and Eve as working hard tending the garden. Milton's fellow Puritans insisted that *laborare est orare*—to work is to pray—or, more pessimistically, that "the devil makes work for idle hands."

These contradictory emotions are just as sharp today. Tom Peters thinks that we live in an age of liberation. Never before have people had more control over their working lives. Many others think that we live in an age of anxiety. The old certainties—a stable job and a stable career—are being replaced by a bombardment of tasks and an all-pervading angst. Even more people are ambivalent. Many celebrate the advances in female opportunities—but lament the rise of BlackBerry orphans. They celebrate the demise of the corporate lockstep—but lament the loss of predictable rhythms. The new world of opportunity is also a world of buzzing uncertainty.

New technology is certainly providing many workers— particularly brainworkers—with freedoms that were unimaginable in previous generations. The Internet puts a world of information and contacts at your fingertips. Free agents can work from home (or office hubs if they crave human companionship). Office workers (including the author of this book) can spend a couple of days a week working from home. In 2009, 1.7 million more American employees worked at home than in 2000, according to the 2009 American Community Survey.[5]

The empowering effect of this new technology is particularly dramatic for women, who have been the chief victims of prejudice and inflexibility in the past, but also extends to men who are trying to juggle child-rearing with work. A growing number of companies are learning to divide up the workweek in new ways— judging workers on how much they work over a year rather than a week ("annualized hours"), allowing them to work nine days a fortnight ("compressed time"), letting them come in early or late ("glide time"), and allowing husbands and wives to share jobs ("family contracts"). Almost half of Sun Microsystems' employees work at home or from satellite offices near their homes. Raytheon, a maker of missile systems, allows workers to take every other Friday off to take care of family business. Ernst & Young, an accountancy, tries to lighten the impact of tax season, which extends from January to April, on families, with personal support and financial relief for childcare expenses.

Some companies are also making their workplaces more family friendly. SAS, an American software developer, is a market leader here. The company employs more than 125 full-time workers whose primary job is to provide childcare, holiday camps,

eldercare, healthcare, or fitness programs. The childcare facilities in the company's North Carolina headquarters have room for
more than six hundred children. The healthcare clinic caters to
dependents as well as full-time workers. Pediatric physicians dispense advice twenty-four hours a day, seven days a week. The
company even employs specialists in looking after old people and
has a "caring closet" that is stocked with wheelchairs, crutches,
and shower seats.[6]

But there is also a dark side to the new world of work. In George
Orwell's *Animal Farm*, the mighty cart-horse, Boxer, inspires the
other animals with his heroic cry of "I will work harder." He gets
up in the middle of the night to do a couple of hours' extra ploughing. He even refuses to take a day off when he splits his hoof. And
his reward for all this effort? As soon as he falters he is carted off to
the knacker's yard to be turned into glue and bone-meal.

For many people, *Animal Farm* looks as much like a parable
about capitalism as one about socialism: they are having to work
ever harder while losing the last vestiges of job security. Workers live ever more frazzled lives. They get home late in the evening, check their email every couple of minutes, and sacrifice
their weekends for corporate travel or conferences. The Corporate
Leadership Council, an American consultancy that surveys 1,100
companies every quarter, reports that the average "job footprint"
increased by one-third between the beginning of the recession and
2010. The Hay Group, a British consultancy that surveyed a thousand people in late 2009, discovered that two-thirds (65 percent)
of workers said that they were putting in unpaid overtime. The
reward for all this effort is frozen pay and shrinking perks.

There are a few signs that companies will ease up a little as
the economy recovers. Companies have learned that "overstretch"
has its downsides. Absenteeism has been on the rise. Low-level

corporate crime has been growing. Corporate loyalty has been plummeting. The Corporate Leadership Council reported in 2010 that the number of workers who are willing to put in "discretionary effort" has dropped by half since 2007, while the number who claim that they are "disengaged" from their jobs has risen from one-tenth to one-fifth, though discretionary effort and engagement are both vital for innovation.

But even if some companies ease up a bit, overstretch is probably here to stay. In the West, companies are trying to do more with less as they cope with slow growth and heavy regulations. In the rest of the world, demand often exceeds supply. And in the public sector, governments are slimming their workforces even as their obligations mount. Everywhere, new technology is allowing work to invade every aspect of people's private lives. The great trio of the wired worker—the computer, the Internet connection, and the BlackBerry—has morphed into a yapping Cerberus, invading people's leisure time and destroying their peace of mind. The old joke at Microsoft is becoming universal: "We offer flexitime—you can work any eighteen-hour shifts that you want."

At the same time people are getting more anxious about work. This is partly because fear of unemployment is pervasive. Most European countries have been stuck with unemployment rates above 5 percent for years. America's unemployment rate hit 10 percent during the recession, and Spain's rate is currently an astonishing 20 percent. But it is also because of changes in the nature of the jobs that remain. Jobs are constantly being reorganized in the name of efficiency (or sometimes just management fashion). Reorganization led to a spate of spectacular suicides and attempted suicides at France Télécom in 2007–08. One man stabbed himself in the middle of a business meeting (he survived). A woman leapt from a fifth-floor office window after sending a suicide email to her father: "I have decided to kill myself tonight . . . I can't take the new reorganization." Most people vent their angst in less extreme ways.

Work is becoming more fragmented as well as more burdensome. Companies may delight in their ability to slice work into its component parts and then distribute it across a globe-spanning production chain, but workers find themselves having to deal with meaningless fragments of work. They have none of the craftsman's pleasure in taking a job from start to finish; instead they are bombarded with slithers and slices. The result is alienation and anomie.

A growing number of working women are confronted with a drastic choice as they enter their thirties—between their careers and children. Many professional women have chosen the former: 40 percent of professional Swiss women are childless. Others delay childbearing for so long that they are forced into the arms of the booming fertility industry. A striking number of women find it difficult to get back into full-time work. An American study of women who left work to have children found that, though 93 percent wanted to return to work, only 74 percent of them succeeded in doing so and only 40 percent returned to full-time jobs.

Women are not alone in finding it hard to juggle jobs and children. Lynda Gratton, of the London Business School, recalls working for a consultancy in the 1990s where overwork was common. Over a period of a couple of months, the human-resources department hired a film crew to go around the world interviewing the young children of senior partners. The crew asked the children to talk about what Daddy was like. The stories they told were of fathers who were frequently absent or distracted, far more consumed by work than family life.

The Levity Principle

A growing number of companies are compensating for all this angst by embracing the cult of fun. The cult started at both ends of the cerebral spectrum. Silicon Valley companies installed rock climbing walls in their reception areas and inflated animals in their offices. Walmart ordered its cashiers to smile at all and sundry. As the cult grew, comedians poked. Homer Simpson's employer, a nuclear power plant, has a regular "funny hat day." One of the most blistering episodes of *The Office* dissects the enforced jocularity of "Red Nose Day."

The cult proved ridicule-proof. Acclaris, an American IT company, has a chief fun officer. Perkins Coie, a law firm, has a happiness committee. TD Bank, the U.S. arm of Canada's Toronto-Dominion, has a "WOW" department that dispatches costume-clad teams to "surprise and delight" successful workers. Red Bull has installed a slide in its London office so that people can slide downstairs. ePrize transforms its headquarters into a giant haunted house every Halloween and awards an "eek prize" for the best Halloween costume.[7]

Fun at work has become a business in its own right. Indeed, a British company called Fun at Work offers you "more hilarity than you can handle," including replacing your receptionists with *Ab Fab* look-alikes. Indian physician Madan Kataria sells "laughter yoga" to a roster of corporate clients. Chiswick Park, an office development in London, brands itself with the slogan "enjoy-work," and hosts lunchtime events such as sheep shearing and goose herding.

Google has long been the market leader in corporate fun. The company has invested heavily in the standard accoutrements of fun: volleyball courts, bicycle paths, a yellow brick road, a toy dinosaur, regular games of roller hockey, several professional masseuses. (The company's massage-addicted founders even toyed with the name "Backrub" before settling for Google.) But now two other companies have challenged Google for the jester's crown—Twitter, up the road in San Francisco, and Zappos, a state away in Nevada.

Twitter employs a team of people whose job is to make workers happy (for example, by providing them with cold towels on a hot day). The company's Web page features workers wearing cowboy hats and boasts that "crazy things happen every day . . . it's pretty ridiculous." Zappos, an online shoe and clothing shop, describes creating "fun and a little weirdness" as one of its core values. Tony Hsieh, the company's boss, shaves his head, spends 10 percent of his time studying what he calls the "science of happiness," and once joked that Zappos had issued a class action lawsuit against Walt Disney for describing itself as "the happiest place on earth." The company practices regular "random acts of generosity," when workers form a noisy conga line and single out one of their colleagues for praise. The praisee has to wear a hat for a week.

The most unpleasant thing about the fashion for fun is that it is mixed with compulsion. Zappos and ePrize don't just celebrate wackiness; they require it. Compulsory fun is not only cringe-making—Twitter calls its office a Twoffice; Boston Pizza encourages workers to send "golden bananas" to colleagues who are "having fun while being the best"—but hollow and contrived. You do not have to look hard to see the crude management thinking behind the "fun" façade—the desire to brand the company as better than its rivals or the plan to boost productivity through team building. "Having fun puts you in the zone and optimizes your brain chemistry for creativity," says Josh Linkner, ePrize's boss.[8]

The Complexity of Careers

The three most striking changes in the world of work—the division of companies into core workers and associates; the growing diversity of the workforce; and the spread of "flexi-working" of one kind or another—are all making careers much more complicated.

Some gurus go further and argue that careers are not so much complicated as dead. This is nonsense. Core workers still spend their lives climbing up the corporate ladder, much as company men once did. They also receive the old-fashioned mixture of monetary and psychic rewards (though membership at gyms has replaced membership at country clubs). Non-core workers also frequently cling to as many vestiges of old-fashioned careers as they can.

But there is no doubt that things are getting more complicated: Tesco profiles and segments its workers in much the same way that it profiles and segments its customers in order to try to understand what is going on.[9] Deloitte claims to practice something called "mass career customization."

The most obvious reason for all this complexity is the feminization of the workforce. Companies are belatedly addressing the fact that women have babies and that babies need to be cared for. Professional service firms are modifying their up-or-out practices. Addleshaw Goddard, a law firm, has invented a "senior assistant" track, as opposed to a partner track, for women who want to combine work with motherhood. Booz & Company, a management consultancy, has identified bits of consulting that can be done from home or during short-stints in the office. Ernst & Young and other accountancies have increased their efforts to keep strong connections with women who take time off to have children and then ease them back into the full-time workforce.

Companies are introducing the equivalent of gap years for veteran employees. John Lewis, a British department store, offers six months' paid sabbatical for people who have been in the company for twenty-five years. Barclays is one of many companies that now allow people to take five years of unpaid leave. Companies are also getting better at managing retirement. Confronted with the imminent retirement of the biggest generation of workers in history—Boeing stands to lose 40 percent of its skilled workers by 2015, for example—companies are rethinking the old model of retirement whereby people worked for forty years and then disappeared, a little worse for their farewell drinks, clutching their gold watches and farewell cards. They are introducing "phased retirement." Abbott Laboratories, a large American healthcare company, allows veteran workers to work for four days a week or take up to twenty-five more vacation days a year. Most consultancies have developed pools of retired or semi-retired workers who can be called upon to work on individual projects. They are also trying to capture all the tacit knowledge that is about to walk out of the door. Construction companies such as Sweden's Elmhults Konstruktions and the Netherlands' Hazenberg Bouw have introduced mentoring systems that encourage prospective retirees to train their replacements.

All these changes mean that the traditional image of careers as ladders is becoming outdated. Lynda Gratton suggests that we should adopt instead the image of "a series of ascending bell-shaped curves—or what's termed carillon curves, in which energy and the accumulation of resources grow and then plateau, only to grow again."[10] Other commentators have suggested the image of on-ramps and off-ramps: women will drive off the career highway, via an off-ramp, in their thirties to raise children and then drive back onto the highway, via on on-ramp, in their forties.

Even these complicated images are far too simple to capture what is going on with the growing cloud of "associates." These associates consist of very different groups, from highly skilled portfolio workers who are giving advice on strategy to garden-variety "somebodies" who are being hired to do more menial tasks. They will also have very different relations with parent companies, ranging from mothers who are taking a few years on half-time to contract workers who are being brought in to do specific jobs. Keeping track of all these diverse people and multifaceted relationships will be a major undertaking in its own right.

One of the oddest consequences of all this complexity is the fashion for Ruritanian job titles. Management gurus love to sing the praises of flat organizations. But in the real world of organizations, title inflation is so rampant that it is producing its own vocabulary—words such as "uptitling" and "title fluffing"—and its own industry. There is even a Web site to help you with the title fluffing—just take your job title and mix in a few more words (such as "global," "interface," and "customer") and you are ready to negotiate with your boss.

The rot starts at the top. Once upon a time, companies had two or three "chiefs"; now they often have dozens. A few companies have more than one chief executive—CB Richard Ellis, a real-estate services firm, has four. A growing number have chiefs for almost every activity or function under the sun, from learning to diversity to apologizing. Southwest Airlines has a chief Twitter officer. Coca-Cola and Marriott have chief blogging officers. Kodak has a chief blogging officer and a chief listening officer. Molson Coors Brewing Company has at least fifteen executives with the word "chief" in their title, including a global chief business development officer and a global chief synergies officer.

And "chiefs" are relatively rare compared with "presidents" and their various declensions (assistant vice-president, etc.). Almost everybody in the banking world from the receptionist on up is a president of some sort. A study of the titles of members of LinkedIn, a professional network, in 2005–09 revealed an inflation rate over four years of 312 percent for presidents and 426 percent for vice-presidents. The inflation rate for chiefs was a mere 275 percent.

Title-fluffing is as rampant among the Indians as among the chiefs. The U.S. International Association of Administrative Professionals—formerly the National Secretaries Association—reports that it has more than five hundred job titles under its umbrella, ranging from front-desk coordinator to first-impressions officer. Paper boys are "media distribution officers." Bin men are "recycling officers." Toilet cleaners are "sanitation consultants." Sandwich-makers at Subway have the phrase "sandwich artist" emblazoned on their lapels. Even the normally linguistically pure French have gotten in on the act: cleaning ladies are becoming *techniciens de surface* (surface technicians).

Up-titling is mainly driven by the very fashion that is supposed to make titles redundant. Workers crave important-sounding titles to give them the illusion that they are making progress. Managers who no longer have anyone to manage are fobbed off with inflated titles, much as superannuated politicians are made chancellor of the duchy of Lancaster or lord president of the council (George McGovern once refused to accept a fancy-sounding job on the sensible grounds that "the longer the title, the less important the job"). All employees, from the executive suite downward, want to fluff up their CV as a hedge against being sacked.

Companies also use fancy job titles to signal that they are *au fait* with the latest fashion. The fashion for greenery is currently producing a new legion of chiefs (such as chief green officer or green ambassador), much as the fashion for corporate social responsibility once did. BP's travails in the Gulf will undoubtedly have the same effect: we can expect a bull market in chief safety officers and chief risk officers. The BBC tries to combat its reputation as a state-funded behemoth by giving its functionaries jazzy-sounding titles such as "vision controller of multiplatform and portfolio."

The American IT sector has been a champion driver of title inflation. Steve Jobs calls himself "chief know it all." Jerry Yang and David Filos, the founders of Yahoo!, call themselves "chief Yahoos." Thousands of IT types dub themselves things like (chief) scrummaster, guru, evangelist, or, a particularly favorite at the moment, ninja.

But leadership in title inflation, as in so much else, is passing to the developing world, particularly India and China, where respect for hierarchy is deeply engrained and labor markets are tight. The result is an explosion of titles. Companies have taken to creating mean-ingless jobs such as "outbound specialist." They have also taken to staging public celebrations of promotions from one meaningless job (additional deputy director) to another (assistant deputy director).

The Social Contract

These profound changes in the nature of work have generated a fierce debate about what might be termed the social contract. What obligations do companies owe their workers? And what role should the state play in this more flexible labor market?

The most popular answer to the first question is that compa-nies owe their workers lifetime employability rather than lifetime employment—or at least a chance to keep their skills up to date. This is becoming widely accepted among workers as well as em-ployers: one survey showed that 94 percent of workers thought that they, rather than their employers, are responsible for their long-term futures. It is also becoming the basis of employment negotiations. The Corporate Executive Board argues that companies that offer workers a chance to fine-tune their skills can attract better workers while also paying them 10 percent less than those that don't.

The emphasis on employability is part of a bigger shift—from long-term contracts between employers and workers to a perpetual negotiation between the two for advantage. This is reflected in the rise of professional social networks such as America's LinkedIn, Germany's Viadeo, and Germany's XING. Job hunters use the networks to advertise their skills and gather information on opportunities and employers, and people who are in jobs can also use them to show that they might be interested in moving if they are wooed hard enough. Social networks not only make the labor market more transparent, cutting out the middleman in the process; they also add to the sense that we are all up for hire, however happy we are in our current jobs.

Good Toad, Bad Toad

The debate about the moral contract between employers and workers points to a further debate about the moral contract between the state and its citizens. There is broad agreement that the state has an important role in making flexible labor markets work efficiently and fairly. Governments have an obligation to provide training for less skilled workers, given that companies have little incentive to invest in people who have few opportunities to move elsewhere, and given that low-skilled workers are also bearing the brunt of economic change, as manual jobs are shifted offshore or mechanized out of existence. But it is also arguable that governments have a further obligation to mitigate the impact of flexible work on family life.

The most perplexing problem with the new world of work is the impact that it has had on children. Even well-off parents worry that they spend too little time with their children, thanks to crowded schedules and that ever-buzzing BlackBerry. For poorer parents, juggling the twin demands of work and child-rearing can be a nightmare. Childcare eats a terrifying proportion of the family budget, and many child-minders are untrained, but quitting work to look after the children can mean financial disaster. British children who are brought up in two-parent families where only one parent works are almost three times more likely to be poor than children in families where both parents work.

A survey for the British Children's Society paints a depressing picture of the consequences of the new world of work. The proportion of mothers of nine- to twelve-month-old babies who do at least some work has increased from 25 percent in the 1980s to 75 percent today. Over the same period, the proportion of children displaying emotional and behavioral problems has more than doubled. Most parents feel that something is awry. The Children's Society survey found that 60 percent of parents agreed that "nowadays parents aren't able to spend enough time with their children." Only 22 percent disagreed. A similar survey in the United States found that 74 percent of parents said that they do not have enough time for their children.

Nor does the problem disappear as children get older. In most countries schools finish early in the afternoon. In the United States they close down for two months in the summer. Only a few places—Denmark, Sweden, and, to a lesser extent, France and Quebec—provide comprehensive systems of after-school care. The result is an epidemic of latchkey children who, at their worst, fuel the sort of social problems that have been portrayed in American television series such as *The Corner* and *The Wire*.

The private sector can be relied upon to solve some of these problems: the war for talent is compelling companies to be more female friendly, and new technology is making it easier to slice and dice work in imaginative new ways. The corporate sector will change even faster as women discover their economic power. Large numbers of talented women are already hopping off the corporate treadmill to form companies that are more sensitive to their needs. Over the past decade, the number of privately owned companies started by women in the United States has increased twice as fast as the number of those owned by men. Women-owned companies employ more people than the largest five hundred companies combined. Eden McCallum and Axiom Legal have applied a network model to management consultancy and legal services respectively, and found that network members work when it suits them and the company uses its scale to make sure that clients get their problems dealt with immediately.

But the private sector will inevitably focus on professional women (who can pay for their own childcare) rather than on working-class women (who, in addition to needing paid child-care, have less value on the market). The state has an important part to play in supplanting the private sector when it comes to poorer women. This will involve restructuring welfare, which was created in a world where most women stayed at home. It will also involve a more active public policy. Some rich countries have done too little to help poorer women combine work with motherhood. The United States spends only 0.5 percent of its GDP on public support for childcare, and is the only rich country that refuses to provide mothers with paid maternity leave (ninety-eight countries provide fourteen weeks or more of paid leave). Even in an era of retrenchment, this needs to change.

The new world of work offers huge possibilities compared with the old treadmill: more people having control over their own lives; more working from home rather than commuting; more glide time and flexitime; a more gentle transition from full-time employment to retirement. At the same time, it also offers huge problems in terms of anxiety and overstretch, problems that can partly be solved by more enlightened company policies but will also require more active state policies.

Philip Larkin once wrote a poem called "Toads" about the "sickening poison" of office life. But he later softened his damning judgment in "Toads Revisited." A master of grumpiness, Larkin nevertheless acknowledged that he rather liked his "in-tray" and his "loaf-haired secretary." "Give me your arm, old toad; help me down Cemetery Road." Turning the bad toad into the good toad is going to be one of the greatest challenges of policymakers of all kinds, public and corporate, in the coming years.

15

The Battle for Brainpower

In a speech at Harvard University in 1943, Winston Churchill observed that "the empires of the future will be empires of the mind." He might have added that the battles of the future will be battles for mind power or talent. To be sure, the old battles for natural resources are still with us: China is busy gobbling up resources across the world, particularly in Africa. But they are being supplemented by new battles for talent—not just among companies (which are competing for "human resources") but also among countries (which fret about the "balance of brains" as well as the "balance of power").

The war for talent is at its fiercest in high-tech industries. The arrival of Google on an already crowded stage in the late 1990s intensified the battle still further. The company has assembled a formidable hiring machine to help it find the people it needs. It has also experimented with clever new recruiting tools, such as billboards featuring complicated mathematical problems. Other tech giants have responded by supercharging their own talent machines and, less inspiringly, suing people who suddenly leave. Yahoo! is fighting for its life by hiring a constellation of academic stars.

But a large and growing number of businesses outside the tech industry are also fighting tooth and claw for brainpower. Consultancies (particularly McKinsey and the Boston Consulting Group) and investment banks (particularly Goldman Sachs) have long prided themselves on their ability to hire the best and the brightest. Now the war for talent is being carried to new extremes by the arrival of high-paying new rivals such as hedge funds.

An Idea Whose Time Has Not Gone

The idea of a war for talent has taken a battering of late. The 2007–08 recession threw millions of people (including 126,000 highly paid Wall Streeters) out of work. Many economists and business people think that the West has embarked on a prolonged period of sluggish growth and depressed labor markets. The left-wing *Washington Monthly* has written the obituary of "the great American job machine,"[1] while the right-wing *Wall Street Journal* editorial page has worried that America is going the same way as Europe, with twenty-somethings spending years on the dole.

Nor does stocking up on talent seem to protect companies from getting it spectacularly wrong. Enron saw itself as the cavalry division in the war for talent. It recruited the smartest guys in the room, as a 2005 documentary on the company put it, hiring up to 250 MBAs a year at the height of its fame. It applied a "rank-and-yank" system of evaluation, showering the alphas with gold and sacking the gammas. And it promoted raw talent much faster than boring old experience. Another corporate disaster, Long-Term Capital Management, was even more talent-heavy than Enron, boasting not only MBAs but Nobel Prize winners among its staff.

There is clearly much more to good management than brainpower. Among other things, it requires rewarding experience as well as talent, cultivating judgment as well as IQ, and applying strong ethical and internal controls. Indeed, talent-intensive businesses have a particular interest in maintaining high ethical standards. Whereas in manufacturing industries a decline in such standards is often slow, in talent-intensive ones it can be terrifyingly sudden, as Arthur Andersen and Enron found to their cost.

Various business gurus have turned against the "talent myth" entirely and launched an all-out critique on the notion of a war for talent. Some gurus point out that companies use the word "talent" to mean all sorts of different things, from alpha workers at the restrictive end to the entire workforce at the meaningless one. Others go even further. Geoff Colvin, a senior editor of *Fortune*, argues that "talent is overrated" in his book of that title.[2] Boris Groysberg subtitles *Chasing Stars*, his award-winning 2010 book, *The Myth of Talent and the Portability of Performance*.[3] And in *Smart Is Not Enough!* Alan Guarino, the founder of Cornell International, a search firm, uses the ominous subtitle *The South Pole Strategy and Other Powerful Talent Management Secrets*.[4]

These critics twist the knife by pointing out that the idea has a dubious history. The phrase was first coined by three McKinsey consultants, Ed Michaels, Helen Handfield-Jones, and Beth Axelrod, whose *War for Talent* was intended to be one of the defining books of the dotcom era, but which unfortunately came out just after the tech bubble burst.[5] The war turned into a rout, and high-priced talent found itself working in Starbucks.

This critique of the war for talent resounds with many people's experience of the dismal job market. It also comes with the endorsement of one of the most successful management gurus in the business, Malcolm Gladwell. But it is far from convincing. Look at the emerging world: successful companies report turnover rates of 40 percent. And look at the market for engineers in the rich world:

companies cannot find any of these among the crowds of media studies graduates. The recession may have complicated the picture somewhat, but the war for talent continues to rage.

The global economy is becoming ever more brain-intensive. Baruch Lev, of New York University, argues that "intangible assets"—ranging from a skilled workforce to patents to know-how—account for more than half of the market capitalization of America's public companies.[6] Accenture, a management consultancy, calculates that intangible assets have shot up from 20 percent of the value of companies in the S&P 500 in 1980 to about 70 percent today. McKinsey has divided American jobs into three categories: "transformational" (extracting raw materials or converting them into finished goods), "transactional" (interactions that can easily be scripted or automated), and "tacit" (complex interactions requiring a high level of judgment). Over the past six years, the number of "tacit" jobs has grown two and a half times as fast as transactional jobs and three times as fast as employment in general. These jobs now make up some 40 percent of the American labor market and account for 70 percent of the jobs created since 1998.[7]

The relationship between brainpower and economic success is becoming tighter. Brains are the price of admission to the world's great money machines, from consultancies to banks. They are also the price of admission to great entrepreneurial clusters in Silicon Valley and Tel Aviv. Today's greatest entrepreneurs have mastered the art of turning brains into gold. Microsoft has ingested about $30 billion of financial capital over its lifetime and has created about $221 billion of shareholder wealth. Google has used only about $5 billion of capital but has created about $124 billion of shareholder wealth.

Traditional talent machines, such as banks and consultancies, do a better job than ever at recruiting and poaching, training and promoting, talent. Goldman Sachs reengineered its recruitment system in 1999, putting more emphasis on formal training, establishing Goldman Sachs University, and telling senior partners to put more emphasis on developing talent. McKinsey has fine-tuned its talent machine, boosting its training budget to $100 million and recruiting people from places other than business schools. Moreover, obsession with talent is no longer confined to blue-chip companies such as Goldman Sachs and General Electric. It can be found everywhere in the corporate world, from credit card companies to hotel chains to the retail trade.

People who dismiss the war for talent have got it upside down. The war for talent in the Western private sector will continue and, indeed, intensify as the economy begins to grow. But that is not the heart of it. The war for talent is going global, driven by a combination of enabling technology and the relentless rise of the emerging world. It is also spreading from the private sector to the public sector. The world's governments are trying to recruit highly talented people as a matter of national policy (Singapore's Ministry of Manpower even has an international talent division). Many government departments are finally beginning to recognize that the answer to their problems lies in being smarter rather than being bigger.

Brains Without Borders

The maharajah's palace in Mysore is one of the architectural wonders of southern India, built to awe the local population as well as to thrill a succession of princes. Yet it is tiny compared with Infosys's Mysore campus nearby, which covers 335 acres, supports a permanent faculty of 250, trains some ten thousand new "Infosysians" a year, and provides advanced instruction for thousands of existing employees. It is awash with swimming pools, gyms, tennis and badminton courts, a multiplex cinema, a cricket pitch, an enormous laundry, and five thousand bicycles.

Everything about the campus is designed to underline the company's claim that it is a world-class rather than just an Indian company. Its mantra is "No caste, no creed, only merit." The buildings are a strange mixture of international styles. One training center looks like a Disneyland version of Washington's Capitol, and the multiplex resembles a giant glass golf ball. The Taj Mahal meeting room sits next to the John Pierpont Morgan lecture hall. To a visiting Westerner this is all rather hallucinatory: you half expect to meet Ken Kesey and his Merry Pranksters. To young Indians on the way up, it proclaims that the world is their oyster. No wonder most Infosysians like to bring their extended families to tour the campus.

Infosys grasped from the start that to challenge global companies such as IBM it would have to attract India's brightest. In 1993, it decided to go public, even though it did not need the cash, in large part in order to be able to build a campus that could rival anything America could offer. It not only paid more than its rivals, it was one of the first Indian companies to issue stock options to its employees, so they would have a much better chance of becoming millionaires than if they worked for a foreign multinational. An interesting symbol of the company's commitment to talent is the fact that it has moved one of its board members, T. V. Mohandas Pai, from chief financial officer, traditionally one of the most prized corporate jobs, to director of human resources to show that it means business.

This investment in talent has paid huge dividends over the past two decades of pell-mell growth. The company's workforce has swollen from 10,000 in 2001 to more than 105,000 today, and its market capitalization has risen to $35 billion. Other companies are now imitating its model. India's office parks and electronic cities are full of training campuses churning out the bright and ambitious citizens of a new and more meritocratic India.

Emerging countries in general—and China and India in particular—boast a huge number of relatively cheap brainworkers. Between them, these two countries produce twice as many people with advanced degrees in engineering or computer sciences as the United States every year (more, if you allow for the fact that 50 percent of American engineering degrees are awarded to foreigners, most of them Indians or Chinese). These brainworkers are both cheaper and more hard-working than their Western equivalents. The cost of an Indian graduate is roughly 12 percent of that of an American one, for example, and Indian graduates work an average of 2,350 hours a year compared with 1,900 hours in the United States and 1,700 in Germany.

Yet the emerging world's rapid growth is threatened by a growing problem: skills shortages. Signs of skills shortages can be found everywhere, sometimes literally: GE Capital displays signs in its Indian office saying "Trespassers will be recruited." Staff turnover in India's and China's high-tech sector has continued to average 25 to 30 percent during the recession. The "help wanted" sections of newspapers continue to bulge.

How can countries such as India and China with billions of people experience talent shortages? One reason is that companies are growing much faster than the education infrastructure. Infosys and Huawei increased their sales by more than 40 percent last year. This is a particularly serious problem in India, where the government is ramshackle and the country's educational system has a long tradition of focusing on a tiny elite. Another reason is that emerging markets started a long way behind the West. ("We've had a couple of hundred bad years," one Chinese person told author Clyde Prestowitz, "but now we're back.") China threw its brightest people in prison in 1966–76. The Indian economy was closed until the early 1990s. Many of the millions of graduates produced by Chinese and Indian universities lack the skills to compete with the world's best. Vivek Wadhwa argues that only 170,000 of the 400,000 "engineers" that India produces every year are really engineers according to Western definitions of the term. McKinsey reckons that only 25 percent of India's engineering graduates, 15 percent of its finance and accounting professionals, and 10 percent of those with degrees of any kind are qualified to work for a multinational company.

Emerging-market companies are making vigorous use of sticks and carrots. China's Haier has made its pay entirely performance-related: screw up and you starve. It also makes extensive use of naming and shaming. Photographs of local managers are prominently displayed in every workplace and marked with a magnetic badge (a red smiley face for a job well done, a yellow frowning one for the opposite). The company also celebrates outstanding innovators by naming innovations after them and honoring them in public ceremonies (it has not yet gone to the lengths of holding shaming ceremonies for outstanding failures).

Other companies reach deep into local traditions to motivate their workers. Brian Gu left school at sixteen and started repairing air-conditioning systems. He is now the boss of Yongguan, one of China's largest shelving companies. One of his biggest problems when he started his business in 1988, he recalls, was the attitude of his workers: they spat on the floor and generally behaved in a disrespectful manner. Gu used a combination of relentless exhortation and Buddhist philosophy to make them more disciplined.

Today, Gu's employees listen to Western classical music as they work. Posters list the times of the next quality-circle training sessions. The walls are plastered with notices about improvement, such as "Quality is our life" and "Concept innovation leads to innovation in management." The factory is laid out according to feng shui principles, with the buildings arranged so that they are full of sunlight. Gu's pièce de résistance is the Buddhist garden next to the factory. The best workers have trees planted in their name. Poor performers are sent to spend time in a temple to contemplate a giant statue of the Buddha.

The best companies in emerging markets treat "talent" as a supply chain that needs to be constantly oiled, not an isolated problem that can be solved on a piecemeal basis. Firms invest heavily in creating future managers: Johnson Electric, a huge Chinese maker of electric motors, has built its own internal leadership school. They also invest in "educational ecosystems." Wipro has created an internal academy, linked to leading engineering schools, to recruit and train non–IT graduates in information technology and engineering. TCS works closely with local colleges and provides financial support for poorer students. Many firms dispatch managers to give speeches at universities. GE, for instance, has charged each of its top ten managers in China with cultivating relations with a particular university. They spot bright youngsters and treat them to tours of their campuses and, if they are lucky, scholarships.

This enthusiasm for education and training is not limited to high-tech companies. Pantaloon, a huge Indian retailer that is opening new shops at the rate of one a week, invests in local business schools. Nor is it confined to first-tier cities such as Shanghai and Bangalore. Intel decided to deal with the problem of labor shortages by setting up an operation in Chengdu, an industrial city that has not so far attracted brain-intensive companies, and improving the quality of local education. The price of high growth is continuous investment in human capital.

Still, there is only so much that companies can do to keep the human supply chain going; in the end they are dependent on the quality of people being produced by schools and universities. This points to the second new frontier in the war for talent: the role of government.

Statecraft as Braincraft

The world's governments are increasingly in the brain's business. Most governments are easing restrictions on the entry of skilled workers. Some are going further and offering incentives. Germany has made it easier for skilled workers to get visas. Britain has offered more work permits for skilled migrants. France has introduced a "scientist visa." Many countries are making it easier for foreign students to stay on after graduating. Canada and Australia have not only tilted their long-established points systems further toward the skilled, they have also introduced more incentives. Canada experimented with a tax holiday for citizens returning from the United States before realizing that this encouraged temporary emigration. Ireland's government works hard to recruit overseas talent.

The most ambitious program for sucking in brains from abroad is—where else?—in Singapore. Lee Kuan Yew, the city-state's elder statesman, has long argued that "trained talent is the yeast that transforms a society and makes it rise." At first Singapore focused on wooing back its émigrés, but now it is going out of its way to import foreign talent. Singapore is particularly keen to attract scientific talent, mainly in biotechnology. Of the 170 staff working in the country's Genome Institute, about 120 are foreigners. Alan

Colman, a member of the Scottish team that cloned Dolly the sheep, is now based in Singapore.

Many countries regard universities as ideal talent-catching machines, not only because they select students on the basis of ability but also because those students bring all sorts of other benefits, from spending money to providing cheap research labor. France is aiming to push up its proportion of foreign students from about 7 percent now to 20 percent over time. Germany is trying to create a Teutonic Ivy League and wants to "internationalize studies in Germany." Both countries are offering lots of courses in English. In Singapore, one-fifth of the students at public universities are foreign, thanks in part to heavy subsidies. Australia and New Zealand have created a ladder leading from universities to the workforce and then to permanent residence. China, which temporarily dispensed with entrance examinations during the Cultural Revolution, is focusing resources on its elite universities.

Some of the best prospects in the competition for talent are émigrés—people who have gone abroad to make their fortune but still feel the home country tugging at their heartstrings. China has introduced a concerted policy of drawing on the brainpower that it has stored overseas. Officials have introduced a mind-boggling range of enticements, from bigger apartments to access to the best schools, from chauffeur-driven cars to fancy titles. The Chinese Academy of Sciences offers fellowships under the "hundred talents program." Beijing has an office in Silicon Valley, and Shanghai has established a "human talent market." China is littered with shiny new edifices labeled "returning-student entrepreneurial building." All this coincides with a dramatic change in the flow of people: China seems to be moving in the same direction as South Korea and Taiwan—first tempting back the diaspora and then beginning to compete for global talent.

India has taken a different approach. The government has relied as much on the goodwill of prominent business people as it has on the wisdom of bureaucrats; it has also cast its net wider, focusing not just on luring back expats but also on putting the wealth and wisdom of the diaspora to work on behalf of the mother country. There are an estimated 20 million Indians living abroad, generating an annual income equal to 35 percent of India's gross domestic product. The Indian government is doing what it can, in its haphazard way, to let them participate in the Indian boom, making it easier for them to invest back home and streamlining visa procedures. There is a special visa for "people of Indian origin." Again, government policy has coincided with a change in the flow of people. Bright Indians, who once had no choice but to make their careers in America or Europe, are now returning home, working for great companies such as Infosys, or creating their own companies.

The success that countries such as China and India are having in tempting back émigrés is changing the nature of the debate about the talent wars. For years, discussion of the cross-border flow of talent has sounded a somber note. For some critics it was nothing less than a new form of colonialism, with the rich world not only appropriating the developing world's best brains but getting them on the cheap, because their educations had been paid for by someone else. One study of fifty-five developing countries found that one-third of them lost more than 15 percent of their graduates to migration. Turkey and Morocco lost 40 percent and the Caribbean countries, 50 percent. Now the gloom has lifted.

In fact, it was always overplayed. Migrants sent huge amounts of money home in remittances: $126 billion in 2004, according to the International Monetary Fund. They also transferred knowledge and connections. The current Indian boom owes much to successful Indians who emigrated in the 1960s and 1970s and who are now determined to modernize their home country. They have formed support groups such as Indus Entrepreneurs, steered multinational contracts to India, established venture capital funds, and helped found business schools. But what has changed the mood is that the flow is no longer one-way. The brain drain is giving way to brain circulation, and returning émigrés are turning into economic dynamos. One example is Dr. Prathap Reddy, a returnee from America who established the Apollo Hospitals Group, one of Asia's largest and the first to attract foreign investment. Another is Dr. Shetty, who spent some time working in St. Thomas' Hospital in London. But they can be found everywhere: one-third of Taiwan's companies were founded by returnees from America.

The global war for talent is likely to intensify. Educated people are already more mobile than their less-educated peers. Two economists, Frédéric Docquier and Hillel Rapoport, estimate that average emigration rates worldwide are 0.9 percent for the low-skilled, 1.6 percent for the medium-skilled, and 5.5 percent for the high skilled. This disparity is likely to intensify as countries simultaneously woo educated workers and build up barriers to less-educated immigrants. Most developed countries are already struggling to find enough doctors and teachers, and are wondering how they will manage when the baby-boomer generation retires. Developing countries, for their part, realize that they will not be able to plug into the global knowledge economy unless they give their people the freedom to move around. A powerful array of interests, from multinationals to city politicians, supports the idea of a global market for the best people. Countries cut themselves off from it at their peril—particularly as hunger for talent is no longer confined to a handful of elite companies.

Everybody Is Doing It

There is nothing new about companies wanting to secure the best talent. The East India Company, founded in 1600, used competitive examinations to recruit alpha minds. The company's employees included James and John Stuart Mill, two of Britain's greatest intellectuals, and Thomas Love Peacock, one of its wittier writers. General Electric has been carefully ranking its employees, with the best groomed for leading positions and the weakest eased out, since the early twentieth century. The company founded its corporate university at Crotonville near New York, often dubbed Harvard-on-the-Hudson, in the 1950s. Jack Welch, the company's legendary boss, spent half his time on "people development" and visited Crotonville every two weeks. As for investment banks and consultancies, they have to be obsessive about talent—what else are they selling?

But the world is also witnessing another new development in the talent wars, along with the creation of a global talent market and the growing role of the state: a much wider range of companies are joining the talent wars. Low-end companies are trying to distinguish themselves from the competition by the careful application of talent. Hotels such as the Marriott Group are putting heavy emphasis on recruitment and training. The boss of McDonald's, Jim Skinner, personally reviews the career development of his company's top two hundred managers. Target has avoided being crushed by Walmart, a company that is more than five times its size, by arranging for some of the world's top designers, such as Michael Graves and Isabelle de Borchgrave, to design some of its products.

One result has been that human-resources departments, which used to be quiet backwaters, have gained in status. A survey by

Aon, a consultancy, identified 172 HR executives who were among the five best-paid managers in their companies, something that would have been unheard of a few years ago. The biggest earners among them worked for some surprising companies, such as Black & Decker, Home Depot, Pulte Homes, Viacom, and Timberland.

Companies with a reputation as "talent masters" have provided both a model and a training school for the rest of the corporate world. GE is America's leadership factory as well as its CEO factory: there are 1,600 corporate universities loosely modeled on Crotonville. Consultancies and investment banks have become finishing schools for future corporate leaders: legendary bosses such as IBM's Lou Gerstner and eBay's Meg Whitman both started off at consultancies, as do 65 percent of the products of top business schools.

Capital One, a credit card company, shows what a difference the application of talent can make to a sleepy market. The company's headquarters, in McLean, Virginia, looks more like a consultancy than a bank. The atmosphere is informal. The staff is young and "data-centric." The formula seems to work: founded in 1995, Capital One is now number four in the American credit card market. The company's success is due to the deployment of lots of brainpower in a business generally seen as unexciting. The founders, Rich Fairbank and Nigel Morris, were both products of MBA programs and consultancies. They decided that they could use mass customization to compete with financial giants such as American Express, recruited a high-powered team of former consultants, and used sophisticated statistical techniques to slice the credit card market into tiny segments.

Companies are beginning to develop some general rules of thumb about talent management. The first rule of thumb is that elitism pays. Companies that have the longest and most distinguished records of managing talent—what Bill Conaty and Ram Charan call "talent masters"—are all obsessed by the "vital few." They relentlessly sort the wheat from the chaff. GE divides its employees, much as Plato divided the citizens of his republic, into three groups based on their promise (Plato's men of gold have transmuted into the less poetic "top talent"). Hindustan Unilever compiles a list of people who show innate leadership qualities (and refers to them throughout their careers as "listers").

Sorting requires measurement and differentiation. Talent masters routinely subject all their employees to performance reviews and progress assessments. But when it comes to high-flyers, they make more effort to build up a three-dimensional picture of their personalities and to provide lots of feedback and mentoring. GE's Jeff Immelt takes pride in his detailed knowledge of the top six hundred people in the company, including their family circumstances and personal ambitions. Hindustan Unilever's bosses build detailed dossiers on their "listers." Novartis asks high-flyers to map out their future careers ("leader plans") and share them with their mentors and contemporaries.

Talent masters also single out high-flyers for special training. GE spends $1 billion a year on training, much of it on Crotonville. Novartis sends high-flyers to regular off-site training sessions. But on-the-job training is even more important than formal training. Many companies speak of "stretch" assignments or "baptisms by fire." P&G refers to "accelerator experiences" and "crucible roles." The most popular stretch assignments these days are overseas: these give future leaders a sense of what it is like to run an entire company rather than just to cultivate your own specialism. They can also include building a business in an isolated village (a popular test for Hindustan Unilever) or turning around a failing division.

A second rule of thumb is that it is essential to plan ahead.

EDS, a giant technology company, has built a global inventory of its 100,000-strong workforce. The company compared the workforce's current skills with its needs in, say, five years' time, and sets about filling the gaps by encouraging workers to acquire the relevant skills. Schlumberger, a Franco-American oil-services group, is preparing for a skills crunch in the next few years, as baby boomers retire, by asking its managers to cultivate successors. It also holds rigorous inquests whenever a high-flyer jumps ship, to discover what it is doing wrong.

A third rule of thumb is that companies need to be more imaginative about recruiting and retention. They need to be more aggressive at hunting for talent: BCG assigns a "captain" to each prospective hire and gives him the job of helping the applicant make up his mind. They need to pay more attention to "passive candidates"—people who are not actively looking for a job but might be open to seduction. Popular techniques include ferreting through lists of people attending conferences in order to button-hole stars, buying information about competing firms (including names of key workers), and searching the Web for people who have created new patents.

Once they have hooked somebody, companies need to pay more attention to making him feel at home ("onboarding"). In the late 1990s, American Express discovered that a striking number of new managers were leaving within the first two years. It now provides them with "assimilation coaches" and gives new arrivals a chance to work on projects that are overseen by the CEO. OhioHealth has a "right at 90" program whereby a senior manager is given the job of looking after new recruits for their first ninety days, guiding them through the corporate maze and sitting down with them every thirty days to tell them how they are doing.[8]

More generally, they need to heed Peter Drucker's advice and treat employees like "de facto volunteers" rather than just wage earners. This means taking the hierarchy out of corporate language (referring to "associates" rather than "hired hands") and removing the starch from organizations. Parties involving bosses and workers; nonfinancial rewards such as handwritten "herograms"; a culture of mutual effort and cooperation—all these things are beginning to characterize the modern workplace in service as well as professional organizations.

A fourth rule of thumb is that internal markets can help circulate talent. Many HR departments routinely look outside for recruits while ignoring internal candidates. Deloitte calculates that the typical American company spends nearly fifty times more to recruit a professional at $100,000 a year than it spends on his or her further training every year. Moreover, new recruits can take more than a year to learn a job. One solution is to establish an internal market, encouraging workers to apply for jobs across the company. Schlumberger encourages its employees to post detailed CVs on the company intranet. McKinsey allows consultants from all over the world to apply for any project within the company. Wipro has created an elaborate internal talent market called Wings Within. The company makes a point of advertising every job that is advertised externally and internally as well. If an existing worker is successful in applying for one of these jobs, his manager does not have the authority to prevent him from moving.

A fifth rule of thumb is that companies should involve senior managers—particularly their CEOs—in talent management rather than handing the job over to human resources. Jack Welch and A. G. Lafley, the former bosses of GE and P&G, respectively, claimed that they spent 40 percent of their time on personnel. Andy Grove, the former boss of Intel, obliged all senior managers, himself included, to spend at least a week a year teaching high-flyers. Nitin Paranjpe, the boss of Hindustan Unilever, visits campuses to look for recruits and frequently drops in on high-flyers. Involving the top leadership helps companies tie talent management to a broader strategy as well as sending a powerful signal that talent matters: P&G's decision to increase its focus on globalization and innovation has been helped enormously by the fact that senior managers choose employees on the basis of their commitment to those twin ideas.

These rules of thumb might not sound very impressive compared with the sophisticated theories being produced by the gurus of finance and IT. One reason for this relative backwardness is that talent is perverse: the more valuable it is, the more difficult it is to manage. World-class talent frequently comes in unexpected guises. Ray Kroc sold milkshake machines to restaurants before starting to build McDonald's at the age of fifty-two. David Ogilvy was a chef, a farmer, and a spy before becoming an advertising genius. Another reason is that solutions that have proved successful in one place do not necessarily work in another. On arriving at Home Depot in 2000, Bob Nardelli was determined to apply the lessons he had learned at GE to reinvigorate the do-it-yourself giant. He appointed a colleague from GE, Dennis Donovan, to run the HR side, and boosted his credentials by paying him the second-highest salary in the company. He replaced the company's ad hoc talent-management system with a much more formal one, creating a leadership development institute, employing more human-resource managers, and imposing an elaborate system of performance measurement. The results were mixed. The company's share price fell, demoralized employees took to calling the company "Home Despot," and Nardelli eventually left.

The debate about how best to manage talent will clearly continue to run for a long time to come. So will an even bigger debate—about the sort of society that this growing war for talent is creating.

The Revenge of the Bell Curve

Francis Galton, a cousin of Charles Darwin, was a Victorian gentleman-scholar of eccentric genius. He devoted his life to measuring everything imaginable—from the frequency of fidgets in a bored audience to the size of the buttocks of a Hottentot woman (from a discreet distance, using a sextant). But what obsessed him above all was mental ability. Why were some people cleverer than others? Why did intellectual distinction run in some families? And how were intellectual abilities distributed in the population?

Galton came to two conclusions: that ability owed more to nature than to nurture, and that the range of mental powers between the cleverest and the dumbest was enormous—"reaching from one knows not what height, and descending to one can hardly say what depth." He put these together to produce a theory of human inequality: the more open society becomes, the more an aristocracy of talent will replace an aristocracy of birth.

Galton's argument contained a good deal of nonsense. He understated the importance of nurture (though not as much as his later critics have overstated it), and he ignored class privileges. But it did offer an important insight: that a free market in talent could end up widening social inequalities. The United States, the country with the world's freest market in talent, is seeing a dramatic increase in inequality. Emmanuel Saez of the University of California at Berkeley and Thomas Piketty of the Ecole Normale Supérieure in Paris have dissected tax records to examine changes in income distribution, and found that the share of income going to the highest-earning 1 percent of Americans doubled between 1980 and 2004, to 16 percent. The share going to the top 0.1 percent more than tripled over the same period, to 7 percent.

Part of the reason lies in social convention: Europeans have strong cultural objections to paying their CEOs the sort of salaries that American bosses get. Part of it is political: inequality has risen faster under the Republicans than under the Democrats. The Obama administration is reining in some of the top earners who did so well under Bush, thanks to higher taxes and a more censorious attitude toward executive remuneration. But a bigger reason is that rising returns to talent and skill, something that is taking place in Europe as well as the United States, and in Democratic eras as well as Republican ones.

Top performers have been doing well in almost every field, from sports to business, and many have continued to pull further ahead of the pack even during the recession. Even universities, which were once bastions of collegial equality, are willing to pay a premium for academic stars—not only because their ideas are so valuable, but also because they will attract other high-flyers. These huge rewards may offend egalitarians, but they make a lot of economic sense. Stars have a dramatic impact on the fortunes of organizations. Alan Eustace, a vice-president of Google, told the *Wall Street Journal* that in his view, one top-notch engineer is worth "300 times or more than the average." Bill Gates says that "if it weren't for 20 key people, Microsoft wouldn't be the company it is today." Success in climbing to the top of an organization requires many kinds of talent. Most consultancies eventually shed 80 percent of their recruits. Only one in ten law students makes it to senior partner at a top law firm. Managers suffer a huge attrition rate as they move up their organizations.

Now the tendency for the best to pull away from the rest is spreading down the corporate hierarchy. Companies are determined to keep their wage bill under tight control because they face competitive global markets, but they are also desperate to keep their best talent from falling into the hands of rivals. So they have been keeping their overall wage bill more or less steady but giving a larger share of it to the top performers. Those differentials could get a lot wider in the future. Academic studies have discovered that the best computer programmers are at least twelve times as productive as the average.

The link between talent and inequality is being strengthened by two things. The first is the tendency of talented people to cluster together. You might have thought that the advent of the Internet would have eroded the connection between place and talent, but in fact the opposite is happening. Bright people gather in university cities such as Boston and San Francisco, or in technology hubs such as Austin, Texas, or Redmond, Washington, or in rural idylls such as Camden, Maine, and Jackson Hole, Wyoming, for the simple reason that they feed off each other's intellects. Christopher Berry, of the University of Chicago, and Edward Glaeser, of Harvard, have studied the distribution of human capital across American cities. They found that in 1970 about 11 percent of people over age twenty-five had a college degree, and that they were fairly evenly distributed throughout the country. Since then the proportion of Americans with college degrees has more than doubled, but the distribution has become much more uneven. Increasing numbers of high-flyers are moving from inland locations to the coasts: once flourishing cities such as St. Louis, Missouri, are losing young talent to New York and Los Angeles. And the epicenters of the talent economy are becoming increasingly unequal, with the talent elite at the top, service workers at the bottom, and nothing much in between. The middle layer is being driven out by sky-high home prices and poor schools. Richard Florida points out that the three most unequal metropolises in the country—Raleigh-Durham, San Francisco, and Washington-Baltimore—are also hubs of what he calls "creative workers." Edward Leamer, an economist at the University of California, Los Angeles, argues that in the heartlands of the talent economy, the workforce is increasingly split between "geeks" and "grunts," with the geeks controlling a growing share of the profits and the grunts keeping them fed and watered.

The second factor that links talent and inequality is that members of the talent elite are good at hogging "human capital." They marry people like themselves. In the heyday of "company man," bankers married their secretaries; now they marry other bankers. They work in jobs that add to their intellectual capital. They live in "talent enclaves," away from ordinary middle-class suburbs, let alone inner-city ghettos. Above all, they pass on their advantages to their children. A striking index of the rise of the hereditary meritocracy is provided by the wedding announcements in the *New York Times*. Couples noisily (and shamelessly) announce their meritocratic credentials—Harvard MBA is marrying Vassar Phi Kappa—in much the same way that their predecessors a few generations ago announced their blue blood.

None of this is peculiar to the United States or other rich countries: the same thing is happening in the developing world, in even starker form. The best and brightest cluster together in high-priced cities such as Bangalore and Shanghai. They then seal themselves off from the masses still further by living in gated communities, some of them with American names such as Palm Springs, Napa Valley, or Beverly Hills, that boast international schools, world-class hospitals, luxury housing, and splendid gyms. And they try hard to give their children every possible advantage. One bestseller in China, *Harvard Girl*, tells the story of two parents who trained their daughter, Liu Yiting, for Harvard from birth, barraging her with verbal stimuli, subjecting her to a strenuous regime of home study, and making her swim long distances.[9] (She predictably ended up working for a management consultancy after graduating from Harvard.) One of the most successful schools at getting students into American Ivy League universities is Raffles Junior College in Singapore.

The talent war is producing a global meritocracy—a group of people nicknamed "Davos men" by Samuel Huntington or "cosmocrats" by John Micklethwait and me—who are reaping handsome rewards from globalization.[10] These people inhabit a sociocultural bubble full of other super-achievers like themselves. They attend world-class universities and business schools, work for global organizations, and speak the global language of business.

Countries that still insist on clinging to egalitarianism are paying a heavy price. Sweden, for instance, finds it hard to attract foreign talent. And across Europe, egalitarian universities are losing out to their more elitist American rivals. But the war for talent produces social maladies as well as economic benefits.

Meritocracy and Its Discontents

In *The Rise of the Meritocracy*, published in 1958, Michael Young, a British sociologist and Labor Party activist, conjured up an image of a society obsessed with talent. The date was 2034, and psychologists had perfected the art of IQ testing. But far from promoting social harmony, the preoccupation with talent had produced social breakdown. The losers in the talent wars were doubly unhappy, conscious not only that they were failures but that they deserved to be failures. Eventually they revolted against their masters.[11]

The rise of the talent elite has bred resistance, starting on the right. T. S. Eliot argued that choosing people on the basis of their talents would "disorganize society and debase education."[12] Edward Welbourne, a Cambridge don, dismissed IQ tests as "devices invented by Jews for the advancement of Jews."[13] But after the Second World War, the resistance spread leftward. Leftists argued that meritocracies were not only unpleasant but unjust. If "talent" owed more to nature than nurture, as many social scientists insisted, then rewarding people for talent was tantamount to rewarding them for having privileged parents.[14]

This resistance has occasionally boiled over into outright rebellion. Young's book was an opening shot in a successful war against the 11-plus, a British school examination that divided children between a gifted elite destined for academic grammar schools and those consigned to run-of-the-mill secondary modern schools. The 1960s saw widespread student revolts against selection and elitism.

There are plenty of signs that another backlash is on the way. Much of this resentment focuses on growing inequalities. People complain that these are straining the bonds of society to the breaking point: a new aristocracy of talent is retreating into golden ghettos and running the global economy in their own interests. "The talented retain many of the vices of aristocracy without its virtues," said the late Christopher Lasch, an American historian, in one of the best analyses of the trend.[15] The logic of talent wars is meritocratic: the most talented get the most rewards. But the reality of democracy is egalitarian: the people can use their political power to defeat the bell curve.

In some ways, things are worse than they were when Young wrote his book. Inequalities are much wider—in both the United States and China they are returning to early twentieth-century levels—and the talent elite has gone global. Young's rebels can now add patriotism (or bigotry) to egalitarianism. Manuel Castells, a sociologist, complains that "elites are cosmopolitan, people are local." The late Samuel Huntington argued that "a major gap is growing in America between its increasingly denationalized elites and its 'thank God for America' public." On American television, personalities such as Glenn Beck and Bill O'Reilly beat the populist drum against those cosmopolitan elites. And on America's streets, angry Tea Partiers complain that the country has been hijacked by a self-satisfied Ivy League coterie that cares more about the good opinion of their fellow meritocrats in the United Nations than about the fate of ordinary Americans. In China, people denounce returning émigrés as "bananas" (yellow on the outside, white inside). Across much of the developing world, the targets of choice for rioters are rich ethnic minorities and foreigners.

But in other ways things have gotten much better. The number of winners now is much larger than it was in 1958. In Young's day, the meritocrats concentrated on spotting recruits for Oxbridge and the senior civil service. The rest were labeled failures. Since then, the United States and Europe have created a mass higher education system, and developing countries are determined to follow suit. When Young was writing, China and India were trapped in poverty. Today they are growing so fast that they, too, are suffering from talent shortages.

Moreover, some problems could prove self-correcting. Many talented people not only create jobs and wealth, they turn their hands to philanthropy, as Bill Gates and Warren Buffett have done. The growing returns to education create incentives for people to get themselves educated, producing a better-trained workforce as well as upward mobility. In China, families spend more on education than on anything else, despite the one-child policy. Multinational companies routinely promote local talent in the developing world, putting an ever more multiethnic face on the global talent elite. Overheated talent markets prompt companies to move production elsewhere—to Mysore rather than Bangalore, say, or Austin, Texas, rather than Silicon Valley. This is the talent economy's way of spreading the wealth about.

Growing wealth also means that society can reward a wider range of talents. "I must study politics and war that my sons may have liberty to study mathematics and philosophy," wrote America's second president, John Adams, and they in turn must study those subjects so that their children can study "painting, poetry, music, architecture, statuary, tapestry, and porcelain." These days, sports stars and entertainers can make millions. There are also ample rewards for all sorts of specialized talents, from the gift of bringing history to life (think of all those well-paid TV historians) to the ability to produce a perfect soufflé (the world is now awash with celebrity chefs). It sometimes seems that there is no talent so recondite that you cannot make a living out of it. Beard-growing competitions are so popular that they are now being televised. Takeru "Tsunami" Kobayashi earns more than $200,000 a year as the world's hot dog–eating champion: he can eat more than fifty in twelve minutes.

The backlash is not inevitable, then. But it is sensible to take steps to prevent it. One popular answer is affirmative action, an idea that is making headway even in that last redoubt of old-fashioned meritocracy, the French establishment. However, experience in the United States— which introduced the practice in the 1970s—suggests that it raises a host of problems. In practical terms, many "affirmative-action babies" fail in highly competitive environments. On a more philosophical note, why should the children of rich blacks be given a head start over the children of poor whites? The biggest problem with affirmative action, however, is that it comes too late. The best way to boost the life chances of poor people is to intervene much earlier in life—to set them on the right path in kindergarten and primary school and reinforce those lessons in secondary school.

Progressive taxation can help. For much of the postwar period most rich countries taxed talent too heavily, causing "bright flight." But in the wake of the Reagan and Thatcher revolutions we may have moved too far in the opposite direction, running the risk of creating a class of trust fund babies whose wealth is unconnected with either merit or responsibility. The best way to head off a backlash is to give everybody a fair chance. This means investing in childhood nutrition and preschool education. It also means repairing the lowest rungs of the educational ladder. Developing countries need to continue the march toward universal primary education: failure to do so will exacerbate skill shortages as well as widen inequalities. Developed countries need to toughen up their schools. In the 1960s, too many schools were lowering standards in the name of child-centered education and shifting the emphasis away from science and mathematics. The chief victims of this were underprivileged children, who could not rely on their parents to make up for the deficiencies of their schools.

The success of advanced economies is increasingly dependent not on their physical capital but on their capacity to mobilize their citizens' brainpower. The rise of a global meritocracy offers all sorts of benefits, from higher growth in productivity to faster scientific progress. It can boost social mobility and allow all sorts of weird and wonderful talents to bloom. The talent wars may be a source of trepidation for companies and countries, but they should also be a cause for celebration.

16

Managing Yourself

Stephen Covey is fond of telling people that he is writing a book on the evils of retirement, called *Live Life in Crescendo*. There is no danger of this particular management guru living life in diminuendo. Covey is working on nine other books, including one on how to stop crime. He also presides over an empire that is even more sprawling than his extended family (he has fifty-one grandchildren at the time of this writing).

Covey has been stretching his brand since *The Seven Habits of Highly Effective People* (1989) turned the cone-head lookalike into a superstar. He followed *Seven Habits* with a succession of spin-offs such as *The Seven Habits of Highly Effective Families* and, irritatingly for people who had shelled out $30 for *The Seven Habits* thinking that they had finally got their life in order, *The 8th Habit* (2004). His other business interests include FranklinCovey, a consultancy that markets successful habits, and a leadership center, which teaches high-flying executives to fly even higher. So far *The Seven Habits* has sold 15 million copies in thirty-five languages, and three of Covey's other books have sold more than a million copies. Coveyism is total-quality management for the character, reengineering for the soul.

Covey inhabits the limbo between two worlds. *The Seven Habits* rubs shoulders in bookshops with books with titles like *Unleash the Thinner You* and *How to Get Rich Without Getting Out of Bed*. The master's lectures are packed with sad-sack people who are looking for a quick fix for their multiplying problems. But Covey is also a paid-up member of the management theory club, with an MBA from Harvard Business School and glowing endorsements from serious thinkers such as Warren Bennis and Clayton Christensen. He claims that one of his biggest inspirations was Peter Drucker, who insisted that "effectiveness is a habit" and provided him one of his seven habits, "first things first," which, for reasons that are never explained, is number three in his list. FranklinCovey claims that 90 percent of Fortune 500 and 70 percent of Fortune 1000 companies are clients.

Covey's life work is an odd mixture of the banal and the serious. Much of his advice is nothing more than a distillation of the wisdom of grandmothers down the ages. Don't waste time. Look after your health. Worldly success means nothing if you die alone. Marry a nice girl (or boy). Make time for family and friends. Don't be so selfish. Covey's attempt to dress this up in the raiments of science, with organizational charts, "EQ" tests, and personality questionnaires, only makes its underlying banality more obvious.

Yet at the core of Coveyism lies a serious point: that character matters. He wrote his PhD dissertation on "American Success Literature since 1776," literature that surely helps to account for America's tradition of upward mobility. He discovered that, for the first 150 years of the republic, most success literature concentrated on questions of character. But shortly after the Second World War, people became more interested in superficial things such as appearance and style. Covey started to preach that people needed to get back to the ancient discipline of character building—and, later, that organizations need to start treating the characters of their employees with the same seriousness that they treat things like cash flows and total-quality management. The building blocks of successful organizations are successful individuals, as he likes to put it.

It increasingly looks as if Covey was ahead of the curve. The questions that lie at the heart of his work—from how you "sharpen your saw" to how you measure your long-term success—are becoming ever more important in management theory.

People are having to take more responsibility for their own lives, as Peter Drucker's "society of organizations" dissolves into a society of ever looser networks. More than 30 million Americans work for themselves or for micro-employers. This means that they have to deal with all sorts of problems—from selling their services to managing huge fluctuations in income—that their corporation-hugging parents never had to confront. And even people who continue to work for large organizations are having to take more responsibility for planning their careers. Big companies expect their employees to take more responsibility for planning their careers and continuing with their training. They also have fewer qualms about sacking them if the weather turns ugly. "Corporate America is not going to cosset you anymore," warns Tom Peters in his inimitable style. "Think of it this way: you've got a new boss. Buy a mirror: it's you."[1]

Most people are also under more pressure at work. Successful chief executives complain that they never see their children grow up. Rising managers fly hither and thither at the behest of their bosses. Everybody suffers from a surplus of information and a shortage of understanding. Burnout is now something that you hear about in Middle Britain as well as in Hollywood therapy sessions. Add to this the fact that people are living much longer and you have a bull market for self-management. Problems that were once rare or nonexistent—moving from one career to another; starting a new life at sixty; having to support yourself in your eighties and nineties—are now becoming commonplace.

The Brand You

The growing demand for advice on managing yourself is inevitably generating a growing supply, and Covey is being joined by a growing number of younger gurus. Some of these gurus belong firmly to the self-help industry. Anthony Robbins, who started life as a school janitor before becoming a "peak performance coach," argues that you can achieve anything you want just so long as you adopt the right attitude. To drive his message home, he encourages his fans (for a fat fee) to walk on hot coals and perform other painful feats of endurance.

Some gurus have one foot in the self-help camp and another in the management theory camp. Marcus Buckingham, a Cambridge-educated Englishman, has pulled off the remarkable feat of colonizing a world that most English people regard as quintessentially American. A former employee of the Gallup organization who has since branched out on his own, he uses a wide range of quantitative data to argue that both workers and managers spend too much time obsessing about what they are bad at rather than focusing on what they are good at. Why sweat to master statistics when other people can be brought in to do the numbers? Why not focus on the one thing that you are uniquely good at? *Now Discover Your Strengths* has sold more than one million copies and inevitably generated follow-ups such as *Go Put Your Strengths to Work: Six Powerful Steps to Achieve Outstanding Performance.* Buckingham commands $55,000 a speech and was one of Oprah Winfrey's favorite guests.

A third group of writers are closer to management theory proper. The *Harvard Business Review* runs a regular series on "managing yourself." The Academy of Management publishes occasional articles in which teams of professors deploy all the might of quantitative method to analyze whether you should join a prospective boss in a drink over dinner (the answer is no). John Moulton, the head of Better Capital, a private equity group, judges CEOs partly on the basis of their marital history: one divorce is good because it suggests that they need a lot of money to keep themselves on the road, but two or three divorces is bad because it suggests a degree of personal instability.

Tom Peters urges people to cultivate their "brand equity" and "renew their core competencies." If "you" are the basic corporate unit of modern society, then you need to run yourself like a company rather than just a working stiff. Robert Reich tells people that they have no choice but to master the art of selling themselves.[2] The man in the gray flannel suit used to want nothing more than to fit in. Now everybody has to try to stand out—by writing a blog, acquiring a Twitter account, appearing on a reality TV show, shouting louder than everybody else, projecting themselves above the crowd. Roberto Alvarez del Blanco, of IE Business School in Spain, puts it succinctly: "brand yourself, or be branded."[3]

This can easily degenerate into banality. We do not need Harvard professors to tell us that it is better to prepare carefully before meetings. But the subject of self-management has also attracted the attention of some of the giants of the management theory industry. These giants have not only demonstrated that you can write about managing the self with the same seriousness as you can write about managing supply chains or inventories. They have demonstrated that Covey was right about one thing: that the boundaries between the personal and the corporate are becoming ever more fluid.

The Meaning of Life

In 1998, having recently moved to Los Angeles for what is arguably the word's best job, *The Economist*'s West Coast bureau chief, I braved the freeway to visit Peter Drucker in his surprisingly modest house in Orange County. You might have imagined that the younger man would have initiated the meeting. But in fact, Peter Drucker took the initiative, after reading an article that I had written in the *Los Angeles Times*, and invited me to have lunch.

The lunch took place in a suburban restaurant with a huge plastic wagon wheel on the wall. The food was as dismal as the décor. But Drucker, who ordered ribs, was undeterred; he talked about people he had met in Vienna and England before the war—Freud and Schumpeter, Keynes and Wittgenstein, Isaiah Berlin and Lewis Namier—sounding like Isaiah Berlin channeled through Henry Kissinger. Drucker also told me his secret of keeping mentally active: find a subject that is unrelated to your main line of work and devote a few hours a day for a year or so to studying it (Drucker was then hard at work on twelfth-century Paris). During the course of a long afternoon spent in his study, looking at his fine collection of Japanese paintings and reminiscing about business people he had known, it became clear that a variety of interests was only one of many techniques that Drucker used to keep his mind refreshed.

Drucker firmly believed that the only way to get the most out of life was to live in many dimensions.[4] He constantly sang the praises of sabbaticals and study programs. He urged people to develop parallel careers. This might mean anything from turning an interest into an expertise to devoting your spare hours to voluntary work. On top of this, he urged people to develop second lives or second identities. He felt that people should take advantage of the fact that human life spans are getting ever longer to pursue two or three careers. This might involve striking off in an entirely new direction—becoming a round-the-world yachtsman after you have retired from running a company, for example. Or it might involve taking one of your parallel careers and turning it into your main thing.

Drucker applied most of these techniques to himself. He combined his first love of writing with teaching and consulting. His collection of Japanese art was museum quality (he first got interested in Japanese art in 1934, age twenty-four, when he ducked out of a rainstorm into an exhibition of paintings in London's Burlington Arcade).[5] In his sixties he decided to turn himself into a novelist, not one of his more successful sidelines. Still, Drucker was a narrow figure compared with his remarkable wife, Doris. Doris earned a degree in physics when she was in her sixties. She invented a voice monitor, called a Visivox, when she was in her mid-eighties and set up a company to market it. She wrote a wonderful book, *Invent Radium or I'll Pull Your Hair*, in her nineties. Now approaching her hundredth birthday, she remains an enthusiastic tennis player and mountain hiker, and a feisty and fascinating conversationalist.[6]

Drucker advanced lots of practical arguments in favor of his notion of living life in many dimensions. People who have a wide range of interests are less likely to be devastated when their job disappears—as so many jobs do these days—and less likely to burn out on the job. They also develop perspectives and contacts that can help them to make a big impact in their main jobs. Drucker's own interest in Japanese management, which helped to give him an edge over his rivals in the 1950s, was an offshoot of his interest in Japanese art. But his basic argument was moral rather than practical: you have a duty to make the most of the gifts God has given you. Cultivate as many talents as you can and your mind will continue to grow. Focus too narrowly on one thing and it will narrow and atrophy.

It is fitting that the greatest businessman of our era, Bill Gates, is also the greatest exemplar of living life in many dimensions. While he was running Microsoft full time, Gates made regular use of "think weeks" or "weeks in the wilderness." He retreated to a log cabin in the middle of nowhere and devoted himself to reading and thinking. At the same time, Gates developed a parallel career as a social philanthropist. He eventually turned his parallel career into his main vocation. In 1998, he handed over the day-to-day running of his company to his long-standing friend Steve Balmer—he continues to be chairman—in order to devote more time to running his foundation. Once again, a similar process of self-renewal seems to be under way: Gates is devoting a growing amount of his time to thinking about energy and handing over his work on healthcare to other people.

Clayton Christensen has also written sensitively on the subject of "managing oneself."[7] Like Covey, Christensen is a devout Mormon (which helps to explain his willingness to blurb Covey's books); unlike Covey, he has a huge reputation in mainstream management theory. The willingness of the God of Innovation Theory to address such a soft subject as "managing oneself" sends a powerful message about the potential seriousness of the subject to his fellow business theorists, not to mention his legions of students at the Harvard Business School.

On the last day of his class (which is predictably one of the most

popular at HBS), Christensen asks his students to turn the "theoretical lenses" that they have spent the past months acquiring on
themselves and ask, How can I make sure that I will be happy in
my career? How can I be sure that my relationships with my family
will be an enduring source of contentment? How can I be sure that
I will stay out of jail?

Christensen started addressing these subjects because he discovered that so many of the HBS alumni who returned for class
reunions had made a mess of their lives, sometimes spectacularly
so. They were some of the most successful people in the world.
They ran huge businesses, commanded armies of thousands, invented new products. Many of them were richer than Croesus. But
they were more often than not personal failures. They were going
through the agonies of divorce. They were estranged from their
children. They measured out their lives in business trips and business meetings. They knew more about the Ritz Carlton's loyalty
program than they did about their children's friends. A startling
number of them had fallen foul of the law. Two of the thirty-two
people in Christensen's Rhodes Scholar class had spent time in jail.
Jeff Skilling had been one of his classmates at HBS.

Christensen explained this in terms of short-sightedness.
The metric that successful people use to allocate their personal
resources—their time, energy, and talent—are dangerously skewed
toward the short term. As high-flying students and business people,
they spend their time fixated on completing the next assignment
and pleasing their taskmasters—first teachers, then professors, and
finally bosses. But they fail to give any serious thought to the purpose of their lives—to think hard about the why and wherefore of
their lives rather than the next task that lands in their In tray.

The problem is a systemic one: people who are driven to excel
in life have an unconscious propensity to overinvest in their public

rather than their private lives. High-flyers need to devote much more energy to thinking about enduring sources of success (Christensen, who is a cancer survivor, repeats the old adage about judging your life from your deathbed). They also need to "create a culture" that emphasizes ultimate things and prevents them from being obsessed with the short term. This sometimes sounds as if Christensen is advising his students to model themselves on him, a father of five who is a devout Mormon and a dedicated member of the Boy Scouts movement. But he is in fact doing something more modest: advising high achievers to spend just a fraction of the time that they spend on their day-to-day obligations to more enduring things.

Machiavelli in the Boardroom

If Drucker and Christensen have taken the high road, teaching their followers how to live more fulfilled lives, Jeffrey Pfeffer, of Stanford Business School, has taken the low road, offering Machiavellian advice on a subject that is probably closer to the lives of most business students, at least when they are young, than that of living a fulfilling life: how to climb the greasy pole and end up in the CEO suite.

All students of business worth their salt are aware of two trends. The first is that the rewards of success have grown dramatically over the past decades. CEOs and other inhabitants of the C-suite have seen their salaries surge at a time when the median wage has either stagnated (in the United States) or grown slowly (in Europe). The same is happening to other top people. Star writers like the journo-gurus are pulling ever further ahead of other authors. Politicians have learned how to bottle their charisma and contacts and turn them into filthy lucre. The Clintons earned $109 million in the eight years after they left the White House. Tony Blair has become a very wealthy man in the years since his forced retirement, writing a best-selling book, giving highly paid speeches, and offering advice to banks. Henry Kissinger once quipped that power is the ultimate aphrodisiac; in fact, powerful people have the best of everything, not just sex: they live longer and healthier lives, have more friends, and suffer from fewer misfortunes.

The second is that the greasy pole is getting harder to climb and, once you've climbed it, more difficult to cling on to. Companies have introduced more complicated structures—removing layers, installing matrixes, replacing hierarchies with teams, dispersing functions around the world. They have also made life harder for CEOs. In the 1990s, it was not unusual to find CEOs who had been in the job for ten or fifteen years. Over the past decade, the average tenure of departing CEOs around the world has dropped and the number of people looking over their shoulders has multiplied. It turns out that it isn't as lonely at the top as most top people would like.

Management gurus are surprisingly disappointing on the subject of climbing the greasy pole, given its overwhelming importance to their clients. Academics and consultants tend to present business as a rational enterprise in which people who play by the rules prosper. Retired business people like Jack Welch are too busy polishing their egos to give helpful advice. In his best-selling autobiography, Lee Iacocca failed to mention his role in creating the Ford Pinto, a car with a gas tank in the back that exploded if it was hit from behind. They almost always gloss over the wire-pulling and backstabbing that was crucial to their rise to power.

Which is why Jeffrey Pfeffer's advice on acquiring power is so valuable. Pfeffer has been teaching a popular course on "paths to power" at Stanford Business School for years. He has also distilled his findings in *Power: Why Some People Have It—and Others Don't*, a book that happily crosses the line between academic tome and how-to book. Pfeffer's first rule is that people who want to wield power need to rid themselves of the illusion that the world is just—that the best way to win power is to be good at your job. This illusion persuades people to misdirect their effort (toward doing substantial things rather than building political power bases) and blinds them to the political land mines that lie strewn in their path. The relationship between rewards and competence is loose at best, nonexistent at worst. Bob Nardelli was a disastrous CEO of Home Depot. But he was paid a quarter of a billion dollars to leave and quickly moved to the top slot at Chrysler, despite having no experience in the car industry. Chrysler then went bankrupt. James Dimon, the head of JP Morgan Chase, is one of the most celebrated figures in the financial services industry, and did better than any of his colleagues during the financial crisis. But he was kicked out of Citibank when he quarreled with the daughter of his boss, Sandy Weill. Pfeffer points out that CEOs who preside over three years of poor earnings have only a 50 percent chance of losing their jobs—and that perfectly successful senior managers are routinely booted out when new CEOs take over and bring in their own people. Between the effort and the reward falls a shadow.

The best way to increase your chances of reaching the top, he argues, is to choose the right department to join. On the face of it, this should not be a very difficult decision. The most powerful departments are the ones that have produced the current bigwigs (R&D in Germany, and finance in America). They are also the ones that pay the most. But the "best" departments tend to be overcrowded with talent. The trick is to find the department that is on the rise rather than one that is saturated. Robert McNamara and his fellow whiz kids flourished in postwar America because they realized that power was shifting from production and marketing to finance. Mike Volpi quickly moved up the ladder at Cisco in part because corporate power was shifting from the engineering function to the business acquisitions function (Cisco bought seventy companies in 1993–2000). The next generation of media honchos will no doubt come from the world of the Internet and multimedia: look at Arianna Huffington's meteoric career since founding the *Huffington Post* on a whim and a prayer, for example.

Once you've chosen the right department, four things matter more than anything else. The first is the ability to project yourself. Warren Bennis suggests that the best leaders are the ones that are the best at playing a role. "I believe in 'possible selves,'" he has written, "the capacity to adapt and change."[8] Andy Grove insisted that brilliant but shy managers attend what Intel called a "wolf school" in order to make them more assertive in public. The second is the ability to "manage upward." This means turning yourself into a successful supplicant, deferential enough to attract the attention of your superiors. Barack Obama asked about a third of his fellow senators for help when he first arrived in the institution. It means mastering the art of flattery. "Never miss an opportunity to flatter" ought to be engraved on every MBA degree: when Pfeffer wrote a note to Jack Valenti, a longtime head of the Motion Picture Association, to thank him for addressing one of his classes at Stanford, Valenti wrote back praising Pfeffer for the quality of his thank-you note. Presumably the exchange of notes could have gone on forever.

It also means pushing flattery beyond what most people might regard as reasonable limits. Jennifer Chatman, of the University of California, Berkeley, conducted experiments in which she tried to find a point at which flattery became ineffective. She failed to find one. (You can try this yourself at work—it's amusing and it might even bring you a promotion.) And it means acquiring an office as near as possible to the boss. In the White House people scramble for broom cupboards near the Oval Office, and realize that a huge suite in the Executive Building is proof that you do not matter. In the corporate world, the best way to understand the balance of power in the organization is to look at the physical distribution of departments. A study of the Pacific Gas and Electric Company found that the engineering department moved ever farther away from the CEO's office as the company grew and eventually ended up in a satellite building miles away from the headquarters (perhaps one day somebody will write a history of the decline of American competitiveness entirely by mapping the physical location of engineering departments). A "decorator at work" sign on an office near the CEO is a sure sign that somebody is on the way up.

The third important thing is the ability to network. Ambitious people need to make as many friends as possible: Keith Ferrazzi, a master of the art, titled his autobiography *Never Eat Alone*, and when he turned forty, had seven birthday parties in cities around the United States. One of the quickest ways to the top is to turn yourself into a "node" in a network by starting a new organization or forging a link between separate organizations.

The fourth quality is a rather more admirable and old-fashioned one: loyalty. Booz & Company, a consultancy, calculates that four out of every five CEO appointments go to insiders, and insiders last almost two years longer in their jobs than outsiders. Both Edward Dolman, the chairman and former CEO of Christie's, and Jim Skinner, the CEO of McDonald's, started on the ground floor and worked their way up. Job hopping is seldom the path to the top.

And what happens if all this loyalty and networking pays off? How do you keep hold of power once you get your hands on it? The old saw about power corrupting has been laboriously confirmed by academic studies of everything from risk-taking to cookie-eating (powerful people are more likely to eat with their mouths open and to scatter crumbs over their faces, researchers have discovered). Powerful people live in a world where everything is done to make their lives easier—where cars are waiting to whisk them to their next meeting, where information is selected to make the world look good, and where everything smells of fresh paint.

The key to keeping power is to understand its corrupting effects. Powerful people need to cultivate a combination of paranoia and humility, two things that do not often go together but that, in combination, can prolong your life at the top by years. They need to be paranoid about how much other people want them out of their jobs. But they also need to be humble about their replaceability. People who do not know when to quit usually crash and burn. People who know when to quit have a good chance of exchanging one aphrodisiacal throne for another when they finally decide that it is time to move on.

Mens Sana in Corporation Sano

This upsurge of interest in managing yourself is more than merely theoretical: a growing number of companies are keen on giving workers the tools that they need to keep themselves in top form (or "sharpen the saw," in Covey's language). Annual checkups and company "wellness programs" have become a familiar part of the corporate landscape. More than half of America's larger companies offer advice on stopping smoking and fighting flab. More than one-third have gyms. Some have rechristened their canteens "nutrition centers." IBM is among a growing band of companies that offer workers financial incentives (such as cheaper medical co-payments) to encourage them to lose weight and exercise regularly. PriceWaterhouseCoopers has appointed "health champions" to promote healthy lifestyles. AstraZeneca has even installed treadmills in its offices so that workers can exercise while holding meetings.

Companies are now also starting to touch on a more controversial area—mental and emotional health. Companies as diverse as BT, Rolls-Royce, and Grant Thornton have introduced mental health programs. These involve everything from training managers to spot problems in their own behavior or that of others to rehabilitating the afflicted. A growing number of boutique consultancies such as Corporate Psychology & Mental Fitness are also offering to improve people's mental well-being.

The fashion is being driven by simultaneous developments in two usually distinct areas—healthcare and management theory. Doctors report that more than one-third of the physical problems that they encounter, including serious ones such as heart disease, have a psychological basis. Britain's National Institute for Health and Clinical Excellence—which establishes best practice for the National Health Service—notes the prevalence of psychological problems in the population and recommends cognitive therapy as a way of boosting productivity.

Management gurus are also focusing on individual psychology. Business professors have taken to littering their texts with references to "toxic organizations" and "emotional contagion." Several psychologists have become influential gurus in their own right. Daniel Goleman, of Rutgers University, sings the praises of "emotional intelligence." Steven Berglas, a psychiatrist turned management professor at UCLA, offers advice on how to "relight the fire" after burnout. Martin Seligman, of the University of Pennsylvania, argues that positive psychology can improve productivity and creativity. There is even a new business discipline, "neuroleadership," that promises to use the science of the brain to improve leadership.

Both doctors and gurus can quote some compelling statistics. The Sainsbury Center for Mental Health estimates that one-sixth of the British workforce suffers from depression or stress, and that mental ill-health costs British employers almost $26 billion a year. American research suggests that "presenteeism" (whereby the walking wounded turn up to work without contributing) costs twice as much as absenteeism. Put these two trends together and you have the making of a new corporate fashion: advising workers on how they can boost their psychological as well as their physical well-being.

So far this trend has been most marked at in the upper ranks of corporations. About 40 percent of the bosses of FTSE 100 companies employ executive coaches, a growing number of whom offer psychological as well as business advice. Grant Thornton, a giant accountancy, sends its partners on a regular two-day program put on by Positive Health Strategies, a London-based company. Positive Health screens people for emotional as well as physical health, and offers advice and counseling for those who feel that they need it. It also offers advice on "optimizing performance" and "staying positive under pressure."

Focusing on the mental health of their stars makes sense for companies. The stars not only represent huge investments; they are also most likely to live under stress but insist on keeping a stiff upper lip. Positive Health Strategies points out that high-flyers are more likely to suffer from problems than also-rans. But focusing on stars also makes sense for the mental wellness movement: the best way to insert yourself into a company's DNA is to seduce the leadership.

This newfound corporate interest in mental health raises some difficult questions. There are questions about the line between the public and the private. Should companies really be prying into people's emotional lives? Can they be trusted with the information that they gather? Should psychologically frail workers put their faith in people who work primarily for their employers (who can terminate their contracts at any time) rather than in their personal doctors? Workers rightly worry that companies will use psychological information in their annual appraisals. They also worry that they will use the movement as an excuse for extending their power over them—persuading them not just to give up smoking but also to adopt a SpongeBob-like "positive" outlook on their work. Warren Bennis has noted that the new "science" of neuroleadership is "filled with banalities." Other people are less complimentary. The discipline of positive psychology operates in the half-world between quantitative science and smiley-faced self-help.

But there are arguments for companies taking an interest in the psychological well-being of their workers so long as they limit themselves to providing them with the tools they need to manage their lives better. There is no doubt that depression and anxiety can take a serious toll on productivity, and that companies bear their fair share of the blame for promoting stress in the first place. There is little doubt that catching psychological problems early can prevent them from escalating. Companies such as Mars UK and BT report that their mental wellness programs have reduced levels of sick leave by between 30 and 50 percent. In a world where the old social contract between employers and employees has been torn up in the name of efficiency, it is only right that companies should provide some of the tools that people need to organize their lives better.

Conclusion: Mastering Management

A few years ago, MBA students spent most of their time stuck in class poring over case studies, most of them devoted to American companies. Today, many business schools are adding tours of the world's management hot spots to their curricula. Students study Devi Shetty and his attempt to apply Henry Ford's system of mass production to heart operations in Bangalore. Or they examine Infosys's system for turning hundreds of thousands of Indians into disciplined Infosysians. Or they wander around Shanghai looking at Nike's superstores and KFC's bustling restaurants.

The list of management marvels that these students can see is endless. There are towns in India that have been summoned up by companies out of nothing. There are factory complexes in China that employ hundreds of thousands of people. There are multimedia studios in Jerusalem where Hasids and Palestinians work side by side on 3-D animation. In a Hindu temple in Bangalore, the chief monk calls himself the CEO and talks about "best-in-class service delivery" as well as reincarnation. In a factory in Shanghai, the boss has laid out the facilities according to the principles of feng shui and obliges erring workers to prostrate themselves before a giant Buddha.

The smartest students are careful not to neglect the old world in their fascination with the new. Toyota's plant in Toyota City is the world's most successful manufacturing plant. McDonald's can recreate any of its restaurants anywhere in the world in its R&D center in Chicago. Boeing's factory in Seattle will take away the breath of even the most jaded student of management.

The old world is reinventing itself at an astonishing pace, too. In Mountain View, California, the inhabitants of the Googleplex are busy spinning information into gold. In Henderson, Nevada, Zappos is determined to prove that delivering shoes and clothes online is the key to eternal happiness—all employees are expected to deliver service with a "wow" and a spring in their step.

A Bizarre Industry

This tour of management theory has been a bizarre experience. Drop in on Michael Porter at the Harvard Business School and you catch sight of the theorist as a respectable academic, churning out articles for learned journals, arguing over the finer points of econometrics, and even doing the regular grunt work of marking students' papers. Visit Stephen Covey's leadership center and you can see the theorist as therapist, encouraging his clients to talk about their innermost feelings. Buy a seat at any Tom Peters seminar to observe the theorist as preacher, telling his audience that the latest buzzword can mean the difference between bankruptcy and unimaginable riches.

Even a brief encounter with the world of management theory leaves you with two immediate impressions. The first is of enormous commercial success. Consultancies such as Accenture or

Capgemini are multibillion-dollar organizations. McKinsey invests $400 million a year on generating knowledge. The most successful management gurus divide their time between giving speeches ($50,000 a speech is not uncommon), offering advice to companies, and running their own companies.

The second impression is that management theory is a mishmash. The books of tenured professors rub spines with those of out-and-out charlatans. Management consultancies can spend a small fortune on some worthy piece of research and then demean themselves with an exhibition of needless hucksterism. In conversation, every guru can move in a flash from a point of genuine insight or scholarship to one of extraordinary banality.

Many management gurus frequently spin their theories out of their own very abnormal experiences. Ram Charan has spent his life preaching the virtues of globalization and flexibility, but nobody in the history of humanity has ever lived a life quite like Charan's. He did not buy his first apartment until he was sixty-seven, spent most of his life living in hotels or bunking down with clients, and got his assistants to keep him supplied with freshly laundered clothes by courier.

The gurus' enormous commercial success and the variability of their output are linked. The combination of easy money and low barriers to entry means that charlatans flock toward the discipline even as genuine scholars flee from it in disgust. So far, management theory has produced only one "great" thinker, Peter Drucker. But Drucker was unique in both his background and his temperament: a Viennese-born intellectual who was introduced to Freud and Wittgenstein in his childhood and who fled Nazi Germany while a young man, he was also an extraordinarily self-contained figure, living most of his life in a modest house in a California suburb. Drucker's fellow gurus are almost always corrupted by the pressure to produce the next "breakthrough" idea. Many jump opportunistically from one "big idea" to another. Their first or second book might include a genuine insight. But pretty soon, surrounded by the paraphernalia of their trade—their own consultancy, the speaking tours, the book contract, the mortgage payments on their third home—they are obliged to spin out "breakthrough" ideas by the yard.

The Case for the Gurus

The existence of so much junk has understandably led many people to dismiss management theory, lock, stock, and barrel. Scott Adams, the cartoonist who invented Dilbert and Dogbert, has made millions out of poking fun at management theorists and their works. "A consultant is a person who takes your money and annoys your employees while tirelessly searching for the best way to extend the consulting contract" is one of his gentler judgments. Mr. Adams's cartoons are syndicated in more than 1,500 newspapers around the world, and his jokes are endlessly repeated around the world's watercoolers, sometimes by the very sort of people who were supposed to be their target.

It would have been easy to continue to bash management theory in this spirit. Management theory *has* been a magnet to a great deal of nonsense over the past hundred years. Management fads *have* torn companies apart. And the language of management theory *is* frequently repulsive. Management scientists have arguably done more damage to the English language than any other group of people.

Yet there is a strong argument to be made in defense of management theory. Companies may be vulnerable to silly fads, but they are also run by intelligent people who are trying to make sense of an infuriatingly complicated world. Business schools may attract more than their fair share of charlatans, but they are also full of whip-smart thinkers who are trying to solve some of the world's most interesting problems.

The most important argument in favor of the management gurus is that the best of them are, indeed, practicing something that can be dignified by the word "theory." General lessons can plausibly be extracted from what companies do and then used to help other companies operate better. Moreover, these general lessons can be refined over time. Successful management ideas are not just bits of local knowledge, fixed by culture and circumstances. They can travel and, suitably modified, can be used to reproduce that success elsewhere—in other countries and industries. Management ideas are not just fads that are taken up and dropped for no better reason than that they are in vogue. They are also techniques that can be modified in the light of rational criticism.

The industry has become much more self-critical over recent years. Indeed, the industry's growing capacity for self-criticism is arguably one of the biggest changes I have observed since John Micklethwait and I wrote *The Witch Doctors* in 1994. The financial crisis produced a wave of soul-searching in the world's business schools. Schools not only examined the techniques that they had been teaching in order to see if they were responsible for the crisis; they also agonized over the "master of the universe" attitude that they had been inculcating. Humility is now in vogue.

The crisis only intensified a process that had been going on for some time. The past fifteen years has seen a fashion for hangwringing books about management. Rakesh Khurana, of Harvard Business School, has bemoaned the unfulfilled promise of management as a profession.[1] Phil Rosenzweig, of IMD Business School, has examined the "halo effect" whereby companies that have a couple of good quarters are treated as repositories of eternal wisdom.[2] *The Academy of Management* and other academic journals are stuffed full of fad-deflating articles.

The management theory industry has also produced a para-industry of people who specialize in deflating its illusions. The reviews of management books are beginning to reflect the frustrations of their readers. Malcolm Gladwell has produced some lacerating criticism of McKinsey ("It never occurred to them that, if everybody had to think outside the box it was the box that needed fixing.")[3] At the *Financial Times*, Lucy Kellaway deserves an endurance award for her ability to mock the excesses, linguistic and otherwise, of the management gurus, week in and week out, even unto the very end of days.

The industry has also profited from the relentless process of specialization and professionalization. Business schools are subjected to growing pressure from their clients to be more responsive and relevant. Consultancies are being forced to be more transparent. The best academic theorists, such as Michael Porter, are judged by the same standards as the rest of the academic community (Porter is one of only twenty Harvard University professors). Even some of the solo gurus are producing interesting work. A man who devotes his life to advising CEOs on how to make the best use of their first ninety days in office may come across as a bit of a monomaniac, but he is nevertheless providing business with a valuable service.

This brings us to the biggest argument in favor of management theory: that it can help to boost productivity. Good companies are constantly borrowing ideas from better companies. Management theorists are constantly searching the world for new innovations and new production techniques. The result of all this constant searching is higher productivity and, every now and again, more contented workers.

Consider Japan's system of "lean production." In the 1950s, Japanese manufacturers were confronted with devastation: much of their industry had been destroyed and they suffered from structural problems (shortages of raw materials and lack of space for storage) that might have rendered them incapable of competing with the American giants. They turned to American quality gurus such as James Juran and W. Edwards Deming. The result was a revolution: they developed a system of lean production that enabled them to produce goods faster than their rivals and with fewer defects. What had looked like disadvantages had been turned miraculously into advantages.

For a while it looked as if the Japanese would drive all before them. America's big three car makers threatened to collapse under the competition. Japanese car manufacturers established plants across the world. But Japan's rivals fought back by learning to imitate Japan's manufacturing prowess. American car companies discovered American gurus that they had long ignored. German car companies established quality circles and just-in-time production.

Not all management ideas produce such happy results. Some techniques have turned out to be duds. Many companies misapply even the most sensible ideas. Public-sector organizations have imposed targets on their employees only to learn that the targets have distracted them from their proper jobs. Banks have "empowered" their front-line workers only to learn that they have made dismal decisions. It is important to remember that Enron was once the apple of every consultant's eye.

But Enron is probably the exception rather than the rule. In general, companies that take management theory seriously have performed better than those that dismiss it. Look at the world's best companies—from America's General Electric to India's Tata Group—and you discover that they have an above-average appetite for management theory. Look at some of the most successful up-starts and you discover that they have a talent for going back to first principles or applying clever ideas from one industry to another. Pixar has applied Toyota's system of lean production to the creative process in an attempt to prevent the company from burning out, and so far it remains the most reliable hit-maker in Hollywood.

This may even be true of countries. There are many reasons for India's current emergence as an economic power, of course, but one of them is surely the country's enthusiasm for studying and adapting management ideas. Indians are some of the world's most enthusiastic students of management theories. The world's business schools are stuffed full of whip-smart Indians; Harvard Business School, the very temple of American capitalism, is now run by one of them, Nitin Nohria. Indian companies seem to be obsessed with hiring gurus and leaping onto the latest fads.

Nor is management theory the intellectual desert that many of its critics imagine. Management theorists have been lucky in their choice of subjects. Over the past decades companies have established themselves as the architects of the future, infinitely more powerful than political parties or public-sector intellectuals. America's politicians have spent the past decade bickering while the deficit explodes and America's power erodes, but companies such as Apple and Google have ushered in a new world of possibilities. Companies have to deliver or die.

The vitality of business ensures that the study of business is equally vital. Management theorists have been grappling with three of the most dramatic changes the world has seen. The first is the impact of the Internet. The Internet is not only producing world-changing companies; it is also changing every aspect of our lives—putting libraries at our fingertips and linking us to armies of like-minded people.

The second is the rise of emerging markets—not just the fabled BRICs but also Indonesia and Vietnam, Turkey and Mexico. The rise of emerging markets promises to be far more revolutionary than the rise of Japan in the 1970s. Emerging-market champions are challenging rich-world multinationals on every front, from IT to manufacturing. They are also producing a new system of production—frugal production—that promises to reduce the cost of many everyday products not just by 10 percent but by 90 percent.

The third change is the rise of social entrepreneurship. Social entrepreneurs are harnessing business techniques to solve social problems that have eluded governments. They are eroding the long-standing barrier between the public and private sectors and between charity and business. They also promise to introduce the same sort of dynamism into the "third sector" that we have long been accustomed to in the private sector.

These changes are confronting management theorists with an astonishing range of new corporate forms and business models. The emerging world is teaming with "business groups" of the sort that used to be common in the West but now survive only in the form of diversified conglomerates such as General Electric: agglomerations of firms that are usually legally independent, diversified across a dizzying range of industries, and tied together by a combination of formal links (equity ties, common board members, common brand names) and informal ties (prominent roles for various members of the founding family).[4] India's Tata Group has subsidiaries in carmaking, agricultural chemicals, hotels, telecommunications, and consulting, and accounts for almost 3 percent of the country's GDP. South Korea's Samsung sticks its brand name on televisions, mobile phones, microwave ovens, and commercial ships. The Philippines' Ayala Corporation has branched out from real estate into telecom, financial services, IT, and electronics.

These groups act as private equity firms, executive search companies, branding consultants, and lobbying shops all rolled into one. They are also adept at mastering politics and shifting capital from one area to another.

Many emerging countries also rely heavily on state-owned enterprises. Not so long ago these state-controlled companies were regarded as half-formed creatures that were destined to die out. But a combination of factors—huge savings in the emerging world, oil wealth in the Middle East, and a loss of confidence in the Anglo-Saxon model—has put them at the heart of the world economy. The world's thirteen largest oil companies, as measured by reserves, are all controlled by governments, and three-quarters of the world's crude-oil reserves are in the hands of state-backed companies. Many of China's best high-tech companies, such as China Telecom and Lenovo, are also state-backed. State-backed companies are the dominant forms in the Mideast and in Russia.

These organizations are not old-fashioned nationalized companies run by the government and designed to control chunks of the national economy, but neither are they classic private-sector companies that sink or swim. Instead, they are peculiar hybrids that have never been seen before, amphibious creatures that flit between sea and land, borrowing money from governments at subsidized rates one moment and plunging into the global market the next. To discover their close relatives, you have to go back not to the twentieth century but to the great European trading companies of the sixteenth to nineteenth centuries, such as Britain's East India Company. Like the old trading companies, they have the trappings of private-sector companies such as boards of directors and listings on the stock market. But, like the chartered companies, they are essentially instruments of state power and state expansion—they roam the world at the behest of their government paymasters and build infrastructure as well as engaging in trade, raising worries, at least for the historically minded, about whether formal empire can be far behind.

The world is also witnessing the rise of a different type of hybrid organization: organizations that straddle the line between the for-profit and the charitable sector. Old-fashioned charities are adopting more business-like methods. At the same time, old-fashioned companies are forming close alliances with voluntary organizations. Unilever has teamed up with NGOs to teach more than 130 million people the importance of washing their hands, conducting perhaps the biggest educational exercise in human history: so far it has taught more than 133 million people about the importance of personal hygiene. And some organizations are blurring the line between charities and for-profit companies even more comprehensively, trying to make money out of doing good. Bangladesh Waste Concern has reduced the mountains of garbage in many of the country's cities by the simple expedient of putting a price on rubbish.

All these developments are introducing an extraordinary amount of uncertainty into the heart of business. Are emerging-market business groups creative responses to their circumstances, as Tarun Khanna has eloquently argued, or are they inefficient organizations that are diverting capital and talent from more productive uses? Are state companies vital challengers to the capitalist system, or are they destined to collapse in a convulsive crisis of state capitalism? Will half-companies, half-charities combine the best of both worlds, or will they prove to be nightmares to manage? Add to these questions the fact that competition has never been fiercer—that companies can be wiped out by interlopers from corners of the world that they had never given a second thought to—and you can see why management theory is unlikely to be short of great subjects.

The opportunities awaiting the management theory industry are well illustrated by the story of Soichiro Honda and the sushi cake. During a visit to Detroit in October 1989, the 82-year-old founder of the car company that bears his name flummoxed his handlers by his emotional reaction to a sushi cake that an American hotel delivered to him as a welcoming gift. The cake was crafted to look like sushi. The baker had made sure that the cake was deliciously soft and healthfully sugar-free in deference to Honda's age. Mr. Honda became fixated on the cake. "You guys think that you have surpassed the Americans," he scolded. "You guys have become too arrogant. Look at this cake. The person who made this cake definitely put his feet in my shoes." Honda summoned the pastry chef and became quite emotional when it turned out that he was a mere twenty-something. "Never underestimate America," he told his bemused handlers.[5]

Mr. Honda used the cake to deliver a lesson to his staff about America, but he might equally have used it to deliver a lesson about management theory: never think that you have discovered the "one best way" of doing things. Your competitors can always imitate your recipes and improve on them. Management theorists, like master chefs, may be irritating in all sorts of ways—bumptious, bamboozling, and overpaid. But it will be a long time before we can dispense with their services.

Notes

INTRODUCTION: THE UNACKNOWLEDGED LEGISLATORS

1. Stefan Stern, "A 100-year health check for Harvard," *Financial Times*, October 21, 2008.
2. Philip Delves Broughton, "Harvard's masters of the apocalypse," *The Times*, March 1, 2009.
3. George Bush earned his MBA in 1975. Dick Cheney ran Halliburton, Donald Rumsfeld ran Searle, and Paul O'Neill ran Alcoa.
4. Gerald Davis, "The rise and fall of finance and the end of the society of organizations," *Academy of Management Perspectives*, August 2009, p. 30.
5. "Oh, Mr. Porter: Schumpeter," *The Economist*, March 12, 2011.
6. See, for example, Mehrdad Baghai, Stephen Coley, and David White, "Staircase to growth," *McKinsey Quarterly*, November 1996; Mehrdad Baghai, Stephen Coley, and David White, "Turning capabilities into advantages," *McKinsey Quarterly*, February 1999.
7. Gary Hamel, *Leading the Revolution: How to Thrive in Turbulent Times by Making Innovation a Way of Life* (Boston: Harvard Business School Press, 2002).
8. Phil Rosenzweig, *The Halo Effect: How Managers Let Themselves Be Deceived* (London: Simon & Schuster, 2007).
9. Sumantra Ghoshal, "Bad management theories are destroying good management practices," *Academy of Management Learning & Education*, 2005, vol. 4, no. 1, pp. 75–91.
10. Rakesh Khurana, *From Higher Aims to Hired Hands: The Social Transformation of American Business Schools and the Unfulfilled Promise of Management as a Profession* (Princeton, New Jersey: Princeton University Press, 2007).

11. Philip Delves Broughton, *Ahead of the Curve: Two Years at Harvard Business School* (New York: Penguin Press, 2008); Matthew Stewart, *The Management Myth: Why Experts Keep Getting It Wrong* (New York: W.W. Norton & Company, 2008).

12. For a classic bit of Kellaway (attacking an Accenture waffle merchant who has a degree in classics from Oxford), see "Accenture's next champion of waffle words," *Financial Times*, January 27, 2008.

13. Leslie Wayne, "A promise to be ethical in an era of immorality," *New York Times*, May 30, 2009.

14. Matthew Stewart, *The Management Myth: Why the Experts Keep Getting It Wrong* (New York: W.W. Norton & Company, 2009), p. 247.

15. Henry Mintzberg, Bruce Ahsltrand, and Joseph Lampel, *Management? It's Not What You Think* (London: Pearson, 2010), pp. 35–36.

16. Rosenzweig, *The Halo Effect*, p. 41.

17. Bain & Company, *Management Tools*, 2005, pp. 1–2.

CHAPTER 1: THE FAD IN PROGRESS: FROM REENGINEERING TO CSR

1. Willy Stern, "Did Dirty Tricks Create a Best-Seller?" *Business Week*, August 7, 1995.

2. Michael Hammer and James Champy, *Reengineering the Corporation* (New York: HarperCollins, 1993).

3. From Tim Hindle, *The Economist Guide to Management Ideas and Gurus* (London: Profile, 2009). Also available online, http://www.economist.com/node/13130298.

4. Hardy Green, *The Company Town: The Industrial Edens and Satanic Mills that Shaped the American Economy* (New York: Basic Books, 2010).

5. See Anita Roddick, *Body and Soul: Profits with Principles—The Amazing Success Story of Anita Roddick and The Body Shop* (London: Ebury Press, 1991).

6. Clive Crook, "The good company: a survey of corporate social responsibility," *The Economist*, January 20, 2005.

7. *Ethical Corporations*, a 35-page collection of studies of "classic CR disasters," can be had for £395.

8. Quoted in Anthony Sampson, *Company Man: The Rise and Fall of Corporate Life* (New York: Times Business, 1995), p. 17.

9. McKinsey & Company, *Shaping the New Rules of Competition: UN Global Compact Participant Mirror*, July 2007.

10. Joseph Schumpeter, *Capitalism, Socialism and Democracy* (London: George Allen & Unwin, 1943), p. 219.

11. Ann Bernstein, *The Case for Business in Developing Economies* (Johannesburg: Penguin, 2010), pp. 149–50.

12. Milton Friedman, "The social responsibility of business is to increase its profits," *The New York Times Magazine*, September 13, 1970.

13. David Vogel, *The Market for Virtue* (Washington, DC: Brookings Institution, 2006), p. 135.

14. Darrell Rigby and Barbara Bilinear, *Management Tools and Trends*, (Bain & Company, 2009).

15. John Browne, *Beyond Business* (London, Weidenfeld & Nicolson, 2010), pp. 194–96.

16. Ed Crooks, "Man in the News: Tony Hayward," *Financial Times*, April 30, 2010.

17. David Brooks, *Bobos in Paradise: The New Upper Class and How They Got There* (New York: Simon & Schuster, 2000).

18. Daniel Isenberg, "Keggfarms (India): Which came first, the Kuroiler or the KEGG," Harvard Business School Case Study.

19. Daniel Isenberg, "Lapdesk company: A South African FOPSE," Harvard Business School case study.

20. Matthew Bishop and Michael Green, *Philanthrocapitalism: How the Rich Can Save the World* (New York: Bloomsbury Press, 2008).

21. Nancy Lublin, *The Power of Zero in Business* (New York: Portfolio, 2010).

22. Jennifer Aaker and Andy Smith (with Carlye Adler), *The Dragonfly Effect: Quick, Effective, and Powerful Ways to Use Social Media to Drive Social Change* (San Francisco: Jossey-Bass, 2010), p. xiv.

CHAPTER 2: THE MANAGEMENT THEORY INDUSTRY

1. Walter Kiechel, *The Lords of Strategy: The Secret Intellectual History of the New Corporate World* (Boston: Harvard Business Press, 2010), p. 243.

2. Ben Schiller, "The rise of the MBA politicians," *Financial Times*, January 16, 2011.

3. Keith Ferrazzi and Tahl Raz, *Never Eat Alone: And Other Secrets to Success, One Relationship at a Time* (New York: Crown Business, 2005).

4. Jay Barney and Trish Gorman Clifford, *What I Didn't Learn in Business School: How Strategy Works in the Real World* (Boston: Harvard Business Review Press, 2010). The novel even concludes with a helpful reading list.

5. Srikant Datar, David Garvin, and Patrick Cullen, *Rethinking the MBA: Business Education at a Crossroads* (Boston: Harvard Business School Press, 2010), p. 18.

6. Ibid., pp. 109–10.

7. Ibid., pp. 117–18.

8. Tom Peters, *Re-imagine! Business Excellence in a Disruptive Age* (London: Dorling Kindersley, 2003), p. 17.

9. Harold Sirkin, James Hemerling, and Arindam Bhattacharya, *Globality:*

Competing with Everyone from Everywhere for Everything (New York: Headline Business Plus, 2008), p. 91.

10. Matthew Stewart, *The Management Myth: Why the Experts Keep Getting It Wrong* (New York: W.W. Norton & Company, 2009), p. 5.

11. Datar, Garvin, and Cullen, *Rethinking the MBA*, p. 17.

12. Sirkin, Hemerling, and Bhattacharya, *Globality*.

13. Chris Zook, *Profit from the Core: A Return to Growth in Turbulent Times* (Cambridge, Mass.: Harvard Business, Press, 2010).

14. Andrzej Hucznski, *Management Gurus: What Makes Them and How to Become One* (London: Routledge, 2007), pp. 191–92.

15. Ibid., p. 163.

16. Gary Hamel, *The Future of Management* (Boston: Harvard Business School Press), p. 6.

17. Emma de Vita, "Do you trust your boss?" *Management Today*, September 2009, p. 44.

18. Bain & Company, *Management Tools and Trends*, 2009, p. 2.

CHAPTER 3: PETER DRUCKER: THE GURU'S GURU

1. See, for example, Elizabeth Haas Edersheim, *The Definitive Drucker: Challenges for Tomorrow's Executives—Final Advice from the Father of Modern Management* (New York: McGraw Hill, 2007).

2. Quoted by Carol Kennedy, *Guide to the Management Gurus: Top Level Guidance on Twenty Management Techniques* (London: Random House Business, 1991), p. 41.

3. Peter Drucker, *Management* (New York: HarperCollins, 1993), p. 14.

4. Mauro F. Guillen, *Models of Management: Work, Authority and Organization in Comparative Perspective* (Chicago: University of Chicago Press, 1994), pp. 45–46.

5. Pauline Graham (ed.), *Mary Parker Follett: Prophet of Management* (Boston: Harvard Business School Press, 1994), p. 27.

6. Guillen, *Models of Management*, p. 224.

7. Peter Drucker, *The Concept of the Corporation* (New York: John Day, 1946), p. 132.

8. Ibid., p. 78.

9. Quoted in Kennedy, *Guide to the Management Gurus*, p. 41.

10. Drucker, *Concept of the Corporation*, p. 132.

11. "Megachurches," *New York Times*, April 18, 1995.

12. Drucker, *Concept of the Corporation*, p. 241.

13. Ibid., p. 241.

14. Drucker, *Managing in Turbulent Times*, p. 104.

15. Ibid., p. 225.

CHAPTER 4: TOM PETERS: MANAGEMENT FOR THE MASSES

1. Stewart, *The Management Myth*, p. 231.

2. You can read all his slides at tompeters.com/slides.

3. See, for example, "Europe outgrows management American-style," *Fortune*, October 1980.

4. Tom Peters and Robert H. Waterman, *In Search of Excellence: Lessons from America's Best-Run Companies* (New York: HarperCollins, 1982), p. xxii.

5. Ibid., p. xxv.

6. Peter Drucker, *Frontiers of Management: Where Tomorrow's Decisions are Being Shaped Today* (New York: Dutton, 1986).

7. David Clutterbuck and Stuart Cranier, *Makers of Management: Men and Women Who Changed the Business World* (London: Macmillan, 1999), p. 218.

8. Thomas J. Peters, *Liberation Management: Necessary Disorganisation in the Nonosecond Nineties* (London: Ballantine Books, 1992), pp. 612–14.

9. Tom Peters, "The Pursuit of Wow" Seminar (London, October 27, 1995).

10. "Who's Excellent Now?" *Business Week*, November 5, 1984.

11. Peters and Waterman, *In Search of Excellence*, p. 215.

12. Ibid., p. 270.

13. Ibid., pp. 106–07.

14. Ibid., p. 30.

15. John Byrne, *The Whiz Kids: Ten Founding Fathers of American Business—and the Legacy They Left Us* (New York: Doubleday Business, 1993).

16. Peters and Waterman, *In Search of Excellence*, p. 55.

17. Ibid., p. 75.

18. Ken Auletta, *Googled: The End of the World as We Know It* (New York: Penguin Press, 2009), pp. 217–19.

19. Ibid., pp 217–19.

CHAPTER 5: FLAT WORLDS, TIPPING POINTS, AND LONG TAILS

1. Adam Bryant, "For Jim Collins, no question is too big," *New York Times*, May 24, 2009.

2. Erin White, "New breed of business gurus rises," *Wall Street Journal*, May 5, 2008.

3. Jason Zengerie, "Geek pop star," *New York*, November 9, 2008.

4. Lawrence Wright, "Slim's time," *The New Yorker*, June 1, 2009.

5. David Plotz, "Why Tom Friedman is America's most important columnist," *Slate*, March 8, 2002. www.slate.com/id/2062905.

6. Danielle Sacks, "The accidental guru," *Fast Company*, January 1, 2005.

7. Zengerie, "Geek pop star."

8. Christopher Anderson, *The Long Tail: Why the Future of Business Is Selling Less of More* (New York: Hyperion, 2004), p. 5.

9. Ibid., p. 37.

10. Ibid., p. 54.

11. Bill Clinton, *My Life* (New York: Alfred Knopf, 2004), p. 137.

12. Robert Reich, *The Future of Success* (New York: Alfred Knopf, 2001).

13. Ibid., p. 73.

14. Robert Reich, *Supercapitalism: The Transformation of Business, Democracy and Everyday Life* (New York: Vintage Books, 2008).

15. Jonathan Rauch, "Robert Reich, quote doctor," Slate, May 30, 1997.

16. Richard Florida, *The Rise of the Creative Class* (New York: Basic Books, 2002), pp. xxiii–xiv.

17. Ibid., p. 9.

18. Ibid., p. 170.

19. Steven Malanga, "The curse of the creative class," *City Journal*, Winter 2004.

20. Lawrence Fisher, "Howard Gardner does good work," *Strategy & Business*, May 29, 2007.

21. Howard Gardner, *Five Minds for the Future* (Boston: Harvard Business Press, 2007), pp. 18–19.

CHAPTER 6: RETHINKING THE COMPANY

1. Auletta, *Googled*, pp. 17–18.

2. Martin Thomas, *Loose: The Future of Business Is Letting Go* (London: Headline, 2011), pp. 181–82.

3. Auletta, *Googled*, p. 21.

4. Steven Levy, "Larry Page wants to return Google to its startup roots," *Wired*, March 18, 2011.

5. Auletta, *Googled*, p. 15.

6. Mark Zuckerberg, speech at Cannes Lions International Advertising Festival, June 23, 2010.

7. Don Tapscott and Anthony Williams, *Macrowikinomics: Rebooting Business and the World* (New York: Portfolio, 2010), p. 253.

8. Nassim Nicholas Taleb, *The Black Swan: The Impact of the Highly Improbable* (New York: Random House, 2007).

9. Tom Peters, "New Products, New Markets, New Competition, New Thinking," *The Economist*, March 4, 1989.

10. Sami Finne and Hanna Sivonen, *The Retail Value Chain: How to Gain Competitive Advantage Through Efficient Consumer Response Strategies* (London: Kogan Page, 2009), p. 6.

11. William H. Whyte, *The Organization Man* (New York: Doubleday Anchor Books, 1957); David Riesman, *The Lonely Crowd* (New Haven: Yale University Press, 1950). The best example of nostalgia is Sampson, *Company Man: The Rise and Fall of Corporate Life* (New York: Random House, 1996).

12. Farok Contractor, Vikas Kumar, Sumit Kundu, and Torben Pedersen, *Global Outsourcing and Offshoring* (Cambridge: Cambridge University Press, 2011), p. 31.

13. Rachel Botsman and Roo Rogers, *What's Mine Is Yours: The Rise of Collaborative Consumption* (New York: HarperBusiness, 2010); Lisa Gansky, *The Mesh: Why the Future of Business Is Sharing* (New York: Portfolio/Penguin, 2010).

14. Charlene Li and Joseph Bernoff, Groundswell: Winning in a World Transformed by Social Technologies (Boston, Mass.: Harvard Business Press, 2008), pp. 7–8.

15. Holman Jenkins, "Google and the Search for the Future," *Wall Street Journal,* August 14, 2010.

16. Michael Burchell and Jennifer Robin, *The Great Workplace: How to Build It, How to Keep It and Why It Matters* (San Francisco: Jossey-Bass, 2011), p. 42.

17. Ibid., p 135.

18. Tim Hindle, *Guide to Management Ideas and Gurus* (London: Economist Books, 2008), p. 310.

19. Harold Leavitt, *Top Down* (Boston: Harvard Business School Press, 2005), p. 49.

CHAPTER 7: ENTREPRENEURS UNBOUND

1. This can be found at www.normanmacrae.com, "The Norman Macrae Archive."

2. Aravind Adiga, *The White Tiger* (New York: Free Press, 2008), p. 4.

3. William J. Baumol, Robert E. Litan, and Carl J. Schramm, *Good Capitalism, Bad Capitalism and the Economics of Growth and Prosperity* (New Haven, Conn. & London: Yale University Press, 2007).

4. Monitor Group, *Paths to Prosperity: Promoting Entrepreneurship in the 21st Century* (January 2009).

5. Amar Bhide, *The Venturesome Economy: How Innovation Sustains Prosperity in a More Connected World* (Princeton, N.J.: Princeton University Press, 2010).

6. Dan Senor and Saul Singer, *Start-up Nation: The Story of Israel's Economic Miracle* (New York: Twelve, 2009).

7. Gurcharan Gas, *India Unbound: From Independence to the Global Information Age* (New York: Penguin Books, 2002), p. xiv.

8. Dan Isenberg, "The global entrepreneur," *Harvard Business Review,* December 2008.

9. Edmund Phelps, "Entrepreneurial culture: Why European economies lag behind the US," *Wall Street Journal,* February 17, 2007.

10. Baumol, Litan, and Schramm, *Good Capitalism, Bad Capitalism,* p. 3.

CHAPTER 8: THE WORLD TURNED UPSIDE DOWN

1. Anil Gupta and Haiyan Wang, *Getting China and India Right: Strategies for Leveraging the World's Fastest-Growing Economies for Global Advantage* (San Francisco: Jossey-Bass, 2009).

2. Nirmalya Kumar, "How emerging giants are rewriting the rules of M&A," *Harvard Business Review*, May 2000.

3. John Hagel and John Seely Brown, *The Power of Pull: How Small Moves, Smartly Made, Can Set Big Things in Motion* (New York: Basic Books, 2010).

4. John Seely Brown and John Hagel, "Innovation blowback: Disruptive management practices from Asia," *McKinsey Quarterly*, 2005, no. 1.

CHAPTER 9: KNOWLEDGE, LEARNING, AND INNOVATION

1. Josh Linkner, *Disciplined Dreaming: A Proven System to Drive Breakthrough Creativity* (San Francisco: Jossey-Bass, 2011), p. 119.

2. Ibid., p. 166.

3. Andrew Harbadon, *How Breakthroughs Happen* (Boston: Harvard Business Press, 2003).

4. Jeremy McCarter (ed.), *Bite the Hand that Feeds You: Henry Essays and Provocations* (New Haven, Conn.: Yale University Press, 2009).

5. Rob Goffee and Gareth Jones, *Clever: Leading Your Smartest, Most Creative People* (Boston: Harvard Business Press, 2009).

6. Ibid., p. 47.

7. Ibid., p. 89.

8. Linkner, *Disciplined Dreaming*, p. 106.

9. Thomas, *Loose*, p. 75.

10. Jonathan Bays, Tony Goland, and Joe Newsum, "Using prizes to spur innovation," *McKinsey Quarterly*, July 2009.

11. Roberto Verganti, *Design-Driven Innovation: Changing the Rules of Competition by Radically Innovating What Things Mean* (Boston: Harvard Business Press, 2009), p. 51. See also p. vii.

12. J. Schumpeter, *The Theory of Economic Development* (Cambridge, Mass: Harvard University Press, 1934; first published in German, 1912).

13. J. Schumpeter, *Capitalism, Socialism and Democracy* (New York: Harper & Bros., 1942).

CHAPTER 10: LORDS OF STRATEGY

1. Henry Mintzberg, *The Rise and Fall of Strategic Planning* (New York: Free Press, 1994), pp. 21–23.

2. Ibid., pp. 62–63.

3. Stewart, *The Management Myth*, p. 186.

4. Walter Kiechel, *The Lords of Strategy. The Secret Intellectual History of the New Corporate World* (Boston: Harvard Business Press, 2010).

5. Michael Porter, "The State of Strategic Thinking," *The Economist*, May 23, 1987, p. 21.

6. Kiechel, *The Lords of Strategy*, p. 3.

7. Ibid., p. 9.

8. Gerald Tellis and Peter Golder, "First to Market, First to Fail: Real Causes of Enduring Market Leadership," *Sloan Management Review*, vol. 37, no. 2.

9. Zook, *Profit from the Core*, p. 1.

10. Steve Lohr, "GE goes with what it knows: making stuff," *New York Times*, December 5, 2010.

11. Siva Vaidhyanathan, *The Googlization of Everything (And Why We Should Worry)* (Berkeley: University of California Press), p. 33.

12. Eric Beinhocker, *The Origin of Wealth: Evolution, Complexity and the Radical Remaking of Economics* (New York: Random House, 2006).

CHAPTER 11: WHAT DOES GLOBALIZATION MEAN?

1. Pankaj Ghemawat, *World 3.0: Global Prosperity and How to Achieve It* (Boston: Harvard Business Review Press, 2011), p. 10.

2. Ian Bremmer, *The End of the Free Market: Who Wins the War Between States and Corporations* (New York: Portfolio, 2010), p. 43.

3. This was reprinted in the *McKinsey Quarterly* for 1984 and is available on the Web.

4. Pankaj Ghemawat, *World 3.0: Global Prosperity and How to Achieve It* (Boston: Harvard Business Review Press, 2011), pp. 26–29, 302.

5. Ibid., p 29.

6. Ibid., pp. 26–29, 302.

7. Nigel Hollis, *The Global Brand: How to Create and Develop Lasting Brand Value in the World Market* (New York: Palgrave Macmillan, 2008), p. 55.

8. Ibid., p. 24.

9. Ghemawat, *World 3.0*, p. 95.

10. Noreena Hertz, *The Silent Takeover: Global Capitalism and the Death of Democracy* (New York: Harper Paperbacks, 2003).

CHAPTER 12: STORM IN THE BOARDROOM

1. Michael Jensen and William Meckling, "Theory of the firm: Managerial behavior, agency costs and ownership structure," *Journal of Financial Economics*, vol. 3, no. 4 (1976).

2. Charles Handy, *Beyond Certainty: The Changing Worlds of Organizations* (London: Hutchinson, 1995), p. 105.

3. Peter Drucker, *Post-Capitalist Society* (New York: Harper Paberbacks, 1993), p. 73.

4. Richard Lambert speech to RSA, *Financial Times*, March 30, 2010.

5. Roger Martin, "The Age of Customer Capitalism," *Harvard Business Review*, January–February 2010.

6. Stefan Stern, "Outsider in a hurry to shake up Unilever," *Financial Times*, April 4, 2010.

7. Vineet Nayar, *Employees First, Customers Second: Turning Conventional Management Upside Down* (Boston: Harvard Business Press, 2010).

8. Francois Brochet, "Information content of insider trades before and after the Sarbanes-Oxley Act," *The Accounting Review*, vol. 85, no. 2 (March 2010), pp. 419–46.

9. Michael Lewis, "O'Neal's agony, or, in the bunker with Stan," Bloomberg, November 6, 2007. www.bloomberg.com/apps/news.

10. Joseph Bower, *The CEO Within: Why Inside Outsiders Are the Key to Succession Planning* (Boston: Harvard Business School Press, 2007), p. 2.

11. Ibid., p. 3.

12. Noel Wasserman, Barrat Anand, and Nitin Nohria, "When Does Leadership Matter?" Harvard Business School Working Paper 01-063.

13. Edward Lazear and Sherwin Rosen, "Rank-order tournaments as optimum labor contracts," *Journal of Political Economy*, vol. 89, no. 5 (1981).

14. Henry Mintzberg, *Managing* (Harlow, Essex: Pearson Education Limited, 2009), p. 1.

15. Ronald Heifetz et al., *The Practice of Adaptive Leadership: Tools and Tactics for Changing Your Organization and the World* (Boston: Harvard Business Press, 2009).

16. William Taylor, "The Leader of the Future: Harvard's Ronald Heifetz offers a short course on the future of leadership," *Fast Company*, May 31, 1999.

CHAPTER 13: MANAGING LEVIATHAN

1. Bernard Marr and James Creelman, *More with Less: Maximizing Value in the Public Sector* (London: Palgrave Macmillan, 2011), p. 3.

2. David Warsh, "A recent exercise in nation-building by some Harvard boys," economicprincipals.com.

3. Michael Porter, *The Competitive Advantage of Nations* (New York: Free Press, 1990), p xii.

4. Marr and Creelman, *More with Less*, p. 18.

5. McKinsey & Company, "The economic impact of the achievement gap in America's schools." April 2009.

6. Clayton Christensen, Curtis Johnson, and Michael Horn, *Disrupting Class: How Disruptive Innovation Will Change the Way the World Learns* (New York: McGraw Hill, 2008).

CHAPTER 14: THE COMMON TOAD

1. Charles Handy, *Myself and Other More Important Matters* (New York: American Management Association, 2008), p. 124.

2. Ken Favaro, Per-Ola Karisson, and Gary Neilson, "CEO succession 2000–2009: A decade of convergence and compression," *Strategy + Business*, Summer 2010, no. 59.

3. Lynda Gratton, *Shift: The Future of Work Is Already Here* (London: Collins, 2011), p. 249.

4. Rachel Botsman and Roo Rogers, *The Rise of Collaborative Consumption* (New York: HarperBusiness), pp. 168–69.

5. Wendell Cox, "Decade of the Telecommute," *New Geography*, October 5, 2010.

6. Michael Burchell and Jennifer Robin, *The Great Workplace: How to Build It, How to Keep It, and Why It Matters* (San Francisco: Jossey-Bass, 2011), p. 24.

7. Linkner, *Disciplined Dreaming*, pp. 95–97.

8. Ibid., p. 101.

9. Gratton, *Shift*, p. 309.

10. Ibid., p. 250.

CHAPTER 15: THE BATTLE FOR BRAINPOWER

1. Barry C. Lynn and Philip Longman, "Who broke America's jobs machine?" *Washington Monthly*, March/April 2010.

2. Geoff Colvin, *Talent Is Overrated. What Really Separates World-Class Performers from Everybody Else* (New York: Portfolio, 2008).

3. Boris Groysberg, *Chasing Stars: The Myth of Talent and the Portability of Performance* (Princeton, N.J.: Princeton University Press, 2010).

4. Alan Guarino, *Smart Is Not Enough: The South Pole Strategy and Other Powerful Talent Management Secrets* (Hoboken, N.J.: John Wiley & Sons, 2007).

5. Ed Michaels, Helen Handfield-Jones, and Beth Axelrod, *The War for Talent* (Cambridge, Mass: Harvard Business Press, 2001).

6. Baruch Lev, *Intangibles: Management, Measurement and Reporting* (Washington, D.C.: Brookings Institution Press, 2001).

7. Bradford Johnson, James Manyika, and Lareina Yee, "The next revolution in interactions," *The McKinsey Quarterly*, 2005, no. 4.

8. Burchell and Robin, *The Great Workplace*, p. 165.

9. Eugenia Levenson, "Harvard Girl," *Harvard Magazine*, 2002.

10. John Micklethwait and Adrian Wooldridge, *A Future Perfect: The Challenge and Promise of Globalization* (London: Random House, 2000), pp. 225–45.

11. Michael Young, *The Rise of the Meritocracy 1870–2033: An Essay on Education and Equality* (London: Thames & Hudson, 1958).

12. T. S. Eliot, *Notes Towards a Definition of Culture* (London: 1948), p. 101.

13. Liam Hudson, *The Cult of the Fact: A Psychologist's Autobiographical Critique of His Discipline* (London: Harper & Row, 1972), p. 47.

14. I have told this story in some detail in Wooldridge, *Measuring the Mind: Education and Psychology in England 1880–1990* (Cambridge: Cambridge University Press, 1994), pp. 253–359.

15. Christopher Lasch, *The Revolt of the Elites and the Betrayal of Democracy* (New York: W.W. Norton & Company, 1996).

CHAPTER 16: MANAGING YOURSELF

1. Peters, *Re-imagine!*, p. 305.

2. Reich, *The Future of Success*, pp. 132–57.

3. Roberto Alvarez del Blanco, *Personal Brands: Manage Your Life with Talent and Turn It into a Unique Experience* (London: Palgrave Macmillan, 2011), p. 1.

4. See Bruce Rosenstein, *Living in More Than One World: How Peter Drucker's Wisdom Can Inspire and Transform Your Life* (San Francisco: Berrett-Koehler, 2009), and Peter Drucker, *Management: Revised Edition* (New York: HarperBusiness, 2008), pp. 481–97.

5. Rosenstein, *Living in More Than One World*, p. 21.

6. Ibid., p. 69.

7. Clayton Christensen, "How Will You Measure Your Life?" *Harvard Business Review*, July–August 2010.

8. Quoted in Tim Hindle, *Guide to Management Ideas and Gurus* (London: Profile Books, 2008), p. 216.

CONCLUSION: MASTERING MANAGEMENT

1. Rakesh Khurana, *From Higher Aims to Hired Guns: The Social Transformation of American Business Schools and the Unfulfilled Promise of Management as a Profession* (Princeton, N.J.: Princeton University Press, 2010).

2. Rosenzweig, *The Halo Effect*.

3. Malcolm Gladwell, *What the Dog Saw* (London: Allen Lane, 2009), p. 374. This essay, "The Talent Myth," was first published in *The New Yorker* on July 22, 2002.

4. Tarun Khanna and Krishna Palepu with Richard Bullock, *Winning in Emerging Markets: A Road Map for Strategy and Execution* (Boston: Harvard Business Press, 2010), p. 156.

5. Michael Schuman, *The Miracle: The Epic Story of Asia's Quest for Wealth* (New York: HarperCollins, 2009), pp. 181–82.

Index